PEOPLE'S
CENTURY
20th

This book is published to accompany the second part of the television series entitled *People's Century,* which was first broadcast in September 1996

Published by
BBC Books
an imprint of
BBC Worldwide Publishing

BBC Worldwide Ltd
Woodlands
80 Wood Lane
London W12 0TT

First published 1996

ISBN 0 563 37025 4

Edited and designed by
B·C·S Publishing Ltd, Chesterton, Oxfordshire

Printed in Great Britain by
Cambus Litho Ltd, East Kilbride, Scotland

Bound in Great Britain by
Hunter & Foulis Ltd, Edinburgh, Scotland

Colour originations by
Fotographics, London-Hong Kong

Jacket printed by
Laurence Allen Ltd, Weston-super-Mare

Set in Bembo and Futura

From the start of the nuclear age to the end of the century

Godfrey Hodgson

Series Consultant
J.M. ROBERTS

BBC BOOKS

Contents

FOREWORD
BY J.M. ROBERTS
6

INTRODUCTION
9

1
FALLOUT
11
The dawn of the nuclear age

2
ASIA RISING
35
Economic boom in East Asia

3
SKIN DEEP
59
The fight against state racism

4
ENDANGERED PLANET
83
Campaigning for the environment

5
PICTURE POWER
107
The impact of television

6
LIVING LONGER
131
Campaigns for better health

7

GREAT LEAP
155

Mobilizing the people of China

8

NEW RELEASE
179

Changing roles for young people

9

HALF THE PEOPLE
203

Women fight for equal rights

10

WAR OF THE FLEA
227

The impact of guerrilla wars

11

GOD FIGHTS BACK
251

Religion on the rise

12

PEOPLE POWER
275

Collapse of the communist empire

13

BACK TO THE FUTURE
299

Towards the millennium

ACKNOWLEDGEMENTS
314

INDEX
316

Foreword

by

J.M. Roberts

If the twentieth century is the first true century of mass history, then in its second half that striking fact was more visible than ever. For a start, there were so many more people alive at the century's end than at its beginning. Population grew faster than ever before. Other historic changes, too, seemed to race along faster than ever. In only a couple of decades, old empires disappeared and scores of new nations came into existence. Science altered daily life beyond all recognition by comparison with the world of 1900 – or even that of 1939, and medicine made advances that changed human expectations of health. New technological devices and new chemistry contributed to an unprecedented material abundance that was experienced by hundreds of millions of people. As a demonstration of what technology could do, men went to the moon in 1969, and within a few years scores of men and women of many nations took part in experiments in space.

One unique aspect of such changes was that most of them were shared as no earlier experience had been. This was true even in the world's poorest countries; while they might share the new abundance of unprecedented economic growth only unevenly, share it they did. With wealth came life: huge numbers of people now lived much longer than their great-grandparents' generation. They also shared the effects of unemployment, crowded cities and more volatile politics.

Experience was shared, too, in another way. After 1950 mass communications (above all, television) became a global fact. Events that at an earlier time would have had only a local or at most regional impact suddenly took on world significance. An almost immediate knowledge of them and participation in reaction to them has been made possible by television. Like many other historical facts, whether that has been for good or ill on the whole can be debated – and at length. It remains one of the facts making recent history unique.

Some years ago, the view was expressed (against the background of the great upheaval as Soviet domination of Eastern Europe crumbled) that we were witnessing 'the end of history'. Many people have been tempted to make phrases and aphorisms about history ('History is bunk,' said Henry Ford, a history-maker if ever there was one), but this must be reckoned one of the sillier ones. History never comes to an end. As the people's century draws to a close it is clear that even more change is on the way: a prospect that, depending on where you stand, may seem inspiring, intimidating, exciting, liberating, oppressive or many other things.

Many changes will turn out to have deep roots in the past. It looked in 1950 as though some of Europe's great problems had been solved forever by victory a few years before; as if a balance of superpowers was now an enduring fact of world politics; as if material progress would continue to deliver better standards of living, without any danger of environmental damage – indeed, the expression was unknown. Now, as the century closes, all such ideas have been blown away. What is more, we see forgotten problems with ancient origins rising again to the surface. They show the weight of the past. The chaos of Bosnia is incomprehensible without taking into account centuries of Turkish rule, or the Serb ambitions that helped to bring Europe to war more than eighty years ago. China's truculence in international affairs has to be understood against the background of the 'Middle Kingdom', a regional superpower and dominant cultural influence in the Far East a thousand years ago. It now seems likely that Islam will have to be taken seriously again; one element in understanding why is the Crusades that took place also a thousand years ago.

There will be nearly six billion human beings alive in the year 2000. We should not be too confident we can guess what will face them, but it will have a lot of history mixed up in it, including unfinished business of our own.

THE PRIME
SHIBUYA 109
日本でUC
UC
UC CARD GROUP
海外でマスター
KEY COFFEE
第一勧業銀行
S・C・V・B
シード コンタクト
三千里薬品
夢枕 獏
菊地秀行
魔界都市
ブルース3
陰花の章
夏の新書・文庫フェア
祥伝社オンステージ'92
評判の店
さくらやは、こちらより歩30秒です。
クスリのことなら 三千里
Mr.shop NOW
レイク
このビル 8F
SHIBUYA 109

LONG LIVE

Introduction

OVER ONE THOUSAND people were interviewed for the television series *People's Century*. This book and its companion volume are woven from their stories. They were not chosen at random. Each of them witnessed or experienced something that changed the lives of thousands, often millions, of others. But in this book they tell the big history of the century through the impact it had on the little histories of their own lives.

The second half of the century, like the first, was violent, unpredictable, full of conflict and change. The plot of the drama became more complicated, as almost the whole of the human race marched up out of the auditorium and took its place on the stage.

After 1950 we lived, more than ever before, in one world – whether we liked it or not. Events, ideas, fashions, products all flashed to the remotest corner of the globe within a bewilderingly short time. Henry Luce, the founder of *Time* magazine, predicted that it would be an American century, and so in some ways it was. The United States remained to the end of it not only the most powerful country militarily, but the most influential in other ways. Yet gradually there were many centres of power and innovation. Where once only Western Europe and North America spoke, and everyone else listened, by the end of the century the people of China, South Asia, Australasia, the Middle East, Latin America and Africa – all the world's people, in fact – were making their voices heard.

The second half of the century promised to be a golden age of prosperity. But in the 1970s what the French called the 'thirty glorious years' came to an end. Inflation in the price of energy and food jolted the wealth-creating machine to a halt. The age of plenty was succeeded by an age of protest. Black people demanded equality with whites; women demanded equality with men. Young people were challenging the authority of their elders. People of all kinds shouted warnings about what we humans were doing to our environment.

You can hear all the voices of this new Babel in this book. Perhaps the most important thing they have to say is that wherever we live and whatever we believe, we all share the Earth and its fate. We also share our own dangerous ability to change our environment more easily than we are able to change ourselves.

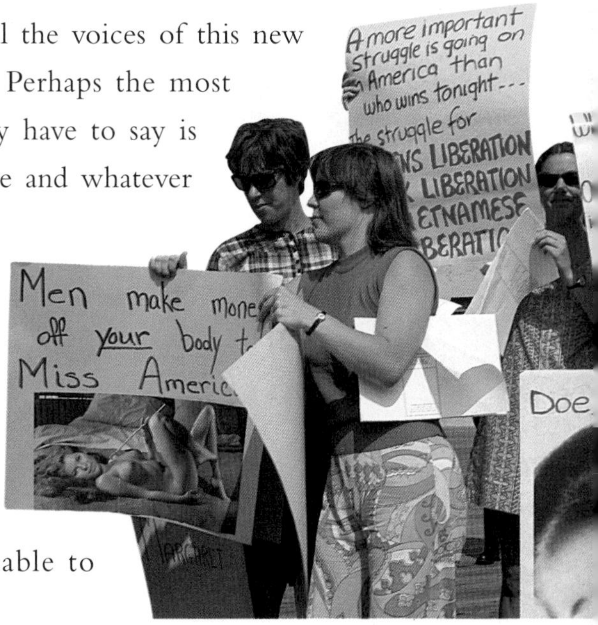

1945 – 1 – 1995

Fallout

The dawn of the nuclear age

THE LAST PEOPLE WHO COULD have prevented the test were the scientists who were monitoring it. But nothing went wrong; as they studied their instruments, at 5.30 in the morning on 16 July 1945 in the desert of New Mexico the world's first atomic bomb was tested. The secret experiment had been codenamed Trinity, and was the culmination of several years' research and development by nuclear physicists.

Berlyn Brixner was the army cameraman assigned to record the explosion. Inside a specially constructed lead and steel shelter, he listened as the countdown began. 'At zero,' he recalls, 'I was temporarily blinded by an intense light. Then I saw a ball of fire rising. It turned from white to a kind of yellow or an orange and then it changed to red before it finally went out amid a smoke cloud....I followed the smoke cloud on up. It was surrounded by a luminous blue haze, blue light due to the high radioactivity.'

The flash from the explosion was bright enough to be reflected back from the moon. No one experiencing the immense heat, the blast, the huge fireball mounting high into the sky could doubt that the test was a spectacular success. 'I was dumbfounded,' remembers Berlyn Brixner. 'I just sat there thinking about the fact that we had made the bomb and that soon World War Two would be at an end....I was extremely excited and elated....We would now use the bomb on Japan and they would have to surrender.'

Some of those who witnessed the test in the desert that morning had mixed feelings. Never before had humans possessed such devastating power. The mushroom cloud came to symbolize a new and dangérous age; the nuclear bomb was for years to cast a long shadow of fear and uncertainty over people's lives. The science that had brought about this momentous event was so complex, and developed in such great secrecy, that most people had no alternative but to trust what they were told by the experts, who predicted an end to the war and raised their hopes by promising that nuclear energy would bring great benefits in peacetime.

EXPLODING INTO A NEW ERA *Nuclear science unleashed vast new sources of energy to be exploited in war and peace.*

“It was like a sea of fire. The ordinary people of Hiroshima who were trapped under collapsed houses were being burnt alive. I could hear the scorching sound of burning flesh. People were calling their children’s names. They were screaming for help.... But the blaze was so intense that we could not do anything for them and had to abandon them.”

AKIRA ISHIDA

DELIVERING DEATH AND DESTRUCTION *In an attempt to shock the Japanese leadership into realizing that further resistance was pointless, pilot Colonel Paul W. Tibbets* (ABOVE, *centre) and his crew were ordered to fly a specially adapted B-29 aircraft, the* Enola Gay, *to Hiroshima to drop an atomic bomb. With an explosive force greater than 20 000 tonnes of TNT, it destroyed two-thirds of the city instantly. The Museum of Science and Industry* (TOP), *gutted by the blast, remains a symbol of that destruction.*

A terrible new weapon

The nuclear age began with an arms race conducted in deepest secrecy. The possibility of building an atomic bomb was known to a few by the time the Second World War began; as it continued, the Allies became determined to produce one before Germany. An atomic weapon would be a major step towards victory.

Research in Germany was originally hampered by the departure of many nuclear physicists during the anti-Jewish purges in the 1930s. Some German scientists had misgivings about supplying the Nazi government with such a terrible weapon, and deliberately slowed the pace of development; this did not diminish the threat perceived by the Allies. The Manhattan Project was set up in the United States as a joint project with Britain specifically to produce an atomic bomb. The American physicist Robert Oppenheimer was appointed to lead it in September 1941, and huge resources – money and manpower – were poured into the project as laboratories were built and equipped. James Hill worked at Oak Ridge, Tennessee, one of the biggest research laboratories – it employed 78 000 people. ‘A large proportion of us did not know exactly what we were doing,’ he remembers, ‘but there was this sense that what we were doing was important to the war effort, and if we succeeded it would make a change.’

They did succeed. Some scientists who worked on the Manhattan Project voiced concern about use of the atomic bomb. They suggested that a demonstration of its power in the desert would be enough to make Japan surrender, but the United States president, Harry Truman, and the British prime minister, Winston Churchill, believed that only a real strike on Japan could bring a swift end to the war. Harold Agnew was a young physicist working on the project. ‘The war had been won, but it wasn’t over and probably wouldn’t have been over for quite a while,’ he remembers. ‘The emperor decided that they would fight to the last Japanese and they had been known to sacrifice themselves, the kamikaze pilots and all the rest.’ Each day that the war continued, thousands more lives were lost.

Two atomic bombs were shipped to the Pacific island of Tinian and prepared for use by a team of American technicians. Harold Agnew, who was among them, recalls, ‘When the bomb was being loaded we had some felt marker pens and almost everybody involved wrote their names on it with some nasty remarks for the Japanese emperor, Hirohito....There was this intense hatred of the enemy.'

At 8.15 a.m. on 6 August 1945 an aircraft called *Enola Gay* dropped the first atomic bomb on the port of Hiroshima. Some 9500 metres (31 000 feet) below, Akira Ishida and his brother were in a tram on their way to work in the centre of Hiroshima. The streets were full of people. 'I saw a bright flash,' he remembers. 'It was like lightning, a thunderbolt. It was so intense I was blinded for a second. I passed out immediately. When I came round my brother and I realized that we were buried under the bodies of all the passengers on the tram who died when the bomb went off. We were suffocating.' When the two brothers managed to crawl out of the tram they were met by a scene of terrible devastation. 'All the houses had collapsed...only a handful of tall chimneys and buildings remained standing....I could see that the entire city had been flattened. I couldn't see any of those people who had been walking in the street. I looked around me and saw slight traces of what looked like round heads, bodies and limbs, all completely burnt, and covered by dust and debris.'

In an instant, an estimated 78 000 people had been killed, and thousands more were horribly injured. 'Sitting on stone steps covered by blackened debris was a woman,' recalls Akira Ishida. 'Her entire body was burnt and her hair was completely charred. She was embracing a red burnt baby in her arms and she was trying to breastfeed it with her red burnt nipples, calling the baby's name again and again.'

Three days later Sumiteru Taniguchi was delivering mail in Nagasaki on his bicycle. He heard the sound of an aircraft and tried to look over his shoulder, but 'Suddenly I saw something like a rainbow, and the next moment I was thrown on to the ground.' A second atomic bomb had been dropped. At the moment of impact 40 000 people were killed. Everyone within a radius of 4 km (2.5 miles) suffered

The day that time stood still

PETRIFIED BY THE BOMB *This watch was found among the rubble and debris at Hiroshima. With its hands arrested by the explosion and still pointing to the moment of impact, it is an enduring reminder of one of the most cataclysmic events in the whole of human history.*

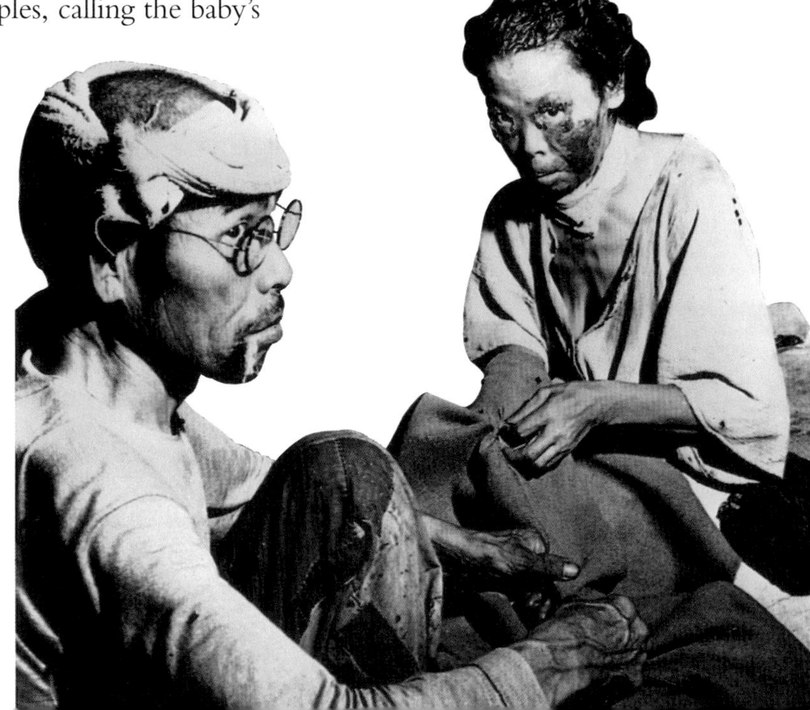

STUNNED SURVIVORS *of the Hiroshima blast. By the end of 1945 some 140 000 of them had died of their injuries or of radiation sickness. Among those who survived the blast in Nagasaki, 70 000 were to die within the next four months. The atomic bombs had devastated two major cities, and more than half the people living in them were either killed outright or doomed to a horrible death.*

Splitting the atom

The development of nuclear power represents perhaps the greatest ever revolution in physics. For thousands of years the atom had been regarded as the smallest unit of matter in the universe; the Greek word *atomos* means indivisible. Yet atoms are in fact not solid matter but minute storehouses of energy.

It was the new understanding of the atom's structure in the early twentieth century that led scientists to explore its potential as a source of huge amounts of energy. Every atom contains a nucleus at its centre, composed of subatomic particles called protons and neutrons. Orbiting around the nucleus are particles known as electrons. All protons carry a positive electrical charge, and would therefore repel each other, but they are bound together by a type of energy known as the strong nuclear force. If the particles of the nucleus are rearranged, some of the energy that binds them is released.

This principle lies behind the development of nuclear power. The energy can be released in two ways: by fission and by fusion. Atoms vary in size and in how stable they are in nature; uranium, used for nuclear fission, is one of the largest, heaviest and least stable of all. It takes the addition of just one extra neutron, colliding with the nucleus of one atom, to start a process in which the nucleus divides and in doing so releases further neutrons that collide with further nuclei; this chain reaction takes place so fast that within seconds huge amounts of energy are released. At the other end of the scale is hydrogen, one of the lightest and simplest atoms; at high enough temperatures – about one million degrees centigrade – hydrogen nuclei can be forced to combine, or fuse.

The new theories about atoms had been proved by scientists before the outbreak of the Second World War, and were well known. It took the terrible needs of war to apply the principles of nuclear physics to develop the technology of the atomic bomb, and later to harness the awesome power of the nuclear reaction to provide energy in peacetime.

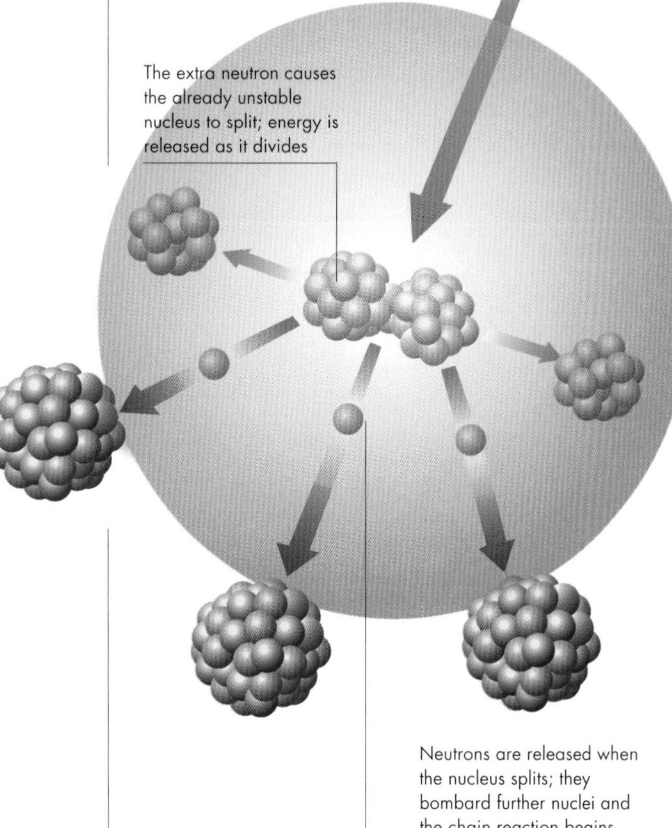

Nuclear fission (left) *releases enormous amounts of energy compared to other processes. One kilogram of uranium can yield more than 10 500 times the energy of an equivalent amount of gas; oil, coal and wood release even less.*

terrible burns from the intense heat and light. All the skin was burnt off Sumiteru Taniguchi's back and his left arm. 'I lay on my stomach unable to move for a year and nine months, waiting for the wounds to heal. I suffered throughout.'

The people of Hiroshima and Nagasaki had little understanding of the new weapon that had been unleashed against them. Akira Ishida fell unconscious for weeks and later lost his eyesight. Over the following months and years the survivors suffered the debilitating, painful effects of radiation sickness from exposure to fallout, the radioactive debris from the bomb.

Five days after the Nagasaki bomb fell, the Japanese surrendered unconditionally; the war was over. The news was greeted with intense relief and euphoria by many in the Allied forces. Sheldon Johnson was a young GI serving in the Pacific. 'I thought it was a beautiful, great thing....It saved my life. I was going to be involved in the invasion of Japan and I knew there was not a lot of chance of my living through that. I was elated. The atomic bomb saved my life and probably a million other soldiers' lives too.'

The race to arms

The bombs that brought the Second World War to an end made the United States the most powerful country in the world. They also brought the fear of another even more terrible war. In the Soviet Union Joseph Stalin, alarmed by the United States' formidable new power, accelerated the programme to acquire a Soviet atomic bomb. Ten secret cities, known as atomgrads, were rapidly built, and thousands of Soviet scientists, engineers and technicians were sent with their families to work in the new laboratories.

WORKING FEVERISHLY *in the Cheliabinsk atomgrad, Aleksei Kondratiev* (BELOW) *was a laboratory assistant to Igor Kurchatov, the leading scientist responsible for the development of atomic bombs in the Soviet Union soon after the war.*

FIRED BY FEAR *the Soviet Union poured huge resources into the development and manufacture of ballistic missiles* (BELOW). *'We believed that the very fact of possessing nuclear arms was necessary to save Moscow from the fate of Hiroshima and Nagasaki,' remembers Lev Altshuller.*

After having fought in the Red Army, Arkadi Brish went to work in an atomgrad situated in the industrial region around the Ural Mountains in the western Soviet Union. 'There was an irresistible desire to make a powerful weapon of our own and catch up with the Americans,' he remembers. 'Starting in 1947, my colleagues and I worked night and day to develop the new science and technology.' It was an exciting opportunity for scientists. Lev Altshuller, who worked in Arzamas 16, another huge atomgrad, recalls, 'The atmosphere was exceptionally fruitful...neither before nor after did I find such perfect conditions for scientific work as there.'

The Soviet scientists worked under intense pressure: as well as a demanding schedule, they were under constant surveillance by the secret police. As Arkadi Brish recalls, 'We were told not to discuss work matters at home. If I shared information with anyone I could be severely punished.' Lev Altshuller agrees. 'The regime of secrecy was very strict....One of our colleagues was banned from work, transferred to the library first, then dismissed. We don't know why. When two men in civilian dress came to arrest him, he withdrew to a back room and shot himself.'

American scientists believed it would take the Soviet Union at least until 1954 to develop the atomic bomb. They were wrong: the Russians were fast approaching their goal by 1949, when the first test explosions took place. Arkadi Brish remembers waiting at the test site. 'We felt great responsibility because a lot of money had been spent and a lot of people were involved. We all realized that any breakdown would have tragic consequences for all of us and for our work.' The test was successful and the Soviet scientists, including Arkadi Brish, triumphant. 'We were swept by a wave of such joy, of such pleasure, such self-confidence,' he remembers.

Now the arms race began in earnest. Both the United States and the Soviet Union, and later Britain, France and other countries, tested larger atomic bombs. The next goal was to develop the first hydrogen bomb (H-bomb), a weapon many times more powerful even than the atomic bomb. In the United States the project caused controversy among scientists, some of whom thought it should not be built. Edward Teller, who became head of the American H-bomb project, had no doubts about the moral issue. 'I believe that he who discovers has no right to make the decision how to use it. That belongs to the people.' But in the Soviet Union one leading nuclear physicist, Andrei Sakharov, publicly expressed his hope that the bombs would never be used; he was told by a senior Soviet politician, 'Your business is to produce. How to use what you produce we can decide ourselves.'

Thomas Saffer *was one of 250 000 American servicemen exposed to fallout to test its effects. 'The ostensible purpose of our being there was to learn about a nuclear war,' he remembers. 'But I am afraid the enemy was our own government, who put us there without our knowledge or consent as to what the consequences would be and could be.' Years later, when thousands of the men began to suffer from radiation-linked diseases, the United States government still denied responsibility.*

While the scientists concentrated on developing more powerful atomic weapons, the military practised the tactics that they believed would be needed in future nuclear wars. Despite the dangers of radioactive fallout – still not fully understood – they planned to use ground troops on the battlefield after a nuclear strike. Experiments were conducted on the troops to find out more about the psychological and physical effects of fallout. In the United States the army and marine corps competed to see how near they could get their forces to an atomic blast.

Thomas Saffer was a young lieutenant in the marines. Early one morning he and his fellow officers were taken by truck to a test site in the Nevada desert. 'Half an hour before the test was conducted a voice from an unseen loudspeaker said, "Good morning gentlemen, welcome to the land of the giant mushrooms. You are going to be closer to a nuclear weapon, or an atomic bomb, than anyone since Hiroshima." That left a very eerie feeling,' he recalls. Some 60 000 men took part in the exercise, all of them wearing standard uniforms without any special protection. Civilian scientists warned that they were too close, but the tests continued regardless.

Thomas Saffer remembers exactly what happened next. 'We were told to kneel, put our forearms over our eyes and close our

CLOUDED VISION *Oblivious to the danger, troops leave their trenches to admire the stunning spectacle of an atomic explosion from what they mistakenly believed was a safe distance.*

WAITING FOR THE BLAST (BELOW) *troops line the trenches just a few kilometres from the point of explosion. After the blast their level of radioactive contamination was measured with a Geiger counter; dusting them off with a broom was expected to get rid of the radiation.*

eyes tightly. Then the countdown started: five, four, three, two, one.... You heard a sharp click and felt this intense heat on the back of your exposed neck. The most shocking part was that you could see the bones in your forearm in a bright red light.... Within a few seconds the shock waves from the bomb hit the trenches and I was immediately thrown from one side of the trench to the other.... I was frightened beyond belief.'

Optimism and ignorance

While people were told little about the military experiments with nuclear weapons, their governments stressed the peaceful potential of the new energy. It was expected to transform medicine and transport, and provide limitless amounts of cheap electricity that would transform industry and bring new prosperity. Canada and France had been involved in the early stages of the Manhattan Project; immediately after the war they both decided to focus on civil nuclear research rather than on atomic weapons. The first Canadian nuclear reactor, at Chalk River in southeastern Ontario, went into operation in 1947. The first French nuclear reactor, near Paris, followed a year later, and by 1952 France had drawn up a complete programme for nuclear power. Britain, which also had ambitious plans for nuclear energy, began to supply electricity to people's homes in 1956. The Soviet Union constructed its first full-scale nuclear power station in Siberia in 1958.

In 1953 President Dwight D. Eisenhower made his 'Atoms for Peace' speech to the United Nations General Assembly. He proposed and later established the International Atomic Energy Agency, which would monitor and control the peaceful spread of nuclear technology. Two years later, when representatives from seventy-three countries attended a conference to discuss how atomic power could be used to enhance people's lives, Eisenhower pledged that the United States would 'find the way by which the miraculous inventiveness of man shall not be dedicated to his death but consecrated to his life'.

The conference was widely reported; within days people all over the world were reading about the benefits to be gained from atomic energy: atomic power would be a cheap, clean substitute for fossil fuels – coal, gas and oil – in the production of electricity; it would also enable countries that lacked other natural fuel resources to accelerate their development.

'DESERTS WILL BLOOM *through atomic power' claimed the advertisement* (OPPOSITE) *promising a new era of prosperity and plenty. Many people believed that atomic power would enrich even the most remote and desolate regions of the world.*

IN THE VANGUARD *of atomic technology in 1965, British workers (*BELOW*) pose before the nuclear reactor at Windscale. Despite potentially devastating accidents, governments continued to assure people that 'Nuclear generating plants are as harmless as chocolate factories'.*

Sheldon Johnson (ABOVE *with his family, and* RIGHT *with his Down's syndrome son) and his wife raised their children in St George, building up a farm to give the boys work experience and for the family to enjoy an outdoor life. Like thousands of others, he was at first oblivious to the radioactive contamination from the nearby test sites. 'We were exposed to the milk you drink and the vegetables you eat and the radiation from the outside atmosphere. We had ample opportunities to receive a full dosage all the time.'*

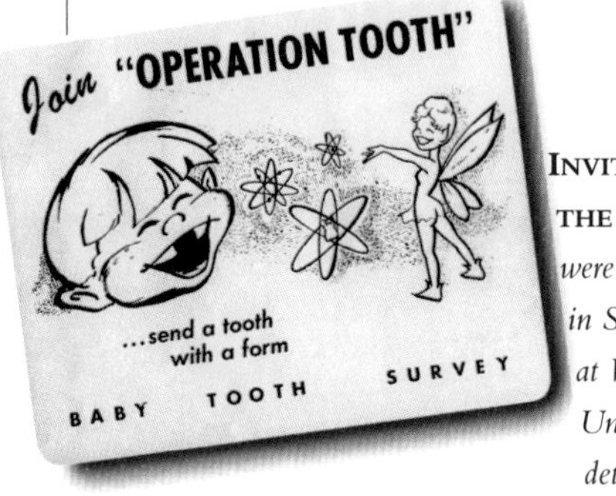

Invitations from the Tooth Fairy *were sent to children living in St Louis by scientists at Washington University. After detailed analysis of tens of thousands of teeth, they concluded that the radioactive substance strontium-90 had entered the food chain, penetrating milk supplies and contaminating children's bodies. The results were ridiculed by the AEC.*

Sheldon Johnson had come home after the war to the small town of St George, Utah. 'I was very thrilled to be part of this great effort to develop atomic energy for mankind's benefit. Atomic energy was going to give us cheap energy for electricity, for building dams and reservoirs and for building roads through mountains...we felt it was just a blessing in our lives.' The widespread optimism about the atomic age was based on ignorance about its implications. Governments did not tell people that the new power stations were also producing plutonium for bombs; nor did they make public the growing awareness of the devastating effects of high doses of radiation.

St George was some 250 km (150 miles) away from the Nevada test site. Although details of the tests were kept secret the inhabitants of the town, and its growing number of tourists, could see the flashes on the horizon. In 1953 they became concerned when the Atomic Energy Commission (AEC) issued a warning that because of a change in wind direction, a fallout cloud from a test bomb, Dirty Harry, would pass over St George. Reassurances were given that there was no danger, though people were advised to stay indoors. Sheldon Johnson heard the broadcast on the radio at his office. 'Most of the people in St George at that time totally trusted the AEC. They totally trusted the people in charge....Why would radiation hurt us? We were not knowledgeable about it at all.' Soon the truth about the dangers of radiation began to dawn on people. For Sheldon Johnson, 'The first time it really hit me was when, in 1954, we had a Down's syndrome son born to us....We found lots of others in the same situation....It came to me that for a small town we had an enormous number of children with mental retardation and various genetic defects who were born around 1954.'

The spiralling development of nuclear weapons meant a corresponding increase in testing, and concern grew about their impact. Barry Commoner was working in the United States at Washington University in St Louis, where his research alerted him to the effects of radiation both on people and on the environment. 'During the 1950s there were almost weekly explosions of nuclear weapons and they caused a great deal of fallout,' he recalls. 'Fallout circled the northern hemisphere, and when there was a heavy rainstorm it would come down and get into the food chain. It would come down on the grass, cows would eat the grass and it would get into the milk....In St Louis we made a serious effort to get powdered milk from Australia to give to the children.' The United States government still denied the danger, but Barry Commoner and some of his university colleagues felt, 'Here was an obligation that we in the scientific community had to the public to straighten out the complete confusion and lies that were emanating from the government nuclear programme.'

An incident in 1954 highlighted the danger, and forced the issue out into the open. A Japanese trawler, the *Lucky Dragon*, strayed close to the danger zone while the United States was testing its largest H-bomb on Bikini atoll in the Pacific. Matashichi Oishi was one of the twenty-three crew members who witnessed the explosion. 'My face came out in rashes and small blisters. Then after a week I started to lose my hair.' All the crew suffered the effects of radiation sickness – nausea, dizziness, diarrhoea and long-term liver problems – and one of them died. The accident provoked outrage and mass protests in Japan, where the truth was beginning to emerge about the numbers of people killed in Hiroshima and Nagasaki and the terrible suffering of the surviving victims. In 1955 a group in Japan set up the Council Against Atomic and Hydrogen Bombs, and demonstrators called on Western powers to stop their tests in the Pacific.

ILLUMINATED BY THE BLAST (ABOVE RIGHT) *A group of spectators at Cactus Spring, Nevada, photographed at night watching an atomic bomb test, 40 km (25 miles) from the point of explosion. Seconds ago it had been pitch dark, but the flash from the blast lit up the surrounding area as if it were midday. When daybreak came the atomic cloud could be seen drifting across the sky* (ABOVE LEFT).

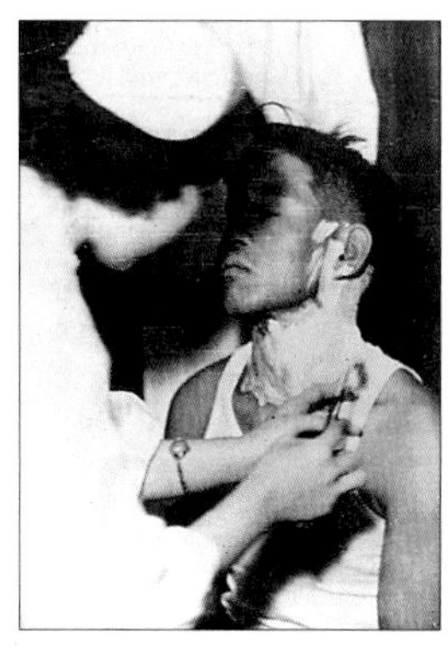

BURNT BY THE RAIN *of radioactive ash from the American H-bomb, the crew of the* Lucky Dragon *receive basic medical treatment; no one could avert the long-term physical effects of exposure. Japan was later paid two million dollars in compensation by the United States government.*

The shadow of the bomb

'In the old days, pre-nuclear weapons, the politicians could start a war, send out young people to kill each other, and nothing happened to them. It was a "no loss situation" as far as their own lives or families or properties were concerned,' Harold Agnew remembers. 'But with a nuclear weapon everybody was at risk.' He was just one among millions of people living in the United States, the Soviet Union and Europe after the Second World War whose lives were overshadowed by the terrible fear of a nuclear war.

In the United States a nationwide 'Alert America' campaign sought to reassure people that simple civil defence procedures would protect them in the event of nuclear war. Booklets and films offered suggestions on how to survive an atomic attack, and trailers and portable exhibits were used by the Federal Civil Defence Administration to familiarize people with images of the catastrophic effects of the atomic bomb, in the hope that this would forestall panic. Millions of comic books were distributed to schoolchildren, teaching them through a cartoon turtle called Bert to 'duck and cover' in the event of an atomic strike. Metal identification tags were even issued in some schools. Towns were equipped with air-raid sirens, and evacuation procedures were also planned.

From 1953, as part of the civil defence programme, a series of test explosions took place in the Nevada desert, watched on television by millions of alarmed people who saw for themselves the atomic destruction of the model 'Doom Town' and its mannequins. But the development of the more powerful H-bomb rendered most measures totally inadequate, and during the 1960s the civil defence focus shifted to the construction of fallout shelters. Many families bought ready-made shelters and equipped them with bedding, basic food supplies and water. The assumption was that people could survive there until radiation had fallen to a safe level.

In the Soviet Union, where civil defence measures were introduced in 1955, people in factories, offices and schools received state training; articles, films and posters were widely distributed and drills were regularly held. An elaborate system of fallout shelters was constructed throughout the Soviet Union, and in Moscow many of the subways were equipped to shelter thousands of people.

The world's largest nuclear shelter was built in Stockholm in Sweden. Capable of sheltering up to 200 000 people, it could withstand any attack apart from a direct hit by an H-bomb. It was part of a highly sophisticated network of civil defence measures that would guarantee the safety of 20 per cent of Sweden's population.

In Britain a shelter programme had been introduced in 1948, and civil defence volunteers were trained to deal with the aftermath. John Hunter was among them. 'We all thought we were going to save the world, initially,' he recalls. 'But after some time, as the years went on, seeing the increase in the power of the bombs, I think we realized that there'd be nobody surviving.' Increasing awareness of what conditions would really be like after a nuclear attack had only heightened people's fears rather than reducing them.

Preparing for Armageddon *Schoolchildren were drilled in basic 'duck and cover' exercises* (ABOVE) *in case a nuclear attack took place, and many families invested in fallout shelters and survival suits* (LEFT). *Mail-order businesses advertised complete survival kits, which included protective suits, masks with respirators and filters, rubber gloves and boots, decontamination powder and handbooks.*

Protests and proliferation

Millions of people in the United States, in divided Europe and in the Soviet Union now lived in fear of nuclear war, and a new type of popular protest began to emerge, showing the depth of public concern about nuclear weapons as the arms race accelerated with the Cold War. Leaders of the superpower states acknowledged that each had the ability to destroy the other and could, in turn, expect to be destroyed. This strategy came to be called MAD – an apt acronym for Mutually Assured Destruction.

Britain's first H-bomb test was also carried out in the Pacific in 1957. With over a hundred American military bases, Britain was expected to be one of the first targets in a nuclear war. It was calculated that a third of its population, some eighteen million people, could be killed in the first few minutes of an all-out attack. At Easter 1957 thousands of demonstrators marched from London to a government nuclear weapons installation at Aldermaston. Some politicians called the marchers naive and subversive; in their own film, the campaigners stated, 'When politicians fail, people must give the lead. Not people of one class, or age, or country, for this is everybody's cause. These were ordinary people, not frivolous or eccentric, but ordinary people with a point of view.' Sally Doganis was one of the marchers. 'We were in at the beginning of history. It was a very simple idea: just no nuclear bombs,' she remembers. 'I suppose it was the people's march. It didn't have anything to do with party divisions, and didn't feel radical.'

Missile power *Moscow citizens watch a Soviet intercontinental ballistic missile being driven past in the annual May Day parade. Some onlookers were bewildered by the show of force. 'I can't explain, and I don't understand why so many bombs were made,' remembers Arkadi Brish. 'There was no need for so many – either for us, or for the Americans.'*

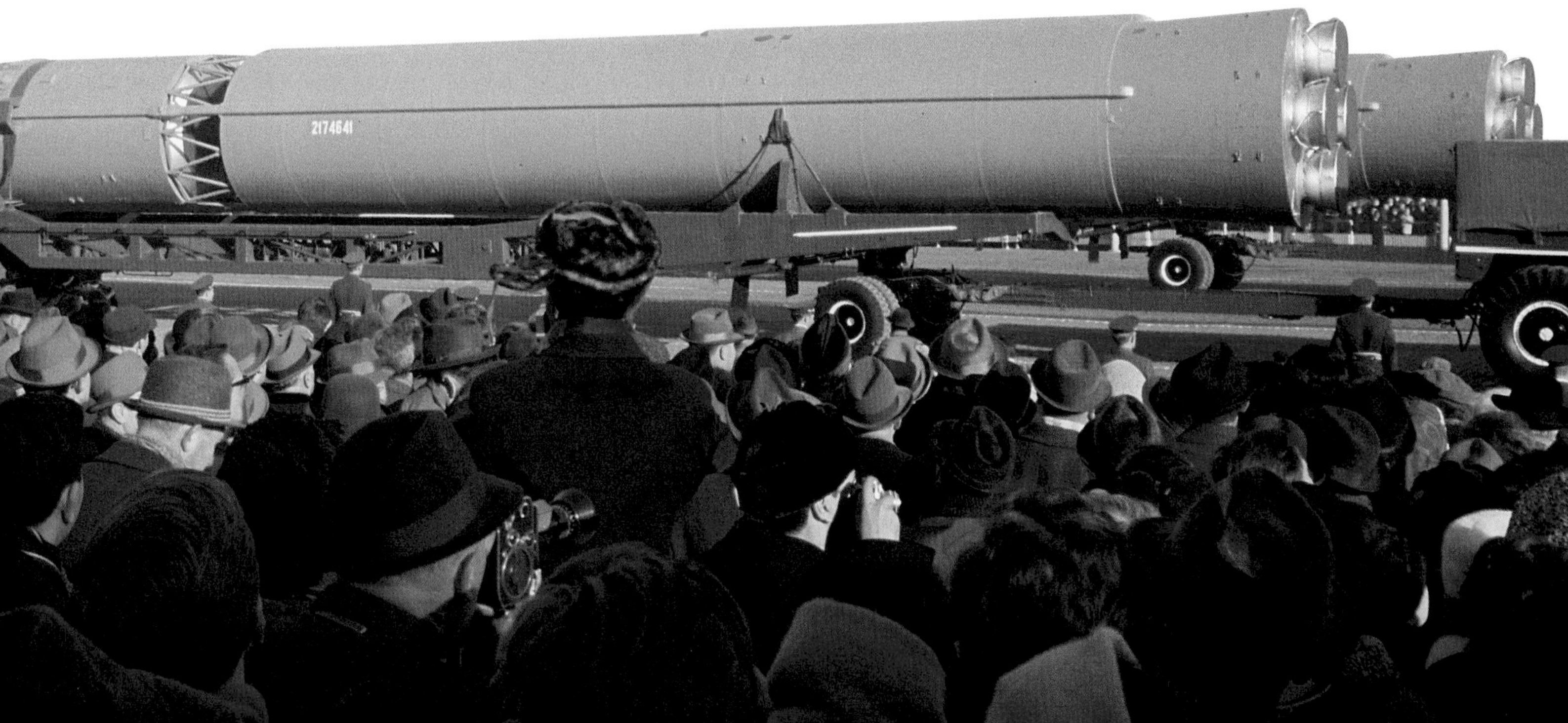

Dr Strangelove (opposite) *was one of many apocalyptic films produced in the 1960s that satirized the strange logic of nuclear strategy. In the film worldwide destruction is triggered by the megalomania of one crazed individual.*

Winifred Howard also took part in the Aldermaston march; she too felt it was a turning point. 'It made many people aware for the first time that there was a problem, that it was a major problem, and that ordinary people had a right to stand up and be counted.'

The Campaign for Nuclear Disarmament (CND), whose organizers led the Aldermaston march, was founded in 1958 in Britain. Its symbol was soon adopted by protesters in Australia, Germany, Scandinavia and the United States, and eventually throughout Western Europe. A protest group also emerged in the United States: the National Committee for a Sane Nuclear Policy (SANE) held national marches and organized demonstrations. Despite all the public protest, governments pressed on with the race to acquire nuclear weapons and the power and status that went with them.

In 1963 the three countries that had first made nuclear bombs agreed not to test them in the atmosphere. In 1968 more than fifty countries signed a non-proliferation treaty intended to prevent the spread of nuclear weapons. It was not very effective. France had an atomic bomb by 1960 and an H-bomb by 1968; China had both types of bomb by 1967; India conducted an underground bomb test in 1974. Israel, Pakistan and South Africa were all believed to have secret weapons programmes, and many other countries were capable of using their nuclear technology to produce weapons.

Symbol of hope

The CND symbol *was inextricably linked with people's fight for nuclear disarmament. With a design based on the semaphore signals for 'N' and 'D', the badges were originally made of porcelain, thought to be one of the few materials able to withstand the heat of an atomic explosion.*

Marching in protest *Fourteen thousand CND supporters from many parts of Britain join the Aldermaston march.*

Accidental fears

Although some governments had responded to their peoples' concern about nuclear weapons, competition to build the largest nuclear power stations was still growing. Increasingly aware of the financial and environmental cost of coal-powered electricity, governments persuaded taxpayers that investment in the nuclear future was essential. At enormous cost, by 1980 some 260 nuclear power plants were in service in twenty-four countries.

In the Soviet Union thirteen power stations were built in eight years. Many were situated close to major towns such as Kiev, Leningrad and Smolensk. Soviet citizens were reassured by government films: 'The station is absolutely safe for personnel and for nearby residents...no dust, no smog, no soot.' Supporters of nuclear power were just as confident elsewhere. 'Formed in the deepest recesses, eons ago,' argued the American Nuclear Society, 'our oil is being consumed at a heart-sickening rate. The nation needs more nuclear power plants. Reactors have proved to be safe, reliable and economical.'

This confidence was not justified; a succession of accidents brought renewed public concern. In 1957 a reactor at Windscale, Britain's first nuclear weapons production plant, caught fire and melted some of the fuel cladding, which contained toxic material. Surrounding farmland was contaminated by radioactivity, and the fallout spread to Belgium, Denmark, France and the Netherlands. The sale and consumption of milk in the surrounding area was banned for twenty-five days, and two million litres (half a million gallons) of it were dumped in local rivers. The following year there was an explosion at a nuclear waste site in the Urals. In 1976 Windscale was again the scene of danger after a leak of radioactive water from the plant.

In 1979 at the Three Mile Island nuclear power station in Pennsylvania radioactive steam escaped, bursting through pipes that contained radioactive water. Without coolant, half the reactor core melted. The radioactive materials were contained and the damage to the environment was minimal, but public awareness of potential dangers was increased further. Each new nuclear project in the West faced public opposition, while the scientists continued to maintain that people's fears were unfounded.

CONTAINING THE CONTAMINATION (ABOVE) *Radioactive waste at a French reprocessing plant at Hague is packed ready for disposal. The transportation and dumping of lethal radioactive substances aroused acute public concern.*

DANGER SIGNS (RIGHT) *Increasing awareness of the dangers of radioactivity led to the adoption of an international symbol that alerted people to the proximity of nuclear installations or the transport of radioactive materials.*

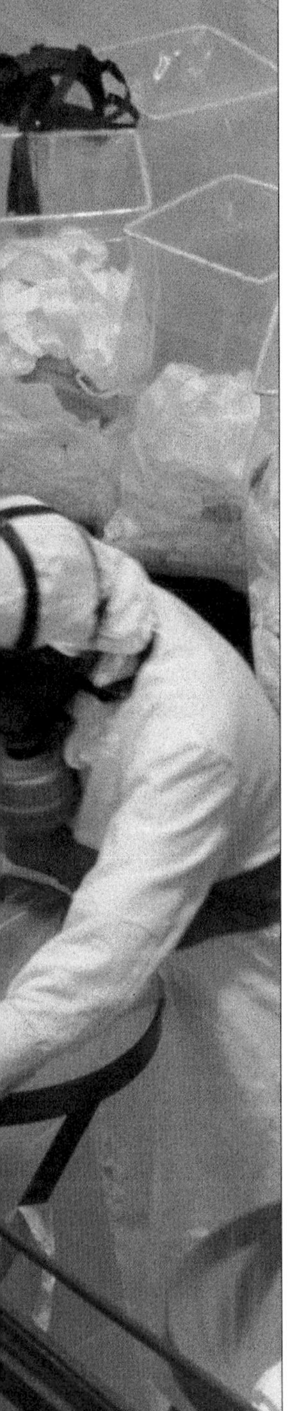

A DANGEROUS LEGACY

THE DANGERS OF RADIOACTIVITY are insidious. 'It is not like an electric current or a hot kitchen stove. You can't see or feel it. You can only see the consequences, which emerge some time later, and these can be tragic or even catastrophic,' describes the nuclear physicist Veniamin Prianichnikov. As more and more nuclear programmes for both civil and military use were established in Europe, the Soviet Union and the United States during the 1950s and 1960s, governments were increasingly faced with the difficult problem of how safely to store or dispose of the highly dangerous radioactive waste produced by atomic processes.

Some countries carelessly dumped nuclear wastes into the land and sea, believing that like other industrial wastes, they would in time disperse or dilute. Some of the waste, such as the gloves, overalls and laboratory equipment used in industry, was low level, and would decay in time, becoming less hazardous. But the radioactivity in some high-level wastes, such as the cancer-causing, man-made plutonium used in bombs, could take hundreds of thousands of years to diminish.

As the full extent of the dangers became more evident, new measures were sought to prevent contamination. In 1975 thirty-three countries banned the dumping of nuclear waste into the sea; Britain, one of the main culprits, continued to do so until 1983. Low-level wastes were stored in containers in concrete vaults; high-level wastes were stored in steel drums for temporary burial at the bottom of the sea or deep under ground. In some countries, the highly radioactive fuel rods used in nuclear reactors were reprocessed at plants such as that at Hague, near Cherbourg in France, or at Britain's Sellafield – but this was a process that created yet more waste.

In the new atmosphere of environmental concern in the 1970s and 1980s, the problem of nuclear waste became a political and moral issue as well as a technical one, as people's perceptions of nuclear power changed. Many took part in demonstrations, opposed to the waste dump sites threatening their communities. When plans were announced in Germany to build new nuclear power stations, there were large public protests.

In the United States intense public opposition successfully halted government proposals to use new sites as dumping grounds in 1986. The Swedish government, influenced by the strength of public feeling, decided to phase out its nuclear energy programme altogether by the year 2010. Yet in France the government embarked on a major nuclear energy programme, and by 1992 fifty-five power stations were supplying 75 per cent of the nation's electricity.

Alternative proposals for the disposal of plutonium have been put forward – detonation, combination with uranium for use as a fuel, conversion to safer substances, and even sending it into space to be dumped in the sun – all of which present further problems. Yet despite the failure to provide a safe long-term solution to the problem of waste, nuclear power stations continue to produce thousands of tonnes of radioactive waste. Matashichi Oishi, who was among the *Lucky Dragon* crew, believes, 'Only when we are certain about how to deal with nuclear waste should we use nuclear power for the advantage of mankind.'

Fighting the fallout (OPPOSITE) *Firefighters at Chernobyl hose down buildings contaminated by radioactivity. Many of the firemen later discovered that they themselves were lethally contaminated. Trained to cope with minor accidents, they were ill equipped and unprepared to deal with such a major emergency.*

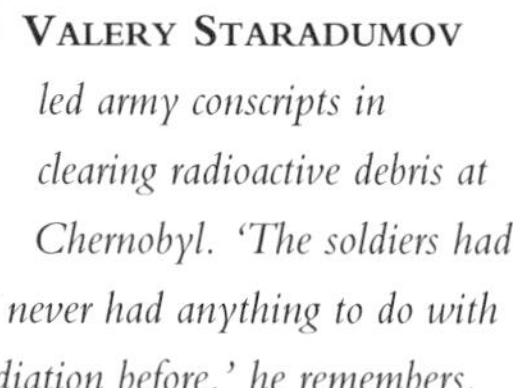

Valery Staradumov *led army conscripts in clearing radioactive debris at Chernobyl. 'The soldiers had never had anything to do with radiation before,' he remembers. 'That's why a lot of time had to be spent on training them before they could fulfil certain tasks. A total of three and a half thousand soldiers worked on the roof in those perilous conditions.... I don't know how carefully their health was followed up.'*

It was in the Ukraine that public confidence in nuclear scientists' ability to control their technology reached a critical point. Chernobyl nuclear power station was 104 km (65 miles) north of Kiev; most of its workers lived in the new town of Pripyat, built just a kilometre away from the plant, which supplied electricity to much of the western Soviet Union. In April 1986 the accident that they had always been told was impossible did take place: an explosion blew the roof off the main reactor.

A helicopter pilot flew over the complex and saw exactly what the experts most feared: the orange glow of fire in the heart of the reactor. Scientists believed they could be facing meltdown, in which the core of the reactor would become so intensely hot that it would melt and burn through the foundations into the earth. If the water table became contaminated, the consequences for the environment would be catastrophic.

Engineers worked frantically to put out the fire and to find out what was happening inside the reactor. They cut through the 3-metre (10-foot) thick concrete lining; one person then had to undertake the most dangerous job of all: going underneath the reactor to see whether the radioactive core was burning through. The volunteer was physicist Veniamin Prianichnikov, who had watched the explosion from the window of his flat two days earlier and knew that a huge amount of radioactivity was being released. 'In my mind's eye I saw all the people of Pripyat, including my wife and my seven-year-old daughter, as living corpses,' he recalls. Now he climbed through the hole in the reactor lining, not knowing what he would find. 'When I pulled open the cover I felt something pouring onto my head. I was wearing just a thin protective cap. I immediately knew that I was in a dire situation, and I was probably finished. I shouted to the people who were

Radiation dispersal (BELOW) *one week after the explosion at Chernobyl. The extent of the fallout partly depended on whether rain brought contamination back to earth from the atmosphere.*

ANGST
TEGEN
KERNWAPENS
de waanzinnig
bewapening
KERN

with me to hand me the meter so I could measure the radiation intensity....The meter showed about two hundred units. It was then I realized that it was all right – I was alive.'

The dreaded meltdown was not taking place, but a massive radiation leak compelled the authorities to evacuate a 32-km (20-mile) zone round Chernobyl, including all the people who lived in Pripyat. As the families left, young army conscripts were brought in to help. The main task was to clear the reactor roof of highly radioactive debris from the core. With no special clothing available they could work only for a single two-minute period in the most contaminated areas. Valery Staradumov, who was in charge of the decontamination, recalls, 'It was clearly everyone's duty to reduce the dangers after the explosion....I am the father of two and I knew that the accident was particularly risky for our children because of the long-term consequences.'

Altogether 600 000 people were directly affected by the Chernobyl disaster. For months afterwards, radioactive dust drifted over western and northern Europe, threatening the health of millions more and contaminating livestock and farmland.

"When the chiefs arrived they first played dare-devils, but after they had driven round the unit, few of them didn't turn pale. The sight they saw was shocking to all. We were absolutely unprepared to face such a tragedy, and we are not prepared now."

VENIAMIN PRIANICHNIKOV

LEONID TELIATNIKOV (ABOVE *and* RIGHT, *in dressing gown) was one of the firefighters at Chernobyl soon after the explosion. 'Over the reactor hall I saw the glow, which was very rich in colour,' he remembers. 'You could see a shining column of white-blue light. You couldn't take your eyes away from it. You felt spellbound.' After just a couple of hours' work, Leonid Teliatnikov felt weak, was short of breath and began vomiting uncontrollably. All his brigade suffered acute radiation sickness; eleven men died.*

The fallout legacy

At the start of the nuclear age no one could have estimated the long-term effects of fallout. The learning curve was to prove costly in terms of both human suffering and environmental damage.

In the United States the desert tests had taken their toll. Many of the soldiers who had been there developed radiation diseases. Thomas Saffer believes, 'We were lied to. Even after the information emerged that these veterans were getting ill...caused by their exposure to radiation, millions of dollars have been spent to defend the government's position....We were sent to a place where no human being should have ever been without being briefed as to what the consequences could be.'

A large number of people living in St George, close to the Nevada test sites, developed cancers, and many of them died. Sheldon Johnson, who has suffered from numerous skin cancers, is well aware of the magnitude of the problem. 'The impact of all this has been enormous – in the sorrow and the pain and the discomfort and loss to many, many people. And I think the thing

STANDING UP FOR PEACE (OPPOSITE) *Dutch anti-nuclear protesters march through the streets of The Hague. As the arms race accelerated and nuclear power programmes expanded, protesters in many countries resorted to mass demonstrations, marches, petitions and civil disobedience to make their views known. The strength of public protest and the ruinous cost of defence spending eventually forced most governments to review their nuclear policies.*

that I feel terribly bad about is that it has lost the confidence in our government. We really daren't trust them any more.'

By 1987 the Cold War had begun to thaw and the leaders of the superpowers, Mikhail Gorbachev and Ronald Reagan, signed an arms reduction treaty in Geneva, amid much celebration. But Arkadi Brish, who had helped to pioneer the Soviet bomb, still believed that a reversal of the arms race was impossible. 'You can never stop designing nuclear weapons, you can only start and go on continuously, perfecting them and moving forward.'

The civil, commercial use of nuclear energy still remained controversial, with governments having to set the strength of popular feeling against the long-term need for electricity. But Hiroshima victim Akira Ishida believed, 'The attitude behind the dependency on nuclear energy is laziness towards the conservation of energy'. He thought that other sources of energy should be developed further. 'If you look at solar energy, for example, there is still so much to improve in terms of both amount and efficiency.' Edward Teller, on the other hand, looked forward to the possibility of electricity being produced by atomic fusion, and claimed, 'Safe fusion will make reactors automatic and inaccessible, and will make the proliferation of weapons difficult'.

In remembrance *Every year, in memory of those who died at Hiroshima, lanterns are lit and floated down the river past the remains of the Museum of Science and Industry in the city's Peace Memorial Park.*

No to nuclear power *Public opposition, and the failure of nuclear power to fulfil its promise as a cheap, clean energy source, increased the need for research into other energy sources such as geothermal, solar, wave and wind power. Diminishing supplies of fossil fuels also forced governments to consider developing them.*

Whatever the long-term use of atomic energy, the effects of nuclear fallout still had to be endured. For Sumiteru Taniguchi, who still continued to receive treatment for his back injuries, 'The war ended fifty years ago, but not for us. We victims have been suffering ever since. And we don't know how it's going to affect future generations.' Despite fierce opposition to nuclear power in Japan, the government continued its nuclear programme, and by 1995 Japan's forty-eight nuclear power stations were producing a third of its power. The experts said that there was no other way of providing for people's needs, but here, as elsewhere, people were no longer sure that experts could be trusted.

1950–1995

Asia Rising

Economic boom in East Asia

It was not until September 1951, six years after the end of the Second World War, that representatives from the governments of Japan and the Western Allies met in San Francisco to agree the final terms of a permanent peace settlement. The Japanese agreed to pay huge war reparations to the countries they had invaded during the war in the Pacific, but regained their independence, bringing an end to the seven-year occupation by the Allied powers.

Since the Japanese emperor, Hirohito, had announced his nation's unconditional surrender in August 1945, hundreds of thousands of United States troops had been stationed in Japan. The future of the country looked dark. Miyoshi Ohba was then a public health nurse in Takaho, a small country village. 'We had lost everything,' she says. When the occupation formally ended on 28 April 1952 there were widespread celebrations in Japan. Under the terms of a separate security treaty, the United States would maintain military bases in Japan, but the San Francisco peace treaty heralded a new era. The Japanese needed to make up for the lost years of development; there was a sense of urgency and collective effort. As Miyoshi Ohba says, 'We had to catch up with the United States... a country that was flourishing. It was like a flea on an elephant.' Standards of living had slowly begun to improve, but cities still needed to be rebuilt, factories were poorly managed and raw materials were in short supply.

Yet Japan did rise again. By the 1990s its people were among the most prosperous in the world. Japan having led the way, prosperity soon spread to other countries in East Asia, whose economies grew faster than those of any other region between 1965 and 1980. Their success amazed people elsewhere, who wondered what it was about the Asian approach and attitude to work that brought them this growth. In what was soon being called an economic miracle they worked hard, ate better, enjoyed better health, lived longer and began to spend as much as, and to save more than, people in the West.

Japanese schoolchildren *are handed American flags to greet the Allied forces who had arrived to occupy their country.*

“We believed that Japan would win, but losing the war was the reality. It was mid-summer, everybody cried because we lost. We were sad and we didn't know what Japan was going to be, we were worried about the future.”

MIYOSHI OHBA

WARTIME DESTRUCTION *hastened Japan's urgent need to rebuild* (BELOW). *Nearly a quarter of its buildings and most of its major cities had been destroyed. When people returned to their homes in urban areas many of them, like this woman in what remains of her Tokyo house in 1949* (RIGHT), *found them in ruins. More than three million people were homeless.*

Recovery and reconstruction

The day after Japan surrendered on 14 August 1945, bringing to an end the war in the Pacific, a meeting was held in one of the few buildings in Tokyo that had not been flattened by American bombing – the offices of the South Manchurian Railway. A group of senior civil servants and economists were starting to plan how the ruined country could lift itself out of the ashes. ‘The Japanese economy will be developed,’ they predicted, ‘through a high level of industrialization and a raising of technological standards.’ Weeks later, Japan's first postwar prime minister, Shigeru Yoshida, noted his hopes for the future: ‘After the rain, sky and land will become brighter,’ he wrote.

Such prophecies seemed highly unlikely. Much of Japan was in chaos, its cities and industrial centres laid waste by devastating incendiary attacks, and by two atomic bombs. At least 2.6 million people had been killed during the war; the survivors, many of them wearing rags, were more concerned about finding food and shelter than mourning their nation's defeat. Yoshiko Hashimoto, who had been evacuated from Tokyo to the countryside, searched through paddy fields for locusts and roaches to feed her baby and her injured sister: ‘Every day you woke up and you had to think about what to eat, how to keep your stomach full. I don't think I thought of anything else.’ Under the direction of General Douglas A. MacArthur, the supreme commander of the Allied powers (SCAP), the occupation forces, most of them Americans, came to disarm and demilitarize Japan, and prevent it ever starting a war again. They believed they could do this by introducing the concept of democracy. But in the first months, what the Japanese needed most was food and medicine.

Unaccustomed to the sight of foreigners, at first many people were both afraid and fascinated by the Americans. The nurse Miyoshi Ohba recalls when they arrived in her village. ‘We thought they were scary people because they had guns....But when we saw the Americans they were nice and generous,

Cooperative spirit (left) *An American soldier and a Japanese policeman stand side by side to direct the Tokyo traffic in the early years of the occupation.*

they gave chocolates to children, and they were smiling and saying "Hello". We were surprised.'

After years of war, Japanese civilians now faced the risk of epidemics, worsened by damaged water supplies and malnutrition. The occupying forces helped to treat the thousands of people afflicted with fleas and lice, intestinal worms and tuberculosis. 'These people were specialists in public health,' recalls Miyoshi Ohba. 'They were great. We were impressed by the democratic way of managing public health.' Hundreds of villagers went to the village hall in an effort to rid them of worms. 'There were so many people with stomach ache,' she says. 'So many worms came out. The largest number was one hundred and eighty. A child came up with the worms in a bowl and he showed it to me. They were wriggling – what a sight! But the child was so proud and happy.'

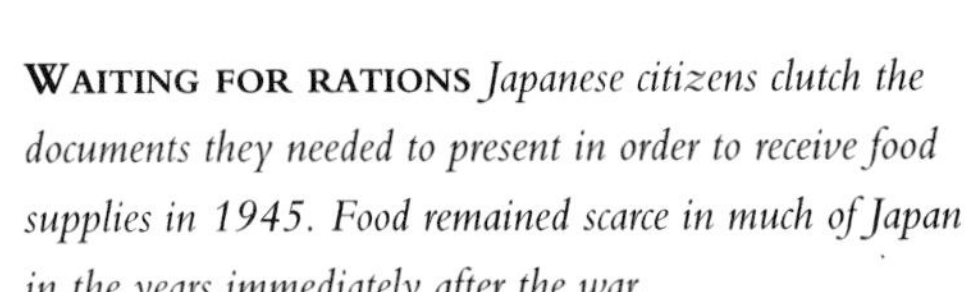

Waiting for rations *Japanese citizens clutch the documents they needed to present in order to receive food supplies in 1945. Food remained scarce in much of Japan in the years immediately after the war.*

In the playground *of a new primary school, pupils take a break among the ruins of Hiroshima, which had to be completely rebuilt after the war. The Americans ordered the Japanese to overhaul their education system, and to stop teaching that the Japanese were a unique people.*

To prevent the Japanese being ruled by militarist leaders who could wage another war, the Americans said the country had to be 'democratized'. Obliged to renounce his traditional divine status, Emperor Hirohito urged the national parliament, 'We must endeavour to understand democracy'. A new constitution was drawn up in 1947. The state Shinto religion was discouraged, and American projectionists toured remote villages showing films about the history of the United States. Schools and colleges were remodelled on American lines. Equal rights for women, including the right to vote, were introduced. In the countryside peasant farmers benefited from land reforms, which broke up the property of landlords and allowed tenants to buy it at a reduced price. In the factories, workers were encouraged to form labour unions; within a year five million of them had become members.

Japan's formerly powerful economy had almost collapsed; the country depended on imported goods. Inflation and prices were high, and nearly thirteen million people were unemployed. There was an urgent need to modernize and rebuild industry.

Expert advice (right) *At the Allied occupation offices of the Antitrust and Cartels Division of the SCAP Liquidation Branch, American officials consult a Japanese specialist over their plans to dismantle the powerful* zaibatsu *(financial clique), private business conglomerates that controlled Japanese commerce, finance and industry.*

The rush for growth

By the early 1950s things were slowly beginning to improve. The United States provided massive financial aid, and also launched a programme of economic stabilization designed to reduce Japan's dependence on foreign imports by helping its industries to develop for export. Instead of punishing Japan by breaking up its remaining heavy industries, with their long-term military potential, the United States increasingly realized that it should support Japan's economic recovery.

The worsening tension of the Cold War between the United States and the Soviet Union was a key factor in bringing this change in objective: as a strong and self-sufficient nation Japan would make a powerful ally against the spread of communism in Asia. American experts visited Japan to introduce modern principles of management and new techniques for industrial production. Funds from the United States helped to establish Japanese banks for reconstruction, development and export. People received vital training in new skills. And before they withdrew in 1952 the Americans gave Japanese industry a further boost: several millions of dollars' worth of orders for military equipment for the United States forces fighting the communist soldiers who crossed from North Korea into the South in June 1950.

In economic terms at least, the Korean war provided a valuable opportunity for the Japanese. The prime minister went so far as to describe it as 'a gift from the gods'. More than a thousand Japanese munitions factories rolled back into steady production of armaments. Building materials, military supplies, general provisions and transport were all needed. The Toyota company's output of trucks leaped from 300 to 1500 a month by 1951. People put up with poor wages, long hours, shortages of goods and difficult working conditions to help meet the growing demand. Yoshiko Hashimoto returned to Tokyo, and found work in a packaging plant. 'The plant started to set up and the work started to pick up. I think it was at that time that life got better,' she recalls. 'The orders were coming in, and as long as we worked hard that meant money would come in and we could eat.'

Japanese industry was privately owned, but government ministries intervened and guided companies in a way that was

Exercise regimen
Men pause for T'ai Chi, an ancient Chinese form of exercise, at the Hamamatsu railway station on the Tokyo–Kyoto line. In the early 1950s many people still suffered from poor health in parts of the country; the average life expectancy was sixty years for men and sixty-three years for women.

U.S. ARMY

unknown in Western Europe or the United States. Planners set targets, and used licences and foreign currency controls to divert investment to where it was needed most. The first priority was the development of heavy industry – coal, then steel, chemicals and shipbuilding. Suezo Uchida was a supervisor at a major shipyard in Nagasaki. It had escaped damage during the Pacific war, which had destroyed three-quarters of Japan's shipping. During the early years of the occupation they were permitted to build only small fishing boats. 'The size of those boats got bigger, and then they remodelled the whaling ship into a cargo ship. Then the real shipbuilding started again,' he remembers.

By the mid-1950s business at the shipyard was booming, and wages began to rise. 'An order for three ships came from the Philippines,' Suezo Uchida remembers, 'and orders came from other areas too....Maybe twelve ships were launched in a year.' Like everyone else, he worked extremely hard. 'I usually went to the company at eight o'clock. I continued working until nine in the evening. That was the usual day. On one day only – Wednesday – I came home at four o'clock. That was the working situation then. I was a workaholic, I worked almost all Sundays, too. I had no time to talk to my wife.'

Rapid expansion in the new car and electronics industries, accompanied by efficient management and production methods, soon followed. There was fierce competition between different companies. At the age of thirty, Akimoto Takehora joined a small new electronics company that was based in a modest two-storey house. 'We worked until seven or eight, and when we were very busy we worked until ten o'clock in the evening,' he recalls. 'We didn't even have a conveyor belt, so we had the product on the table and then it was passed to the next person. Each day we could make only five hundred units with thirty people working.' When they acquired a moving conveyor belt, production increased. More orders were coming in from abroad, and the renamed Sony Corporation quickly expanded. In

"The economy was growing in Japan, so maybe we played a part in it. At that time we only had Sundays off...that was a lot of work."

MASAAKI ICHIHASHI

HARD AT WORK *in a small Japanese factory. Alongside the key heavy industries that were being developed, small companies continued to manufacture goods for markets at home and abroad.*

LIFTING A PROPELLER (OPPOSITE) *at the busy Tsurumi shipyard near Tokyo. After receiving American technical assistance, the Japanese reorganized their shipyards and built large ships more cheaply than anyone else. By 1956 they had become the world's leading shipbuilder.*

September 1955 they released a transistor radio onto the market. 'I was sure this would sell well,' remembers Akimoto Takehora. 'We thought, "This will be the trend"....At that time portable radios were four or five times as big, so its small size had a great impact.'

From 1952 Japan's average annual rate of growth – more than 9 per cent – was the highest in the world. The economic 'miracle' was the result of hard work by educated, well-trained workers and managers in an environment moulded by the government to favour industry: low taxation, low inflation, high savings and high investment. In the early years left-wing trade unions tried to fight the companies for higher wages and more control. The showdown came in 1953, when the industry-wide car workers' union took on three car manufacturers; by 1954 the strike had been broken. From then on Japanese manufacturers created their own 'company unions', and averted further strikes by improving cooperation between management and workers.

Vogue product

THE TRANSISTOR RADIO, *first made in Japan by the Sony Corporation in 1955, was an innovation that played a major part in Japan's successful electronics industry. Four years later this compact model, the TR610, small enough to fit into a shirt pocket, was exported to the United States.*

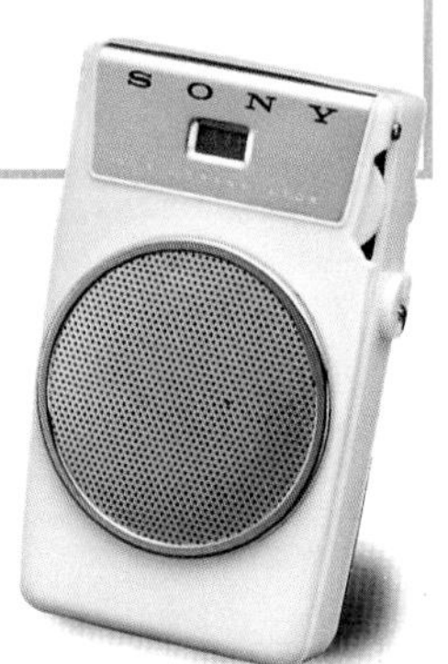

In 1956 the Japanese government announced that the 'postwar period' was now over: living standards were back to prewar levels, and industrial output was reaching the high target set. Japan had overtaken both Britain and West Germany in shipbuilding; new offices and factories were being built; cameras and watches were being manufactured. In the towns people's standard of living had improved. As new industries began to develop, more labour was needed. The result was an exodus of people from the countryside: some four million young people left their homes in the space of five years to take up jobs in the new factories and offices. As the decade came to a close the Japanese were living far better than anyone had imagined would be possible only ten years before, and in 1960 the new prime minister, Hayato Ikeda, made a promise to the people of Japan that in return for their efforts their earnings would double within the next ten years.

LINES OF PRODUCTION (ABOVE) *in a camera factory. At first Japanese camera manufacturers concentrated on exporting their products, helping to establish a new reputation abroad for quality in Japanese goods. By 1964 half the Japanese population also owned cameras.*

TEAM WORK (RIGHT) *An early morning line-up outside the MK Taxi Company, one of many Japanese businesses that engaged staff in drills and routines designed to heighten their sense of belonging, loyalty and corporate commitment.*

Warriors in Business

LONG HOURS OF WORK for six days a week were standard for Japanese workers, regardless of status, during the 1960s. Following the series of major strikes that shook Japan in the early 1950s, industry-based unions had declined and were partly replaced by 'enterprise unions'. Large companies offered their employees steadily increasing wages, lifetime employment, pensions and various fringe benefits. Strong corporate loyalty was encouraged: many employees were expected to wear company badges and to sing the company song before work each day. In return, companies avoided layoffs, and redeployed workers to other areas if orders fell.

Companies provided annual workers' outings and a range of benefits. Employees could eat in company canteens and sleep in company dormitories. Young married couples could move into company housing at greatly reduced cost. Holiday allowances were allocated according to seniority. Many factory workers looked to their company superiors to fulfil the traditional role of matchmaker in arranged marriages. As employees in large corporations were paid a salary that increased according to seniority and long service, rather than as a reward for merit, they had a strong incentive not to change jobs.

While large Japanese companies were good, if paternalistic employers, only a third of the Japanese labour force was employed by larger firms. Small companies offered less favourable terms of employment, and many temporary or part-time workers earned lower wages, with no bonuses or job security, and were deprived of the guarantees or pension rights offered to white-collar workers – the *salarriimen* – in bigger companies.

Women workers were paid less than men, and had far fewer opportunities. Of the sixty million people employed in Japan in 1990, twenty-four million were women, but only 1 per cent of them were in managerial positions. The majority of 'office ladies', or OLs as the young women were called, worked in junior office jobs for low wages; they were referred to as 'flowers of the office'. Several large manufacturing firms made it their policy not to hire women at all.

In 1986 an Equal Opportunity Law prohibited employers from forcing women to retire when they married or had children, though the practice was still quite common. As industrialization spread to other parts of East Asia, employers treated women in much the same way. In Malaysia women in electronics factories were encouraged to give up work after four years to get married – at about the time that their eyesight would start to deteriorate after constantly working with microscopes.

For their dedication and intensive working patterns Japanese men were called 'business warriors'. Only one in three workers expected to take a two-day weekend. In 1987 company employees took an average of only eight days' holiday a year, and by the 1990s the Japanese were working between 200 and 500 hours a year longer than their Western counterparts. It proved too much for some of them: cases of *karoshi*, deaths among workers as a result of stress and overwork, were on the increase.

The rewards of prosperity

The Japanese were delighted with their new prosperity and the new things it could buy. Soon almost every family had acquired the 'three sacred treasures' – a television set, refrigerator and washing machine. For Yoshiko Hashimoto, who had always washed her clothes by hand using cold water and a washing board, life became much easier. 'Among all the electrical consumer goods washing machines were the best, even better than television,' she recalls. 'When I bought the washing machine I was so happy, I couldn't stop laughing. At that time it was quite expensive, so you couldn't pay in one go, it was like a loan. But even so, I was happy.' Then there were fans and electric rice cookers, followed later in the 1960s by air conditioning units, colour televisions and cars.

The major Japanese car makers, led by Nissan and Toyota, were producing more cars than ever before, and more people were learning to drive. After working at the Toyota factory for six years, Chikara Abe could afford to buy a car at the age of twenty-four. 'I went up to heaven when I bought the car,' he remembers. 'I was single and I had an apartment and the parking place was a little way from the flat. Every day when I woke up I checked to make sure it was still there. Every day I washed the car with water.'

Japan's population had grown to 100 million, an increase of thirty million since the end of the war. As people continued to leave the countryside, where standards of living were lower, in the towns housing shortages and high rents became more common. To meet the crisis, new apartment blocks – *danchi* – were built in Tokyo and other cities with government funding. With their modern fittings and bathrooms they became very popular. People had to apply up to thirty times before they were allocated one of these small flats. Taisuke and Nobuko Sato applied eighteen times, and then won a new apartment in a Tokyo *danchi* through a lottery draw in 1965. They were one of the first families to move in. Their two children were fascinated by the number of light switches in their new home. 'In the old apartment there was just one light,' Taisuke Sato remembers, 'but in

Sitting exams *Japan had high literacy rates and rigorous standards in education. Despite the pressure of so-called 'examination hell', the proportion of pupils who voluntarily went to high school after completing compulsory middle school rose from 43 per cent in 1950 to 55 per cent ten years later and 82 per cent in 1970. More than a hundred new universities and colleges were built during the 1960s.*

Old and new (below) *These wooden homes were among those built in Tokyo immediately after the war to house the city's millions of homeless people. Work on the modern apartment blocks in the distance began in 1954, as the demand for housing increased in the overcrowded city.*

Changing lifestyles *Car ownership spread in the 1960s* (FAR LEFT, ABOVE), *and many of the* danchi, *the new apartment blocks* (LEFT) *included space for parking. When Nobuko Sato* (FAR LEFT, BELOW) *moved with his family into a new* danchi, *he was impressed by the amount of space. 'From one room to three rooms,' he says, 'and there was a bath in the flat.'*

Showcase of success

THE TOKYO OLYMPIC GAMES signalled Japan's readmission to the international community after the Second World War. The city had been due to host the Games in 1940, but they had been cancelled. In October 1964 some 8000 competitors and about 80 000 spectators were among those who flocked to Tokyo to take part in or to watch the first Olympic Games ever to be held in Asia. Residents of Tokyo were actively encouraged to offer them a warm welcome. As the emperor declared the Games open, 10 000 coloured balloons were released and explosions of a thousand firecrackers could be heard.

The preparations had been immense. In the final hours before the opening ceremony was due to take place, bulldozers and an army of construction workers were still feverishly working to complete the Olympic sites and the new highways linking them to the airport and to the city centre. A total of £700 million was spent, some of it on building a 13-km (8-mile) monorail, on widening twenty-three newly designated Olympic roads, on 145 km (90 miles) of new motorway in Tokyo, on modern hotels and on the impressive Olympic stadia themselves.

The Olympic complex in Komozawa Park was the largest sports stadium in the region. It was designed by the architect Kenzo Tange around an open spectator area that featured traditional Japanese elegance in grey stone and pebbles. It included a soccer stadium with seating for 80 000 people under a petal-shaped overhanging roof, a £3 million swimming pool with enough space to seat 15 000 spectators, and an octagonal wrestling and martial arts hall. Here the Japanese sport of judo – which had been prohibited for a brief period as part of the drive to eliminate the military tradition in Japan – made its debut at the Olympic Games.

Japan had not been a particularly successful competitor in previous Olympics, but in Tokyo Japanese athletes excelled before the home crowd and the hundreds of millions of television viewers throughout the world. Tremendous enthusiasm was roused by the Japanese women's volleyball team, which played against women from the Soviet Union in the final. When the Japanese team won, many of the spectators burst into tears of happiness. In the end, largely owing to their successful performance in the martial arts, the Japanese tally of medals was exceeded only by those of the United States, the Soviet Union and West Germany.

As the final competitions took place, the veteran American president of the International Olympic Committee, Avery Brundage, called them 'the greatest Olympics ever held'.

this flat there were several switches.' Her husband was most thrilled with the bath in their new apartment. 'In the old days we used the wooden bath,' says Nobuko Sato. 'For the first time, it was my own bath, my own flat, and the bathroom was inside the flat.'

BEACON OF PROGRESS *Yoshinori Sakai, who lit the Olympic flame at the start of the Games* (LEFT), *was born in Hiroshima on 6 August 1945, the day the atomic bomb was dropped there. In nineteen years his country had made enormous strides, and now proudly hosted an Olympics that reflected its achievements. The National Gymnasium* (BELOW) *was built on a site formerly used to house American troops.*

RUSH HOUR SHOVE *Wearing white gloves, 'pushing boys' were hired to squeeze passengers onto congested commuter trains.*

With growing industry and a powerful economy now established, more money could be allocated to the development of public services and utilities. In the cities new schools and universities, motorways and subways, as well as hotels and office blocks, were being built. In the countryside most villages had electricity, and television was now reaching them too. By 1964 Japan displayed its progress and new prosperity to the world when it hosted the international Olympic Games in Tokyo.

Between 1965 and 1970 Japan's economy grew at a startling average rate of 13 per cent – it was almost doubling every five years. Japan's economy had overtaken that of Britain in 1962 and of West Germany five years later, becoming the third largest in the world. Growth at such a consistently high rate fostered optimism, optimism encouraged investment, and investment first encouraged and then absorbed the world's highest rate of saving – more than 20 per cent of disposable income. People's earnings had already doubled – even earlier than Prime Minister Ikeda had predicted they would.

With their new wealth the Japanese began to spend more money both on consumer goods and on entertainment. They also began to adopt many features of the modern Western lifestyle – there were new fashions, new tastes in food and popular music. From the early 1970s many people chose to replace their traditional futons with Western-style beds, and spent more time and more money playing golf and taking holidays abroad.

TAKUNORI NAGAOKA *was one of the drivers on Japan's new electric 'bullet train'* or shinkansen. *At a speed of 200 km (124 miles) an hour, it was the fastest express train in the world when it first ran in 1964 between Tokyo and Osaka.*

New ways of living

Taisuke Sato can remember the first time she tasted meat at a Chinese restaurant in Tokyo, shortly after she was married in 1960. 'I had never seen so much meat before,' she says. 'Though I finished it all myself, I was shocked.' By the 1970s and 1980s, as the proportion of people working on the land in many East Asian countries dropped – in Japan from 50 per cent in 1945 to 10 per cent, and in South Korea and Taiwan from 60 per cent to 20 per cent – there were more imports of food and other goods from the West.

Among these meat, bread and dairy products such as cheese and butter were new to the Japanese diet, which previously consisted largely of fish, rice and vegetables. As the influence of the West became more pervasive in Asian countries, some people began to use knives and forks for the first time instead of chopsticks, and drank coffee and whisky rather than their traditional tea or *sake*, rice wine. Hisako Sugawara had her first taste of a cola drink at the Sony company where she worked. 'We were asked to try a cola, and it was a brown liquid, it tasted like medicine,' she remembers. 'I just couldn't finish it.' The American fast food chain McDonald's opened its first outlet in Japan inside Tokyo's Mitsukoshi department store in 1971, adopting the selling line, 'If you keep eating hamburgers you will become blond!'

With higher incomes more people could afford to eat out and to go on holiday. In 1985 more than 8.5 million Japanese travelled abroad, most of them to Hawaii, Hong Kong, South Korea and Taiwan. Traditional extended families were affected by overpopulation in the cities, which hastened an increase in small, single-family homes. The average number of people living in a household fell from five in 1920 to three in 1985. When birth control had first been introduced in country areas of Japan in the 1950s, health workers used special methods to overcome the shyness of village women. 'Until then,' says Miyoshi Ohba, 'women didn't know what a condom was....There was this 'love box' filled with condoms. You put money in and took one out without other people noticing.'

The best proof of the effect of improving diet and health care came in the statistics about the Japanese themselves: research in 1976 showed that the average height of a seventeen-year-old male had increased by nearly 7 cm (2.75 inches) since 1950. There was also an increase in life expectancy: by the 1990s the Japanese, with average life expectancies of seventy-four years for men and eighty years for women, were living longer than any other people in the world.

Dining out *in one of Tokyo's many restaurants catering for people's new tastes.*

Street crossing *in the Shibuja district of Tokyo. The city's growing number of high-rise buildings, businesses and shops reflected Japan's economic success and status as a centre of world commerce. By 1986 eleven million of the Japanese population of 121 million lived there.*

By the 1970s there were visible signs that Japan's growth was causing problems. In the rush to industrialize, severe environmental damage had been inflicted by factories and chemical plants across the country. There was widespread pollution of the air, of rivers, and of the sea. And as Tokyo, Yokohama and other smog-filled cities went on expanding, people had to put up with cramped, expensive apartments and slower journeys to work.

Despite these hazards the economy continued to grow. By the 1980s Japan's Gross National Product (GNP) had overtaken that of the Soviet Union. As the yen continued to strengthen, the average Japanese income overtook that of Americans. In 1985 the United States, the world's largest creditor, became the world's largest debtor; most of that debt was owed to Japanese banks.

Years of austerity

Jang Chang Sun had wrestled for South Korea in the 1964 Tokyo Olympics and won a silver medal. When he arrived in Japan to prepare for the Games he had been very impressed. It was the first time in his life that he had used an escalator. 'Thinking about it now, it seemed like a paradise,' he reflects. 'There were a lot of tall buildings, there were highways, there were overpasses, there were things you couldn't see in Korea....People said that we were thirty years behind, but I felt we were behind at least fifty years.'

Despite its proximity to Japan and its status as a former Japanese colony, South Korea was still living in another era. If the Korean war had been a macabre 'gift from the gods' for Japan, for Koreans it was a tragedy, devastating their land, killing a tenth of the population, and leaving millions homeless. The division of the peninsula into two states within opposing spheres of influence – China and the Soviet Union for the communist north, and the United States for the People's Republic of Korea in the south – also divided millions of families, and cut off South Korea from the natural resources and limited pre-1945 industries in the north.

Most people in South Korea remained desperately poor throughout the 1950s. Under the corrupt regime of Syngman

"In those days there were no such things as refrigerators. You would put your food outside the window when it was cool, and sometimes it would rot because it was too warm."

YEON BONG HAK

BURDENS OF LIFE *South Korean basket weavers in Seoul in 1963, some with their babies on their backs, wait for the bus to take them to nearby farms, where they hoped to sell their baskets to rice farmers.*

Rhee the economy remained static, sustained by the American aid that paid for essential imports. There was no electricity in the countryside, where two-thirds of the expanding population lived, and many people still went hungry. Most goods were in short supply. Kim Bok Soon, who was then living in Inchon, a seaport city near the capital, Seoul, remembers how hard it was to feed her family of eight with the limited amount of rice available. She measured out a strict daily ration. 'I subtracted eight spoonfuls a meal,' she remembers. 'Because of our thrift we could live for one month on the rice that we would earlier have used up in only fifteen days.…In the evenings we didn't eat a lot.' They used ashes rather than soap to wash their clothes, and walked or cycled long distances to work. While people in Japan were becoming more prosperous, in South Korea there were no televisions, few people owned cars, and even clocks, radios and watches were regarded as luxuries. Political instability led to a series of demonstrations and public disturbances.

Changes began to take place in 1961 when an army general, Park Chung Hee, seized power in May. Establishing a dictatorial and authoritarian regime, he launched a process of modernization and reform. Park's government adopted many of the methods that had successfully been used in postwar Japan. The government kept a tight reign on imports and foreign exchange, and concentrated on export industries. There were mass literacy campaigns for adults as well as children. People flocked to the towns and cities to work on ambitious construction projects. What was different from Japan was the speed and drive that came from above. General Park believed that the army was the most efficient force in the country. Generals were put in charge of building new roads, railways and ports, power stations and oil refineries. Most people worked for nearly sixty hours a week. 'Everyone was constructing,' recalls Kwak Man Young, who helped to build a new motorway between Seoul and Pusan. 'I worked day and night. I would work for a week with almost no sleep. There was no such thing as a vacation.'

Agricultural production was also boosted by government action. In 1971 the Saemaul Undong, or New Village Movement (NVM) was launched in the countryside. It urged people to improve farms, repair homes, install running water and electricity, plant trees, build roads and bridges. Kang Sung Ro, a university student from Seoul, became active in the community movement in the village where he spent his holidays. In the morning they were woken up by songs and slogans beamed from loudspeakers. 'Each person would come out with a broom or a shovel and we would sweep or mend the road,' he recalls. Every morning there were group exercises. 'They were called "rebuilding exercises". And right after the exercises we would start cleaning the village.'

The NVM's policy of national self-improvement through individual self-discipline was echoed in its slogan: 'We too can live well if only we try hard'. In the interests of the nation's economy people were encouraged to eat coarse food grains instead of rice, and to give up alcohol. Women were urged to wear short skirts – not to show off their legs but to save cloth. 'You could make them faster,' says Kim Bok Soon, who became one of the community

BUILDING WORK (TOP) *On government orders, Korean workers clear away the remains of slum dwellings in the early 1960s to make way for new buildings.*

TRAILER RIDE (ABOVE) *Mechanized cultivation methods in South Korea brought new means of transport to people living in the countryside.*

movement leaders in her village. 'You needed less fabric.' To save money so that more would be available to invest in developing industries for export, the government reduced imports of consumer goods and discouraged people from wanting to buy them. 'We learnt that we should not use foreign goods and we should make our own. Although the quality might be poorer, if we used our own goods we would feel happy, we would feel proud,' says Kim Bok Soon. Everybody scrimped and saved and tightened their belts. Mass weddings were held to reduce the cost of getting married, and special awards were given to thrifty housewives.

South Korea, like Japan forty years earlier, began with light industries. Textile factories were built that could take advantage of cheap labour and find a ready export market. Yi Chong Kak worked at a textile factory in Inchon. Wages were low, and the working conditions terrible. 'The first day I got there,' she recalls, 'I thought, "This is hell itself". There were huge machines as big as houses, and there was so much noise you couldn't hear anything. You pulled thread out of cotton and that caused a lot of dust.' Yi Chong Kak worked ten, sometimes twelve hours a day. The women workers were scolded by the managers if they failed to keep up or arrived late. In the summer they worked in extreme heat under fluorescent lamps. As they could not stop to eat regular meals, many of them developed stomach ulcers, and constant exposure to the dust led to outbreaks of tuberculosis. Foot fungus, caused by wearing rubber shoes all day in the heat, was common. 'We all worked like machines,' says Yi Chong Kak. 'We worked to our full capacity, and we produced a lot.'

Heavy industry in South Korea had to be built from scratch. Much of the technical aid and vital materials needed for producing steel, building ships and later making cars came from Japan. Labour and construction costs were kept to a minimum. Yeon Bong Hak began work on the construction of a major new steelworks in Pohang in 1971. 'There were no buildings on the site. We didn't even have a place to change or eat lunch,' he says, 'and each time the wind blew, sand would fly all over the place and would get into my eyes.' As a shelter in which to eat his meals and change his clothes, he commandeered two large crates that had been used to transport machinery. The work was demanding: if

Material for trade (above) *Textiles and sports shoes were among the consumer goods made in South Korea for export.*

Car boom (below) *Hyundai Motors produced vehicles for export while people in South Korea could still only dream of owning a car. When wages increased, a 'My Car' campaign enticed people to buy cars, and banks offered 'My Car' savings accounts to help them.*

part of the foundations were found to be faulty they would have to be strengthened at once, even if it meant working a twenty-four-hour day. If workers complained to the foreman that they lacked the right tools, they were advised to make them themselves.

Since 1968 the government had poured $3.6 billion into the Pohang Iron and Steel Company, known as POSCO. When the plant opened in 1973 it had the capacity to make one million tonnes of steel a year. It could hardly have been a worse time: within two months the world economy was crippled by the oil crisis. Yet the plant was profitable from the start. People like Yeon Bong Hak created the economic miracle by the sweat of their brows. They were helped by the financial strength of the *chaebols*, conglomerates such as Daewoo, Hyundai and Samsung, many of which also profited from exporting the nation's prime asset – its disciplined labour force – to Middle Eastern construction sites.

Yi Chong Kak *and her fellow workers at the textile factory in Inchon* (BELOW) *encountered harsh opposition when they formed a women workers' union in the 1970s to protest over poor working conditions. 'In those days we were given just enough salary so that we wouldn't starve to death,' she recalls. 'I was so tired of the poverty, I just wanted to make more money. I thought if I worked hard I would be able to live well.' Following her arrest Yi Chong Kak spent nine months in prison.*

Face to face (above) *Students in Seoul confront the forces of power in 1987 to protest over the arrest of a student leader. There were widespread demonstrations in cities across South Korea as opposition to the autocratic rule of President Chun Doo Hwan mounted.*

"There were guards on the gate who would stop you if your hair was too long. We nicknamed them 'Emperors of the Gate'."

Hwangbo Gon

The government also decided that South Korea should go into shipbuilding. In 1973 Hyundai Heavy Industries started work on a new shipyard. The first ship to be built was one of the largest in the world – a supertanker. For the workmen pressure became intense as the launch date approached. Yi Sung Hwan from Ulsan was one of the team leaders: 'Work and sleep was the only thing. We didn't have time to take a break.' The deadline for completion was eight o'clock in the morning. At midnight they started welding the last plates into position; by four in the morning they had finished. Then they had to take X-rays, but the steel was still hot so the film kept sticking to it. 'The developing centre was behind the main office,' Yi Sung Hwan recalls. 'It takes twenty minutes on foot. I rode the bicycle as fast as I could.' By seven o'clock the hull was ready for painting. When they finished, on time, 'All the strength drained out of me,' says Yi Sung Hwan. 'I hadn't slept for three days, and I lost consciousness. When I woke up I was on the sofa in the office.'

Signs of change *in 1984 in the Itewan shopping district of Seoul, where foreign influences and new consumer goods appeared as people's affluence grew.*

For many people the relentless work and the lack of civil rights took their toll. Workers who joined a union or went on strike were dealt with harshly by the government. In the late 1970s there were more protests, and South Korea's economy came under threat as debts soared during the world recession. In 1979 another general, Chun Doo Hwan, took over. Martial law was imposed in 1980, and uprisings were brutally suppressed.

In the early 1980s a new generation of American-trained economists and civil servants began to liberalize trade and privatize banks to open up the economy. Political democracy did not come until 1987, under President Roh Tae Woo. By then the rate of growth was increasing rapidly. In less than ten years Hyundai had become the world's leading shipbuilder, and by 1983 POSCO was pouring 9.1 million tonnes of crude steel a year. Three years later it entered into a joint venture with an American company seeking to modernize one of its plants. Now it was South Koreans who were supplying the United States with capital and technology.

As in Japan, South Korea's economic success began to be reflected by changes in people's lifestyles. More modern apartments were available; people had their own private bathrooms instead going to public baths, and they no longer had to carry gas canisters upstairs for cooking and heating. As incomes continued to rise, here too people could buy the televisions, refrigerators and washing machines now on sale. More people could afford to buy a car of their own. When the wrestler Jang Chang Sun began his career as an athlete, $300 a year was considered a good income. Now average earnings were more than $10 000. By the time the 1986 Asian Games were held in South Korea, as Jang Chang Sun says, 'We caught up with the Japanese and we won first place over all.' The next games to be hosted by Seoul were the Olympics.

KANG SUNG RO *worked as a door-to-door salesman for Hyundai Motors in Seoul. He travelled by bus for several years until he could afford his own car. 'In those days there were no other cars in the area, so I would honk my horn on the way home and my wife and children would know that it was me,' he recalls. 'People would all come out to see my car.'*

The Asian tigers

By that time the world was beginning to talk about the 'Four Tigers' following the trail Japan had blazed. Like South Korea, Hong Kong, Singapore and Taiwan had also grown at astonishing rates, partly stimulated by Japan's success and by foreign investment in their industries. By the 1990s they were followed by other newly industrial countries in East and Southeast Asia, especially Indonesia, Malaysia, the Philippines and Thailand.

Since the series of peace treaties had been signed between Japan and its former wartime enemies in Asia in the late 1950s, a Japan-centred economic system had developed in the Pacific region. Between 1982 and 1991 Japan replaced the United States as the biggest exporter to the Philippines, South Korea and Taiwan, and became the largest importer and investor in the region as well.

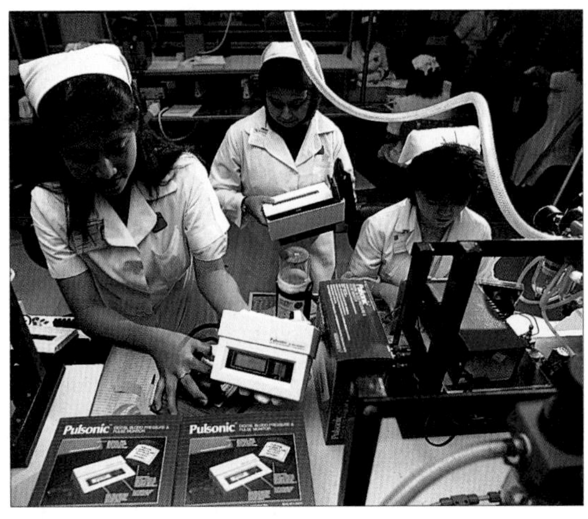

BUSINESS OF EXPORT *At one of the many manufacturing plants in Singapore, women workers produce electronic medical equipment to supply companies abroad. By the 1990s Singapore had become one of the richest countries in Asia.*

Such high success rates had dramatic effects on people's lives. In Malaysia the proportion of those living in 'absolute' poverty – lacking food, clean water and shelter – dropped from 37 per cent in 1960 to less than 5 per cent by 1990. That was achieved by hard work, especially by thousands of young, single women working in the garment trade or manufacturing silicon chips for computers.

As elsewhere, prosperity came at a price. Over-population and pollution threatened the quality of people's lives. In Taiwan there was concern about cancer rates, which had doubled since the 1970s; the number of cars in Hong Kong since the 1960s had risen by 700 per cent. The governments of Malaysia, Singapore and Thailand exercised tighter controls over their peoples.

For most people the benefits outweighed the drawbacks. Over half a century, first in Japan, then in Hong Kong, Singapore, South Korea and Taiwan, and eventually in almost the whole Pacific region, economic transformation was helped by people's frugality and hard work, by high-quality education and training, and by governments that protected their home industries until they could become fully competitive. The people of Asia had always known how to work. Now their efforts brought them a growing share in the wealth of the modern world. That wealth could be measured not just in the shiny products of industry, but in real improvements in the lives of millions of people.

CONSTRUCTION ALL ROUND (OPPOSITE) *in Indonesia in 1995, the next country in line for economic growth.*

1 9 4 8 – 3 – 1 9 9 4

Skin Deep

The fight against state racism

EARLY ONE AFTERNOON IN March 1960, thousands of men, women and children gathered at the black township of Sharpeville, near Johannesburg, in South Africa. They were staging a peaceful demonstration against the law requiring every black African to carry a passbook. These passbooks restricted the rights of blacks to enter 'white' areas, and were the latest in a long series of legal limitations imposed on black South Africans by the minority white government.

The demonstrators were unarmed, but as they approached the police station the officers of the white police force panicked, and began to fire at random into the crowds. Constance Maysiels was there. 'Shots started to be fired,' she recalls. 'People were running into houses.... The shots flew right across the street, killing children, killing adults.' At least sixty-seven Africans were killed, most of them being shot in the back as they fled, and nearly two hundred more were wounded.

The following day images of the victims' coffins, lying in a row like piano keys, appeared in newspapers across the world. Shocked by the violence, many people expressed concern, and the United Nations Security Council urged the South African government to review its racial policies. For the black Africans themselves the massacre at Sharpeville was further proof that the minority white regime was determined to go on denying nine million people whose skin was not white the same voting rights, welfare, education and jobs as they wanted for themselves.

The belief that the law could still be used to legitimize racism was not limited to South Africa; the law still treated blacks and whites as different in many of the southern states of the United States in 1960. But the experience of American blacks and South Africans was to be very different. In the United States a massive popular campaign within ten years succeeded in securing radical changes to the law. For South African blacks the oppression worsened, and it would be another thirty years before the white government finally conceded the principle of equality and majority rule.

FLEEING FOR THEIR LIVES *Peaceful demonstrators in Sharpeville, South Africa, scatter under police fire.*

Black workers *packing grapes in a vineyard shed in Cape Province. There was no opportunity for the black men and women who worked for white farmers to share in the nation's wealth.*

Segregation in South Africa

When the Nationalist Party gained power in South Africa in 1948, twelve million people came under its control. Two million whites of European origin dominated the rest of the population – eight million black Africans, one million Coloureds and 300 000 Asians. Despite the inequalities, many whites believed the Africans had a good life. 'I think the native, left to the people who know how to handle him, is a fine fellow,' stated one white farmer in a government film. 'If you can measure happiness,' said another, 'they are above us. They don't read the papers about the atom bombs and everything.... They're children of nature.'

Millions of black Africans working for white employers saw things differently. Elizabeth Shuba worked for a white farmer for some twenty years. 'The white children always came around and smacked me for not doing things the way they wanted them done,' she remembers. 'Their father would come and finish the beating with a whip. We used to work from 3 a.m. to 10 p.m. with no break. We never received money. We were paid with over-processed milk.'

In the cities as well as in the country, every aspect of people's lives was defined by race. Nomathamsanqua Koha grew up in Johannesburg, where she was taught to make way for white people

Banished from the towns *Millions of black families lived in cramped, makeshift accommodation in shantytowns on the outskirts of cities. Unemployment and poverty contributed to a soaring crime rate.*

The Prelude to Apartheid

South Africa was a nation divided by wealth, power, laws and religion, and above all by race. It was a nation that, although it claimed its people lived in racial harmony, was a segregated society in which only those with white skins could enjoy freedom and acquire wealth.

There had long been divisions not only of race but also within the different racial groups that had settled in South Africa. The Nationalist Party drew its support from Afrikaners. They made up about 60 per cent of the white population, and were descended from seventeenth-century Dutch settlers (known as Boers) in the Cape. The remaining 40 per cent of whites were descendants of the British settlers who had come to South Africa after it had been declared part of the British empire in 1810. The discovery of diamonds and gold in South Africa during the second half of the nineteenth century had exacerbated existing tensions between the two groups, culminating in the Boer War of 1899–1902. Despite the legacy of mistrust resulting from the war, the white peoples attempted to bury their differences in 1910 when an independent Union of South Africa was declared. The new constitution gave even greater power to white South Africans.

The majority of Afrikaners were members of the Dutch Reformed Church, which argued that the Bible demonstrated the superiority of Afrikaners: as God's chosen race they were destined to rule over black peoples. Their view was supported by notions then widely accepted that different racial types had distinct physical, mental and moral characteristics and capacities.

Before 1910 there were already laws discriminating against black South Africans: pass laws to restrict their movements, masters' and servants' laws, special taxation. Further laws were enacted to ensure that blacks could not compete economically with whites: the 1913 Native Land Act prohibited Africans from owning land except in specially designated 'reserve' areas; the Native Urban Area Act of 1923 extended residential segregation to towns. In the 1920s white workers reacted violently when the mining industry attempted to use black Africans for semiskilled work, which might have threatened their own employment.

While the policies of various governments often differed, they had in common the deliberate maintenance of white supremacy. With almost complete power in their hands, the whites were able to lay the foundations for the legal structure of apartheid.

Clearing rubbish *from a coastal street at Strand, near Cape Town, a black worker passes a sign reminding him that only white people could use this stretch of beach for recreation.*

Mining for diamonds *in perilous conditions, thousands of Africans are employed on meagre wages and overseen by their better-paid white colleagues. As more black Africans worked in the mines, racial tension increased, particularly when black workers were trained to improve their skills.*

by stepping off the pavement and walking in the road. 'You would rather be knocked down by a car as you made room for the white to pass than bump into him,' she recalls.

In many parts of the world there were racial inequalities and conflicts; the South African government took this further by incorporating racial segregation into the country's legal system. Laws had already been passed to separate the races, but it was in 1948 that the Nationalist Party, led by Dr Daniel Malan, came to power in a general election for the first time. The Nationalists represented Afrikaners – whites originally of Dutch descent who spoke a form of Dutch called Afrikaans – and drew most of their support from among white farmers. The party's slogan was, 'The kaffir [African] in his place', and the new government pledged to consolidate legal divisions between different races. This doctrine became known as 'apartheid'.

To support apartheid a pseudoscience of racial theory was developed. Quentin White was made director of the South African Institute of Race Relations. Interviewed at the time, he

Hitching a ride *to work (*RIGHT*). Black workers often had to travel long distances on crowded trains to get to work from the townships where they lived. Travelling on the couplings between carriages was a way to save money.*

said, 'Apartheid is intended to keep the races apart in all sorts of ways,' he said. 'The attempt now is to separate out your Coloured people (mixed bloods), your Indian group, your African group, so that they're residentially apart.' And not only residentially: Africans were soon to be prevented from living alongside whites in other ways – in schools and colleges, at work, in hospitals and in all other public places.

Within months of the election, a series of racial laws was passed by the Nationalist government to enforce apartheid: the Population and Registration Act labelled all South Africans by race, making skin colour the most important legal definition of a person; the Group Areas Act ruled that separate urban areas should be given to each racial group; the Immorality Act made sexual relations between the races illegal; and the limited voting rights of some Africans, Asians and Coloureds were abolished altogether.

The government left no detail unattended to keep the races separate. Even blood supplies for transfusions in hospitals were kept apart according to their 'racial origin'. Blood containers had to be coded: A for blood from Asians, B for Bantu (black Africans), C for Coloureds and W for whites. Nomathamsanqua Koha worked in Frear hospital in Johannesburg. 'Black blood would never, never be given to a white person,' she says. 'Black blood would be given to a black person, and white blood would also sometimes be given to a black person.'

Lashing out (below) *with her stiletto-heeled shoe, a white woman threatens an African in the street after a disagreement over a scooter. Retaliation by the African could lead to imprisonment or even death.*

Education also reflected apartheid. Tandy Gcbashi was one of millions of young Africans taught only domestic skills. 'The idea behind Bantu education at that time,' she says, 'was to teach young African women and men how to do the menial jobs in society – how to be good servants and good labourers.' Subjects such as mathematics and science were considered irrelevant to the lives of most African children.

In the 1950s the government consolidated the legal pillars of apartheid, and many whites were able to reap rich rewards from exports of South Africa's diamonds and gold, uranium, industrial metals and tropical crops. Meanwhile, blacks were systematically stripped of their political and civil rights, and without them found it increasingly difficult to challenge what was happening to them.

Americans campaign for civil rights

In very different circumstances, the blacks of the United States – 12 per cent of the population – also faced legal discrimination. But while the black majority's plight was worsening in South Africa, American blacks were about to realize that it might be possible for them to shift the racial legislation that had kept them as second-class citizens, even after slavery had been abolished in the nineteenth century and despite the fact that the Constitution declared all people to be equal.

In most southern states racial segregation was enforced by local laws known as the 'Jim Crow' system. There was segregation in almost all public places and many private ones – the armed services, hospitals, housing and schools, drinking fountains, playgrounds and swimming pools, buses, taxis and trains, churches, restaurants and theatres. When the code of subordination – the taboo on sexual relationships in particular – was thought to have been broken, gangs of whites carried out beatings, burnings and lynchings of blacks while officials looked the other way.

With so much discrimination, the opportunities for young blacks were limited. By the mid 1930s in seventeen southern states only 6 per cent of students in higher education were black. For every seven dollars spent on the education of white children, only two dollars were spent on blacks, who had to go to separate schools and were prevented from attending whites' universities, technical institutes or military colleges. Laws discriminated against blacks becoming policemen or local officials.

After the Second World War many African-Americans who had travelled abroad during their military service were no longer prepared to tolerate legal discrimination at home. In the late 1950s new independent black nations were emerging in Africa, and in the United States itself the issue of racial discrimination came to the fore. Ann Pratt, a young black mother in Montgomery, Alabama, recalls the mood. 'I was boarding the bus downtown. I had my son on my arm and I was climbing on to the bus holding on with the other hand. There was a Caucasian coming behind me. He tried to swirl me around. "You don't go on the bus before I do, nigger," he says. And I said, "Watch me!" And I hoisted my baby on my shoulder and got on the bus.'

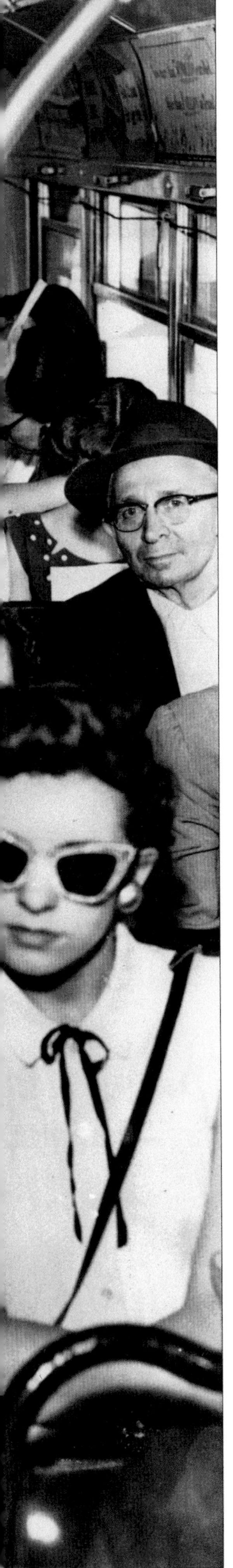

In 1954 the United States Supreme Court declared that separate education was unequal, and therefore illegal. All over the South, black people began to assert their newly declared rights, and to challenge local race laws more aggressively. Civil rights and church leaders in Montgomery called for a boycott of the city's segregated bus system. For maids such as Zekozy Williams, that meant walking to work or organizing a car pool. 'I would get up early,' she recalls, 'fix my husband's breakfast and get him off to work. Then I would set off in my car, picking people up and taking them to work.' As soon as she finished her own job, at four o'clock, Zekozy Williams would start driving again until everyone had been collected and taken home.

SILENT TREATMENT (ABOVE) *Waitresses at a 'whites-only' lunch counter would refuse to serve black college students. Bernard Lafayette* (RIGHT), *who was trained not to react to hostility from whites, recalls that, 'When we were finally served it meant that we were respected as human beings and as equals'.*

One of the leaders of the Montgomery bus boycott was a young Baptist minister called Martin Luther King, who had been impressed by the non-violent approach of Mahatma Gandhi in India. Soon ministers, students and many other black people in the southern states were putting non-violent protest into effect.

In Nashville, Tennessee, a group of students organized a workshop to practise self-discipline if they were subjected to racial violence. Bernard Lafayette was one of the students. He had his training put to the test when he entered the 'whites-only' lunch counter at a local department store. 'We took our seats quietly at the lunch counter,' he remembers. 'We were not to say anything until we were asked to be served. The waitress was very panicky. She was walking up and down, very confused about what she was going to do, but very clear that she was not going to serve us. And there were these fellows walking behind us. They would make cat-calls and say, "What are you doing in here, jungle-bunnies! Get out of here! You're not going to be served!" '

SITTING APART (OPPOSITE) *in a Texan bus. The notice displayed above the rear window reminded black passengers that they had to occupy the rear seats while white people sat at the front. Anyone disobeying the regulations could be fined.*

Another student, Frankie Henry, was very frightened. 'I was praying,' she says, 'when this white lady came and put her cigarette out on my arm. So I calmed myself down. While I was calming

'I HAVE A DREAM'

IT WAS THE POWERFUL RHETORIC of Martin Luther King that made his contribution to the American civil rights movement so formidable. His message, though rousing, was one of peace as he supported – and increasingly came to lead – campaigns of non-violent civil disobedience in the struggle to eradicate racial inequality in the United States.

The son of a prominent Baptist minister and teacher, King became a minister too. His first church was in Montgomery, Alabama, where he helped to organize the bus boycott that captured the nation's attention. Before long he emerged as the most eloquent of the new generation of black Christian leaders. In 1957 he founded the Southern Christian Leadership Council (SCLC), which was to become the focus of his civil rights activities over the following decade.

These activities culminated in the march to Washington on 28 August 1963. That morning the government ordered the National Guard to patrol the city's streets, as officials were nervous about what might happen when thousands of protesters descended on the capital. Its fears proved unfounded. By the afternoon some 200 000 people, blacks and whites, thronged the streets of Washington. They were disciplined and peaceful as they listened to Martin Luther King speaking from the steps of the Lincoln Memorial.

'I have a dream,' King declared, 'that one day this nation will rise up and live out the true meaning of its creed....I have a dream that one day sons of slaves and sons of former slave-owners will be able to sit down at the table of brotherhood....We will be able to transform the jangling discords of our nation into a beautiful symphony of brotherhood. And all God's children – black, white, Jews, Gentiles, Protestants and Catholics – will join hands and sing "Free at last! Thank God almighty, we are free at last!" '

In 1964, after the Civil Rights Act was passed, King was awarded the Nobel Peace Prize. He continued to organize marches and demonstrations until the Voting Rights Act was secured.

Despite these victories, King faced many challenges to his leadership. Younger, more radical campaigners demanded black power, not shared power, and some believed that he was too conservative and too willing to compromise with whites. Nevertheless, his assassination in April 1968 provoked nationwide rioting. Bernard Lafayette remembers that on the day Martin Luther King was killed, 'He was telling us, "Whatever you do, don't abandon non-violence". He was telling us we must have confidence and stay the course, because non-violence will have its moment.'

LEADING THE PROTEST *Martin Luther King* (ABOVE, *centre foreground, in a dark coat) leads an estimated 10 000 civil rights marchers in Montgomery, Alabama. He rallied massive support for the campaign, despite attempts by the Federal Bureau of Investigation (FBI) to discredit him.*

Ernest Green (BELOW) *was among the first nine black students to enrol at Little Rock Central High School. 'We spent three weeks being barred from the school,' he remembers. His colleague Elizabeth Eckford* (BOTTOM) *was turned away from the school by armed soldiers of the Arkansas National Guard.*

down she lit the rest of her matches, pulled my poncho out and dropped the lit matches down my back.' Outraged by the group's daring, some of the white bystanders decided to make an example of one of the students. 'Paul La Pratt was pulled off his seat at the lunch counter,' says Bernard Lafayette. 'He was kicked and beaten on the floor.... Ten minutes later they took us all to jail.'

In 1957, following the Supreme Court's decision that segregated education was unequal, nine young black students tried to enrol at the all-white Central High School in Little Rock, Arkansas. 'It was the premier high school in the mid-South, turning out large numbers of Merit scholars,' remembers Ernest Green, one of the nine students. 'But there was a barrier. Because I was a black kid, I couldn't attend there.' The state governor ordered soldiers of the National Guard to keep the black students out. But because of the Supreme Court's decision, President Dwight Eisenhower felt obliged to send in the army to escort the nine students in to school. Ernest Green was in a station wagon

with one army jeep, mounting a machine gun, in front of him, and another behind. 'A cordon of soldiers surrounded us,' Ernest Green says. 'We went up those steps. It really was an exhilarating feeling that you had finally accomplished something. You could see the cameras and the people across the street. And all of it was focused on the nine of us going to school.'

"The most amazing thing was that through all the turmoil, the pain and the physical abuse that we took, we outlasted our enemy and we achieved something. I was able to stand there with my cap and gown, with my diploma, as a graduate of that school."

ERNEST GREEN

Ten years earlier a group of radicals, blacks and whites, had tried to draw attention to segregation in the South by going on what they called a Journey of Reconciliation. Their leader had ended up on a Georgia chain gang. In 1961 their way of protest was revived. A civil rights group called the Congress of Racial Equality organized Freedom Rides. It sent two busloads of 'riders', some young black students and some older white pacifists, to test the segregation of southern bus stations. Jim Zwerg was one of the white riders. For much of the journey, the state police tried to protect the demonstrators from the anger of local white residents. 'As we looked out of the windows we were kind of overwhelmed at the force,' he remembers. 'There were police cars with sub-machine guns attached to the back seats, and planes overhead.'

Floyd Mann was an officer of the Alabama state highway patrol. He and his colleagues had arranged for sixteen car loads of state troopers to drive in front of the buses, with sixteen more behind. They also had air reconnaissance overhead. About halfway between Birmingham and Montgomery, Floyd Mann was told that there would be no police in Montgomery from the City Police Department to protect the riders. Anticipating this, he had arranged for a hundred state troopers to be ready there. 'I knew we were caught up in one heck of a dilemma,' he admits. 'We had a governor who had just got elected with the support of the Ku Klux Klan.' (The Ku Klux Klan was a secret, racialist organization of Protestant whites.) When the Alabama attorney general tried to serve an injunction on the crowd of white protesters waiting for the Freedom Rider buses, people began throwing bottles and bricks at him. Floyd Mann radioed for the troopers, but before they arrived the violence escalated, with the whites attacking the riders. 'They were hitting them with bats,' he recalls. 'I had to take my gun and put it to the ear of a man and say I would blow his brains out if he swung his bat one more time.'

RESISTING CHANGE *White students in Pontiac, Michigan, protest against the court order to integrate buses, carrying banners urging their fellow students to join them.*

Bernard Lafayette was at the Montgomery bus station. 'All of a sudden we saw this mob burst out of the doors....First they went straight to the reporters and started beating the newsmen and cameramen,' he recalls. The Freedom Riders began to sing the civil rights hymn, 'We Shall Overcome'. Within minutes they were attacked by the mob. 'There was a frenzy,' Bernard Lafayette says. 'They just went wild. It was absolutely out of control....They got a young guy, about eighteen years old, and they threw him to the pavement. They had this lead pipe, and they put a foot on his neck and they tried to force this lead pipe down his ear. They were so inhumane.' The Freedom Riders were taken to jail, but they had achieved their aim of bringing more publicity for the continuing evils of southern segregation.

Most white Americans, in the South as well as in the North, were outraged when they saw television reports of the violence used to suppress the protesters. Public opinion demanded that

Floyd Mann (RIGHT *and* BELOW) *tried to contain the violence between blacks and whites. As clashes spread, violent incidents such as the 'arrest'* (BOTTOM) *of a photographer by troops of the National Guard in Cambridge, Maryland, became more frequent.*

something be done. The march on Washington that took place in the summer of 1963 to pressurize the United States Congress into passing a civil rights bill proved to be the largest demonstration in the history of the nation. That summer President John F. Kennedy finally committed himself to asking Congress for new legislation that would guarantee an end to segregation in the South and make discrimination on the basis of colour an offence in law.

It was an exhilarating feeling for black Americans to see that the federal government seemed ready to keep its promise and use its power to attack the long-entrenched customs and practices that supported inequality. The following year a civil rights bill became law. As a result, voting rights were extended, equal employment opportunities were introduced, and segregation was prohibited in public facilities and in public education. It was huge step forward.

Some people were determined to resist integration. In many southern states white bureaucrats made it almost impossible for blacks to register for voting. Zekozy Williams tried to register several times. 'Every time you went down there, they would make you come back,' she says. 'People were told: "Come back in two months" or "Come back next year". They intimidated us so much that some people just wouldn't go back.' In Alabama a group of black teachers was barred from even entering the registration office. When the Reverend C. T. Vivien demanded justice from the sheriff he was dragged away and then attacked by the police. 'The idea was to beat people down, destroy them physically,' he remembers, 'to destroy their right even to work in a town if they had the courage to try and register to vote.' Many Americans, black and white, were horrified by the violence. Subsequent protest marches attracted widespread support, and in 1965, in response to public demand, Congress passed the Voting Rights Act, guaranteeing the vote to all black people living in the South.

The determination of African-Americans to acquire equal rights had proved stronger than attempts to suppress them. By 1965 the 'Jim Crow' system had been dismantled. Although full equality was to remain beyond their reach even many years later, at least the government had now acted to declare that as far as the law and the state were concerned all people should be regarded as equal, whatever their race.

Black citizens *of Somerville, Massachusetts, queue up to register on the electoral roll. After years of oppression some black people needed encouragement to exercise their newly gained voting rights, but many were not deterred even when they encountered opposition.*

United in the cause (OPPOSITE) *More than 200 000 civil rights demonstrators from all over the United States gathered at Washington's Lincoln Memorial in August 1963 to hear Martin Luther King proclaim his vision for the future.*

The struggle against apartheid

While the civil rights movement in the United States gathered momentum, the white minority government in South Africa remained intolerant of opposition and continued to consolidate its power. But events in the United States did have an impact on South Africans. Michael Weeder was a Coloured boy growing up in Cape Town at that time. He understood even then that black Americans still experienced hardships in the United States, but he and his friends were excited and optimistic about the changes that were taking place there. 'We saw the examples of Martin Luther King, the examples of triumph,' he remembers. 'And for us, who were not very politicized or organized, those glimpses of black America made a very positive impression. It was the pop culture – the Jacksons, Stevie Wonder – that made me more positive about my own brownness. It gave me guts.'

For some white South Africans apartheid posed a moral dilemma. Hugh Lewin remembers being told by his father, an Anglican priest, that in God's eyes everyone was equal. 'But as a white South African,' he explains, 'blacks didn't exist for me other than as servants.' It was not until he began visiting Sophiatown, the black neighbourhood closest to white Johannesburg, that his ideas began to change. 'I saw people who were real, who were families and not just servants.... There was colour there, there was noise, there was singing, there was life,' he remembers. 'And there were all colours, mainly black, and it was something that was tremendously powerful. For me it was a complete

awakening, because there for the first time everyone was together. That was the beginning of my political awareness.'

Some of Sophiatown's inhabitants were quite prosperous and had bought substantial houses, but to the government the very existence of Sophiatown was an affront. The Group Areas Act had been designed to keep whites and blacks well apart from each other, with blacks living in distant, 'containable' townships, and being allowed into white urban areas only to work. Eventually the government simply closed Sophiatown. 'One morning the trucks came in,' recalls Hugh Lewin. 'Everyone was loaded into trucks, and the whole town was moved out. People were driven twenty-five miles southwest to Meadowlands and moved there.' Albertina Sisulu was a nurse in Sophiatown, and recalls the scene. 'We saw the people being bulldozed,' she says. 'It was terrible to see them being pulled out of their houses, their furniture thrown outside in the yards, and the children crying aloud. There were women with children on their backs who were lying dead. We saw it.'

By the early 1960s, after the massacre at Sharpeville, South Africa was in turmoil. Yet many whites appeared to be unaware of the daily despair the black majority had to endure. A reporter at the time asked a white woman on a Cape Town beach, 'Do you think the South African government's racial policy is right?' 'I really do,' she replied, 'because we cannot mix with the lower races.' A man on the same beach was asked, 'Do you feel that the white minority can continue their position?' 'Most decidedly,' was the answer. 'Forever.'

White confidence and complacency depended on the power of the police force. When David Bruce joined the police in Cape Town it was really a force just for the white community. He reluctantly found himself having to enforce apartheid laws such as pass control. 'I must say we felt pretty uncomfortable arresting a person two or three times our age – we were a very young police force.' When he arrested someone for not being in possession of a passbook, he would handcuff them and then, as he describes, 'you would trudge through the city until you found another person who had transgressed the law, and he'd be handcuffed too. At the end of the day you'd be walking with a whole string of a dozen people behind you.'

Leaving home (above) *Watched by armed police, a family prepares to move out of Sophiatown, the black neighbourhood near Johannesburg from which the government evicted the entire population from 1955.*

Placards of protest (left) *A crowd of demonstrators takes to the streets of Johannesburg to demand change.*

Dawn raids *on black townships, such as the Durban shantytown of Cato Manor* (above)*, became more frequent as levels of unrest rose. Documents were confiscated and arrests were made to prevent strikes and other protests. Detectives, security branch men and uniformed police were all involved. David Bruce* (right *and* below) *felt it was his duty to uphold and enforce the law: 'In police work there isn't very much discretion'.*

As the grip of apartheid tightened, Africans found it even more difficult to express their opposition to it or fight it without breaking the white South Africans' laws. Unable to vote – and therefore to have an effect through parliament – they turned to the African National Congress (ANC), founded in 1912. One ANC member, the man who came to symbolize the black majority's yearning for freedom, was a young black lawyer, Nelson Mandela. In 1962 he was arrested with other black leaders and put on trial for conspiracy to overthrow the government. They expected to be given a death sentence. One of the others accused was Walter Sisulu, Albertina Sisulu's husband. 'When the trial began,' she recalls, 'everybody was angry. In fact when the judge came in, some of us did not even stand up. We were prepared to die in court that day, because we were so angry.' Nelson Mandela used the trial as an opportunity to state in public his own beliefs and the ideals of the ANC. 'I have carried the ideal of a democratic and free society in which all persons live together in harmony,' he said. 'It is an ideal for which I am prepared to die.'

The judge did not sentence the men to death. When he read out the sentence the wife of Dennis Goldberg, one of the defendants, could not hear it. She shouted, 'Dennis, what is it?' And he shouted back, 'Life! Life! To live.' For Nelson Mandela that meant twenty-seven years on Robben Island, a prison run by Afrikaner warders 29 km (18 miles) out at sea from Cape Town.

With the opposition apparently crushed, its leaders either in jail, in exile or dead, the white South African government was convinced that it could succeed in maintaining apartheid. But a new generation was growing up in the townships, one that would not accept that its enemies had won. All the old injustices rankled. Africans hated the pass laws and the Group Areas Act, which relegated them to the townships and added long hours of travelling to their working day. They resented their lack of voting rights, the

Symbol of segregation

ALL AFRICANS OVER THE AGE OF SIXTEEN *were compelled by law to carry a passbook issued by the Native Affairs Department. The pass stated where the bearer lived, who their chief was and whether they had paid the annual poll tax, which was levied only on Africans. White employers, policemen and civil servants could demand to see the pass at any time. Failure to produce one could lead to arrest and a heavy fine or even to imprisonment.*

CROUCHED OVER SLATES (RIGHT) *black schoolchildren struggled to gain a basic education without the facilities and funding enjoyed by young white children.*

BURNING INJUSTICE (BELOW) *Black protesters in 1961 defied the law by setting fire to their passbooks.*

poor-quality education given to their children, the restrictions on where they could live and what they could own, and above all the assumption that they were innately inferior to the white race.

In the townships into which black people had been herded a new wave of protest erupted in 1976. The latest grievance was the government's declaration that African children should be taught in Afrikaans instead of in English. Magdeline Choshane was at school at the time. 'Afrikaans was difficult as a subject,' she points out. 'We couldn't imagine having to do subjects such as history converted into *histidones*, or mathematics as *verskinde*. So we had to indicate that we didn't want Afrikaans. Initially our aim was not to destroy – the aim was a peaceful demonstration.'

VIOLENCE ERUPTS (ABOVE) *in Soweto in June 1976. Rioters used cars as roadblocks against the police, who retaliated by using firearms. The uprising triggered riots and student boycotts across South Africa.*

MOURNING THE MURDER *of Stephen Biko, supporters turn their grief into anger and energy. 'Don't mourn – mobilize!' became the rallying cry. Biko made a powerful impact on rebellious young South Africans such as Alaim Zende: 'They were preaching black consciousness, and this was the only power that appealed to us.... We understood that we were being oppressed and we had to fight,' he recalls.*

In June 1976 students from Orlando high school in Soweto took to the streets to protest against being taught in Afrikaans. Soweto was a township that had swollen in size until it became a huge, impoverished African city, dwarfing nearby Johannesburg. Thousands more young people took to the streets. Suddenly the police fired tear gas to disperse them. Eric Rothele was among the crowd. 'We didn't understand what tear gas was. Tempers flared. We started throwing stones at the police.' Nomathamsanqua Koha saw what happened next. 'The children were running around, running away. The policemen were pointing guns at them, and we were shouting, "Hey! Stop it, stop it!" ' Twenty-five people were killed that day. Before the year ended a further 284 people had been killed and 2000 more wounded.

In 1977 Stephen Biko, an African youth leader, died in police custody after being tortured and beaten. By this time a new generation of Africans, bolder and more impatient with their elders' fatalistic endurance of apartheid, had concluded that violent rebellion was the only answer. With the ANC now committed to

Aboriginals and Maoris fight back

It was not only in South Africa that the lives of the original peoples of the country were disrupted by the arrival of Europeans. In Australia and New Zealand, too, domination by whites brought discrimination and a long struggle against it.

The Aboriginals of Australia did not understand the European concept of land ownership, believing that they belonged to the land rather than that the land belonged to them. When British settlers arrived in Australia from 1788 they took what land they wanted, by force if necessary. Conflict and European diseases, to which the Aboriginals had little resistance, took their toll: the native population shrank from about 350 000 in the late eighteenth century to 40 000 by 1961.

As a society modelled on the West developed in Australia, the Aboriginals suffered increasing legal and social discrimination. They were herded into land reservations and denied the right to continue their semi-nomadic way of life; their culture was suppressed, and eclipsed by Western values; and they were denied many of the benefits enjoyed by the white settlers – good housing, health care and education.

By the 1960s some strong Aboriginal leaders were beginning to emerge who publicized the plight of their people, and forced the issue of land rights to the fore. It was not until 1962 that Aboriginals were able to vote in all elections; they appeared in the census for the first time in 1971. By 1975 public opinion had forced the government to set up the Land Fund Commission, which bought land and restored it to Aboriginals.

A similar movement took place in New Zealand, where about 200 000 Maoris lived when European settlement began in the early nineteenth century. The Maori chiefs had ceded New Zealand to Britain by the treaty of Waitangi in 1840. In return, they were guaranteed possession of their lands, forests and fisheries, and granted the same rights as British citizens. These rights were not always respected, and by the beginning of the twentieth century conflicts over land and the effects of European diseases had reduced the Maori population to some 42 000.

The Maoris began to recover their population and their rights only gradually. Some measure of self-government was gained before the First World War, and their cultural identity was strengthened by a new Maori religious movement, the Ratana Church. But it was not until 1935 that the Maoris could gain from welfare reforms in education, social benefits and land settlement. By the 1970s the Maori population had grown to 400 000, and a radical group of young Maoris, frustrated by the slow pace of change, embarked on a hard-hitting campaign to highlight their cause.

Campaigning for land rights *An Aboriginal protester wearing his protest on his T-shirt, depicting Ayers Rock in Australia. 'You are on Aboriginal land', it declared.*

"Many of those people were wanted for criminal activity...it struck me that it wasn't so much the political person that was rising up against the police but a person with a lot of grudges...lack of opportunity, lack of jobs, lack of decent housing...all those things that people want."

DAVID BRUCE

armed struggle, some of them went abroad, to train as soldiers who would return to South Africa to fight for freedom. Alaim Zemde went to Angola. 'I didn't have a chance to say goodbye,' he remembers. 'My parents wouldn't have understood that I had to leave, because they thought I was very young, that I wouldn't be able to survive where I was going. So I arranged with some of my friends to come to my home, and I passed some of my clothes through the window. Then I told my parents that we were going to the cinema to watch a film. That's how I left home.'

Nomphiti Radebe went even farther from home – to the Soviet Union. 'We went to the armoury,' he recalls, 'to see the famous AK-47 and to learn the automatic and single-shot fires. We were all looking forward to going to the shooting range to use the weapon ourselves.' Many of the young rebels felt they were on a mission from God. 'I felt like Jesus,' recalls Alaim Zemde. 'I was coming to preach the word of liberation, and giving people the means of liberating themselves....Our presence really gave our people hope. This gun in my hand was my Bible.'

The government responded to the growing violence in the townships with a massive display of force. 'The police were always outnumbered,' remembers David Bruce, now a colonel in the police force. 'It meant you had to use firearms.' When tear gas and smoke grenades failed to disperse the crowds, rubber bullets were fired; when the police were fired on, they fired back with live ammunition. In Cape Town in 1985 young priests led a protest march. One of them was Michael Weeder. 'We were given two minutes to disperse,' he recalls. 'There were thousands behind us. We knelt down to pray. We were singing, "Our Father who art in heaven, hallowed be Thy Name". We didn't get any farther than that. We were about to sing, "Thy kingdom come, Thy will be done", when they were among us. I saw a nun being battle charged. The policeman was grinning as he hit her across the breast. They came with their dogs. They shot tear gas, they beat us up.'

FIGHTING TO RESTORE ORDER *during the rioting in Soweto, white policemen try to arrest ringleaders among the protesting students. The ANC organizers joined the protest. Mass funerals for the victims of the violence later became further rallying points for resistance.*

The road to change

By the late 1980s the violence had escalated in the townships, not only between white policemen and black people, but also between supporters of the ANC and Zulu members of Inkatha, the Zulu movement headed by Chief Mangosuthu Buthelezi. To contain the violence, a state of emergency was declared in thirty-six South African districts. With the country now diplomatically isolated, many whites began to realize that South Africa could not continue with minority rule and apartheid, in defiance of the rest of the world. The economic sanctions that had been imposed by the international community harmed black Africans most of all, but together with anti-apartheid demonstrations in the West they did put extra pressure on the government to yield. The fears of white South Africans that they would be submerged by a communist revolution directed from Moscow were allayed when communism collapsed in Eastern Europe in 1989.

In September that year the parliamentary elections in South Africa were followed by a general strike in which three million

MY FREEDOM IS YOUR FREEDOM *Students demanding the release of Nelson Mandela demonstrate in Cape Town in 1988. Without the release of Nelson Mandela, the road to change remained blocked.*

CELEBRATING FREEDOM *Nelson Mandela addressing the audience at a concert held in his honour in London in April 1990, which was televised worldwide. He thanked all those opposed to apartheid who had worked for the release of political prisoners and had supported measures to end oppression in South Africa.*

"Going to the voting booth was like going to a very private chapel. There was an element of great joy in knowing that this was the burial of something very evil."

MICHAEL WEEDER

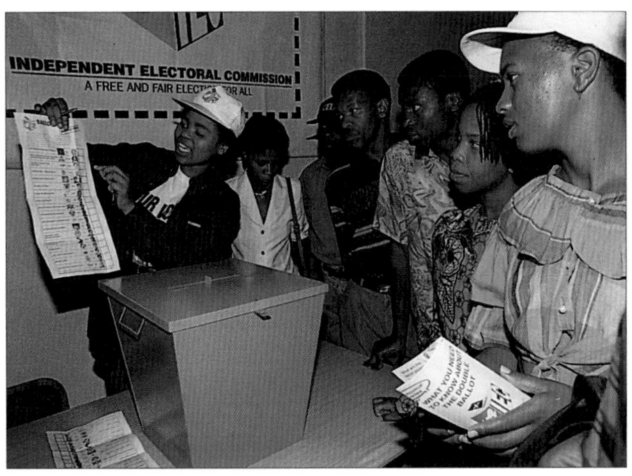

SOUTH AFRICA'S NEW VOTERS (ABOVE) *were offered special tuition to guide them through the voting procedure. The ballot paper listed each party, giving its symbol and a photograph of its leader. Nomathamsanqua Koha* (ABOVE LEFT), *now a hospital matron, began to believe after Nelson Mandela's release that change really might be possible. She was thrilled to be able to cast her vote for the first time.*

QUEUEING TO VOTE (OPPOSITE) *For the first time in their lives, black South Africans line up outside a polling station to cast their vote. A few practical problems with misplaced ballots and pirate voting stations did not diminish the excitement of election day.*

blacks stopped work. It was one of the country's largest protests ever. As more white people joined the protests, pressure for reform intensified. By the time F. W. de Klerk (who as education minister had unleashed the Soweto rebellion by imposing Afrikaans on African schoolchildren) became state president, the demand for action could no longer be ignored, and the worst excesses of apartheid began to be dismantled. On 11 February 1990 he lifted the bans on the ANC and other political organizations, and made an announcement that no one expected to hear: 'I wish to put it plainly that the government has taken a firm decision to release Mr Mandela unconditionally.'

The whole nation was watching on television as the arch-enemy of apartheid, aged seventy-three, made his first appearance for twenty-seven years. 'The day when Mandela was released,' one old miner remembers, 'nobody ate food in the house. Everybody was very, very, very happy – nobody felt like cooking.' Albertina Sisulu's husband Walter Sisulu had already been released. 'Sometimes,' she says, 'when you are excited it is accompanied by tears. It was just like that: it was mixed. You could feel the tears coming, and the joy stopped the tears.'

It took years of complex, tense negotiations between Nelson Mandela, F. W. de Klerk and the other parties before a route could be agreed to introduce one man, one vote, and a new parliament in which the black majority could exercise power. The first free, multiracial, democratic general election in South Africa took place on 27 April 1994. When the great day came, queues of people waiting patiently for their turn to vote stretched across the veldt and through the streets of the townships. Nomathamsanqua Koha describes her emotions. 'You went in, and when I was behind that screen I said, "I'm voting! Me! Voting!" I could hardly believe it. And you say, "Where is the ANC? I mustn't make a mistake. My 'X' must really go in the space provided"....It was wonderful!'

Long before the election results came in it was clear that the ANC would form the next government, and on 10 May 1994 Nelson Mandela became president. It would be a long fight to gain economic equality and equal access to education, housing and jobs, but at least all South Africans, of whatever colour, were now equal before the law, and state racism had finally been overturned.

4

1950–1995

Endangered Planet

Campaigning for the Environment

The most awe-inspiring experience in space for the astronaut James Lovell came in December 1968 aboard *Apollo 8*. As the spacecraft first orbited the moon he put his thumb against the window and found that he was able to conceal the entire earth behind it. 'Now you had to think about that for a little bit,' he reflects. 'It gave you a feeling of just how insignificant we are on earth compared to the rest of the universe.' Later, as the spacecraft began its long journey back home, 'The earth came out of the horizon – and it was earthrise'. The astronauts' powerfully vivid photographs of the fragile planet floating in the darkness of space were brought to people around the world.

Richard Ayres, a law student living in the United States, was one of them. 'We were the first kids to see pictures of our planet taken by another human being. It made us feel how small the planet was.' For Bonnie Campbell, who grew up in the polluted industrial Midwest, seeing the earth was a turning point. 'You were watching TV, and here is a picture of the earth looking back at the earth. Here's a living planet, and the blue ocean,' she recalls. 'It really made you think, "Here we are; maybe this is the only place in the whole universe where life can exist, so let's take better care of it".'

The *Apollo 8* photographs fixed an image and caught a mood; they helped to focus attention on the earth and on its vulnerability as the dangers associated with industrial pollution became more evident. People's concern about environmental issues, which grew throughout the 1960s, was heightened in the following decades by a series of unnatural disasters and disturbing new discoveries.

Governments, politicians and industrialists were forced to listen as people around the world began to take direct action, joining new groups dedicated to protecting the environment and participating in mass protests. As local threats to the planet's health assumed global proportions, these people's commitment helped to spread a new awareness of the dangers of uncontrolled commercial exploitation.

Earthrise *Seen beyond the surface of the moon, the image of the fragile earth inspires a new environmental awareness.*

"We had no concern about industrial waste...there was no environmental ethic at that time. We were concerned and preoccupied with developing our industrial base and having jobs. The environmental concern was largely irrelevant because it was not even thought of."

CARL BAGGE

WASTED WATERS *of Minamata Bay, heavily polluted with over 600 tonnes of methyl mercury by the Chisso Corporation, were no longer safe for fishing. Hiroki Iwamoto was among the many local fishermen and fishmongers who were forced out of business. 'Our lives have always depended on the sea. The sea – which should be a great treasure for us to pass on to future generations – is damaged and we have lost our livelihood,' he says. 'My anger is beyond expression.'*

DIRTY BUSINESS (OPPOSITE, TOP) *Toshio Hanada, a resident of Minamata Bay, surveys the unhealthy scene of the huge Chisso factory complex from the top of a nearby hill. 'In those days, smoke and toxic gases would pour out of the factory,' he remembers. 'Even in the middle of spring, the lovely green leaves would turn yellow and the hill would become almost bald.' Smoking chimneys were a familiar feature of industrial landscapes everywhere.*

The dilemma of development

One of the first sinister episodes to prompt people's questioning of scientific progress took place in a little fishing port on the south coast of Japan. In the middle 1950s Japan was just beginning to rebuild its mighty industrial machine. A new factory belonging to the Chisso Corporation, a chemical company, had been built on the shores of Minamata Bay, where the fishermen continued to take their boats out on to the water to fish for octopus, squid, and other species of fish and shellfish as they had always done.

The first sign that anything was wrong came when the other fish-eaters of Minamata, the cats, began to behave in an odd way, staggering with what the fishermen and their families called 'dancing cat disease'. And then they died. Soon humans also began to be affected. Tsuginori Hamamoto had fished with his father since he was a child. At night they cooked bait made from wheat bran and dried bugs, and in the morning carried the heavy pots of bait down to the boat. But one morning Tsuginori Hamamoto stumbled and fell. 'I put the yoke back on my shoulders and put the bait-baskets back on the yoke, but as soon as I reached the beach I fell over again. Finally I realized what was happening: my whole body was trembling and numb.'

As more and more fishermen became ill, doctors from the local university came and filmed their shaking fits. They suspected that the cause was metal poisoning. Before long, babies were being born partially paralysed and suffering from other birth defects. Eventually it became clear that the disease was caused by methyl mercury discharged into the sea from waste pipes by the Chisso factory. The mercury entered the food chain: it was absorbed by the plankton on which the fish fed, and then by the cats and the humans who ate the fish. It damaged the nervous system, affecting people's ability to talk, see, hear and walk. Contamination from the fish eaten by pregnant women was absorbed by their unborn babies, causing severe brain damage. Soon no one would buy the fish at the local market. People's livelihood, long dependent upon the sea, was under threat.

At first the Chisso Corporation denied all responsibility. Tests confirmed that mercury was the cause of 'Minamata disease', but the company covered up the results. Hidenori Yamashita worked in the Chisso laboratory at the time. 'The management didn't give a damn about pollution or about the environment, and the workers didn't give a damn either, and even if someone did they were just ignored.' Besides, he adds, 'Chisso helped the town a lot. People thought they might as well put up with it'. As the company continued to dump its highly toxic waste into the bay during the next ten years, more than seventy people died as a result of the poison, and thousands more suffered from its effects.

During the 1950s many people throughout the industrial world regarded smoke and dirt as an inseparable part of industry and progress – a price that had to be paid for the security of a job. Carl Bagge grew up next to a steel plant in northern Indiana. 'We accepted this as part of life in industrial America – the stench, the smoke, the absolute filth that filled our lungs. We thought this was the way life was, the way God intended, and the way prosperous America could survive.'

Hidenori Yamashita *and his colleagues in the Chisso laboratory tested the water to try to prove that Chisso was innocent of the accusations made against it by the local press. 'One of my colleagues was in charge of the experiment that found poisonous mercury in the sludge,' he recalls. 'I saw it with my own eyes.'*

Catalyst for change

In the United States many people could now afford to buy new consumer goods – domestic appliances that used more electricity, and cars that consumed more oil and polluted the atmosphere. Electricity was generated by nuclear reactors in new atomic power stations, and scientists countered public fears of radioactive fallout with assurances of their safety. On the land too, science offered progress in the form of agricultural chemicals, which were widely used during the 1950s. For farmers, new pesticides such as DDT offered an effective method for controlling pests, and so helped to increase crop yields. But the chemicals could kill birds as well as insects, and pollute land and streams as well helping crops to grow.

SMOG SCREEN *Breathing problems were one of the consequences of the grey smog familiar to Londoners; it grew worse during the 1950s as traffic emissions increased. Some pedestrians covered their faces to protect their lungs from the thick smog – a mixture of smoke, fog and chemical fumes. After some 4000 Londoners died as a result of respiratory and heart problems in 1952, the British government passed a Clean Air Act.*

Trust in scientific progress was challenged in 1962 with the publication of a book entitled *Silent Spring*. Its author, the American biologist Rachel Carson, argued that far from being a harmless blessing, pesticides were inflicting irreparable damage on the environment. 'Unless we bring these chemicals under better control,' she proclaimed, 'we are certainly heading for disaster.' She asked whether anyone could believe it was possible 'to lay down such a barrage of poisons on the surface of the earth without making it unfit for all life'.

Despite attempts by industry and by science to deny and discredit her warning message, Rachel Carson succeeded in shaking public confidence and alerting the American people to the hazards of chemical pollution. Her prophetic book became a best-seller, and made many people aware of the way in which uncritical scientists in the service of business or government might damage the environment. At about this time Walt Patterson, a Canadian living in Britain, decided to become involved in campaigns to protect it. 'We thought things were getting out of hand,' he recalls. 'We thought that the people who were supposed to be in charge weren't in charge, they were actively aggravating the problems.' As public concern grew, an investigation into the dangerous side-effects of DDT and other pesticides was launched.

By this time petrochemicals had become the lifeblood of the modern world. The oil needed to power factories, fuel the growing number of vehicles and heat homes was being shipped across the seas from the Middle East and other oilfields in huge supertankers. In March 1967 the *Torrey Canyon*, fully laden with 120 000 tonnes of crude oil, hit the rocks off the south-west coast of England. Nothing like it had ever happened before. At first bombs were dropped in the hope of burning off the oil. Jonathan Tod, a British pilot, was part of the mission. As he flew south over the Scottish border, 'Looking up ahead of us we could see a large black cloud going up to at least thirty thousand feet...it made one realize very clearly the magnitude of the task that we had to undertake and the potential hazard that it could become for the environment as a whole. What we had there was in many ways an environmental time bomb,' he recalls. As his bombs hit the tanker, he saw a huge billow of smoke and a bright red flame leaping 300 metres (1000 feet) into the air.

The bombing did not succeed in burning off all the thick oil from the ship; it was washed onto the nearby beaches, polluting the water and sand, killing fish, shrimps, oysters and other forms of marine life, and fouling the seabirds. People moved by the plight of the birds struggled to rescue them. Olga Penrose was one of hundreds of volunteers who did their best to clean them. 'You looked in a box, and it

CLEAN-UP CAMPAIGN (BELOW) *on the coast of Brittany, where 100 km (60 miles) of beaches were affected by the* Torrey Canyon *oil spill. Volunteers such as Olga Penrose* (BOTTOM) *worked hard to rescue the oil-soaked seabirds.*

DISASTER AT SEA (LEFT) *A column of black smoke pours from the* Torrey Canyon, *the first super-tanker to run aground, and the first of many oil spills. Walt Patterson remembers it well: 'It was an image that was burned into the brains of people...that the industrial reliance on oil brought with it the possibility of this kind of environmental catastrophe.'*

"Earthday gave people all over the country an opportunity for the first time to express their concern, which they did in huge numbers."

GAYLORD NELSON

was a ball of tar and a beak sticking through. You literally had to scrape this ball of tar off until you got to the actual bird, and that was really horrific. You knew that the oil was burning the bird, so you tried to get it off as quickly as possible. It made you feel so inadequate, and very angry, to think that man had done this.'

The fate of a group of brown pelicans at Anacapa, an island off the Californian coast, brought yet more alarming evidence of the harmful nature of chemicals, though this time the cause was less visible. Lloyd Kiff was a member of an expedition sent to discover why the pelicans at Anacapa were not breeding. He climbed the steep cliffs to the pelican colony on the uninhabited island. 'It was an absolutely perfect scene, the gulls in the air screaming, the wind blowing, the ocean breeze, and five hundred pairs of pelicans, their nests all adorned with flowers. An untouched island. And then we looked into nests and all the nests contained broken eggs. And in that whole season, where there were twelve hundred nesting attempts by pelicans, they produced only two young,' he remembers. 'This was a horrifying scene to us. I can't describe how moved we were, that something so insidious could be changing the world like this.'

EGG CURATOR *Lloyd Kiff made dedicated efforts to rescue the pelicans' fragile eggs on the island of Anacapa from reproductive failure as a result of DDT. It had taken some twenty years for the full extent of the damage caused by the pesticide to emerge.*

Lloyd Kiff had been aware of Rachel Carson's book, and he knew that DDT was now banned in several European countries, in Canada and in the North American state of Wisconsin. He also knew that when it entered the food chain DDT caused a decrease in eggshell weight. DDT had never been used on Anacapa itself, but minute traces of it had found their way from distant rivers into the pelicans' food chain, making the shells of their eggs too thin to bear the weight of the parent birds during incubation. It was just as Rachel Carson had predicted.

It was becoming clear that many of the products of modern industry – aerosols, fertilizers, pesticides, petrochemicals and other substances – were causing not just local problems but a threat to the whole planet. Maurice Strong, a Canadian industrialist with a deep commitment to environmental issues, sensed the changing mood: 'Industrial activities were giving rise to local air and water pollution, and residents were...increasingly sensitive to it. People saw some of their favourite recreational places – beaches, natural areas – being desecrated, waters being contaminated.'

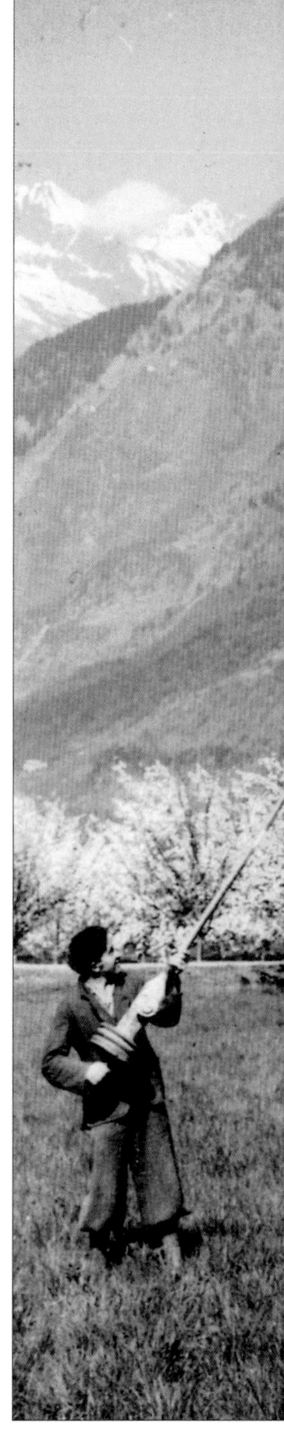

CHEMICAL KILLERS *such as the DDT being sprayed in this orchard in northern Italy were at first hugely beneficial to farmers, but they were environmentally disastrous. As insects built up resistance to DDT it accumulated in their body tissues, and was passed on to predators. DDT was later banned in many countries.*

A grass-roots movement

The growing concern for the environment was first shown on a national scale in the United States on 22 April 1970. Denis Hayes was one of the organizers of the demonstrations held on that day. 'Earthday was the most massive outpouring of human beings that had ever surrounded any issue up to that time,' he remembers. 'We had twenty million Americans drawn from all walks of life, turning out in these huge events in every major city and most of the minor hamlets across the country, to protest the direction that the world seemed to be headed.'

Earthday was devised and organized by Gaylord Nelson. 'I was creating an event in which the people at the grass roots could participate on their own,' he says. 'It worked because the grass roots responded and was interested and concerned.' Helped by the immense participation of the American public and the wide media coverage that it received, Earthday marked the beginning of the people's environmental movement, forcing the issue onto the agenda of American politics. The United States president, Richard Nixon, could sense the pressure. The great question of the 1970s, he told the nation, was 'Shall we make peace with nature, and begin to make reparations for the damage we have done to our air, our land, and to our water?' He announced the establishment of an Environmental Protection Agency, and persuaded a willing Congress to enact a Clean Air Act. An advertisement featuring American Indians echoed his pronouncement. 'Some people have a deep, abiding respect for the natural beauty that was once this country,' it ran, 'and some people don't. People started pollution, people can stop it.'

VISION OF THE FUTURE
A young demonstrator at Earthday in New York in 1970 adopts a gas mask as a symbolic warning message of the implications of continued urban air pollution for people and their environment.

By the 1970s, people's new awareness of the dangers, and their impatience with the reluctance to act of industries and governments, was no longer confined to the United States. In India, educated campaigners for the protection of the environment joined voices with villagers concerned at the danger to their livelihoods posed by the pollution of forest, land and water. In Japan there was an equally new mood among the people of Minamata Bay. They had formed an association to take action against the company that had consistently denied responsibility for their plight. Still partly paralysed, Tsuginori

Making waves

In 1971 a small group of men and women decided to join forces to oppose nuclear weapons testing by the United States in the Aleutian islands, west of Alaska. Twelve volunteers, armed with cameras and tape recorders, hired a small boat and sailed to the test site in the North Pacific. The resulting media attention triggered a tidal wave of concern over the testing, rallying public support for their cause. More than 177 000 people signed a telegram of protest that was nearly a kilometre long and took four days to transmit to the White House. Although one bomb was eventually detonated, the rest of the test series was cancelled. Robert Hunter took part in that first mission. 'As far as we knew it was the first time the anti-war and the environmental movements had found a common cause – thus the name Greenpeace.'

The Greenpeace movement began as an informal committee with few resources. 'There was virtually nothing, there wasn't a single typewriter, there wasn't an office, people just met in each other's living rooms or basements,' recalls Robert Hunter. 'There was nothing except everybody's common desire.' The movement quickly grew, its campaigners seeking, among other goals, a worldwide ban on nuclear testing and an end to the dumping of dangerous waste at sea. Small groups of protesters, following a guideline of 'direct, non-violent action', risked their own safety by plugging industrial pipes to prevent the flow of toxic waste, spray-painting seal pups to render their fur worthless, and challenging large whaling ships in small dinghies. One American volunteer, Patty Hutchison, boarded a Japanese whaler in the Pacific Ocean, made her way to the massive harpoon, chained and padlocked herself to it and then, in full view of the ship's crew, threw the keys overboard. 'If you saw an injustice you could try to stop it,' she says. 'A small group of people, or even one individual, could make a difference.'

By 1995 Greenpeace had become one of the world's largest non-governmental organizations (NGOs) with a fleet of sea vessels, a research station in Antarctica, a steadily growing membership of five million people and a network of bases in thirty countries around the world. It offered a public forum for people who as individuals might have gone unheard, but collectively exercised increasing influence.

Pressure groups *such as Friends of the Earth, founded in Britain in 1971, and Greenpeace attracted widespread international support; they produced their own publications as well as organizing demonstrations.*

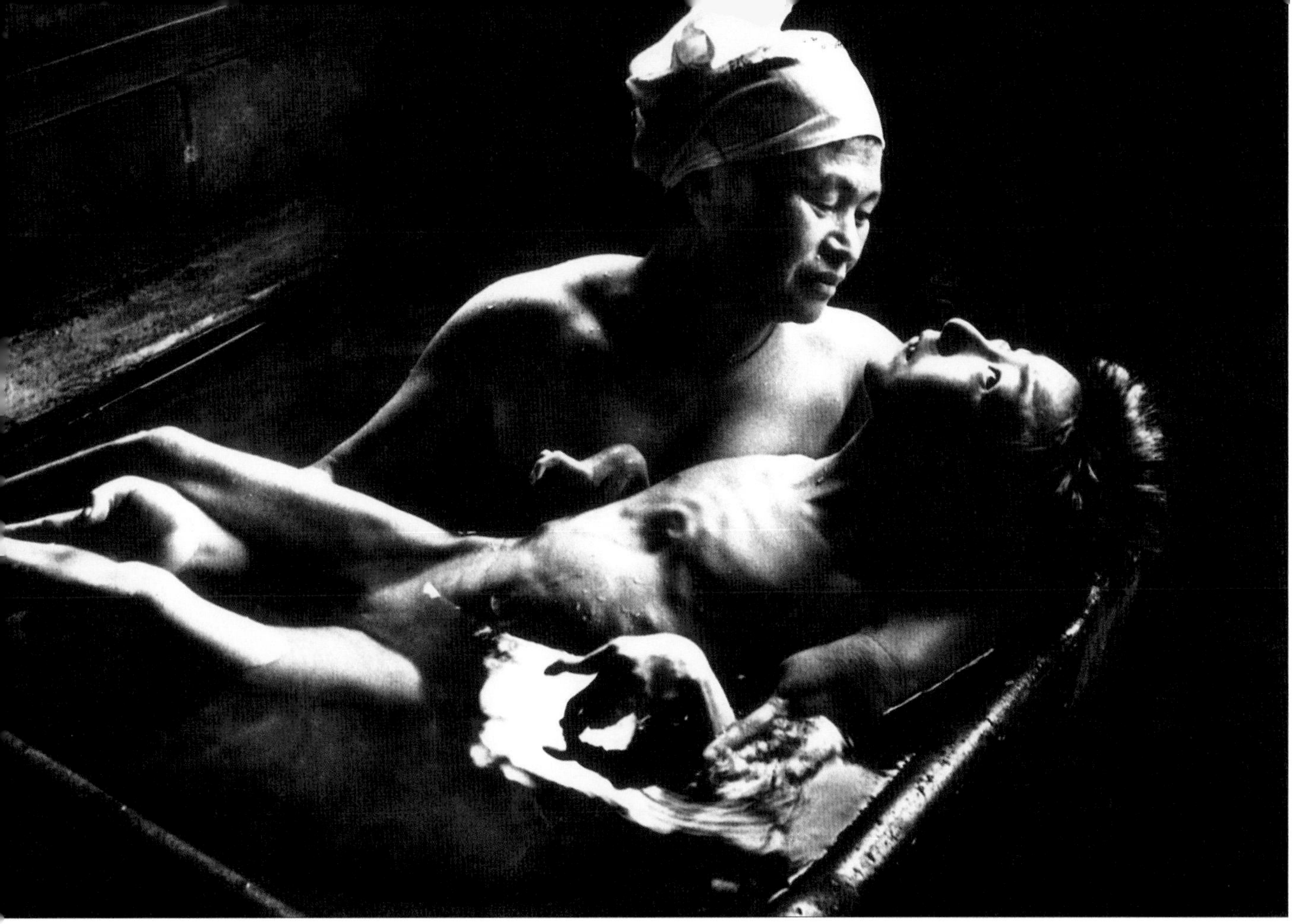

Hamamoto, the fisherman who had been one of the first to be poisoned, led a group of victims trying to reach a settlement. 'It was very tough, though we had doctors looking after us. They gave us injections and medicines while we stayed up all night negotiating with Chisso. We were exhausted, and felt absolutely disgusted with Chisso's uncompromising attitude,' he remembers. Under intense public pressure, the company was finally forced to make concessions. Its president performed the *dogeza*, bowing down to the ground in a formal gesture of submission, an act that would once have been inconceivable for a powerful Japanese industrialist.

Representatives from Minamata were invited to the first international conference on the environment, organized by the United Nations and held in June 1972. Delegates from more than a hundred countries met in Stockholm to describe and debate the damage that was being inflicted in and to their own countries. The meeting was chaired by Maurice Strong. 'This issue came from the grass roots,' he reflects. 'The issue of the environment really came from the growing perceptions of people that their lives were

THE CRIPPLING CONSEQUENCES *of Chisso's dumping of toxic waste were visible to all in the fate of Japan's thousands of poison victims. Born brain-damaged, deformed and unable to see or talk, one young sufferer* (ABOVE) *is bathed by her mother. Their plight helped to stimulate public outrage. Angry demonstrators in Tokyo* (BELOW) *demand justice from the company, which eventually yielded in 1971, awarding 664 million yen ($5 million) in compensation to the victims and their families after a fifteen-year battle.*

Forest of doom
Clearing forested areas helped many developing countries to reduce population pressure and economic difficulties by freeing land for farming and ranching, and providing timber for the world market. But as rich and delicate self-sustaining forest ecosystems were destroyed, the exposed soil became vulnerable to drought and erosion, endangering the survival of countless species of animals and plants as well as of indigenous forest peoples.

being impacted....Politicians didn't perceive this and then inform their people that this was a problem...it was quite the other way, this was always a people-based issue.'

As a result of the Stockholm conference, the United Nations Environment Programme (UNEP) and several national environmental agencies were established to monitor pollution levels and implement new policies. Popular involvement was still needed to effect change, as Anil Agarwal, a young Indian writer attending the conference, recalls. 'I did not come back with the impression that it was governments who were taking the issue very seriously.' He did have 'a very strong impression that the younger generation in Europe was taking it very seriously. Essentially it gave me the feeling of a new form of democracy beginning to emerge.'

EMBRACING THE FOREST

IN THE HIMALAYAS, source of India's sacred river Ganges, villagers took a direct part in a campaign to preserve their livelihoods and their surroundings. For thousands of years the people, plants and animals of the forest lived in harmony, the mixed forest supporting wildlife and protecting the steep mountain slopes from the eroding impact of heavy rain, the local people taking from the forest what they needed without over-exploiting its resources and disturbing its fragile ecological balance. Like other forest dwellers, their way of life depended on trees to provide them with the raw materials for their tools and homes, and to supply food for themselves and their animals.

The forests became government property under British colonial rule, and were regarded more as a commercial resource to be exploited than as life-sustaining habitats. The programme of deforestation was accelerated after India's independence. Much of the remaining forest was 'developed' into cash-yielding pine plantations. Pine needles could not offer the umbrella-like protection of broad-leaved trees, which reduced the impact of falling rain. The result was torrents, flash floods and even landslides as the water ran rapidly down the bare hillsides. Within a century, the stability that had been sustained over thousands of years was being destroyed.

HUGGING THE TREES (RIGHT) *in non-violent defiance to protect them from loggers in the Himalayas. Although at first it was mostly women who took the lead, men joined the Chipko movement too. Its success inspired similar ecological movements in other parts of India as well as in Australia and the United States.*

The peasant women living in the foothills of the Himalayas, whose job it was to collect essential fuel, water and fodder for their animals, were worst affected by the changes. In 1973, when the forestry department allocated the Chamoli district's ash trees – from which the villagers made their tools – to a large commercial company, they decided to take a stand. Inspired by Mahatma Gandhi's methods of non-violent resistance, the women flung their arms round the trees, shielding them with their bodies and challenging the woodmen from the logging companies to use their axes. The woodmen could not get past the Chipko (literally 'tree-hugging') people, and left without felling a single tree.

Inspired by this initial success, other villagers also began to resist, and the Chipko movement quickly gained momentum. Within five years it spread to eight districts in the Himalayas, covering an area of 51 000 square kilometres (19 700 square miles) with a population of nearly five million people. The landslides of 1978, which affected villages up to 500 km (310 miles) downstream, alerted the government to the scale of the destruction in the Himalayas, and helped to convince them that decades of rest and rehabilitation were now needed. A complete ban on the commercial felling of trees was imposed.

Although most of its initial demands had been met, the Chipko movement did not die out. Its intensive campaigning continued to spread environmental awareness in the region. Anil Agarwal, an Indian journalist, remembers, 'When the Chipko movement came in it gave us a very clear message, that if you destroy the environment you will inevitably create social injustice by affecting the survival base of the poor.' With the support of the Chipko movement, local people turned their energies to reforestation, continuing to play an active part in ensuring a future for the forest and for their descendants.

Acting for the environment

New environmental pressure groups were being established that were concerned with wider ethical issues such as nuclear testing, the waste of natural resources and the treatment of animals. One of the issues tackled at the UN conference was the problem of species whose survival was being threatened by the continuing exploitation of wildlife. Many species of whale, for centuries hunted and slaughtered in huge numbers for their blubber, meat and oil, were now facing extinction. There were once so many blue whales that 100 000 of them were caught every year in the southern Pacific and Antarctic oceans by the factory ships of Japan, Norway, the Soviet Union and elsewhere. Yet in 1970 only twenty-three blue whales could be found. At the UN conference there were calls for a ban on the killing of certain species, but the international commission representing the whaling countries continued to allow the slaughter.

Waste not want not *Recycling and conservation joined the environmental agenda. When the leading British drinks manufacturer, Schweppes, announced plans to abolish returnable drinks bottles in 1971, a small band of people from the new Friends of the Earth group dumped 15 000 empty bottles outside their London headquarters in a challenging media stunt.*

Now the Greenpeace movement adopted the whale as its new mascot, and decided to tackle what governments were failing to achieve. One of its early members, Robert Hunter, was sent as a reporter to cover Greenpeace activities; he stayed to become an activist, and led a Greenpeace expedition that tracked down Soviet whalers in the Pacific. The activists tried to get between the whale and the harpoon by using themselves as human shields. 'As these were 250-pound explosive harpoons with a steel cable we were obviously at risk,' he remembers.

Action was needed not just to prevent the possibility of new threats but also to force the authorities to rectify their past mistakes. Poisonous waste carelessly dumped in rivers, lakes and under ground all over Europe and the United States was now threatening the communities living nearby. At Love Canal, an industrial suburb in upstate New York, the Hooker Chemicals Company had buried 20 000 tonnes of highly toxic waste between 1942 and 1953 in the land surrounding the plant. A school was built on the landfill site, and a residential neighbourhood around it. Barbara Quimby grew up nearby. 'The chemicals and vapours would fill your house...it became unbearable in there....It would make you cough and choke and you'd have burning eyes, but it was just something people were used to, that's just how we lived.'

Demonstrating their concern (opposite) *for whales at a Greenpeace protest rally in Glasgow, men and women of all ages take to the streets with badges and banners in a determined effort to stop the slaughter of whales.*

GREENPEACE
GREENPEACE
MATLOCK SUPPORT GROUP
GREENPEACE
CHESTERFIELD LOCAL SUPPORT GROUP
SAVE THE WHALES
VICTORY FOR THE WHALES
STOP THE SENSELESS SLAUGHTER
VICTORY

EXPORTING POLLUTION

SOME OF THE WORST environmental conditions in the Americas developed within a few kilometres of the United States–Mexico border. Dangerous chemicals leached into the soil, polluting water supplies and exposing people on the Mexican side of the border to metal poisoning and other serious health hazards. Yet the underlying cause of these problems was a process that boosted the Mexican economy.

From 1965 numerous foreign-owned factories were established in the border area. Most of these were run by American manufacturing companies taking advantage of low Mexican wage rates and avoiding the cost of increasingly stringent health, safety and environmental standards in the United States. The factory assembly plants, known as *maquiladoras*, imported components to be assembled into finished products such as cars, televisions and clothing for sale back to the United States, in foreign markets and later in Mexico itself. The reduced running costs enabled such companies to compete with low-cost Asian producers, while the Mexicans benefited from American technology and marketing expertise.

The *maquiladoras* provided badly needed jobs for hundreds of thousands of people. Despite low wages, there was never a shortage of labour, with hundreds of people arriving every day from all over Mexico, eager for a chance to work in an American factory. But the pollution of air, land and water and the degrading living conditions in the nearby shantytowns exacted a terrible toll. The growing number of people suffering from birth defects and rare cancers provided living proof of the serious damage being inflicted.

The explosion of the Mexican *maquiladora* industry was just part of the growing flight of heavily polluting industries from the developed to the developing world, the undoubted short-term economic advantages of these collaborations blinding both rich and poor nations to their potential human cost.

CONDITIONS OF LIFE *for the Mexican* maquiladoras *workers, housed in settlements often without proper sanitation or rubbish disposal, could be even more unhealthy than conditions within the workplace. Yet people living here were fortunate compared with those living in the disease-ridden shantytowns.*

Leaving town (above) *A father clutches his children during the evacuation of Three Mile Island in Harrisburg, Pennsylvania, following an accident at a nuclear generating plant in 1979. The relocation of families from Love Canal was largely due to the determination of residents like Lois Gibbs* (right, above) *who helped to form community associations and organize protest meetings* (right, below).

In the late 1970s the steel drums containing the factory's waste began to rust, and the poison they contained seeped out. Children were burned after playing with explosive phosphorous rocks in the streets, and the rubber soles of their sneakers dissolved in the chemicals on the playground. The local postman drew attention to the dangers by wearing a gas mask to deliver the mail.

When Lois Gibbs moved to Love Canal with her healthy one-year-old son she thought she was buying into the American dream. 'That consists of a husband, a child, a house, a station wagon, a dog, a white picket fence. I had all of those things, and that's what I wanted to do: be a full-time homemaker, raise my children, take care of my husband.' Within five years her son had developed epilepsy, a liver disease, a urinary tract disorder and severe asthma. She decided to do something about it, and grew 'from a very shy individual to a very angry woman. My goals changed, my priorities changed...no longer did I care whether my floors were clean'.

The Love Canal residents, led by Lois Gibbs, organized themselves into a group and set out to persuade the government to relocate them to new homes. After resistance and repeated delays from state authorities and politicians, the women decided to take direct action. They took hostage several officials from the government's Environmental Protection Agency. Lois Gibbs called the White House and said, 'I'm calling to tell you we're holding these Federal officials hostage and we're not going to let them go until you release the Love Canal residents from these poisons'. She gave them a deadline, noon the following Wednesday. 'At noon I was sitting by the phone praying – I'm not a big religious person, but I was praying they would call. When the phone rang we all jumped out of our skin. And it was the White House calling to say that all residents at Love Canal could be evacuated.' Nearly a thousand families were evacuated in 1978. Lois Gibbs had learned an important lesson. 'You don't have to be a scientist with a PhD, you don't

have to be wealthy, all you have to be is active,' she says. 'If you take one or two little steps you can change the world.'

By the late 1970s grass-roots campaigns were achieving results all over the Western world. In Europe the Green movement, focusing initially on nuclear energy, acid rain and pollution of the countryside and the rivers, entered mainstream politics. But not everyone benefited from the new environmental legislation. Some people felt threatened by the confrontational new style of those who wanted to save the earth. When a copper-smelting plant at Tacoma in the northwest United States was closed down after fears that it released arsenic into the atmosphere, hundreds of workers found themselves without a job. One of them was Chuck O'Donahue. 'They came, they attacked it and they cost us our livelihood,' he says. 'There are people from the smelter who haven't worked a day since that smelter closed down.'

Green goods

ENVIRONMENTALLY FRIENDLY *detergents and other household products appeared on many supermarket shelves during the 1980s, as people began to take more care over the effects of the products they used. Some of the names and colours chosen for these consumer products reflected the new environmental ethic. There was also a growing demand for used materials such as glass and paper to be recycled rather than thrown away.*

Carl Bagge, who had been raised in the smoke and grime of Gary, Indiana, later became president of the National Coal Association; he spent twenty years attempting to save the coal industry from environmentalists who wanted to bring change. By the 1970s, he believes, 'This benign environmental ethic had mushroomed into a pervasive religious zealotry'. The government passed environmental legislation that damaged the producers of high-sulphur coal as well as the communities who were dependent on producing it.

PLEASE DON'T PANIC! (RIGHT) *advises a banner displayed by protesters outside a nuclear power plant in Germany. As the dangers of radioactivity were more clearly understood, anti-nuclear campaigners became part of the wider effort to protect the environment.*

GREEN POLITICS

THE RELUCTANCE of established political parties to respond to environmental needs led some groups to seek their own political representation. Nearly a million people voted for the new Green party – Die Grünen – in the 1979 federal elections in West Germany. Although this fell short of the 5 per cent of the total vote needed to obtain seats in parliament, the voting did reflect the growing concern for environmental issues. In the 1983 elections the Greens passed the 5 per cent barrier, becoming the first environmental party to win representation in a national government. In another four years more than 8 per cent of the German people voted Green.

During the 1980s people throughout Europe began to look to politicians who would give priority to the environment. Green parties won national parliamentary seats in eight western European countries: Austria, Belgium, Finland, Germany, Italy, Luxembourg, Sweden and Switzerland. In the 1989 elections to the European parliament, too, the people of Belgium, Denmark, France, Germany, the Netherlands and Spain all elected Green party members; their voting system, based on proportional representation, reflected the number of votes cast. In Britain, which has a different voting system, the Green party succeeded in polling 15 per cent of the vote but failed to win a single seat. The electoral successes of Green parties depend upon proportional representation, where the support of individuals is not lost.

Public support for the new Green parties was viewed with alarm by the major political parties, all of which were losing votes. They began to realize that to regain their voters they would have to include environmental issues in their own agendas. It was the votes of millions of individuals, who showed that for them the dangers to the planet's health were an issue of real importance, that brought environmental policies into mainstream politics.

COLLECTIVE CONCERN *for the environment is the focus of debate at conferences held by the German Green Party, which offered a new channel of hope to many young people. Founded by Herbert Gruhl in 1979, it became a national party the following year.*

For Carl Bagge, 'As a guy fighting for the coal industry it was a total, unmitigated disaster, because all the people who had been lobbying for environmental organizations were now in positions of power, they were the people I had to make my pleas to on behalf of coal. It was awful,' he says ruefully. 'I didn't want to get up to go to work in the morning. These guys were extremists, there was no balance at all.'

Drumbeat of disasters

Blinded at Bhopal (above) *by a toxic leak at a chemical plant, local women wait patiently for treatment to relieve their painfully burning eyes.*

The 1980s began with a backlash against the environmental movement, initiated by a new United States president who felt that concern for nature had gone too far. 'There is environmental extremism,' announced Ronald Reagan sceptically. 'I don't think they'll be happy until the White House looks like a bird's nest.' It was a much happier time for Carl Bagge. 'When Reagan came in and we had people that I would say were more balanced – from our standpoint, a balanced point of view,' he recalls, 'I didn't mind getting up in the morning. I would even bounce to work because I was talking to people who would listen to your story.' But a spate of disasters showed that the risks were as great as ever.

There had been leaks of poisonous gas at industrial plants in the past, but nothing could compare with the explosion at the American-owned Union Carbide factory at Bhopal in central India in 1984. The plant was situated in the middle of a poor neighbourhood of the city, and more than 2000 people were killed outright by the poisonous fumes. A further 20 000 were blinded or severely disabled. Eventually, in an out of court settlement between Union Carbide and the Indian government, the company paid $470 million compensation. (The question of responsibility and compensation arose again when the *Exxon Valdez* oil tanker ran aground in Alaska, causing devastating pollution in a pristine wildlife area. The clean-up operation cost Exxon $2 billion and, though nobody was killed, $5 billion in compensation.)

Toxic cargo (right) *A train crashes in Livingstone, Louisiana in 1982, emitting hazardous smoke into the atmosphere. The risks of storing and transporting potentially dangerous substances increased as industrial production grew.*

In 1987 there was another explosion at a chemical works, near Basle in Switzerland. Toxic chemicals were washed into the

Buckets of oil (right) *are collected by relief workers after the supertanker* Amoco Cadiz *ran aground on the coast of Brittany, northern France in 1978. It had been carrying twice as much oil as the* Torrey Canyon*; the oil quickly spread over fishing grounds and oyster beds.*

C-6

PROFESSOR F. SHERWOOD ROLAND (RIGHT, *seated and* BELOW RIGHT), *whose research into CFC gases led to his alarming predictions for the future. 'There are three major consequences that we realized at the time for ozone depletion: ultraviolet effects on humans, ultraviolet effects on biology other than human, and the possible changes in the structure of the atmosphere itself.'*

Rhine, and poisoned fish all the way down the river through Germany into the Netherlands. These accidents highlighted the now global effects of environmental damage. Lakes and forests in Canada and northern Europe were dying because of gases from power stations in other countries, hundreds of kilometres away. Pollution could no longer be seen as a local issue.

There was another new danger, one that could not yet be seen, felt or heard. Professor F. Sherwood Roland, a chemist at the University of California at Irvine, was carrying out research into chlorofluorocarbons (CFCs), chemicals widely used in aerosol cans and refrigerators. 'We were proceeding along with essentially an innocent problem, just trying to find out what happens to the CFCs,' he describes. Then he discovered that when the harmless CFCs pass through the ozone layer (a narrow band in the atmosphere that shields the earth from harmful ultraviolet radiation) they break apart. Highly reactive chlorine atoms are released, starting a chain reaction that would ultimately destroy the ozone layer. 'I came home one night,' says Sherwood Roland, 'and my wife asked me how the research was going, and I said, "I think the research is going fine, but it looks like the end of the world".' Satellites soon began to gather evidence establishing that the theory was becoming fact. In 1985 a hole – in fact a dramatic thinning – appeared in the protective ozone layer above Antarctica.

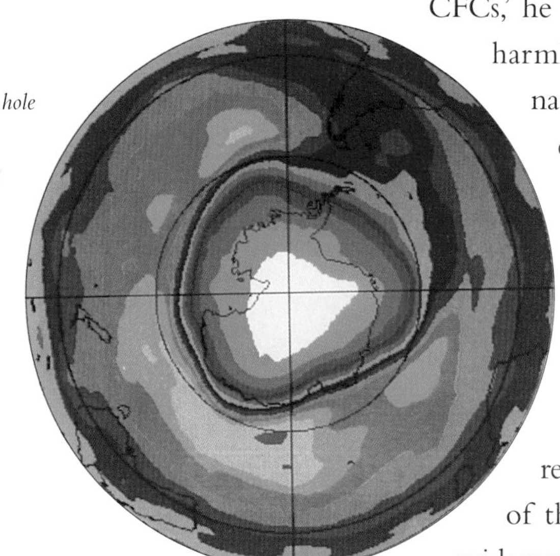

GLOBAL ALERT *The gaping hole in the protective ozone layer above the surface of the earth is the result of CFC gases escaping into the atmosphere. Proof of their damaging effects led many countries to ban the use of CFCs, and to introduce measures to monitor and reduce levels of pollution.*

At about the same time scientists discovered that the level of carbon dioxide gas present in the atmosphere was steadily rising, threatening to change global climate patterns through the 'greenhouse effect'. The tens of thousands of hectares of rainforests being burned in Africa, Central and South America and Indonesia were partly to blame; the carbon dioxide released by burning oil, natural gas and coal in the power stations, factories, vehicles and homes of the West was the worst culprit.

Consumption of fossil fuels was rapidly increasing, and the

Sustaining a future

New dangers and risks continued to emerge in the 1980s, and demands on the earth also continued to increase as populations grew and their aspirations rose. Some people realized that the unlimited exploitation of limited resources could be permanently damaging to the earth.

The idea of sustainable development – managing the earth's resources so that present needs are met in ways that will not prevent future generations from meeting theirs – was introduced in 1980 by the World Commission on Environment and Development. A proposal for how this could be achieved – Agenda 21 – was put forward at the 1992 United Nations Conference on Environment and Development (UNCED) in Rio de Janeiro. It recognized the need for a global alliance to tackle the difficult problems of poverty, development and the environment.

At national and local levels, too, a new attitude began to emerge that encouraged efficiency, self-renewal and conservation alongside economic growth, as awareness grew that the use of recycled materials and renewable sources of natural energy (biomass, geothermal, hydro, solar, tidal and wind power), the reintroduction of traditional methods of farming that would replenish rather than deplete the soil, and the enforcement of restrictions on hunting and fishing, could all contribute to a gradual reversal of long-term ecological decline. Instead of building more power stations, nations could concentrate on ways of saving energy – reducing consumption levels, introducing local energy-sharing schemes, designing cars that consumed less fuel, and insulating buildings.

There were public demands for government initiatives to deter polluters and encourage 'greener' industries that would regulate their economic development in terms of sustainability. In Sweden, where a million people lived in communities devoted to sustainable living, the Natural Step programme established links with industry and education to devise new strategies for environmental change.

The need for sustainable development was also being tackled in the developing world, as countries with rapidly growing populations and few fossil fuel and mineral resources searched for affordable alternatives. By 1995 more than 90 per cent of the energy in Ethiopia, Nepal and Tanzania was supplied by burning vegetable matter, and in Brazil alcohol produced from sugar cane was used to fuel vehicles. The introduction of more efficient cooking stoves led to a 30 per cent saving in fuelwood in Sri Lanka, and reduced Kenya's demand for charcoal by the equivalent of one and a half million tonnes of trees a year. Nepal, a country highly dependent on its natural resources, established a National Planning Commission to integrate the need both for conservation and for development.

Conservation of the natural environment, economic development and the need to solve the problem of rising world population – growing at a rate of some ninety million people a year – could no longer be tackled separately; environmental needs would be met only if the huge problems of hunger and poverty were also addressed. Power elites, military aggression and a global market regulated by profit and competitiveness all raised obstacles to effective sustainable development, which required international agreement and an understanding that the health of the planet could not be separated from the well-being of all the people living on it.

Holding on to earth *A child clutches the hand of a walking exhibit at the Earth Summit that took place in Rio in 1992.*

problem of pollution could no longer be confined to the richer, industrialized nations. In developing countries, especially the nations of Asia, where more than half the world's people lived, there was rapid industrialization, and billions of men and women looked forward to the lifestyle already enjoyed by people in North America, Europe and Japan. To meet their needs would mean more cars and lorries, more power stations and more factories – all discharging more carbon dioxide into the atmosphere.

'We have a real dilemma,' says Maurice Strong. 'On the one hand, we have no right to impose constraints on the developing countries in pursuing their development, we have no right to deny them the right to grow....At the same time, if they follow the path that we followed, it's going to be disastrous for them and for us.' In India Mukesh Gupta, who was manager of a foundry in the outskirts of Delhi, saw the problem in more practical terms. 'About fifty men work in this foundry. Altogether they support probably four hundred people. The livelihood of these families depends on us,' he says. 'I'm sorry if our pollution harms the environment, but you must realize that we have to meet our basic needs.'

Trying to breathe *Children in the Czech Republic wearing face masks on their way to school to protect them from the poor air quality. Eastern Europe became one of the world's most polluted regions as a result of rapid industrial development, and many people living there suffered from various pollution-related health problems.*

Dying trees *became common in Europe's forests, where millions of hectares faced destruction from acid rain falling as a result of pollutant gases from industry and vehicles collecting in the atmosphere. The severe damage caused to soils, lakes and rivers in Europe, in Canada and the United States continued to spread farther afield.*

The fishing families of Minamata had their own answer to that. The mercury still lay on the seabed; they would never be able to fish in the bay again, and had to take their boats far out to sea to earn their living. Their experience was a microcosm of what was happening all over the world. Popular concern might have forced business and government to acknowledge the dilemma of progress, but the damage continued all the same. In the forty years to 1995 a fifth of all the earth's species of plants and animals either became extinct or were threatened with extinction. Half the rainforests were lost. Thousands of lakes, rivers and coastal areas were poisoned. Tomiji Matsuda, brain-damaged and blinded by the mercury at Minamata, understood the implications, and urged caution: 'I think people must be very careful about progress. It doesn't just bring benefits: it brings danger as well.'

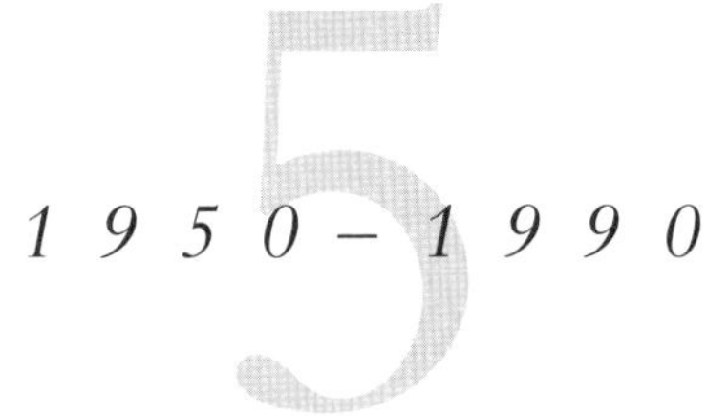

1 9 5 0 – 1 9 9 0

Picture Power

The impact of television

In Fort Wayne, Indiana, Elizabeth Fincher Dobynes had taken the day off work to make Christmas wreaths at home. With one eye she was watching the television set she had bought with her wages as an elevator operator in a local department store. 'Why were they pushing and rushing?' she thought. And then they announced that the president had been shot. 'I dropped everything and I found myself on my knees....I was praying. My eyes were bathed in tears.'

In every corner of the United States the assassination of President John F. Kennedy by Lee Harvey Oswald on 22 November 1963 in Dallas, Texas left an indelible emotional imprint. Within an hour some 90 per cent of Americans had heard the news. Millions of people grieved in front of their televisions as they watched the live coverage that followed. 'I think all our lives were centred round that four days. We watched the funeral and we watched the whole thing from beginning to end,' remembers Marjorie Brandt, who also lived in Fort Wayne. 'It was a very mournful thing to observe, and we realized history was being made and that we were a part of it. That was the beauty of television – we didn't have to read it, we saw it.'

People all around the world were similarly stunned as they shared the immediacy of the news of the president's death. 'It made me realize that the news belonged to television now,' reflects Conrad Frost, who had been a London newspaper journalist for most of his life. 'It didn't belong to newspapers any more. You could never get the impact that you got that night, you could never get that from a newspaper.'

On the day that Kennedy was assassinated, television was just over a quarter of a century old. In the decades that followed, it continued to grow to become the world's preferred source of news, information and entertainment, a giant industry and powerful global medium watched by people everywhere. It was no longer just a spectator or critic of the human drama: increasingly, television was becoming the stage on which a good part of the human drama was played out.

The unforgettable moment *of the assassination of United States President John F. Kennedy is caught by the camera to be watched by millions.*

An early spectacle

> *"Television was a tremendous novelty ...there was a great anticipation of seeing it for the first time."*
>
> TONY CLARKE

Technically, television had been on its way for a long time. As early as the 1880s scientists in parts of Europe and the United States had been developing the technology to transmit pictures as well as sound. By 1923 John Logie Baird was working on an early television set in London, and two years later the Bell Telephone Laboratories in the United States began research into television. By the end of the 1920s a number of inventors were hard at work on various television systems in Britain, France, Germany, Japan, the Soviet Union and the United States.

The world's first public television service was launched in Britain in 1936, with regular broadcasts of drama, game shows, music and sports programmes. 'At that time,' remembers Conrad Frost, who was one of the first people to buy a television set, 'people who had television regarded it as cinema. You put all the lights off to watch it, you had a special room for it – it was the television room.' Early televisions were designed as a piece of furniture and sold as complete cabinets that contained radios as well. Television was welcomed by those who could afford it; for most people it remained a novelty. When Tony Clarke first saw a television set at a neighbour's house, he tried to persuade his parents to buy one too. 'The first moments of actually seeing a live picture on a screen in somebody's house...that was a tremendous thrill,' he recalls. 'The television set was put smack in the middle of the room, the chairs were carefully arranged around it. It was *the* feature!'

PEERING AT THE SCREEN *of a television set displayed at a London exhibition in 1936. Like many early models it was contained in a wooden cabinet with the speaker below. By then, of the two main television systems competing in Britain, Marconi-EMI was favoured above that of Baird Television.*

At the electrical goods shop in Windsor, near London, where Harry Dix worked, they had been so busy selling radio sets that they hardly bothered with television at first. Eventually they decided to promote it by opening their showroom to customers during the evening. 'We used to provide as many chairs as we could, but often we had people standing as well,' remembers Harry Dix. 'People were really impressed by what they had

seen...so that did an awful lot for television sales.' By 1939 500 television sets were being sold in Britain each week.

Elsewhere, television was also making an impact – in Germany and in France, where television had been demonstrated as early as 1931, it was the star attraction at the Paris World's Fair in 1937. A regular French television service was launched in the following year. In the Soviet Union television broadcasts began in 1939; in the same year television transmissions in the United States made their debut at the New York World's Fair. Thousands of people caught their first glimpse of television among the stands and pavilions where the most modern scientific innovations were on show. 'It was absolutely amazing,' remembers John O. Brown, who visited the fair. 'They would take your picture in one room and then you could see it in the other room. And they said, "You know this is going to be something that we're going to have in every household soon." And I just couldn't believe it.' Don Hewitt, a picture editor at a news agency, was equally sceptical at first. 'I thought it was literally out of this world,' he says. 'I thought this is all a lot of experimental stuff, and it's great at a World's Fair and it's very amusing, but it's never going to be part of our lives.'

At the time of the World's Fair there were fewer than 200 television sets in the whole of New York, and sales remained low. Commercial television broadcasts began in 1941, only to be closed down a few months later as the United States joined the Second World War. Two years earlier, the picture had faded in Britain, too. 'I remember switching on one evening,' says Conrad Frost, 'and they said, "This is going to be the last television programme," and you suddenly realized that there was going to be a war....The first thing it meant to me was that I wasn't going to have television any more.'

Vision of the future *A crowd gathers at the site of a television exhibit at the New York World's Fair in 1939* (LEFT). *Three years earlier, television cameras brought live coverage of the Olympic Games* (RIGHT) *to Germans watching in twenty-eight halls across Berlin.*

A new pastime

It was not until 1946 that television broadcasting was relaunched in Britain. The announcer jauntily introduced the first programme with the words, 'Hello. Remember me?' In the years immediately after the war, television was still a luxury. The national television service was run by the British Broadcasting Corporation (BBC), and funded through an additional licence fee charged to anyone who owned a television. At first it was confined to the London area. Peter Robinson was a schoolboy when the first television sets appeared in Preston, an industrial town in the north of England. 'We would go on the bus to town, have a wander round, and then see the television on in the shop window and stand there with the rest of the people,' he remembers. 'It didn't start until a quarter to eight in the evening and it closed at about ten past ten....We put up with the cold weather just to watch it.'

When Japanese television began regular broadcasting in 1953, with both public and privately funded stations, fewer than a thousand people had bought their own television set. Instead huge crowds gathered at street corners and in parks to watch it. Public viewing was also common in France and Italy; in the Soviet Union, where television was controlled and rigorously censored by the government, large monitors were installed in public places for collective viewing.

In 1947 there were only 60 000 television sets in the whole of the United States. When television did finally take off, though, it did so with tremendous speed and success. In the first half of 1950 alone, more than three million television sets were sold, most of them on credit. Unlike Britain, television in the United States was a commercial business, depending on advertising revenue and commercial sponsorship rather than public funding. By the mid-1950s there were more than 500 different commercial stations.

Fort Wayne, in the Midwest state of Indiana, was one of the last American cities to have its own television station. It caused a sensation. Until then, the few people who owned television sets had had to contend with poor reception from stations in distant cities. 'We were trying to put out as many television sets as we could,'

Public viewing (above) *Customers at an American steak house pause to watch television. By 1953 half of American families owned their own sets at home.*

Essential commodity (opposite) *A German magazine featured television on one of its covers in 1952, the year regular broadcasts began in Germany.*

Window shopping *in Britain* (below) *where 2 per cent of the population owned a television in 1950. Peter Robinson* (left) *worked in a shop that sold televisions. 'People would come in just out of interest after seeing the set in the window,' he remembers. Sales swiftly improved by the mid-1950s.*

THE POWER TO SELL

TELEVISION PROGRAMMES were costly to make, and in countries where they was not funded by viewers or by government, commercial advertising and sponsorship provided the necessary revenue. In New York on 1 July 1941 people watched the first advertisement ever shown on American television: the Bulova Watch Company paid $9 for a ten-second spot. The need to attract large audiences and bring in the maximum income governed what programmes were made. They were interrupted by frequent spot advertising for the new consumer goods available after the Second World War. Television and advertising formed a mutually beneficial alliance. Manufacturers and businesses gained a unique advantage by selling their consumer products and services to a large and instantly accessible audience, and advertising revenue was used by television stations to produce and distribute programmes. From the start, the many competing television stations in the United States were supported by advertising and sponsorship.

In Britain television was seen as a public service that should not be driven by the need to deliver ever higher ratings. A licence system similar to that of the BBC was introduced throughout Western Europe – in France, Germany, Italy and the Netherlands – and in Japan. Only after a long political battle was a commercial channel allowed in Britain; when the first commercial channel, Independent Television (ITV), was launched it charged advertisers £438 for a fifteen-second, peak-time advertisement. People tuned in to the new station for the first time on 22 September 1955, and saw advertisements for beer, chocolate, margarine and soap.

As television ownership assumed global proportions in the 1960s and 1970s, it far surpassed radio and magazines as the leading medium for advertising, and advertising rates consequently soared. Specialized agencies were employed to create hard-hitting advertisements; market researchers and consumer experts analysed audiences to determine what brand of coffee or toothpaste they might be persuaded to buy. In the United States, where advertisers and sponsors were exerting a greater degree of control over programming content, advertising increased sixfold in financial terms between 1965 and 1985. For just a few seconds of air time, companies paid several thousands of dollars. By 1989 advertising expenditure worldwide had reached $250 billion.

As it developed, television advertising attracted criticism: television commercials were blamed for encouraging unnecessary purchases and creating social envy. When the same techniques began to be used to sell Western-made pharmaceuticals and powdered milk to poor people in developing countries, there were protests. Codes and standards to regulate what was advertised, and how, were introduced by most countries. In 1981 the United Nations and its World Health Organization established international guidelines for marketing products such as baby food. Alcohol and tobacco advertisements were banned from television in several countries. In Japan and the Netherlands advertisements for confectionery were accompanied by reminders to children to brush their teeth, and in Australia, Canada and New Zealand advertisements targeting children were limited to certain hours and certain days.

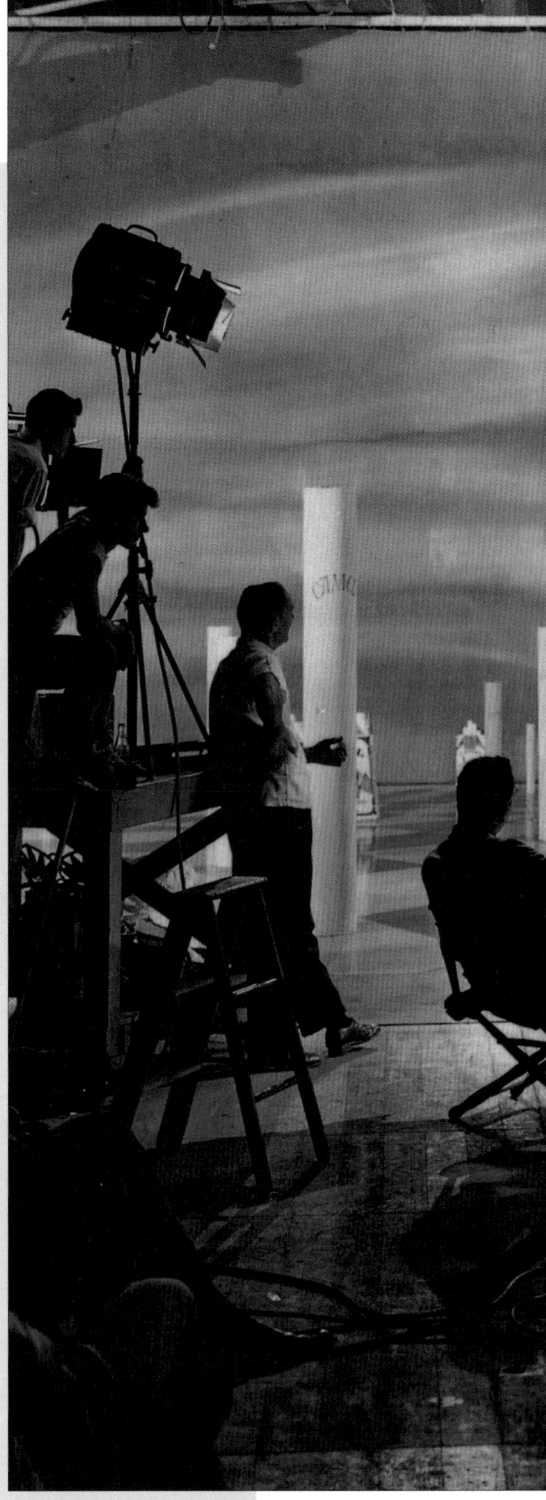

COMMERCIAL SET (ABOVE) *A television advertisement for cigarettes being made by a New York film company. Thirty-second commercials could cost hundreds of thousands of dollars to make.*

remembers James Huhn, who was working at Rarick's, a local television store. 'Our advertising was such that we tried to entice people to buy them in the summertime at a special price and be ready when the station came on the air.' Everybody wanted to get a set, and as they did, everything in town was set to change in one way or another.

Marjorie Brandt and her husband had bought a television by the time WKJG Fort Wayne went on the air. 'Our first television set was a console set, and we also had to have an antenna and a rotor to be able to operate it. It dominated the room. Everything faced that set because it was an important part of our life in those days,' she remembers. 'It was our recreation and our channel to the outside world.'

As more and more people bought television sets, cinema audiences and library loans dwindled; radio and comic book sales decreased. As they stopped going to the cinema, young couples no longer needed to hire babysitters. 'We didn't call people on the telephone because it would interrupt a favourite show,' remembers Marjorie Brandt. The pastor of St Paul's Lutheran Church, Edwin Nerger, found that many of the popular programmes conflicted with church services. 'Services had to be changed, dropped. Some of the services were discontinued,' he remembers. 'The church had to do a lot of adjusting. Not only our church, but practically all the churches in town.'

Others, like Alex Azar, personally discovered the possibilities of commercial television. He decided to advertise his new 'Big Boy' hamburger restaurant on Fort Wayne's new station. 'When we first opened,' he says, 'we were lucky to do a couple of hundred dollars a day. We were brand new, people had never heard of us. They had never seen us.' The advertisement simply showed a well-known television announcer eating a Big Boy double-decker hamburger, with sauce and lettuce and mayonnaise. 'He just sighed that it was so good, and we all wanted one,' remembers Marjorie Brandt. Alex Azar's business boomed after that. 'The cars kept

Switching on to TV (Right) *An American advertisement of the 1950s compares the number of hours a person would need to work in order to earn a television: from 1224 in the Soviet Union to 1170 in Denmark, 529 in France, 513 in Britain and 136 in the United States.*

coming and the people kept coming,' he says, 'and it continued for years. We had more business than we could accommodate.'

As more and more families everywhere bought television sets, their lives changed in much the same ways. They ate meals around it and rearranged their furniture around it. 'We didn't play as much because we watched the television,' remembers Wendy Vause. She was eight years old when she saw one for the first time, on a visit to her grandmother's home in Preston. 'Going to the theatre obviously stopped, going to the pictures some nights stopped.…I stopped reading.'

Wendy Vause's grandmother was one of millions of people in Britain who decided the time had come to buy a television in the summer of 1953, shortly before the coronation of Queen Elizabeth II. 'They were selling like hot cakes,' remembers Peter Robinson. He now worked as a television dealer. 'In the weeks leading up to the coronation, things got very busy indeed. The rigger putting up aerials was working from the early morning until late at night.…We were installing sets as fast as we could.' Those who could never have gone to London to watch the festivities in person took a renewed interest in the royal family. More than twenty million people saw the coronation on television at home, in pubs and clubs, or gathered in small crowds to watch through the windows of other people's houses.

By 1955 there were 37 million television sets in the United States and 4.7 million in Europe. 'Television was kind of a space-age thing then,' Joe Abrell had felt when he first saw one at a local store in Miami. 'Everybody would stand around the store window and look in and watch baseball games in the evening. I think that's when we really began to feel that television was here to stay and was going to become a part of our lives.' Within a year the number of sets outside the United States had doubled, and sales in Britain rose when commercial television was launched there. Television was launched in Australia in 1956, with commercial and national networks, in time for the Melbourne Olympic Games that year. As television reached many other parts of the world – from Algeria, China and India to New Zealand, the Philippines and Thailand – it had a similar impact.

TV guides

WEEKLY MAGAZINES *providing television viewers with full programme listings were quick to appear wherever television became available. Some, such as the American* TV Guide *and Britain's* Radio Times, *developed huge national circulations. There were similar periodicals all over the world. Columns devoted to television listings and programme reviews were also featured in daily newspapers.*

BARGAIN SALE (ABOVE) *Some people queued outside this London store all night to take advantage of the remarkable offer of a television set for only £1. Television sales peaked in Britain in the build-up to the Queen's coronation in 1953. Viewers in the United States were able to see a film recording of the ceremony, broadcast the following day.*

A platform for politics

By the 1960s watching television had already become the main leisure occupation for most families in the developed world. As well as entertainment shows, millions of people watched the evening news, and news presenters achieved celebrity status. In the socialist bloc and in many newly independent countries, television was regarded as too important to be left to the market; it was seen as a tool for political control as well as mass education. In Cuba, Egypt and Eastern Europe, it carried speeches by party leaders and reports of record harvests and new industrial achievements. 'We had no freedom – we were under the constant control of censorship,' says Kamila Mouchkova, a news reporter in Prague. 'There was a man with us from the Ministry of the Interior whose job was to go through every news story before we went on the air. If he approved of it, he stamped the script and we could then broadcast it. Without that stamp, we couldn't broadcast anything.'

In the West, television was being used by politicians in an increasingly sophisticated way. It played a growing part in election campaigns, and politicians began to manipulate the news coverage by orchestrating 'picture opportunities' at which they were seen against helpful backgrounds. Speeches were written to include the soundbites that television used. American politicians spent millions of dollars buying themselves advertising space. Television became a

WAVING THE CZECH FLAG (ABOVE), *a man leaps onto one of the Soviet tanks that rolled into Prague on 20 August 1968 to reassert Soviet power over the country. Newsreader Kamila Mouchkova* (RIGHT) *was ordered at gunpoint to stop broadcasting as the TV studios were occupied.*

NEWS ANCHOR *Walter Cronkite* (BELOW), *the principal presenter in the United States, began to read the evening news on the Columbia Broadcasting System (CBS) network in 1962. He was held in such high regard that it was even suggested he should run for president. Television quickly overtook radio and newspapers as the preferred source of news.*

main political forum when the first debate between presidential candidates was held on television. The Republican Richard Nixon appeared in a studio confrontation with Senator John Kennedy, the Democratic candidate. Don Hewitt, who now worked for a television company in Chicago, was the producer of the debate. He remembers the moment when Nixon, recently recovered from an illness, arrived: 'He came to the studio looking like the cat dragged him in – kind of green,' he says. Kennedy, on the other hand, had been campaigning in an open convertible in the California sunshine, and 'looked like Cary Grant'.

Elizabeth Fincher Dobynes, who would be voting for the first time, watched the programme in Fort Wayne. 'Before the debate I didn't know who to vote for,' she says. 'That was a turning point in my life. I was completely sold on that young man.' Most of the 115 million people who watched the debate felt the same. 'When it was over,' Don Hewitt recalls, 'people who heard it on the radio thought Nixon won, people who saw it on television thought Kennedy won....By the next morning everybody was saying, "Jack Kennedy is the next president of the United States". Nobody even waited for election day.'

Kennedy's television success helped to win him the election. Over the next three years his life, and then his death, were closely followed by the nation

THE FIRST TV CONTEST *for the American presidency, held on 26 September 1960, was seen by millions of families across the country* (BELOW). *When Alex Azar* (LEFT) *watched the debate from his home in Fort Wayne, like many others he felt surprised by Nixon's appearance. 'It wasn't too inspiring. He looked tired and haggard, and Kennedy looked young and vibrant,' he describes. 'I came away thinking that maybe Kennedy was the better of the two.'*

on their television sets. 'We were all just fascinated,' says Dorothy Berger from Cleveland, Ohio. 'We had a real affinity for the Kennedy family – it was brought to us, right into our homes.'

Until the early 1960s television's development had taken place within national boundaries. Transmitters had a limited range, and viewers could follow events in distant countries only with filmed reports. This began to change when the first communications satellites began to allow direct links between continents. In 1962 *Telstar*, in orbit around the Earth, made it possible to receive and transmit television signals across the Atlantic. In Britain Peter Robinson watched the satellite broadcast from his local club. 'There was a tremendous cheer, and of course we had quite a few drinks after that,' he remembers. 'It was an exciting night to see those first pictures across the Atlantic, and it certainly reduced the size of the world.'

As the satellite system was extended, television organizations mounted a series of international programmes to demonstrate what was now possible. 'Our World' in 1967 linked The Beatles singing in London, folk singers in Mexico and babies being born in Japan. 'Town Meeting of the World' showed discussions about the future taking place between political leaders. The satellites made the most difference to news programmes, allowing pictures from distant places to be shown each day.

In the United States evening news bulletins were extended from fifteen to thirty minutes, and presented a less sanitized view of the world. One of the most significant events to be covered in the 1960s was the country's involvement in the war in Vietnam. Although television did not portray the full horror, it did bring disturbing images into people's homes, helping to turn public opinion against the war. 'I was against it,' says Dorothy Berger. 'We were all against it. If you watched television, you heard it every night and that was really gruesome.'

In the same way, television news reports of the civil rights demonstrations in the South helped to raise people's concern. 'I was so mesmerized with what was going on,' Elizabeth Fincher Dobynes recalls, 'and it was due to television.' Her local newspaper had failed to cover the events. 'Without television there would have been no civil rights movement, nobody would have known.'

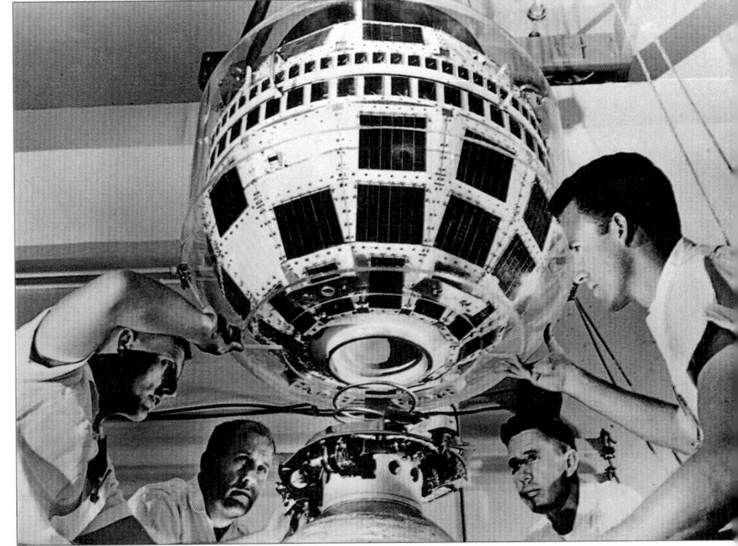

EXTRATERRESTRIAL COMMUNICATIONS
The pioneering Telstar *satellite* (ABOVE) *is inspected by technicians before being launched into space from Cape Canaveral in the United States in July 1962. Weighing only 77 kg (170 lb), the satellite orbited the Earth at the same speed as the Earth itself rotates, maintaining a stationary orbit above the Atlantic. Among the earliest transatlantic satellite pictures it beamed to television viewers across Europe* (RIGHT, *from top to bottom*) *were the American national memorial at Mount Rushmore in South Dakota, a Chicago baseball game and a view of the New York skyline.*

MOONWATCH (ABOVE) *Hundreds of people gathered in front of a giant screen in London's Trafalgar Square to watch the moon landing on 21 July 1969. Everywhere celebrations marked the historic moment, which had been preceded by four days of television coverage of the journey to the moon.*

COLOURED VISION (LEFT) *A family gazes at its latest acquisition in a poster promoting colour television. Technically it was developed at an early stage, but was not widely taken up until the 1950s and 1960s. Through colour, television gained in impact. In Britain the TV licence fee was increased to take advantage of the change.*

Views of the world

By the end of the 1960s, progress in satellite communications meant that a much wider range of programmes could now reach people across the world. New colour monitors and transmissions in colour boosted television sales. 'When it first came and you first saw it, you kind of went "Oh!", remembers Wendy Vause. 'Once you had seen colour television you didn't want to go back.' And as television was introduced to more and more countries during the 1960s and 1970s – to parts of Africa, Asia, Central and South America and the Middle East – the numbers of television viewers everywhere soared. Before long, television cameras would even enable people to see live pictures from space.

In 1969 some 723 million people in forty-seven countries – a fifth of the world's population – watched the landing of the *Apollo 11* spacecraft on the moon. 'We had the television on the patio,' recalls Edwin Nerger, who was visiting his in-laws in Dallas that summer. 'It was a very clear night. The moon was just as big and bright as it could be. And we were looking up at the moon, and we were watching the moon landing on television....And when you realized that we were not the only ones watching, but the whole world was watching, it was a tremendous event.' All over Europe people stayed up into the early hours of the morning to watch their televisions. 'I couldn't believe the pictures were from the moon to begin with,' says Wendy Vause in Britain. 'That day I felt that I watching television for the first time....It was almost unbelievable.'

"I loved every minute of watching that man walk on the moon.... When I thought my grandmother was in a log cabin and here I was seeing a man on the moon!"

MARJORIE BRANDT

The same satellites were now increasingly used to beam sporting events, including international soccer and boxing, to audiences around the world. The largest audiences so far were expected for the Munich Olympic Games in the summer of 1972. 'There was an uplifting atmosphere,' recalls Hans Klein, a sports journalist who attended the opening ceremony. 'Everybody was aware that eight hundred million people via satellite were watching this fantastic event.'

In Cleveland, Ohio, Dorothy and Benjamin Berger had a special reason for watching the Games from Germany: their son, David, was competing in the Israeli weightlifting team. 'We came downstairs about eight o'clock for breakfast, which we usually do, turned on the television, and we saw one of the weightlifting coaches being interviewed,' remembers Dorothy Berger. 'Then we heard something about hostages.' They soon heard the news that the entire weightlifting team had been kidnapped by Palestinian terrorists demanding the release of prisoners being held in Israel.

What had begun as a major sporting event quickly became an international crisis covered live on television by the world's media. 'All day long we watched television to see what would happen,' says Dorothy Berger. 'We didn't hear from anybody; we didn't hear from the Israeli government. Pretty soon we began to realize this is not good. We just watched television all night....Nothing that day ever came through any source but television.' At 11 o'clock that night there was a

VANTAGE POINT *Cameras of the world's media* (BELOW) *focus on the scene of alarm at the Munich Olympics caused by the kidnap of Israeli athletes by Palestinian terrorists, while security forces disguised as athletes* (RIGHT) *try to keep the kidnappers surrounded. Dorothy and Benjamin Berger* (TOP), *parents of one of the hostages, anxiously watched the news reports from their home in the United States.*

news flash. It announced that all eleven hostages had been killed. 'That's when we heard it,' says Benjamin Berger. 'We watched very briefly and then turned the set off.'

Captured on camera
The stabbing of a Japanese politician, Inejiro Asanuma, at a rally in 1960 was one of a growing number of violent incidents now seen live on television.

The hostages had been seized because members of the Black September group knew they would gain international attention. 'We were aware right from the beginning of the great influence of television,' says Abu Daoud. 'Our aim was to make the international community aware of the Palestinian cause....After the Munich operation, there was a great interest from the media in our cause and in the Palestinians.' And after Munich, where television itself had been hijacked, other terrorist groups found that they too could use the worldwide reach of television by staging incidents to draw attention to their cause.

Many people believed that television was not being used to its full educational potential, and in 1975 the boldest satellite experiment so far was launched. The United States agreed to loan a satellite to India as part of a national programme to improve the lives of millions of poor farming families. In India television was mainly available to people in towns and cities. Much of India's vast countryside was not covered by television transmitters, and many people had never even seen a television. With the new satellite, programmes could be beamed directly to remote rural regions.

The Indian government delivered television sets and satellite dishes to schools in 2400 villages, where families gathered each evening to watch programmes on better farming methods, family planning and health care. Madan Lal Joshi was a schoolteacher in the village of Bichoon. 'When people first assembled here we were not sure whether the programmes would appeal to them,' he recalls. They did take an interest: 'Like the farmers, who were taught about new agricultural implements and seeds. Whatever they were told they wanted to incorporate in their day-to-day life.' The programmes were broadcast to six states in six different languages. 'We were told about medicines, about pesticides for crops,' Radah Krishen, a cobbler, says. 'It was really a new thing!'

Remote reception
Members of an Aboriginal family gather outside their home in central Australia to watch television. The sheer size of the country meant that its availability was limited in some places.

Television games
A football match is being watched by sports journalists, not on the nearby pitch but on a multitude of television monitors. As well as reducing public attendance at games, television meant new competition for newspapers. 'Television was a great intruder,' remembers Howard Kleinberg, a sports writer in Miami since 1949. 'We had the locker room to ourselves, we had the post-game conference to ourselves, but along came this camera and this other person who always set up in front of us.'

Sport on screen

Businessmen, sponsors and sports promoters soon realized that television, with its capacity to engage and thrill audiences, was made for the world of sport. 'You could listen to a baseball game if you were a sports fan, or listen to a heavyweight championship fight, but you couldn't see it,' Reese Schonfeld, then an American television reporter, recalls. 'The seeing of it was absolutely wonderful, it made it much more real.'

From the intricate detail of golf to the gladiatorial contests of tennis or boxing, and from the fast-moving action of football to the grand sweep of the Olympic Games, sport offered an immediacy that hundreds of millions of viewers could share, full of conflict, passion and drama.

The first transmission in the world of team sport was the Japanese broadcast in 1931 of a Waseda University baseball match. The 1936 Olympic Games, held in Berlin, were watched by 150 000 people on special demonstration sets provided in schools and halls around the city, and in the following year in Britain there was live coverage of the Wimbledon tennis championships.

As television ownership everywhere increased, so too did the variety of sports that could be watched from home during the 1960s – major league baseball, cricket, professional football, ice hockey, soccer, swimming and sumo wrestling. Players sometimes wore new patterned clothes so that they could be identified and distinguished on black and white televisions; rules were simplified; the timing of some sports was altered. Show jumping and snooker in Britain, and American football in the United States, became more popular as a result of television. Live satellite broadcasting attracted millions of sports viewers, and television companies were paying first thousands, then millions of dollars for exclusive broadcasting rights of major international sporting events. In 1972 ABC secured exclusivity in the United States to the ill-fated Munich Olympics for the sum of $7.5 million; twenty years later, NBC broadcast the Barcelona Olympics for $420 million.

Televised sport had become big business. High-earning players and sports personalities doubled their incomes with sponsorship contracts, advertising, and personal appearances. Satellite and cable companies created sports-only channels for paying fans, and began to monopolize sports coverage. Tobacco companies, banned from advertising on television in several countries, poured money instead into sponsoring sports such as cricket, golf, motor racing and tennis. Television was transforming the world of sport.

Prime time viewing

By the 1980s television had become a global force and a powerful industry. By 1981 there were regular television broadcasts across 137 countries. One of the most popular programme formats, which captivated television viewers everywhere, was the 'soap opera'. Originating in the United States, where they had been used to sell soap powder by radio, and then adapted for television, these highly popular serial dramas drew huge audiences all over the world – in Australia, Germany and Japan, in India and Central and South America.

Catering for convenience

THE 'TV DINNER', *along with TV chairs, TV lights and even TV trays, was a must for television viewers who did not want to miss their favourite evening show. As television became the centre of family life for many people, it altered patterns of eating. Easy to prepare in a matter of minutes, these rapid meals could be consumed in front of the screen, instead of at the dining table.*

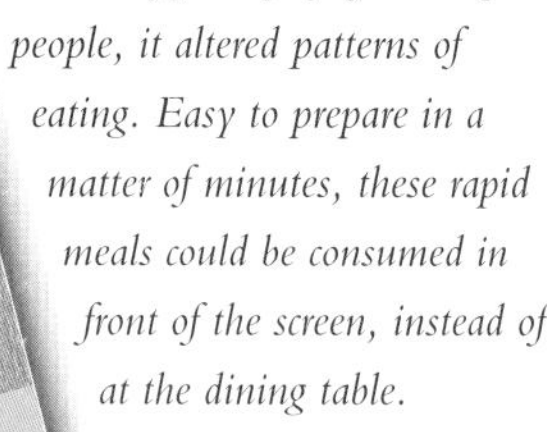

Brazilian soap operas, *telenovelas*, were among the world's most successful. Watched regularly by 65 per cent of the Brazilian population, these long-running narratives of romantic comedy, interwoven with historical, mythical or political drama, could be seen three times a day, six days a week. Diaz Gomes wrote many *telenovelas* for Brazil's TV Globo since they were first produced in the 1960s. At one time, he says, the ratings for one drama reached 'one hundred percent, which means that all of the television sets turned on at that moment were tuned to the same *novela* – to the same channel, the same story, the same scene,' he remembers. 'The *novela* stopped the country. You went out on the streets and the streets were deserted.'

THE *TELENOVELA* (OPPOSITE), *advertised in a poster marking its appearance on German television, was popular with European viewers as well as South American audiences.*

ROLE PLAYING *Larry Hagman, who starred as J. R. Ewing in the American* Dallas *serial, distributes imitation dollar bills bearing his image. Soap opera characters were so popular that they sometimes acquired a life off the screen as well as on it.* Dallas *was dubbed into ninety different languages, allowing Steliana Stefonoiu* (RIGHT) *to watch it in Romania.*

They did not just appeal to Brazilian audiences. By exporting its *telenovelas* to more than a hundred other countries, TV Globo became one of the most successful television companies in the world. In much the same way, Australian soap operas were enjoyed by British audiences, and people in France and Italy watched American ones.

In the United States, *Dallas* was one of Elizabeth Fincher Dobynes' favourite soap operas. It was about the glamorous, feuding family of a Texas oil baron. 'I fitted my schedule to watch these shows,' she says. 'There was no VCR, nothing of that nature, I made sure I watched. I didn't have to ask anybody what had happened.' In Germany Alexandra Benes followed *Dallas*

RAQUEL glaubt an ihre Tochter Fatima und an das Gute im Menschen.
IVAN will um jeden Preis Karriere machen. Raquel steht dabei im Weg.
CESAR, der Dressman ohne Erfolg,
verbündet sich mit Fatima.
ALFONSO glaubt, es sei Liebe.
VALE TUDO
Die neue Telenovela der Gegenwart
Montags bis Donnerstags um 16[30] Uhr, im 1.
ALLES IST ERLAUBT - UM JEDEN PREIS"

Epic viewing in India

One bride was late for her wedding. Two ministers were late for their own swearing-in ceremony. All over India life had come to a standstill. The explanation was simple: everyone was watching *Ramayana*. 'The sale of televisions shot up at that time. People thought that they have got to watch this serial,' remembers Shyam Sunder Arora, a television salesman. 'There were instances when people asked trains to be stopped so that they could watch *Ramayana*.'

This thirty-minute, weekly television series that took the country by storm when it was first shown in 1987 was based on an epic poem taken from a classic Hindu text. The televised drama of the familiar and well-loved story of the life of the Hindu god Rama was shown every Sunday morning on the state-run television station, Doordarshan, and all over the country people stopped what they were doing to watch it.

Source of unrest *A scene from the* Ramayana *drama series, which had a far greater popular impact than any other programme shown on Indian television.*

When *Ramayana* began there were only about ten million television sets in India, but as many as seventy million people are thought to have watched the series. In some villages the television sets were placed in front of temples by the Brahmins, for all the villagers to watch together. For some among the millions of Hindu followers of the series, *Ramayana* became more than just a television drama. Believing the television actors to be incarnations of the gods they portrayed, many pious Hindus worshipped *Ramayana*, and burned incense or hung garlands around their television sets. While some of the actors were worshipped as gods; others were elected to parliament because of their popular role in the series.

As the potent force of the religious epic reached the villages and the urban streets it affected many people's lives. In the northern city of Jammu, angry *Ramayana* fans occupied a local power station after a blackout caused them to miss an episode. There were local reports of hospital patients being abandoned by doctors and nurses while *Ramayana* was being shown. As the end of the series approached, threats of civil unrest and strikes in some parts of India by people demanding that it should be continued persuaded Doordarshan to double the number of episodes. An appeal to extend the series had even been raised in parliament.

Ramayana had a powerful effect in politics. It boosted public support for the militant Hindu parties, especially the Bharatiya Janata Party (BJP). The series provoked religious riots, and some television stations were occupied and vandalized by extremists insisting that their Hindu festivals be broadcast on television. The wave of Hindu piety raised by the series led to criticism of Doordarshan by people who claimed that it represented a breach of the public network's commitment to avoid extended coverage of any one religion or political group. *Ramayana* was nevertheless the most successful series – commercially as well as in popularity – to be shown on Indian television.

Glued to the set
The number of television sets and transmitters in India grew as a result of government policy, and both popular series as well as educational programmes reached even larger audiences.

every week without fail: 'Everybody was talking about it in the office....so I thought, I just have to watch it.' In communist Romania, where food queues were part of people's everyday life and they could not enjoy the freedom to travel abroad, watching *Dallas* enabled some to catch a glimpse of life beyond their own country. It was a welcome change: 'There were lots of episodes,' remembers Steliana Stefonoiu, 'and as we watched we became acquainted with the American way of life: how Americans dressed, how they lived, how they managed their finances. Everything was new and special for us, and therefore there was a lot of interest in this series.'

Within a few years, however, Steliana Stefonoiu could no longer watch her favourite programmes from the West. In 1983, in an effort to reduce the nation's foreign debts, television transmissions were gradually rationed by the government, along with food and clothing, to only two hours of viewing a day.

Sesame Street (OPPOSITE) *was launched in 1969 in the United States, becoming popular with young audiences all over the world. Puppets and games were used to teach preschool children about numbers and the letters of the alphabet.*

A television revolution

After the Romanian president, Nicolae Ceausescu, had introduced rationing, television featured dull documentary programmes and news items interspersed with patriotic songs. 'There were shows worshipping the presidential couple in all aspects of their public lives,' remembers Badea Anghel, whose job was to sell televisions in Bucharest. 'There were very few programmes about science, professional training, or on life in other countries, not to mention movies. Everything went in one single direction: the worship and glorification of the dictator.'

For many people, television simply ceased to exist. Instead they read books, listened to the radio or, like Steliana Stefonoiu, took up needlework. Some resorted to other means. 'People watched Bulgarian, Yugoslavian and even Russian television, which showed different kinds of programmes,' says Badea Anghel. 'This almost turned into a large-scale industry – manufacturing aerials and other equipment to receive neighbouring television stations that could meet people's need for information, music, movies.' This was illegal, and it also meant that people had to follow programmes in foreign languages – still preferable to the constant propaganda of national television, and a source of information about what was going on elsewhere. And in Eastern Europe things were changing very fast in the last months of 1989, as communist governments began to crumble.

In December 1989 viewers were watching a live broadcast of Ceausescu making a speech when the audience in Bucharest's main square began to boo him. It was unprecedented. 'He was speaking from his rostrum and suddenly the transmission was cut off,' says Steliana Stefonoiu. 'We realized that something was going on. From that moment on we stayed glued to the television set.' Outside, a revolution was erupting as people demonstrated in the streets. They soon seized the television studios. 'It was sensational!' recalls Felicia Melescanu, who worked in the newsroom. 'We quickly organized a studio...and we started to talk. A colleague, who was principal newscaster and who had sworn to wear a navy blue suit only on the day that Ceausescu was overthrown, quickly went to put his blue suit on. He came back and started telling people, "Romanian television is free!" '

"We all experienced the joy of participating in history, and the awareness that we were making history, and that television was making history."

FELICIA MELESCANU

TRIAL BY TELEVISION *For five days Romanian television stayed on the air with live coverage of the dramatic fall of the communist regime. After twenty-four years in power, the dictator Nicolae Ceausescu and his wife Elena were shown on national televison in the last few hours before their execution.*

FILMING REVOLUTION (OPPOSITE) *A television crew in Bucharest records violent scenes between civilians and armed forces during the upheaval in Romania. Most people learnt of the revolution by watching it on television.*

The centre of attention (opposite) *for these men in the Zambian capital of Lusaka is the football match they are watching on television. By the 1990s the advent of satellite broadcasts and the rapidly expanding global network of dishes and cables meant fewer and fewer limits to what people all over the world could watch.*

Teleshopping *on the QVC home shopping network was one of the numerous choices open to target audiences. With access to television, and with just a telephone and credit card number to hand, anyone could make a purchase from the wide range of products being advertised.*

Media war *From its start in 1991 the Gulf War following the Iraqi invasion of Kuwait created instant and sensational news. As its full drama and horror unfolded in front of camera crews, televison viewers everywhere checked its daily progress.*

Channel to the world

Television played an active part as the communist empire was dismantled. The new political situation was debated, and the new freedoms tested and demonstrated, on television. The entire course of the Romanian revolution was brought into living rooms around the world. Lightweight cameras and electronic methods of recording made live media coverage much easier, and round-the-clock international news channels such as the Cable News Network (CNN), founded in the United States in 1981, continued to bring people coverage of international events as they unfolded. Soon the letters CNN were as famous as any logo in the world: by 1990 it could be viewed in more than ninety countries

CNN was just one of a new generation of international broadcasters whose programmes could be picked up around the world, through domestic satellite dishes or relayed through the rapidly extending cable systems. Cable had once been used to give better transmission of broadcast television. Now higher capacity cable systems began to carry channels dedicated not to news but to cartoons, children's programmes, movies, sport and even shopping. In Miami Howard Kleinberg, who since the 1950s had watched television come of age, received several hundred channels. 'We've got a golf channel, we've got a food channel, we've got a travel channel,' he says. 'I can buy anything.'

In half a century television had become a formidable force: it was used to sell products to people, to educate, entertain and inform them. Elections were contested on it, votes were won on it, and leaders could be created or deposed by it. In the age of global television, it was harder for dictators to control what people watched, when with direct satellite dishes they could pick up international broadcasts from the sky.

By 1990 there was a television receiver in 98 per cent of homes in the developed world, and about 2.5 billion people in the developing world had regular access to one. From the start, people had instinctively understood that it would change all our lives. 'It has made all of us more aware of other nations, other people,' says Alex Azar. 'I didn't know a whole lot about areas outside the state of Indiana. And today – why, the world is part of our neighbourhood....I don't think the world will ever get along without it.'

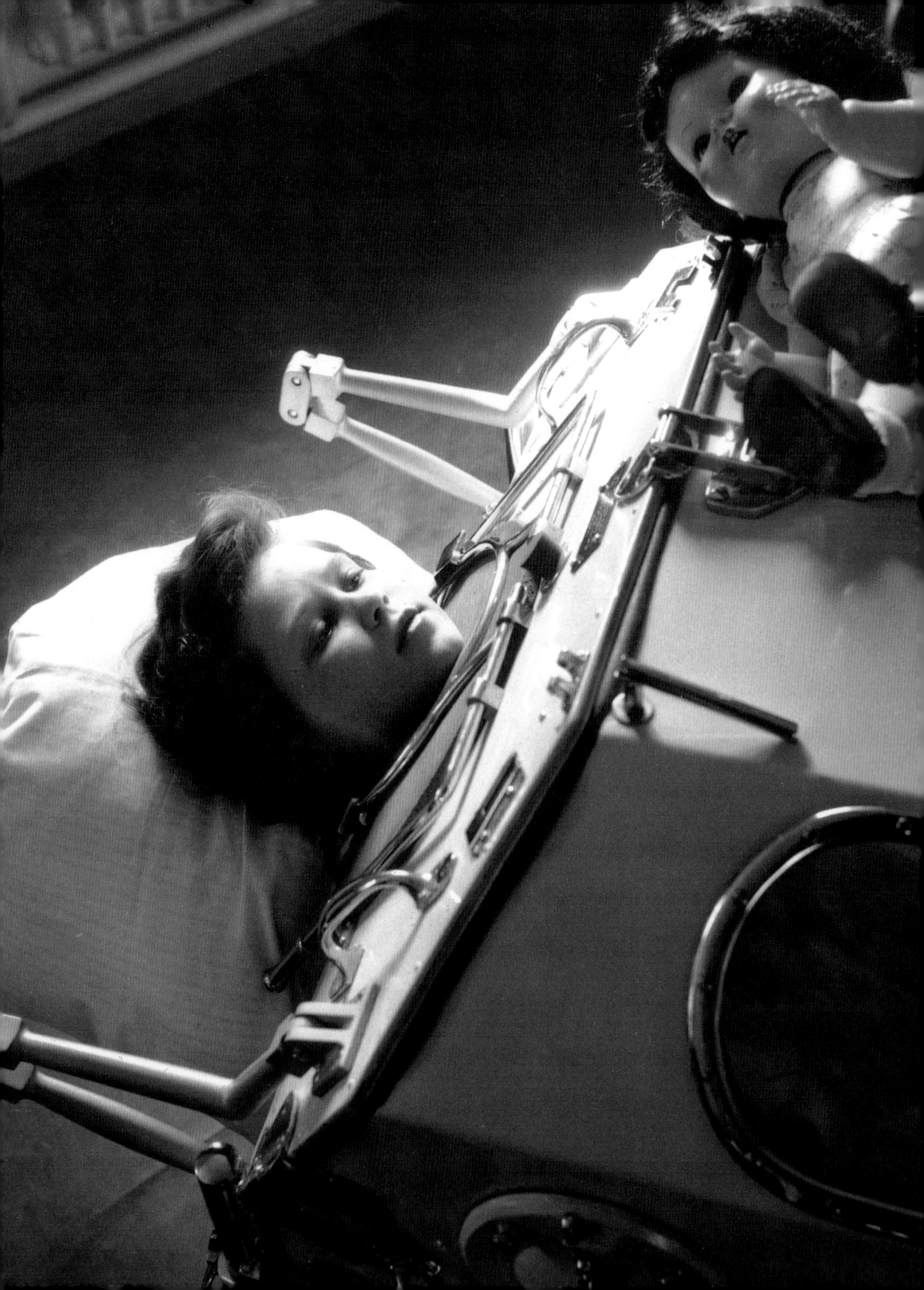

6

1945 – 1995

Living Longer

Campaigns for Better Health

'It's 1954, it's Brooklyn, trees, school, friends, the sun was still yellow, and suddenly that world ended,' remembers Sharon Stern. She was nine years old when she woke up one Friday morning in October with a severe headache. Her mother kept her home from school that day. A few days later she became extremely ill and was taken to hospital, and was diagnosed as suffering from polio. When her left leg became paralysed and she began to have trouble breathing, she was placed in an 'iron lung' – an airtight metal cylinder that enclosed her body right up to the neck, allowing her to breathe artificially. She was to spend the following nine months inside that machine. As she still vividly remembers, 'It's very frightening to a child, to be suddenly taken out of that little world that you're growing up in. I'm in this strange place, among strange people, and I have no control over my body or my breathing.'

Sharon Stern was just one among several hundreds of thousands of children all over the world who suffered from the debilitating effects of poliomyelitis right up until the 1950s. Within a few months of her own struggle with the illness, a preventive vaccine finally became available after many years of intensive medical research. It would relieve millions of parents and their children from the fear of infection.

In the three decades after 1945, medical science and improvements in public health care seemed to be overcoming one after another of humanity's oldest enemies. As more and more of the world's epidemic diseases were conquered, people increasingly began to rely on the successful methods of prevention and cure that scientists and doctors were now able to offer. Protected from many major diseases by immunization in their first year of life, millions of people could expect to lead longer and healthier lives. But as populations around the world began to increase ever more rapidly, unforeseen health problems as well as new diseases emerged, reducing the effects of the progress that scientists had brought as well as challenging them to find new solutions.

Life saver *A young polio victim rests, trapped in the iron lung that is keeping her alive.*

Health for all

"It was a miracle drug....A lot of infections responded to penicillin that we had never been able to control before."

JAMES LEWIS

At the turn of the century the millions of people throughout the world who suffered from the infectious diseases that threatened their lives could expect little by way of treatment. Only a few drugs were available to combat the scourges scientists were trying to cure – among them cholera, diphtheria, influenza, malaria, scarlet fever, typhus, yellow fever and whooping cough. Advances in antenatal care and obstetrics had begun to reduce the large numbers of women who died in childbirth. But millions of people were still afflicted by the often deadly viral and bacterial infections that spread ever more rapidly in the increasingly densely populated cities. At that time the number of years people could expect to live was relatively low: average life expectancy at birth in the United States was only forty-seven years, while in India it was as little as twenty-five years.

WAITING ROOM (ABOVE) *A mother prepares her children for a checkup in the Infant Welfare Clinic at Britain's first All-In Health Centre. Before the nationalization of health care, free medical treatment had only been available for the poor or homeless. After 1948 everyone became eligible.*

During the 1920s and 1930s several drugs were discovered, including insulin for treating diabetes, and new ways were found both to treat and to control viral diseases. In some countries mass screening was introduced to identify and control early outbreaks of disease. Vaccines were introduced to prevent diphtheria, influenza, tetanus and yellow fever. One of the most significant breakthroughs was made accidentally at a London hospital in 1928 when a British scientist, Alexander Fleming, spilled some mould onto a dish containing a bacterium, killing it. Further research in 1939 profited from that discovery to develop a powerful new drug – penicillin, an antibiotic agent that helped to fight infections.

By 1941 penicillin was being mass produced in Canada and the United States for military use, to treat soldiers wounded in the Second World War. It was used in large quantities to combat gangrene. James Lewis, an American army doctor, realized its value when he was working in an emergency operating theatre in northern France after the D-Day landings. 'I was treating serious abdominal wounds, chest

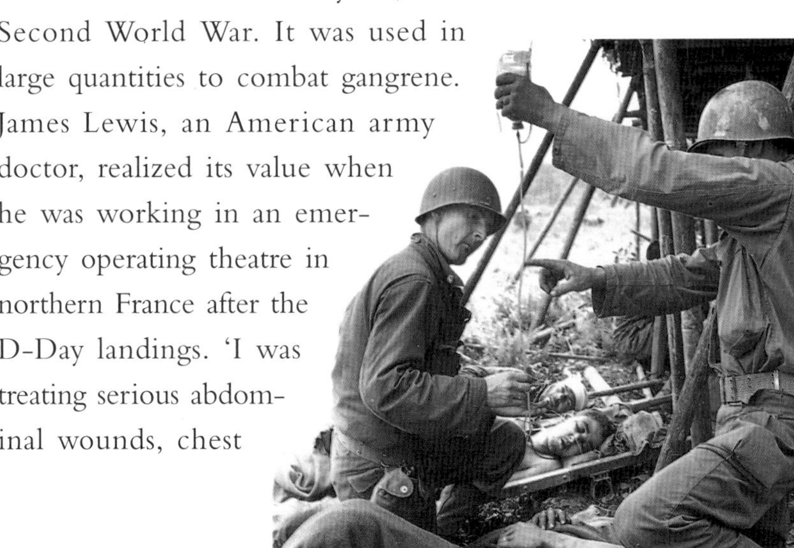

WARTIME WARD (RIGHT) *in northern Burma, where medical personnel of the United States army treat war casualties in a tent. American interest in the development of penicillin, stimulated after the Japanese invasion of Pearl Harbor, continued after the war when the United States became the largest producer of the new drug. Among the many infections it combated, penicillin proved remarkably successful in treating venereal diseases, a common wartime affliction.*

The Health of the People

During the century most Western governments saw that they had to take on responsibility for their people's health, and introduced new measures to improve access to health care. The earliest of these was Germany's Sickness Insurance Act, introduced in 1883, which became the basis for national health policy there. With money raised through contributions from employers and employees, the scheme began by offering medical care to those who were most vulnerable. It was later extended to provide health benefits for most of the population, and included dental care, maternity care and annual preventive health checks.

Japan turned to Western medical practice and introduced an Employee's Health Insurance scheme in 1922 based on the German model. At first limited to urban workers, it was extended during the 1930s and again in the 1960s to give compulsory coverage for the whole population.

In the Soviet Union, where people had suffered from frequent epidemics of cholera, typhoid, dysentery and influenza before the revolution, the new communist government undertook direct responsiblity for public health. The Commissariat of Health, set up in 1918, established compulsory health clinics, centres and programmes, improved standards of hygiene and sanitation, and offered free medical care to all. A similarly comprehensive approach was taken by Britain's Labour government with the establishment of the National Health Service. It took effect in 1948, offering free medical and dental care to everyone – regardless of age, race, income or occupation – in hospital and out of it. Private medical practice continued for those who could afford it, but thousands of hospitals in Britain were nationalized.

In the United States, federal grants for maternal and child health care and mass screening were introduced during the 1930s, but attempts to pass national health legislation through Congress repeatedly failed. Some companies that had set up workers' medical schemes during the war continued them in peacetime, but most people had to take out their own health insurance to pay for health care from private sector doctors and hospitals. In the 1960s national Medicare and Medicaid programmes were set up to care for the elderly, the disabled and the poor, but with the exception of some public hospitals, private sector health care was still more common.

Most developed nations chose national health provisions based on these methods, or a combination of private and public schemes. Their impact was considerable, setting new standards for millions of people who benefited from greater access to health care: a hundred years after the introduction of Germany's Sickness Insurance Law, Germans lived on average about twice as long; in Russia there was a sharp decline in mortality generally, while infant mortality had dropped by 90 per cent since 1913.

Developing countries had neither the money nor the trained medical workers to approach these levels of health care. By the 1990s even in wealthier nations the availability of treatment and hospital beds for larger and increasingly ageing populations was coming under threat as the cost of health care continued to rise.

Health policies *of Britain's Labour government were a central feature of its welfare reforms after the war that promised social security and family allowances as well as free health care for the young, the old, the homeless and the unemployed.*

wounds, amputations and head wounds, where the potential for infection was very great,' he remembers. 'I had one casualty who'd been hit by a shell that had blown his thigh open and blown manure into it, which had to be scraped out with a brush. These are potentially terrible infections, and penicillin played a big role. It was a miracle drug.'

After the war, millions of civilians were able to benefit from the new drugs that had saved the lives of so many soldiers. In 1945 many European countries were facing a public health emergency.

Drives to combat disease (above) *Mobile X-ray units were used in 1951 to encourage people to come forward for tests in Glasgow, which had the highest number of tuberculosis cases in Britain, as part of the city's campaign to defeat the disease. X-rays helped doctors to discover the disease at an early stage by showing the shadow on the patient's lungs.*

A German child, *displaced by the war from her home in Czechoslovakia, is deloused with DDT spray by a worker at a medical centre run by the United Nations International Children's Emergency Fund (UNICEF), before setting off to a new home.*

Millions of refugees were on the move. Food shortages and a lack of clean water made people particularly vulnerable to disease. Over pictures of bombed-out families taking water from a drain, a newsreel commentary warned: 'In biblical days his name was pestilence. His modern name is epidemic disease. His shadow is in the sewer water of a thousand towns. These people slake their thirst with typhoid fever and dysentery, with infectious jaundice and possibly with infantile paralysis.' DDT, a pesticide developed in 1944 to protect soldiers in the tropics, was now used to fight the spread of lice and ticks, typhus and malaria in the ruined cities.

In the postwar years, as standards of living began to improve, people in the West began to look to their governments and their employers for better health care. State-sponsored health provision and insurance schemes were set up, while insurance companies did their best to persuade those who could afford it to take out private health insurance. In 1948 a specialized agency of the United Nations, the World Health Organization (WHO), was established with twenty-six member states to promote better health for everyone. Internationally, the priorities were to continue medical research and to use the newly available medicines to stamp out old infectious killer diseases everywhere. In industrialized countries the worst of these was tuberculosis, known and feared as TB.

Cures for life

Fifteen-year-old Marjorie Cave grew up in the overcrowded East End of London. As her father was ill and her grandparents had come to live with them, she had to share a bed with her mother. 'My mother was very ill, and I saw her have haemorrhages and breathless attacks, fits of coughing in the night,' she remembers. 'It was very frightening.' After her mother died Marjorie Cave herself grew thinner, paler and more breathless. Then she also began coughing. 'I thought, "This is it, I'm the next," and I was right.'

Tuberculosis, a potentially fatal disease that principally affects the lungs, flourished where people lived in poor, overcrowded conditions. Hospitals were filled with its victims, and it had caused millions of deaths. 'The whole outlook was very bleak,' Marjorie Cave recalls. 'That is, of course, if you survived. They thought I wouldn't live three months.' She stopped going to school, and instead was taken first to a local sanatorium and eventually to Papworth, a sanatorium near Cambridge specially built to care for tuberculosis victims. It was five years before she fully recovered.

Marjorie Cave *feels fortunate to have recovered from TB. 'You were terrified of catching it. You couldn't mix freely with people, it wasn't very pleasant. You were very, very thin, pale, you sometimes had a horrible cough,' she says. 'Nobody really wanted to know you...except those who were very fond of you.'*

Until the 1950s there was no effective cure for people who were suffering from tuberculosis. They were instead encouraged to rest, follow special diets and spend plenty of time in the open air. Some patients received far more drastic treatment. When Les Ellis, who was serving in the British army, found it difficult to keep up with the drills, he was given an X-ray examination and was then referred to the military hospital. 'I didn't know what it was all about,' he remembers, 'but when I got there they said, "Well, you've got TB".'

Two months later Les Ellis was also moved to Papworth Sanatorium; the doctors told him he was to have a thoracoplasty. The idea was to collapse the lung so that it could rest. First they took out two of his front ribs, and when that did not work, they took out two at the back and one more in front. As he was given only a local anaesthetic, Les Ellis can remember the details of the operation. 'Dr Murphy, he was holding my hand as high as he could so he could get at the ribs. He made the incision and said, "You'll hear a crack. Don't worry about it, it's just one of your ribs". And there was this great bang, just like someone breaking a piece of wood.'

Queueing for protection (right) *Children await their turn at one of the emergency polio vaccination centres in Chicago in 1956.*

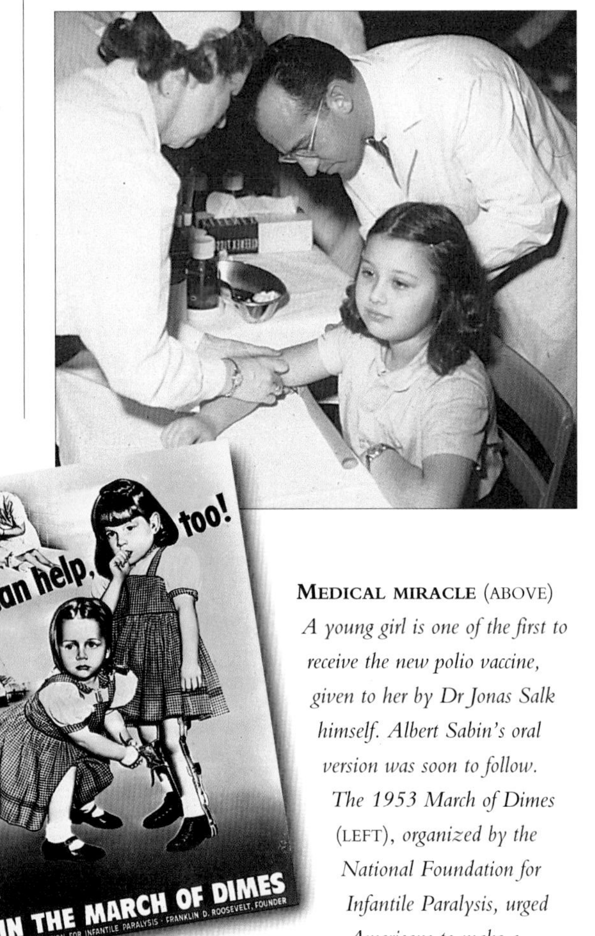

Medical miracle (above) *A young girl is one of the first to receive the new polio vaccine, given to her by Dr Jonas Salk himself. Albert Sabin's oral version was soon to follow.* *The 1953 March of Dimes* (left), *organized by the National Foundation for Infantile Paralysis, urged Americans to make a donation to the campaign to fight polio. This poster, featuring two children affected by the crippling disease, was distributed throughout the United States.*

A few years later, once penicillin was in general use, new drugs specific to tuberculosis were discovered: Streptomycin in 1944, PAS in 1946 and INH in 1952. Together, they successfully inhibited the disease, curing all but the most advanced cases. 'It came a bit too late for me,' says Les Ellis. 'It would have been nice to have been saved all that surgery.' For millions of others, the 'white plague' of tuberculosis was no longer a threat.

People did continue to fear polio, a viral infection that destroyed the nerves, causing its victims – who were most often children – to lose control of their muscles and become paralysed, and in some cases to die. In the United States, where polio reached epidemic proportions in the early 1950s, 40 000 cases were reported each year. 'Everybody was frightened of polio,' remembers Deborah Runkle, who grew up in Minneapolis. 'The mothers were frightened and they made the children frightened.' In 1954 came yet another wonder drug, an anti-polio vaccine developed by Dr Jonas Salk at the University of Pittsburgh. It was followed two years later by one that could easily be swallowed on a lump of sugar.

The new vaccines could not cure polio, but they did prevent it from spreading, and immunization was introduced in several European countries, and in Australia, Canada and South Africa as well as the United States. In the early months, when supplies of the vaccine were still limited in Minneapolis, Deborah Runkle's father managed to reserve some for his daughter. It was a big day

"Polio was a sort of disease of the day. It was the top contender that everybody was frightened of getting, because it could strike anybody at any time."

VIRGINIA GRANATO

for them. 'We went and got the vaccine, and then it was over. That was the fix. There was no more polio. There was no more worry.' In Eastern Europe and the Soviet Union, where more than 115 million people were vaccinated, polio was almost completely eliminated by the end of 1960.

By the 1960s almost all children in the richer countries could expect to lead long and active lives. Western governments had the resources and the organization to make sure that everyone benefited from the new drugs. In developing countries, where more than three-quarters of the world's population lived, things were very different. In spite of the Indian government's efforts to improve health care for its people, poor sanitation, polluted water, poverty, overcrowding and hunger, and the lack of medicine to combat infection, left many of them vulnerable to disease. With a population of 500 million, basic resources were in short supply.

In Tegu Raghuvir's village in Uttar Pradesh, northern India, there was no hospital and no doctor. 'We used to go running to fetch a herbalist, but by the time we got back the patient would be dead,' he recalls. 'Smallpox, measles, cholera, plague, influenza – these were fatal diseases.' As many babies and children died, people tried to have large families, partly to help supplement the family income. Only six of Tegu Raghuvir's nine children survived. 'Some people had this fear that, "If I just have this one child, and if he dies, then my family will be finished". And some people kept having daughters hoping they would have a son.'

DEBORAH RUNKLE *(ABOVE and with her brother, RIGHT) was eight years old when polio inoculation began in her home town, Minneapolis. 'I remember it so very well,' she says. 'I think it took a year or two to get enough vaccine for everybody....At first, one day you could get it and the next day it was gone.'*

Search and containment

In India, as in much of Asia and Africa, smallpox was the disease people feared most of all. A potentially fatal viral infection, it affected people of all ages, causing high fever and making the body break out in pustules that gradually dried up, turning to scabs. After two weeks the scabs were shed by the scarred victims, and the infectious stage was over. 'The pustules were enormous,' remembers Dhanari Devi, who caught smallpox in his village of Rohaki. 'They were all over the body. It was a dreadful sight.' Another villager, Bi Karma, suffered such a massive attack that his eyes were forced shut by the pustules for eight days. 'When the pox receded, water oozed out of the pustules so profusely that I could wipe it down my limbs. The upper layer of the skin began to peel off. It was very painful. I felt I wouldn't live.'

The face of smallpox *An Indian child is cradled by his mother, the disfiguring signs of his illness clearly visible. As well as a characteristic rash that turned into pustules, smallpox also inflicted on its victims fever, headaches, pains and sometimes vomiting and convulsions.*

The only protection against smallpox was vaccination. Immunization, begun in the nineteenth century, had succeeded in controlling the spread of the disease in many countries that had the necessary resources. But the virus was still rampant in every continent apart from Europe and North America, affecting more than ten million people a year and killing an estimated two million in 1967 alone. In India, where the government was determined to get rid of smallpox as other countries had done, a programme of mass vaccination was introduced, but there were still epidemic outbreaks. In 1966 an international campaign to eradicate smallpox from the entire world was launched by the WHO. It achieved considerable success: by the end of 1973 smallpox was restricted to the Indian subcontinent and parts of Africa. In India the WHO tried a new approach. Instead of trying to vaccinate everyone, teams of medical workers would search for individual cases, isolate them for the incubation period, and then vaccinate everyone within 3 km (1.9 miles).

Sick room (below) *With an earthen floor and corrugated iron roof, a smallpox emergency ward in the Pakistani capital of Karachi houses victims of the disease during the necessary incubation period. Despite often limited medical resources, many countries made huge efforts to combat infection.*

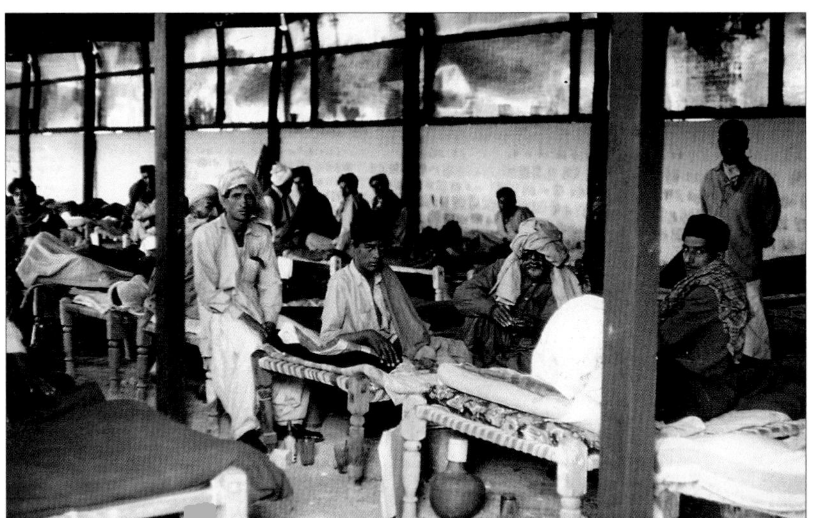

Thousands of people set to work in villages and markets, the start of a long and difficult process. 'It was during the hotter season,' remembers Bohumir Kriz, a Czech doctor helping the Indian authorities. 'We were living in the villages, sleeping in the villages, eating in the villages, working for

Dangerous games *in Calcutta. Children's play could have catastrophic consequences, as poor sanitation and contaminated water contributed to the frequent epidemics of smallpox and cholera that claimed many lives.*

eighteen to twenty hours a day. Everybody was dedicated.' He and his colleagues would find an outbreak, contain it and move on to the next one. Every district health centre had a smallpox room, with a map to trace the spread of the infection.

Panchu Ram remembers the day a medical team arrived in his village. 'There was general excitement. The children and the women all came pouring out of their homes....Everyone, the young and the old, flocked to the village centre and arrangements were made for the vaccination of one and all.' There were some obstacles. In remote villages where smallpox had become an accepted part of life, people regarded the disease as a sign of the goddess Sitla Devi. Victims were thought to be blessed by her, and pilgrims came from all over India to worship at her temple in Varanasi. Many looked to prayer rather than medicine for cures. 'When I started to vaccinate a woman she was so angry she spat in

MALARIA'S DEADLY BITE

In 1939 some 700 million people in the world were suffering from the effects of malaria, an ancient parasitic disease that strikes at humans' internal organs. The parasites are carried by mosquitoes, and are introduced into people's bloodstreams when they are bitten by the female mosquitoes. The toxins released produce extremely unpleasant symptoms – shivering cold followed by chronic fever, sweating and vomiting. If the disease is untreated the spleen may be affected, and a quick death can follow.

The long struggle against malaria achieved its greatest success during the 1940s and 1950s. New drugs were developed that proved effective in both preventing and curing the disease. Until then, clearing swamps and marshes infested with mosquitoes had been the only method of controlling malaria. Chloroquinine was developed in 1943 by the United States army, and DDT was widely used during and after the Second World War, especially in subtropical areas, where it was sprayed in homes and in the mosquitoes' breeding grounds. By 1955 staff at the WHO believed that it would prove possible to eradicate malaria all over the world. It had already been banished from the middle west and south of the United States, and from both Greece and Italy.

By 1960 it looked as though this widespread disease had almost been conquered. But although most developed countries were malaria-free, the scientists had miscalculated. In those parts of the world worst affected by malaria – Africa, Asia and Central and South America – severe shortages of resources and equipment hindered the eradication campaigns. There were further setbacks when both the parasite and the mosquito itself developed immune strains resistant to medical and chemical treatment. Chloroquinine began to lose its effectiveness as a result of over-use, and DDT was found to be highly toxic, damaging to humans and to the environment. By 1976 a WHO official reported that 'the entire population living in the original malarious areas is now at malaria risk'. In the four years between 1972 and 1976 the number of reported cases of malaria in the world more than doubled – from 3.2 million to 7.6 million.

Malaria's growing resistance to once-effective drugs postponed hopes of its permanent eradication. In the meantime, alternatives being researched included the use of an ancient Chinese remedy and a trial vaccine developed in South America.

With ever greater numbers of people on the move as a result of political upheaval, famine and poverty, the disease continued to spread as it became more difficult to treat. In the tropical world tens of millions of people still suffered from malaria; more than two million of them died each year.

Mosquito nets *treated with insecticide, first introduced in The Gambia and subsequently in Ghana, Kenya and Tanzania, offered effective protection from malarial mosquitoes, but in poor countries most people could not afford to buy them.*

my face,' remembers Zafar Husain, a paramedical assistant. 'I didn't say a word. But other people in the village were very upset by her behaviour. Later on everybody in the village was vaccinated.' In an attempt to overcome people's fear, rewards of ten rupees were offered to those who reported cases of smallpox.

The new approach worked: by 1974 the search had been narrowed down to the last few cases. One of them was a young girl living in Pachera, a small village in Bihar, north and west of Bengal. Zafar Husain was absolutely determined that she would be the very last case in his region, and spent fifteen days at her home, sleeping on the veranda to ensure that no one came into contact with her. 'I was completely confident that after this child the infection would not spread farther,' he recalls. 'The last scab shed in front of me and I destroyed it. Then I knew that the infection would not spread!'

In 1977, after two years of surveillance, India was officially certified as free from smallpox by the WHO. Bohumir Kriz was making plans to close his office in Delhi, discharge the staff and hand over the equipment, when he received a telegram asking him to report to Somalia, in eastern Africa, within a week. 'We hardly knew where it was, and of course we had no idea that there was smallpox there. We thought India was the last place with smallpox, that the whole thing had finished,' he remembers. 'We started again from scratch.'

The outbreak in Somalia proved to be a serious one, and the programme went on for several months. There were not enough medical staff in some of the more remote areas, and it was difficult to isolate smallpox cases among nomadic people moving from place to place. In this Muslim country some of the men refused to be vaccinated by women, and some women to be vaccinated by men. 'They were sometimes frightened,' remembers Bohumir Kriz. 'We assembled the whole village with the village chief, we talked to them, we explained to them what we would be doing, why we were doing it.' By October the virus was confined to one person: Ali Maalin, a twenty-three-year-old hospital cook. 'I never thought that I would live,' he remembers. His was the last case of smallpox in Africa. 'I saw it as a victory,' says Ali Maalin. 'The fear was no longer there. We realized that if enough effort was made against disease we would eventually be successful.'

In 1980 the WHO announced that smallpox had finally been eradicated from the world. Bohumir Kriz and his team could now return home. 'Our boss brought from Geneva a case of champagne. We were celebrating. We were happy. But later that night we were a little sad, because it was clear we would all be disappearing to all corners of the world. And at that moment somebody said, "Well, I wonder what mother nature will prepare for us next?" '

"The search started in 1973, and in 1975 we saw through the last case. A disease that had been going on for ages was eradicated."

ZAFAR HUSAIN

POINT OF RECOVERY
Malaysian children (RIGHT) *line up for their vaccinations, supplied by the WHO in 1982. Berber tribesmen and their families* (BELOW) *in the remote valleys of Morocco are given antibiotic ointment for conjunctivitis. Since medical teams supplied with UNICEF drugs first arrived there in June 1953 they have achieved considerable success in keeping the seasonal infection at bay.*

A people's programme

The attacks on major killer diseases such as polio, smallpox and tuberculosis on a world scale, and the introduction of new public health measures, were proving successful – so successful that every year millions more children survived into adulthood, and millions more adults were also living longer. However, one result was a sudden, dramatic explosion of population that in some countries threatened to overwhelm food supplies, health care provisions, and even the survival of governments hard-pressed by the needs of ever more people.

Nowhere was the problem more acute than in China, where there were more people – including more babies – than in any other nation on earth. For centuries the Chinese had wanted large families, and in the countryside families with four children were common. In an effort to control the population, the communist government had launched several birth control campaigns in the 1950s and 1960s. In 1979 a new official policy of 'one family, one child' was announced. Women were forced to have abortions, and fines were levied on parents with more than two children.

ONE FAMILY, ONE CHILD *'for today but especially for tomorrow', is the message on a Chinese poster promoting family planning. Reproductive rules for Chinese parents were introduced in the late 1970s, as mounting population pressure precipitated the urgent drive for national birth control in the hope that China's huge population of one billion would eventually be reduced to 700 million.*

FUTURE REFLECTIONS *A boy gazes at a poster bearing the symbol of India's birth control campaign – the red triangle. The campaign was widely promoted through community education, at health centres and in family planning clinics. Some people resisted it. 'You had many children,' says Amravati Devi, 'because suppose you had four and each one of them contributes a penny, then you would have four pennies. They would help you on the farm.'*

In the Caribbean, South America, sub-Saharan Africa, and especially the Indian subcontinent, governments faced the same imperative: to control the mounting tide of births or risk all the progress that had been achieved through investment in economic development and improved health care. Between 1947 and 1975 the population of India grew from 350 million to 750 million. As a government film acknowledged, 'Fifty-five thousand babies are born in India every day – two births every three seconds, straining our resources of food, shelter, clothing, employment and welfare.'

In the early 1950s a series of programmes was launched in India to offer advice and information on family planning methods, but with little success. From the 1960s the campaign intensified. The prime minister, Indira Gandhi, announced, 'Family planning is an accepted official policy in India, but our programme will not succeed if it remains only an official programme. Family planning is truly a people's programme. Its success rests on individual citizens. They have to be approached, persuaded, prompted, and helped to practise family planning.' At local rallies the campaign elephant distributed condoms held in her trunk, and then set out

তিন বছর যাক হেসে খেলে
দুটি সন্তানের জন্মের মধ্যে ব্যবধান রাখার
উপযুক্ত ও কার্যকর পন্থা হ'ল লুপ
(W.B.M.O
সরকারী অনুদান:—
ভেসেকটমির ক্ষেত্রে প্রত্যেককে নগদ
(যাতায়াত খরচ ও জলযোগের জন্য বরাদ্দ
টিউবেকটমির ক্ষেত্রে প্রত্যেককে নগদ
ও বিনামূল্যে হাসপাতালে অপারেশন.ওষুধপত্র ও খাদ্য
তা ছাড়া:—
লুপ গ্রহণের ক্ষেত্রে প্রত্যেক মহিলাকে
সরকারী অনুদানের ব্যবস্থাও আছে
যে কোন হাসপাতাল বা
স্বাস্থ্যকেন্দ্রেই এই সুযোগ পেতে

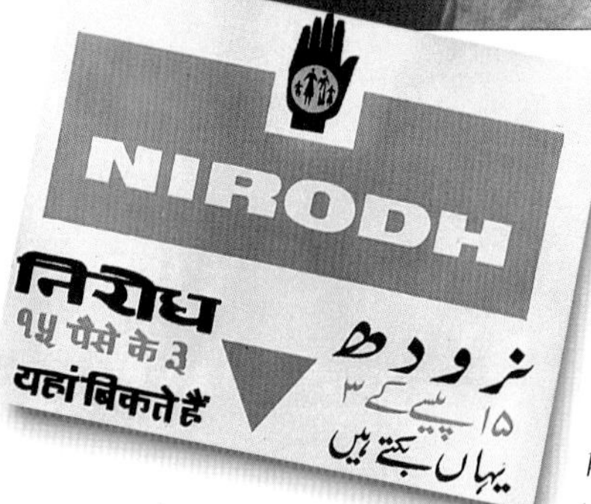

Before and after *Women stand waiting to be sterilized* (ABOVE)*, while those who have already undergone the brief operation rest on the floor before returning home. Sterilization camps for both women and men were set up throughout India, and methods of contraception were widely promoted. Millions of condoms were freely distributed by the Nirodh campaign* (ABOVE LEFT)*; the word means to stop or control.*

> *"Now people are going in for sterilization most willingly. They know that a small family is a happy family."*
>
> VASANTI SRIVASTAVA

to spread the message through thousands of villages. 'You have two, that will do' was the official slogan, similar to the message of the Chinese authorities.

India's democratic government did not feel it could use the same methods as the Chinese had done, but there were other ways of persuading people to have fewer children and even to undergo a sterilization operation, as one Indian doctor, Kalpana Bhatt, found. 'To attract patients,' she remembers, 'the workers would tell them that they would have a small injection, and they would go away walking, no need for rest or anything. And then the patients were given money – a hundred rupees – so they came for the money's sake. Sometimes they were already operated on, and they would come a second time. Even the bachelors would come sometimes.'

As the campaign was stepped up, millions of people across India volunteered. Dutta Pai, one of Bombay's leading sterilization doctors, was in charge of the Control of Population programme. 'Everybody worked hard. I remember those days – 1967 to 1974. The programme was being implemented with tremendous zeal, great conviction. A lot of effort was made to communicate the message to the minds of men and women, and we succeeded.' There were family planning clinics all over Bombay – at railway stations, in converted buses, and on street corners. Between 1971 and 1973 alone, more than five million sterilization operations

TOO MANY PEOPLE

IN THE EARLY 1930S the population of the world was about two billion; it had taken the whole of human history to reach that size. Since then there has been a dramatic explosion of population. In under fifty years the world's population doubled to four billion; by 1993 it had reached five and a half billion and was continuing to rise, being estimated to reach a peak of ten billion people by the year 2050 before beginning to level off.

Improvements in health care, nutrition and sanitation, the control of epidemic diseases and higher standards of living all contributed to the plummeting death rates and high birth rates that resulted in this population explosion by the early 1960s. Alarmed by the threat to food supplies, many governments increased funding for population control programmes, with a particular emphasis on family planning. Birth rates decreased in a number of countries, though the annual rate of population growth – some 100 million people – remained alarmingly high, with the greatest pressure in Africa, Asia and Central and South America.

The result was increased pollution, environmental degradation, and continuing poverty and hunger. In many developing countries there was concern that resources would be overwhelmed as millions more people needed food, health care, living space and work. In 1950 there were only three cities in the world with more than ten million inhabitants. By the end of the century it was expected that there would be twenty such cities, most in developing nations. In the 1990s many of the twenty-five million inhabitants of Mexico City lived in extreme poverty. With a land area roughly the same as that of the United States, China already had four times as many people, and far fewer resources of fertile land, fuels and minerals to support them. Its population was expected to rise to at least one and a half billion; some experts believed that the population of India, about 850 million, might exceed that of China within fifty years.

Billions of dollars were spent on population programmes in Africa, Asia and Central and South America. In 1994 the United Nations Population Fund initiated a world plan of action designed to stabilize population growth by the year 2050, through family planning and universal education. Experts were in no doubt that the population explosion would soon end; the question was whether it would come humanely, as a result of lower birth rates, or tragically through increases in death rates as a result of epidemics, starvation or war. By the 1990s many people had come to believe that the need to reduce birth rates, to increase food production while preserving the natural environment, and to distribute food and other necessities to all those who needed them, had become the greatest challenge of their time.

THE ESCALATING SCALE *of the population problem was worst in developing countries, which were less able to cope with population growth, but it was the world's wealthier nations, where consumption was much higher, that placed the greatest strains on the earth's resources.*

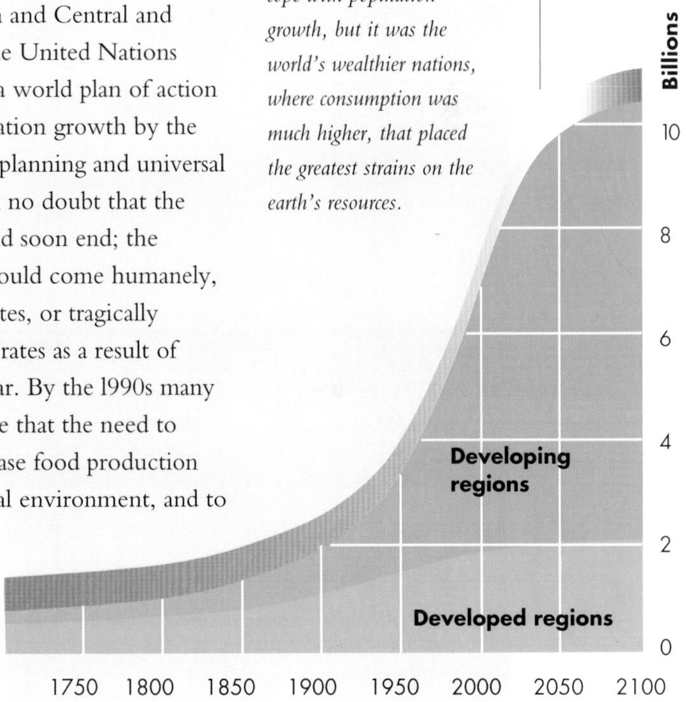

were performed, thousands of them by Dutta Pai. But, he says, 'Some people went too far, and this effort on the part of some misguided people led to a backlash....They tried to give greater incentives – people talked about giving away watches and this and that, so people who were not properly motivated came under the knife.' As more people claimed they had been coerced into having operations, the campaign became unpopular. 'In 1976 there was so much talk against male sterilization and family planning,' Dutta Pai says, 'that democracy won and family planning lost the battle.'

New epidemics, new diseases

In many parts of Africa, Asia, South America and the Caribbean, populations were rising almost as fast as in India. Now that viral diseases such as smallpox had largely been conquered, dangerous waterborne bacterial infections – typhus and cholera – posed the greatest threat to human health in poorer, overcrowded environments. The cholera epidemics that affected parts of Asia and Africa during the 1970s and 1980s, prompted by monsoon floods, famine and war, were an age-old problem.

In 1980 the WHO estimated that some twenty-five million people were dying every year from diseases caused by dirty water and lack of sanitation, six million of them children. Despite a drop in overall mortality rates in many developing countries, infant mortality was still high and continued to encourage larger families. The only way to prevent the spread of infections such as cholera was to provide clean water and sanitation, and to improve public hygiene and health as well as curing disease. In 1981 the International Drinking Water Supply and Sanitation Decade was announced by the United Nations, an ambitious programme to provide clean water and sanitation for everyone by 1990. In ten years, thirty-five billion dollars were spent, mostly on local schemes. Villagers helped to drill wells, install hand pumps and dig cesspits.

Sources of infection *Mexican villagers carry out their daily chores around their local water supply. Installing village pumps meant that people no longer had to carry water so far, and provided them with safe drinking water. This helped to prevent waterborne diseases from threatening many communities.*

In Peru, which had one of the highest birth rates, the size of the population was overwhelming the resources of the cities. Rubbish collection, water and sewage provision simply could not keep up. Standards of living and conditions of health and hygiene were poor. In the overcrowded shantytowns around the capital, Lima, people lived among their own rubbish and washed and cooked with water contaminated by untreated sewage. Cesar Queverdo Linares worked on a project to provide drinking water for the residents of Cajamarca in northern Peru. 'The drinking water system had been designed to supply the needs of places with 200 to 2000 inhabitants,' he remembers. 'The systems we installed there were calculated to last for twenty years, and our twenty-year

plan allowed for a fifty per cent growth in housing,' he remembers. 'But subsequently there was a population explosion and the drinking water system we'd installed proved inadequate.'

In 1991 a cholera epidemic broke out on the Peruvian coast, and quickly spread inland among people living in the Andes. In February, a month of carnival celebrations, Sennefelder Silva Marin was working at the hospital in Cajamarca, a town northwest of Lima. 'After the carnival we were surprised to learn that people had been admitted to the hospital with cholera, an illness none of us knew anything about, and which we'd never had to treat before,' he recalls. 'Never before in Cajamarca had there been an epidemic of such appalling proportions.'

In just over one year, 9500 people in Cajamarca caught cholera. Teams of emergency workers went out to treat them. 'It was an illness characterized by violent vomiting and diarrhoea,' says Sennefelder Silva Marin. 'It was a truly horrific illness.' When Maria Llana Rudas' husband fell ill with cholera, she had no idea what was wrong with him. 'His stomach hurt, his head hurt, he

Breeding ground *for infection. Smoky Mountain in the Philippine capital Manila, where nearly half the city's inhabitants lived in poverty in makeshift homes with no sanitation or rubbish disposal. Here as elsewhere, deprivation and overcrowding contributed to disease.*

Honouring the dead (above) *A family in Lima visits the grave of a relative, one of the thousands of victims of the Peruvian cholera epidemic. 'There were some who'd bury their dead straight away,' says Luis Correa Camacho, 'others who would refuse to bury them and who would leave them where they were because it was cholera.'*

Helping hands (above) *Western aid workers carry away the dead to prevent further spread of infection in the Kibumba refugee camp, where an epidemic outbreak of cholera in 1994 killed thousands of displaced Rwandans fleeing from the bloody ethnic fighting in their country.*

didn't speak to me, he didn't say a word. Even his faith seemed to have gone,' she remembers. 'My eldest son helped me take him to the hospital. We thought he might get better, but he didn't. We took him away dead.'

Part of the difficulty was to help people understand the infection so that they could avoid catching or spreading it. Although there was no cure for cholera, lives could be saved by quick treatment administered by trained staff, but both were in short supply. Sennefelder Silva Marin had the help of only three colleagues. 'Then we were joined by two more doctors sent by the Department of Health,' he remembers. 'So there were six of us fighting to save three and a half thousand lives.... We treated people morning, noon and night, working in shifts.' Things were made worse by the local custom of holding a three-day vigil before burying the dead. Luis Correa Camacho, a former mayor of Otuzco village, attempted to persuade one family to bury their dead relative immediately. He even threatened to call the police.

Mouths to Feed

One million people – men, women and children – seeking refuge from civil war died of starvation when famine broke out in Biafra, Nigeria in 1968. While epidemic diseases were successfully being fought, many people's lives in Africa, Asia and South America were still threatened by hunger and hunger-related illness, despite a steady rise in the amount of food being produced in the world as a whole. Many developing countries, with relatively weak economies, political instability and poor conditions for farming, became increasingly burdened with the task of feeding their rapidly growing populations.

Food production in industrialized countries soared during the 1970s and 1980s with new advances in agricultural science that enabled farmers to produce high-yielding, fast-growing crops. There were hopes that increased foreign aid to developing countries and the new 'Green Revolution' would solve the world's food problems: Mexico's wheat harvests increased threefold, and Pakistan stopped importing its wheat from the United States. But in the poorer countries most farmers could not afford the fertilizers, pesticides and modern machinery that were required by the new intensive methods of farming.

As people in developed countries enjoyed more food than ever before, there was less food available to many of those living in Africa and parts of Asia. By relying more heavily on foreign aid and food imports, the economies of developing countries began to be overburdened by massive debts and soaring interest rates. To repay the debts, governments spent less on health services, housing and welfare, leaving their most vulnerable people, many of whom were too poor to buy or grow their own food, unsupported. In some countries farmers were encouraged to produce cash crops for export – coffee, cotton, sugar and tobacco – to help alleviate foreign debts, rather than growing food for local people to eat. Food shortages worsened as areas of once-fertile land turned into desert as a result of over-development.

During the 1980s a series of droughts in sub-Saharan Africa caused crops to fail, killed livestock and precipitated widespread starvation in the region. In Ethiopia five million people, many of them refugees from war, were threatened by famine; starving people fell ill after eating unfamiliar wild plants. Media attention, particularly to the suffering of the children, prompted a vast international relief effort in 1984 as the daily death toll rose. Aid arrived from European countries and from Australia, Canada and the United States, while charities and rock musicians banded together to raise funds and collect food and clothing.

The scale of the Ethiopian famine alerted the world to the sobering fact that in the face of drought and conflict, not even modern technology, greater food production and international aid could solve the problem of hunger. In 1991 civil war in Somalia left 250 000 people without food. Seven million people in Sudan faced hunger while the government used the country's resources to finance war. The physical and mental development of millions of children, and ultimately their whole future, was affected. By the 1990s, in a world of plenty, 800 million people continued to go hungry.

Barren desert (below) *Weary from hunger, heat and exhaustion, refugees carry their few possessions on the long and difficult journey through the semi-arid Sahel region on the southern rim of the Sahara. Frequent droughts killed large numbers of cattle, devastated crops and brought widespread famine.*

'They ignored me. They kept vigil, chewing coca, and they prayed and chanted,' he recalls. 'Then suddenly – boom, the dead man exploded, faeces and guts all over the mourners, and by seven in the morning about eighty per cent of them had cholera. It was dreadful.' There were some 50 000 cases of cholera in the Peruvian epidemic, and more sporadic outbreaks continued elsewhere.

While the worst of the traditional killers were being driven back by vaccination and public health campaigns, a deadly new disease surfaced that was to threaten people in the developed and the developing world. Acquired Immune Deficiency Syndrome (AIDS) was first formally identified in the United States in 1981, though it had been spreading in some populations before then, particularly in parts of Africa, where it reached epidemic proportions in the 1980s. Caused by the human immunodeficiency virus (HIV), which damages the immune system and leaves its victims vulnerable to even minor infections, AIDS was easily transmitted through sexual intercourse and infected blood, and from mother to infant.

Ribbon of awareness

THE RED RIBBON *was adopted in the 1990s by AIDS campaigners trying to raise awareness about the disease. Part of the worldwide campaign against AIDS and HIV, the ribbon became a symbol of understanding and an expression of support and sympathy for its victims. Ten million ribbons, folded by volunteers, were produced for distribution all over the world – including China and India – through charities and other organizations such as schools and scouts clubs, in the army, at AIDS meetings and other public gatherings. The campaigners hoped that by prompting people's curiosity the red ribbon would help to save lives by giving more people accurate information about the disease.*

Everyone was frightened of catching the new disease. In Kenya Rowlands Lenya found that he was HIV-positive in 1989. 'I announced it to some friends, I went to the police and they took my photo, then the problems started,' he recalls. 'At my place of work, my colleagues did not want to share with me the usual office facilities. At home many of my friends stopped coming to our house. In school my children were abused by other children....So the situation became very difficult.'

By 1988 there were 120 000 reported cases of AIDS in 138 countries around the world; millions more people were infected by HIV. In the West, where major infectious diseases had long been brought under control and age-related illnesses posed the biggest threat, AIDS prompted a public health crisis. At first homosexual communities were thought to be most vulnerable to the disease, but it soon became clear that everyone was at risk. In

the United States 50 000 people had already died from the disease as medical scientists raced to discover new drugs for its treatment. Education, screening programmes and counselling facilities were set up, and many governments launched campaigns encouraging 'safe sex'. In 1990 the WHO reported that between eight and ten million people in the world were infected by HIV.

As the disease continued to spread, scientists were still unable to find a cure. 'My experience was that almost everything you could get was curable and easily treatable,' says Peter Staley, who became infected in 1985. He joined other sufferers in the United States, attending conferences, forming self-help groups and demonstrating in Washington. 'We had a sense of optimism that as long as we shook the trees of the scientific establishment, the cure would fall out,' he remembers. 'Unfortunately it didn't happen that quickly. A lot of people lost hope, a lot of people died. I don't know if science is going to be able to defeat this in time for me and my friends.'

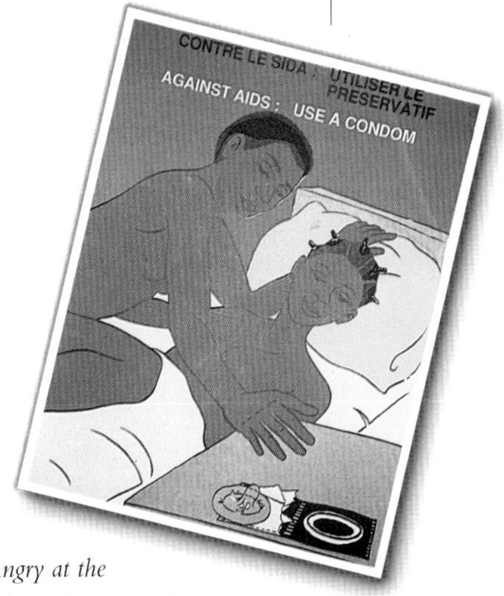

AGAINST AIDS (RIGHT)
A French poster produced for a Paris AIDS conference in 1990 promotes the use of condoms to prevent the spread of infection. Angry at the failure of the United States president, George Bush, to initiate a national plan against AIDS (BELOW), *crowds demonstrate in Washington in 1991. Peter Staley* (LEFT) *and his fellow AIDS sufferers took an active part in such demonstrations. 'I would survive the crisis just by shaking the tree, just by demonstrating, just by screaming,' he says.*

New hopes and old fears

It was a discouraging thought that new diseases such as AIDS could arise, and age-old diseases that doctors believed had been conquered could reappear. Yet that is just what happened. After forty years in decline, tuberculosis was once again threatening lives. By weakening their resistance to infection, HIV made many people more susceptible to TB. The disease that struck Marjorie Cave and Les Ellis in the 1950s killed nearly three million people in 1990; by the mid 1990s, people were beginning to realize that the high hopes and ambitions of medical science in the 1950s and 1960s might have to be abandoned.

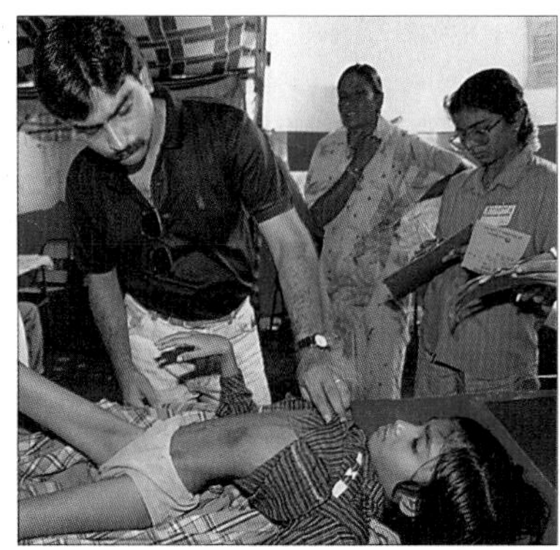

Medicine by train *A doctor from the Life Line Express examines a young patient in a nearby tent. India's hospital trains brought medicines and medical care by rail to people living in remote areas.*

Deborah Runkle, who was among the first to receive the new polio vaccine in the United States, grew up believing that medicine held all the answers. 'I never knew anybody with a bad infectious disease. If you got sick, the doctor would prescribe something and it was over in three days.' But the spread of AIDS raised new doubts in her. 'I wonder, will polio come back? Are my children safe? What about my grandchildren?' she asks. 'I am not so positive any more. I think we had a lucky twenty-five years and I am not so optimistic about the future.'

From 1945, progress in twentieth-century medicine and health care was largely responsible for the threefold increase in the world's population. That success created new burdens, but it also improved countless numbers of lives. In India, Budu Harku was able to receive proper treatment for his cataracts. 'In the old days there were no eye operations,' he remembers. 'Once you were old, you became blind. But now, if you have even a minor eye problem you get your eyes fixed, and then you can look after yourself again.' Amravati Devi has also witnessed the dramatic changes. 'There is not so much disease now. Smallpox is gone. There is much less cholera and plague. People used to die of TB, that's also reduced. When the women came out of labour, they would get a kind of fever – and that's gone as well. Now there are doctors and medicines available in every village.' Since the early years of the century, average life expectancy everywhere had increased. In India by the 1990s it had risen to fifty-eight years, while in rich countries the average span of life was seventy-five years. For the majority of people, living longer was no longer a dream.

Three generations *of a Japanese family pose for a wedding photograph* (Opposite). *By 1993 life expectancy in Japan was the highest in the world. As elsewhere, the growing percentage of elderly people in the population created new social and economic burdens.*

保衛世界和平
慶祝中國人民政治協商會議成功
中華人民共和國中央人民政府成立
擁護中央人民政府
擁護人民民主專政

1 9 4 9 – 7 – 1 9 8 9

Great Leap

Mobilizing the People of China

The communist soldiers of the People's Liberation Army reached the city of Shanghai on 27 May 1949. Ma Gennan and her fellow factory workers rushed into the streets to welcome them. 'There was an endless stream of people, some playing military band music, some dancing,' she remembers. 'The great joy was indescribable.'

After the years of fighting, China's bitter civil war had at last ended, bringing victory for the communist forces. 'What the liberation meant to us was the collapse of the "three mountains"– feudalism, imperialism, bureaucratic capitalism,' recalls Ma Gennan. 'It was under the leadership of the Communist Party that we had succeeded in toppling the three mountains: in the countryside we had been subjected to the repression and exploitation of feudal landlords; in the factories we were suppressed by capitalists and foremen. Now we were to be liberated.'

Four months later, on 1 October, hundreds of thousands of people congregated in Tiananmen Square in the capital city, Beijing (Peking), to hear their new leader, Mao Zedong (Mao Tse-Tung), proclaim the People's Republic of China. Huo Buo was one of the official photographers there that day. The atmosphere was so electric that she found herself in tears. 'As soon as the broadcaster announced "Chairman Mao has arrived", the square was immediately seething with excitement. The crowd was chanting, "Long live Chairman Mao".' They listened intently as he declared, 'The People's Republic of China is now established. Chinese people are now standing up.'

This day had not come easily, but China's communist revolutionaries had proved to be an irresistible force. As a result, a way of life and a society that had continued almost unchanged for hundreds of years was about to be shattered. As their leaders set the Chinese to achieving their vision of a socialist utopia, and to building China into a strong power, people were to be swept into an unprecedented form of revolutionary mania, and subjected to new tests of endurance.

The communist flag is raised *as people celebrate the triumph of the Chinese revolution in the city of Shanghai.*

The turning point

The upheaval had been coming for a long time. China had been ruled by its imperial dynasties for more than two thousand years. Millions of people endured harsh poverty, barely able to survive. Ninety per cent of the population still lived on the land; peasants were pushed into debt by government tax collectors and by their landlords, who imposed high rents. Child labour was normal, and women were subjected to forced marriage or concubinage.

"I wove cloth day and night to make ends meet.... In the old days there was justice for the rich but none for the poor."

HU BENXIÜ

A series of uprisings and organized rebellions had begun to challenge China's rulers during the nineteenth century, but the possibility of real change came with the death of the empress dowager in 1908. The Manchu dynasty was overthrown, and a republic declared in 1911; a period of instability and suffering followed, as rival political groups and regional warlords fought for control. By the late 1920s there were two major forces in the struggle for power: the Guomindang (Kuomintang) nationalist forces led by Jiang Jieshi (Chiang Kai-shek), and the Chinese Communist Party (CCP), which was founded in 1921.

During the chaotic years of the 1920s and 1930s there was little improvement in living standards. For many people, like Hu Benxiü, who grew up in the southwestern province of Sichuan, life in the old society was very hard. 'My mother looked after our three sisters. She had bound feet so she couldn't go to work in the field. Our life was very poor. As the landlord took away our land, we had to earn a living by spinning.' They were able to buy only a small amount of rice with their earnings. 'Struggling not to starve,' she says, 'we couldn't afford to take care of what we wore.'

PLIGHT OF POVERTY *China's large population of illiterate peasants endured a life of continuing hardship and suffering. Many of them died of starvation or disease.*

China's cities were expanding as the country began to industrialize, but conditions there were little better. Ma Gennan's parents sent her from the village to work in a Shanghai factory. 'Once recruited to the factory we weren't allowed to return home and we had to live inside the factory,' she recalls. 'The place we lived in was a straw shed....We ate stinking vegetables and salted fish. At mealtimes, everybody fought for more food. Our monthly wage was only about twenty fen, not even enough to buy a roll of toilet

The Long March

The bitter fighting between the nationalists and communists intensified in 1930, when Jiang Jieshi launched a series of extermination campaigns against the Red Army soldiers. As they drew the noose tighter round the communist mountain enclave in southeastern Jiangxi province, by the summer of 1934 it looked as though China's communists were about to be wiped out. They decided to retreat.

On 16 October 100 000 soldiers, remnants of a far larger communist army that had been whittled away in the fighting, attempted a break-out. Joined by thirty-four women, including Mao Zedong's pregnant wife, and a few children, they began one of the most challenging feats of the century.

Over the next year they made their way in a great arc from southern China almost to the borders of Tibet, then north across great rivers, snow-covered mountain passes and vast, uninhabited, swampy grasslands. On the way they came under frequent attack from the nationalists, but were supported by the peasants, who responded to their disciplined, courteous behaviour. The communist soldiers' courage and endurance was often tested, as when they reached the Dadu river, a tributary of the Chang Jiang (Yangtze), where the only crossing was over a bridge, suspended by chains and laid with wooden planks, high above a deep mountain ravine. Many of the planks had been removed by the nationalist forces waiting on the other side.

The exhausted soldiers at last reached the sanctuary at Yan'an in the remote northern province of Shaanxi, 368 days after they set out. They had walked some 40 km (25 miles) each day, with little food, and fought many battles along the way. On the Long March – in all covering some 9600 km (6000 miles) – only 30 000 of them survived the hardships of the journey and the fighting. They formed a stronghold at Yan'an, building up power to continue their struggle.

What had begun as a retreat from an advancing enemy became a show of great strength and unity that safeguarded the communists and ensured their survival. The Long March also gave Mao new standing as the undisputed leader of the Party, and assured both Mao himself and the other campaign leaders of lasting prestige.

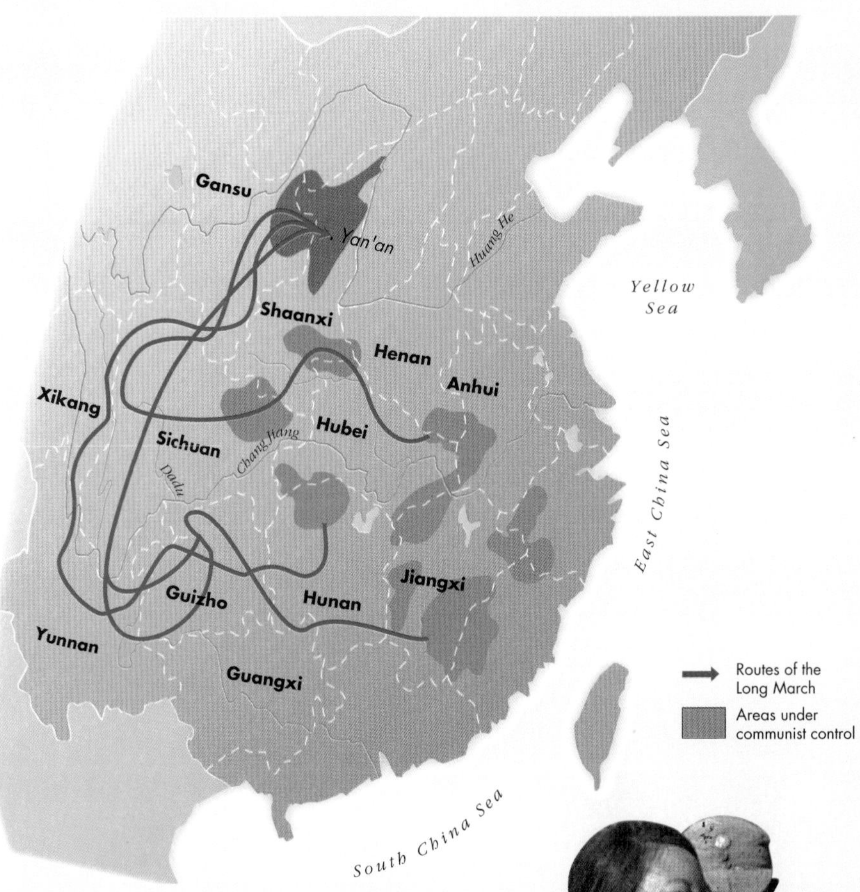

The perilous trails (above) *of the Long March wound from south to northwest China. From three starting points the communist soldiers followed different routes through the harsh terrain, establishing communist bases along the way, until they reached safety at Yan'an.*

Peasant support (below) *was a vital factor in the communists' victory, and a key aspect of Mao's revolutionary strategy. In contrast to the often harsh treatment meted out by nationalist soldiers, the communists treated the peasants well and even offered recompense for their hospitality.*

paper. If you didn't do your work well, the foreman would hit you with an iron rod wrapped in cotton flannel.' But for the wealthier middle classes life was very different, as Jin Jingzhi, whose husband ran an advertising company in Shanghai, remembers. 'We had many social engagements....My husband always paid great attention to his dress when going out....When he returned home in the evening, I made him really comfortable....I was very happy.'

"We saw the People's Liberation Army sitting by the road. They didn't even ask for a cup of water or food, they asked for nothing at all. They were very disciplined."

REN FUQIN

It was to the huge peasant majority of the population that the communist leader Mao Zedong now looked for support. He believed that revolution would come through them. The communists promised them land and an end to poverty and oppression, and managed to establish local control in parts of the country they called 'liberated areas' as bases from which the revolution could spread. Pamphlets were secretly distributed among workers and peasants. 'We thought that what was said in the leaflets was right,' says Ma Gennan. 'We lived a bitter life, like beasts of burden, enduring hard labour but earning no money.'

The communists fought a fierce guerrilla war, both against the nationalists and against the Japanese troops who had in 1931 seized Manchuria in the northeast, and in 1937 launched an attempt to annex China itself. For a time the communists and nationalists formed an uneasy united front against the invaders, but after Japan's surrender at the end of the Second World War, full-scale civil war resumed in 1946. Victorious in Manchuria, and now armed with captured Japanese weapons, the strong, newly

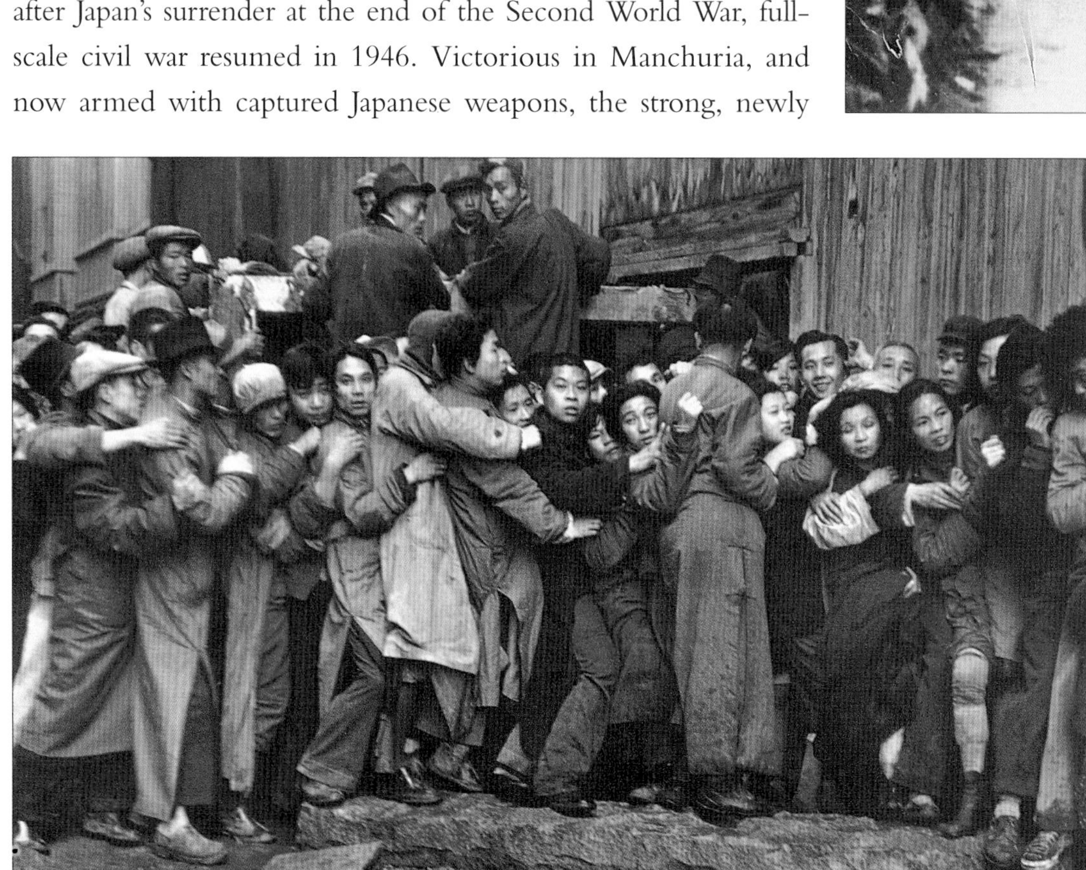

CLASS STRUGGLE
Alarmed at the now real prospect of a communist victory, prosperous Chinese citizens jostle in a queue at a Shanghai bank in late 1948 to convert their savings into gold. When the communists took over, hyperinflation worsened China's already weak economy.

formed People's Liberation Army seized one area after another. By October 1949 Mao and his lieutenants were celebrating their final triumph in Tiananmen Square in Beijing, while the nationalists fled to the island of Taiwan.

When Hu Benxiü witnessed the arrival of the communist soldiers in Sichuan she was frightened of them at first, but as they visited people's homes they told them, 'We are your own people!' The general mood went from one of daunting fear to euphoric joy. 'We danced and paraded in the streets,' Hu Benxiü describes. 'We also sang a song which went, "The East is red, the sun is rising, and there is Mao Zedong in China, he creates happiness for the people".'

Standing guard
Soldiers of the invading Japanese army watch over the citizens of Tianjin in 1939. 'Opposite our house there was a post where the Japanese set up checkpoints,' recalls Ren Fuqin. 'Any Chinese who went through it had to bow to the Japanese. If they forgot, the Japanese would make them kneel down with a heavy barrel of water on their heads.'

> *"We would follow the Communist Party wherever it directed us, and would do whatever the Party instructed us to do. Now we were the masters, and our life was to be secured from the cradle to the grave."*
>
> MA GENNAN

Mobilizing the millions

At first the revolution was widely greeted as a liberation. When the communists came to power China's economy was in ruins; most of the railways and main roads had been destroyed by the war, and disease and hunger were widespread. To implement the new socialist ideal and fulfil the promises of the revolution, productivity on the land and in the factories had to increase. It was the communist intention that the people should bring about the changes by their own efforts. Their energy and resourcefulness were to be tapped, and directed into building a healthier and stronger country.

VILLAGE SPECTACLE (ABOVE) *in the northern province of Henan, where a man is publicly tried for attempting to sell one of his relatives, the young girl seated on the stool in the centre. Under the communists, women's lives underwent dramatic changes.*

REVOLUTIONARY PYRE (OPPOSITE) *of former land deeds and other official documents seized by the communists in 1951. As many as a million landlords are thought to have been killed after the communists came to power, and much of their land was redistributed.*

Mao had taken the decision to rely on the peasants, not on the urban workers, and they had fought for him. To reward them, land was confiscated from the landlords and given to the peasants: 43 per cent of China's land was redistributed to 60 per cent of the people. For the landlords, who became targets of blame and hostility, it was a frightening time. They were dealt harsh penalties at village 'people's courts'. The communists also organized 'speak bitterness' meetings, at which the landlords and the former village chiefs were publicly denounced before being imprisoned. Many were tortured or killed. Party activist Luo Shifa attended one of these meetings in Sichuan: 'We first asked the tenant farmers to make speeches denouncing the landlords.' The landlords were rounded up, bound hand and foot, and made to listen to the denunciations. 'We called it "eating bitterness",' describes Luo Shifa. 'Then it was time to chant slogans. We redistributed the land and farming tools. Peasants were very happy after the land redistribution as they could plant their crops in their own land.'

The communists also introduced a Marriage Law in 1950, which awarded equal rights to women and abolished child marriage and concubinage; people were discouraged from holding traditional arranged weddings. Prostitutes were cleared from the

The great helmsman

From the beginning of the Chinese liberation, the nation's attention was focused on one towering figure: Chairman Mao, or the 'great helmsman', as he came to be known. Jiao Shouyun had been brought up to revere Chairman Mao. Each school morning she and her fellow pupils would stand in front of his portrait to recite passages from his writings. 'I had always cherished, since I was little, a feeling of great esteem for Chairman Mao, and dreamed that one day I could meet him.' A few years later, at a rally in Tiananmen Square, she did. 'I shook hands with Chairman Mao three times,' she remembers. 'I was simply intoxicated with great joy and happiness....I would follow Mao everywhere, do whatever he asked me to do.' Afterwards, everybody wanted to shake her hand, the hand that Chairman Mao had touched.

The man who cultivated this adulation, and who worked to use it to his own political ends, was born in Hunan province in south-central China in 1893, into a family of well-off peasants. Mao received a basic education in the Confucian classics before serving briefly as a soldier. In 1918 he qualified as a teacher from a school in the provincial capital, Changsha, where he came into contact with Western ideas and writings and began to shape his own ideas about revolution.

Mao realized that the time for profound change had arrived, and was determined to be one of its agents. From the 1920s he slowly emerged as a leading figure in the Communist Party. In 1927 he organized the Autumn Harvest peasant uprisings in Hunan and Jiangxi provinces. After the success of the Long March in 1935, he became chairman of the Party. A firm believer in Karl Marx's analysis of class and the need for class struggle, he tried to adapt the Soviet model of revolution to China's different circumstances by putting the peasants, rather than the workers, at the centre of his struggle, spreading his powerful guerrilla army among them 'like fish in the sea'.

After Mao led the communists to power, the entire country became steeped in his thinking. Young children were taught to sing, 'Father is dear, mother is dear, but Chairman Mao is dearest of all'. Adults learned that, 'All our victories are victories of the thoughts of Mao Zedong', and crowds of young people wished him, 'Ten thousand years of life!' The cult of Mao reached its height during the Cultural Revolution in the mid-1960s, when his image appeared on countless badges and posters, his quotations were broadcast on loudspeakers, and his thoughts were circulated in his published writings.

Through his mastery of propaganda and his personal charisma, Mao managed to dominate the Party and the nation until his death in 1976 at the age of eighty-three. Despite the ruthlessness and failure of some of his policies, Mao continued to portray himself as the father of the people, and many of them continued to adore him even though he had subjected them to great suffering.

Leading the Chinese people (below) *Mao Zedong appeared at the centre of propaganda images encouraging people to devote their energy and enthusiasm to building a new China.*

Shao Ai Ling *took this personal photograph of Mao at the moment of their meeting. 'When I was told that Chairman Mao was going to receive me, I was tearful and sleepless,' she describes. 'I felt that for the rest of my life I should serve the people better.'*

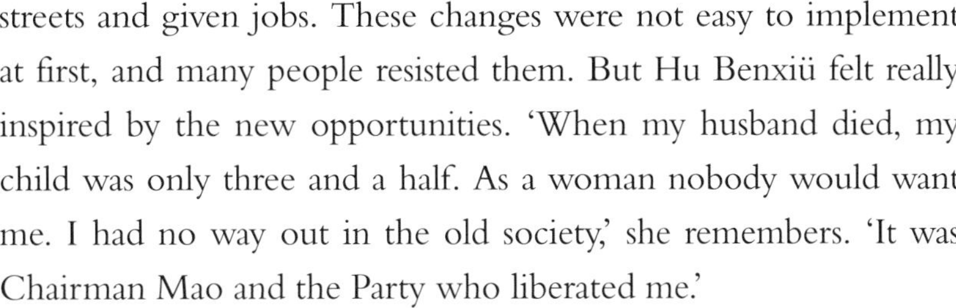

streets and given jobs. These changes were not easy to implement at first, and many people resisted them. But Hu Benxiü felt really inspired by the new opportunities. 'When my husband died, my child was only three and a half. As a woman nobody would want me. I had no way out in the old society,' she remembers. 'It was Chairman Mao and the Party who liberated me.'

Public health was one of the Party's top priorities. Mass inoculation campaigns were introduced all over the country, and people were urged to observe cleanliness and hygiene, and to spit in their handkerchiefs instead of on the ground. In occupation, the Japanese had referred to the Chinese as the 'sick men of Asia'. Now, Ren Fuqin remembers, 'We used this as an example to mobilize everyone to participate in the public health campaigns.' As a local public hygiene worker, Ren Fuqin and her colleagues brushed the walls with water and stuck up posters. One read, 'Everyone takes part in exterminating the four pests: bedbugs, flies, mosquitoes and rats'. Schoolchildren would proudly present their teachers with boxes of dead insects. Ren Fuqin also had to inspect people's homes. 'We would put our hands in the dustbins to see if they were clean. We mainly examined whether the table was dusty or not,' she remembers. 'Families that had done a good job would be given a little flag.'

Field work *A farm worker is treated for a minor injury by one of China's new 'barefoot doctors'. With a little training, a health manual and a few basic medicines, they set about providing health care for their fellow workers in often remote rural areas. Under the communists people received free medical care.*

There were campaigns for literacy, too. People were not only taught how to read and write, they were pressed into service to teach other people. One of them was Guao Xiuying. 'I used a wooden door as my blackboard. I wrote words on it and they copied them. Some of those who were learning had to carry their babies with them, breastfeeding them while studying.' People were encouraged to learn as they worked on the land or in the factories. 'I still remember what we learnt to read: "We are all Chinese; we are workers; we are peasants",' says Ma Gennan. 'I enjoyed studying. There were five girls in our family, all of us illiterate. Now, as

37

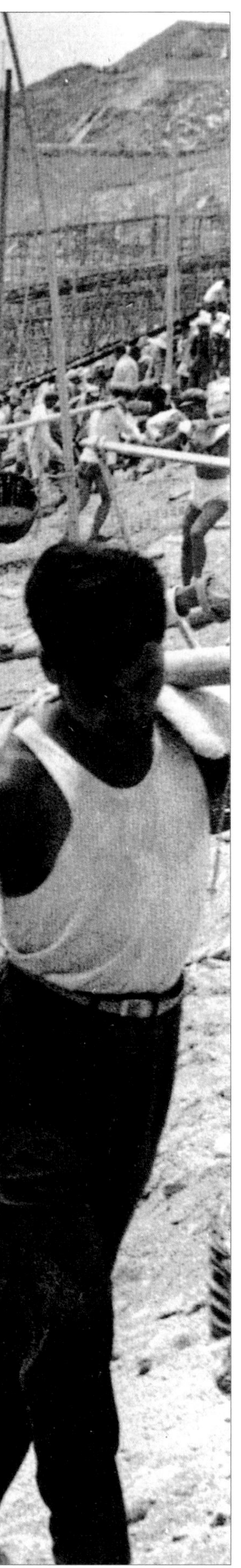

a factory worker I had the opportunity of free classes, so I really wanted to learn.'

Heroic workers *of Tachai are commemorated in a poster* (ABOVE) *following the successful completion of an ambitious project to build walls to control the annual flooding of a river. Several irrigation projects involving thousands of workers were launched* (OPPOSITE). *The Red Flag Canal project, begun in 1960 in Henan province, took more than 70 000 workers ten years to build. Numbers alone were not enough – China needed modern technology as well.*

Private enterprise in the cities was allowed to continue at first (though it was closely controlled by the state) in an attempt to stabilize industrial output, but by 1952 people had to relinquish their businesses to the nation. Jin Jingzhi and her husband had to adapt to the new social order. 'I was very worried at the time,' she remembers. 'I thought that the Communist Party spoke on behalf of working-class people, and I didn't know how people like us would be treated.' She later attended a local residents' meeting, and then became involved in the household committee.

People were rallied into collective action by means of huge posters and banners, newspapers, loudspeakers or at public meetings that spread the communist ideology of class struggle and delivered a new political consciousness into the minds of millions of people. Mao's power and status quickly grew, and in 1954 he became chairman of the republic as well as the Party. Shao Ai Ling was a teacher in Shanghai. 'We constantly filled the minds of our pupils with Mao's political thoughts, and held him up as a figure of authority. To our minds Mao was our paramount leader, a great man. As a result the students soon came to realize that the changes taking place in our city, in our families, in the school, were brought about by Chairman Mao. They knew that Chairman Mao was our great saviour.'

Gradually the gigantic process of the revolution worked itself out in every corner of the country. Reconstruction, helped by aid from the Soviet Union, was under way. The bulk of the rural population was organized into cooperatives and collective farms; factories were taken over and run by state enterprises. The Party's will reached out into every village in the vast countryside, and every alley in the great cities; the Chinese people, some joyfully, some in fear and doubt, transformed themselves into revolutionary workers. By 1956 food output had grown by over 70 per cent. Yet Mao was not satisfied; by 1958 he was worried. China was not moving fast enough, and it was losing sight of its revolutionary goals. His solution was a new campaign for growth in both agricultural and industrial production.

New opportunities *A schoolgirl practises on an abacus, demonstrating her knowledge to her uneducated grandmother. In 1950 only one in five people could read. Many people benefited from the education policies introduced by the communists.*

'Greater, faster, better'

The new campaign was known as the Great Leap Forward. It called for renewed efforts in town and countryside alike. Banners exhorted the Chinese to work so hard that China would soon be able to catch up with the West. But behind this push for greater production was a second motive: to complete the revolution. Collectivization was speeded up and expanded. The family was no longer to be China's basic social and economic unit, as it had been for thousands of years. Instead, millions of people found themselves marshalled into enormous, unfamiliar and labour-intensive communes where they lived and carried out public works projects, manufactured industrial goods or farmed.

Communal life *Children living on one of the large new communes are looked after while their parents are at work.*

Twenty-four thousand communes were set up in the first two months of 1958 alone. Unlike cooperative farms, communes housed everyone, not just farm workers. In them, all aspects of people's lives were effectively 'collectivized' and regimented. Communal nurseries freed the women from looking after their children and communal dining halls fed their families, so they could devote all their time and energy to working under strict discipline. Instead of money, residents of the rural 'people's communes' were provided with six community services absolutely free: education, food, funerals, haircuts, health care and movies.

Zeng Guodong was a Party cadre, one of many officials assigned to implement policy and encourage others to do so. He participated in the transformation of eight agricultural cooperatives into communes in

New lines of communication *were opened in 1956 with the completion of a railway across a mountainous landscape to link the southwest and northwest regions of China. Workers applaud one other at the site of a monument to their labour, as a train makes its first journey towards the city of Chengdu.*

Tianjin. 'There were about two hundred and seventy thousand people in two big communes,' he describes. 'Big communes could deal with big projects. With several hundred thousand people to do a job, things were completed in next to no time.' One of Zeng Guodong's duties was to organize the dining halls. 'There was one big dining hall for every hundred households, and each dining hall catered for several hundred people,' he recalls. 'In this way, we managed to assemble the working forces and have food at the same time.' It was Qin Yongchang's job to serve the food in a commune in Henan province, where they were first established. 'When the village bell rang, people would return from the fields and come to the commune's dining hall,' she remembers. 'We would cook noodles, sweet potatoes, and bread made from wheat husks.'

> *"Other workers asked to rest, but I didn't want to leave the "battlefield" and continued to work by the furnace."*
>
> LIAN TIANYUN

STEEL-MAKING COUPLE *He Jin Lua and Lian Tianyun* (LEFT), *who worked feverishly to outproduce one another in the steel-making campaign during the Great Leap Forward. As steel production targets continued to rise to meet China's growing industrial and agricultural needs, people in villages throughout the country were urged to contribute by using domestic 'backyard' furnaces similar to the idealized version depicted in propaganda pictures* (TOP). *In 1958 the Chinese claimed that steel production was more than double that of the previous year.*

All this was part of the policy called the General Line and the Three Red Flags: 'Go out, aim high, and achieve greater, faster and better results in building socialism'. One of the most extraordinary campaigns launched during the Great Leap Forward was intended to double China's steel production. Zeng Guodong helped to spread Chairman Mao's message. 'I didn't think China would be a powerful nation if it was without iron and steel. Building machines, ships and trains all needed steel,' he says. But instead of building new steelworks, Mao planned to mobilize the peasants once again. Small 'backyard' furnaces sprang up as people began to smelt iron and contribute to the target of ten million tonnes of steel a year. The demand for scrap iron was so great that peasants were persuaded to give up their cooking pots and tools to be melted down.

Shortly after He Jin Lua and Lian Tianyun got married in Henan province, they threw themselves wholeheartedly into the steel-making campaign. 'Those who were less productive would be seen as good for nothing,' He Jin Lua remembers. 'We were determined to follow the Party's instructions. We were willing to do whatever the Party asked us.' Her husband made a bag by tying up the legs of a spare pair of trousers, and filled them with all the scrap he could find to hand over to the factory. He Jin Lua cut off her pigtail, using her hair to reinforce the furnace, which was made of earth. Assigned to different work groups, the young couple competed furiously. 'If his group produced more we had to outdo them,' He Jin Lua remembers. 'I used to have sleepless nights after our tiring meetings discussing our strategy.' Steel-making took precedence over everything, even starting a family. 'How could we have time for children?' she asks. 'We didn't even visit our parents when they were sick, because we devoted everything to steel-making.'

The campaign at first appeared to achieve astonishing results: China's steel output was said to have doubled in a single year. Mao's attention again turned to accelerating agricultual output. To meet the absurd production quotas that were set, some people resorted to trickery. 'We removed all the ready-planted rice from the fields and replanted it in a show field so that we would reach our quota,' remembers Zeng Guodong. But the densely planted rice did not grow. 'Before long the rice rotted, and the peasants got angry. They said, "If you take all the rice and waste it, what will we eat in the autumn?" ' Extravagant targets also encouraged the tendency to boast. Many Party cadres and farmers falsified their achievements, exaggerating national production figures. Of the 375 million tonnes of grain said to have been produced in 1959, only 275 million tonnes were actually harvested.

Nothing was permitted to stand in the way of high yields – not even the birds. 'The word came down from above to mobilize the masses to kill the sparrows,' remembers Hu Benxiü, who helped to organize a 'kill sparrows' campaign in her village. 'Villagers old and young joined in. We were so busy that we even had to take turns to eat,' she describes. 'The trees were really high, and hard to shake, but everyone made an effort to do their best, so the sparrows could not land on them. We also used catapults to shoot them down. Some people used guns.... Those who killed the most sparrows were praised and given rewards. Those who caught smaller numbers were criticized, and encouraged to do better the following day.'

Despite the nation's huge efforts the Great Leap Forward was a failure. Fewer sparrows meant more insects, which did more harm to the crops than the sparrows had. The steel that had been enthusiastically produced in backyard furnaces at low temperatures

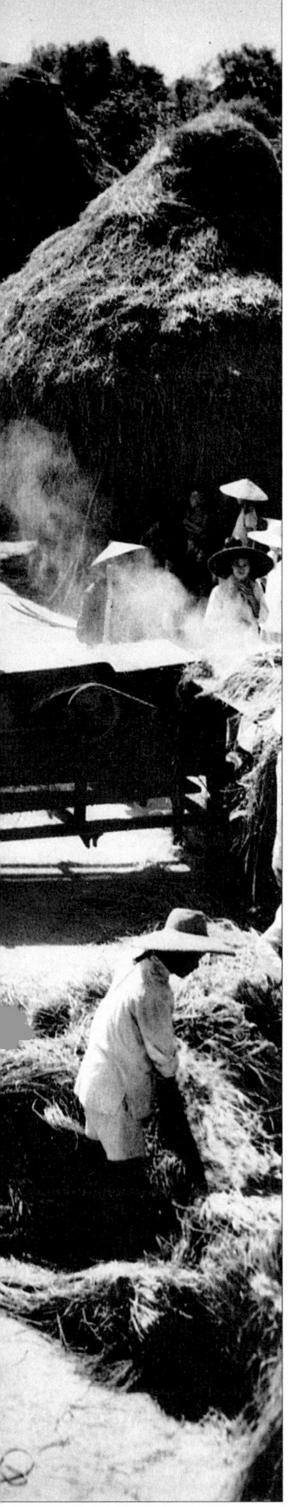

Harvesting hopes
United by their efforts to produce ever greater yields, commune workers (ABOVE) *deal with the rice crop, while young girls tend a sweet potato field on an agricultural cooperative* (LEFT)*.*

turned out to be useless, and, as Zeng Guodong came to realize, the campaign to make it had diverted millions of agricultural workers. 'As a result, wheat and sweet potatoes were left to rot in the fields,' he admits, 'The loss was very great.' To make things even worse, a series of droughts, floods and typhoons beginning in 1959 caused immense damage. The excesses of the Great Leap, combined with these natural disasters and then the withdrawal of Soviet aid after a rift in Sino-Soviet relations, were followed by what may have been the worst famine in Chinese history.

Food was in desperately short supply. To avoid starving, people ate any kind of vegetable they could find, such as cabbage roots or sweet potato vines. Others lived on fermented earth dried into biscuits. Times were hard for factory workers in the towns. 'We overcame the shortage of food by tightening our belts. We ate the stem from a green vegetable – *won*. We called it "seamless steel pipe". We first smashed the stem and then mixed it with flour,' Ma Gennan remembers. 'Chairman Mao assured us at the time that all would be well after this period of natural disasters, so we must follow Chairman Mao's instructions to get over this hurdle.'

In the countryside the effects of the famine were far more devastating. 'We simply had nothing to eat,' remembers Ren Yangchen, a worker on the Red Flag Canal project in Henan province. 'We had to eat wild vegetables or herbs. We ate elm bark and leaves from the trees. We ate almost anything in order to survive.' When Luo Shifa made his way back to Sichuan from Beijing, he found that people were dying from dropsy, severe bloating brought on by starvation that was made even worse by the consumption of wild vegetables. 'In our commune sixteen hundred people were starving,' he remembers. 'Some people fell over from weakness and were lying in the road, others were already dead. When the peasants saw me they began to cry. I cried too.' In the three years after 1959 more than twenty million people are thought to have died in the famine.

Victims of famine
In China's long history there had been many disastrous famines and mass starvation. Under the rule of the communists, people did not expect to suffer a similar fate.

The Abode of Snow

On 7 November 1950 the People's Liberation Army entered Tibet, known as the Abode of Snow. Its people differed greatly from the Chinese ethnically, in language and in religion, and did not welcome the communist 'liberators'.

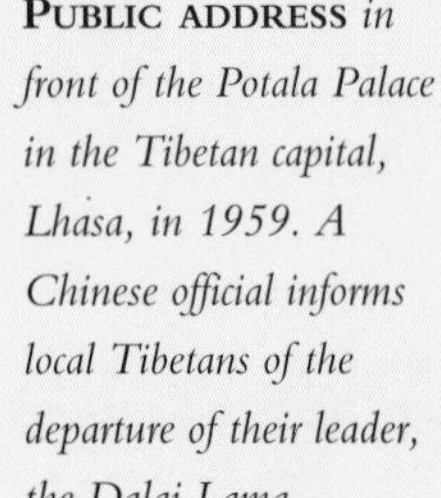

Public address *in front of the Potala Palace in the Tibetan capital, Lhasa, in 1959. A Chinese official informs local Tibetans of the departure of their leader, the Dalai Lama.*

Until the early years of the century the Tibetans, sheltered by the highest mountains in the world, had lived in peaceful isolation, though the Chinese emperors claimed that they were subjects of Beijing. People in this religious, feudal society lived under the rule of their king and spiritual leader, the Dalai Lama, working as serfs for Buddhist monasteries or for secular landlords. Trouble had begun when a British expedition crossed the Himalayas from India into Tibet in 1904. Tibet became caught up in quarrels between Britain, the Russian empire – which was expanding into Mongolia – and China. The British accepted China's suzerainty over Tibet, which Tibet refused to acknowledge; with the collapse of the Manchu dynasty, Tibet tried to assert its independence.

When China's internal conflicts ended, Tibet was again drawn into China's orbit. After the invasion in 1950 the Chinese promised to respect its status as an autonomous region, and the rule of its lamas. But instead they treated Tibet as an integral part of the People's Republic. Collectivization was enforced on its people, monks were coerced into marriage and work, and monasteries were closed down.

Chinese rule was so unwelcome that in 1959 Tibetans organized a revolt, which was brutally put down. Thousands of people were executed, arrested and deported, and about 80 000 Tibetans, including the Dalai Lama, fled to safety over the mountain passes into India. Communist rule was forcibly imposed. Buddhism was outlawed and temples destroyed. Local people were forced to carry identity cards, and large numbers of Chinese settlers arrived. When the Red Guards came in 1967, during the Cultural Revolution, they set about ravaging any remnants of Tibetan culture and tradition.

The severity of China's attempt to transform Tibet into a province of China was relaxed during the 1970s, and tourism and economic development were permitted. But when the Tibetans rebelled again in 1987 many were executed, tortured and imprisoned. China was willing neither to leave Tibet alone nor to allow its people to live as they had for centuries. A poor and isolated country, Tibet's once stable agricultural economy was sacrificed to Chinese collectivist dogma. The Tibetans remained bitterly resentful that their religion had been slighted and their culture undermined for a period of almost fifty years.

Rallying to the cause (left) *Armed with uniforms and the Little Red Book of Mao's thoughts, student Red Guards attend one of many mass rallies that took place during the 1960s. As the shock troops of perpetual revolution, they caused immense chaos and destruction, turning people's lives upside down.*

Thought reform (below) *Students sent to work in the countryside pause to study the writings of Chairman Mao.*

Rekindling the revolution

In 1962 Mao had to admit defeat. The suffering and destruction caused by the Great Leap fuelled opposition to his policies both within the Party and in central government. He issued a public 'self-criticism' acknowledging the failure of his economic policies, and a programme of recovery was launched by the more pragmatic leaders: Deng Xiaoping, the former secretary-general of the Party, and Liu Shaoqi, who had been appointed chairman of the republic in 1959 following Mao's resignation from that post. Nevertheless, Mao was still a powerful figurehead. At the age of sixty-nine he retained the chairmanship of the Party and was still supported by hardline radicals and the army.

Mao did not stay in the background for long. To regain a tight rein over the country and re-establish his power, he began a campaign that turned into the Great Cultural Revolution. In its earliest stages, it seemed to reassert an ideological and cultural revolutionary spirit. With the help of the Gang of Four – a group of hardliners that included Mao's third wife, Jiang Qing – millions of copies of a 'little red book' containing selected *Quotations from Chairman Mao* were distributed, and the *People's Daily* newspaper reiterated the message. At first, tendencies that were thought to be

"There were several hundred Red Guards with their armbands. Some had scissors in their hands and wanted to chop people's hair. They regarded me as an anti-revolutionary reactionary simply because I didn't carry Chairman Mao's Red Book with me that day."

Shao Ai Ling

Targets of abuse *Three people accused of being anti-revolutionaries are paraded on the back of a truck through the streets of Beijing. Forced to wear dunce's caps that bear their names, they are publicly denounced as a crowd of jeering Red Guards looks on.*

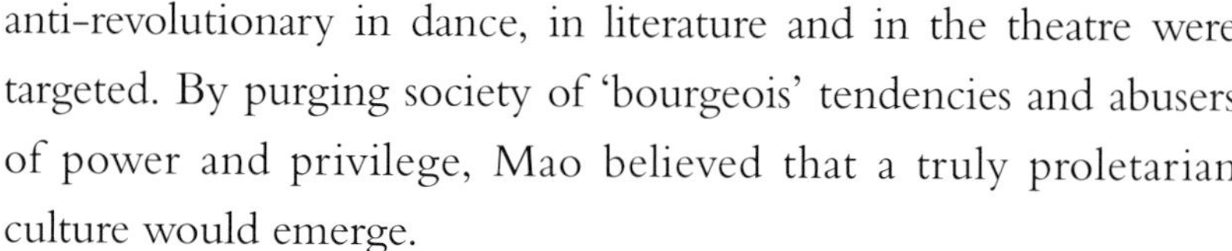

anti-revolutionary in dance, in literature and in the theatre were targeted. By purging society of 'bourgeois' tendencies and abusers of power and privilege, Mao believed that a truly proletarian culture would emerge.

In 1966 the Cultural Revolution began to speed up. Backed by the army, Mao took the opportunity to denounce and discredit his political rivals, Deng Xiaoping and Liu Shaoqi, and assume power once again. This time it was young men and women to whom Mao appealed. They attended mass rallies and flocked to Beijing in their thousands to listen to his speeches, which whipped up their enthusiasm. With Mao's support, students who had begun to call themselves 'Red Guards' took the lead. The movement grew so fast that there were soon up to twenty million Red Guards in cities across China. Zhang Pingan was one of them. 'We thought we were spearheading the revolution, responsible for clearing all obstacles to the revolutionary cause. We felt we were the vanguard of the Party and of Chairman Mao, and we were proud of our role.' Mao told them, 'The Chinese future is with you'; they responded by carrying out his revolutionary will. They were provided with free food, accommodation and transport.

What had begun as an ideological campaign soon descended into a dangerous hysteria as the increasingly militant Red Guards set out to search for and denounce 'enemies' of the revolution. 'Anyone in power became a target, whether they were right or wrong,' Zhang Pingan confesses. 'Our teachers and the principal were not really bad people, in fact they were quite progressive, but we had to find a target, otherwise we would be in trouble. So we organized ourselves and targeted them. We ordered the principal to confess, but he said he had nothing to confess. We thought he was dishonest, so we began to beat him up. We dragged him from place to place until he had a heart attack.'

Shao Ai Ling, who had become the principal of Shanghai Number Six Girls' School, was also denounced by her students. Several hundred student Red Guards came for her, some wearing armbands, some military belts. 'They chopped off my hair and beat me with sticks,' she remembers. 'They told me that revolution means rebellion, and that it is not soft-hearted. They ordered me to produce the Red Book. But that day I was wearing a white

Bible of the masses

The 'little red book', *as the* Quotations from Chairman Mao *was popularly known, was published by the Chinese army in the mid-1960s to draw mass support for Mao's ideological Cultural Revolution. Hundreds of millions of copies of the book, containing a selection of Mao's writings, were printed and distributed to the vast Chinese population, who were urged to study and recite from its passages of Maoist doctrine. There was virtually no other reading matter available at the time. The pocket-sized version of the book was produced so that people could always carry a copy with them.*

Peking Opera

THE CHANGES BROUGHT by the 1949 revolution were at first welcomed by China's actors and singers, who had lived humbly in the old society. 'Although we could earn quite a lot of money, our social status was very low, and people despised us,' remembers Tong Xiang Ling, who was a performer in Shanghai's Peking Opera. Under the communists, he says, 'We were told that we artists were the engineers of human souls. We didn't perform only to earn money, but had a serious responsibility to educate people through our art. We felt a strong sense of emancipation, not economically but ideologically.'

The Peking Opera was the finest of many provincial opera schools of this highly popular Chinese art form, which dated back to the thirteenth century. After the revolution the communists objected to many aspects of traditional opera, and began a programme of reform. Some operas were revised so as not to give offence to revolutionaries. The characteristic clashing cymbals, symbolic, stylized gestures, rich costumes and dramatic makeup were toned down in favour of a new simplicity and directness.

By the early 1960s Mao thought that social transformation in the arts was too slow in coming. 'Isn't it absurd,' he asked, 'that many communists are enthusiastic about promoting feudal and capitalistic art, but not socialist art?' Mao's wife, Jiang Qing, herself a former actress, took an active role in transforming the theatre. 'The grain we eat is grown by the peasants,' she said. 'The clothes we wear are made by the workers, and the People's Liberation Army stands guard for us. Yet we do not portray them on the stage.' Peking Opera's centuries-old plays about Chinese history and legend were replaced by new operas commemorating revolutionary feats and proletarian virtues.

During a national festival in 1964 more than seventy theatrical groups performed about 7000 shows of the 'revolutionary' operas to audiences totalling seven million people. The most famous of these was *Taking Fierce Tiger Mountain with Wise Strategy*, in which Tong Xiang Ling felt honoured to play the role of the hero. One night, Chairman Mao and Premier Zhou Enlai were among the guests of honour. 'We were told that the fate of the play would be determined that day,' he remembers. At the end of the show, as the curtain was lowered, the perfomers waited anxiously on the stage. 'My heart was beating really fast. When the announcement about Mao's approval was made, I couldn't help jumping up,' remembers Tong Xiang Ling. 'That night was the happiest moment of my life.'

Peking Opera faced its most critical test in 1966, as it fell victim to the Cultural Revolution's vengeful assault on traditional culture. During the convulsions that followed, the Red Guards were turned loose on actors and singers, no longer 'engineers of the human soul' but anti-revolutionary reactionaries. 'One morning my wife telephoned me, asking me to go to the Peking Opera troupe immediately,' Tong Xiang Ling remembers. When he got there he found huge denunciation posters that read, 'If Tong Xiang Ling doesn't surrender, he will be exterminated'. He could not understand what it was that he had done wrong. 'In the past I played emperors and feudal gentry, but now I played heroic revolutionaries. Even so, I was being targeted.' Many popular actors and singers were killed or committed suicide in a desperate last act.

TONG XIANG LING *the Peking Opera star, stands proudly next to Chairman Mao* (TOP, *left of picture in leopardskin costume*). *He was later branded an enemy of the people after being denounced as an anti-revolutionary and forced to attend gruelling denunciation meetings.*

ROLE REVERSAL *Uncharacteristically, the male parts in this Peking Opera production staged after the revolution were played by women. Chinese women traditionally did not appear on the operatic stage, so all the female roles had to be played by men.*

shirt with no pockets, so I hadn't got the Red Book with me. They said, "If you are not carrying the Red Book, that means you are not loyal to Chairman Mao.... You deserve to be overthrown!" It was December in Shanghai and very cold. They ordered me to stand outside the playground from morning to night. But then they thought the punishment was not severe enough, so they got a big blackboard and pressed it down on me. One of them stood on it on the right side and one on the left, like a seesaw, and I was squashed in the middle.' Shao Ai Ling survived the torture, but was left with permanent injuries to her face.

Many others did not survive. Thousands of people were killed or committed suicide; thousands more were relentlessly persecuted by the fanatical Red Guards. Luo Shifa had supported the Cultural Revolution, but he too was confronted. 'I knew I hadn't done anything wrong. I had always followed the mass line,' he says. 'I answered to whatever name they called me: landlord, anti-revolutionary, capitalist-roader....I knew it was just a routine I had to endure. At the denunciation meeting, they slapped my face and forced me to kneel down. Kneeling on hot charcoal and broken glass was almost a daily routine, so I put a soft pad inside my trousers and that made it easier when I was forced to my knees.' Luo Shifa was paraded through the streets with a denunciation placard hanging from his neck. Even the Party cadre, Zeng Guodong, was attacked. The Red Guards twisted his hands behind his back and forced him to bend over, sometimes for as long as three hours, while they denounced him.

As former capitalists, Jin Jingzhi and her husband were also sought out. Their home was searched for ten days. 'I was confined to one room and my husband to another. They didn't allow us any contact. They bombarded us with questions day in, day out,' she recalls. 'If they suspected that something was hidden in the ceiling, they would rip open the ceiling. All the trees in my garden were uprooted, but they found nothing and finally left.'

The Cultural Revolution affected almost everyone. The way people cut their hair or the clothes that they wore could easily give them away as 'bourgeois reactionaries'. A Red Guard slogan said that China had to be rid of the 'four olds' – old habits, ideas, customs and culture – so ancient temples, museum artefacts

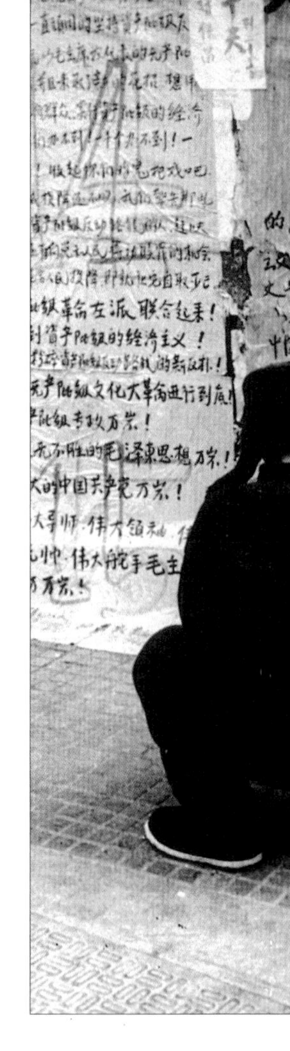

Critical times (right) Dazibao *or handwritten 'big character' posters denouncing enemies of the revolution were a familiar sight on public walls in the late 1960s. The one in the centre accuses Mao's rival, Liu Shaoqi. Shao Ai Ling also fell victim to them. 'For a middle school principal, big character posters were mainly confined to the campus,' she says, 'but in my case they were put up in the People's Square, the Great Shanghai Cinema and the Great World Amusement Centre.'*

The Gang of Four (below), *largely responsible for the upheavals of the Cultural Revolution, are the subject of a 1976 poster illustrating their downfall.*

and countless other examples of China's heritage, as well as signs of foreign influence, were destroyed. Books printed before 1949 were burned, scientists and scholars attacked. People argued in the factory and at factory gates. Husbands argued with wives, parents with their children. Everywhere people were debating, discussing, quarrelling, putting their thoughts into slogans on 'big character' posters for everyone to see. The country ground to a halt. Farmers stopped planting, workers stopped producing. Hospitals could not function without the doctors who had been discredited and sent away, schools could not teach without teachers.

By 1967 China had slipped into something like anarchy. The British embassy was burned down, and foreign diplomats were attacked. In some places Red Guards split into factions and fought each other with machine guns and artillery. Mao responded by calling in the army to restore order, and despatched millions of young people to the countryside to learn from the peasants.

From 1969 the zeal and excesses of the Cultural Revolution dwindled, but Mao still held on to power into the 1970s. He had purged both the Party and the government of his political rivals, and now ruled with the help of his lieutenant Zhou Enlai and the Gang of Four. In 1976, the Chinese year of the dragon – which was traditionally a time of great change – both Zhou Enlai and Mao Zedong died. 'I didn't know what would happen to China,' remembers Zeng Guodong. 'All those people who shared Mao's vision were gone. Who would lead the Communist Party now? Nobody had the power and the authority to unify China as Mao did. I felt at a loss.'

END OF AN ERA (BELOW) *Thousands of people publicly mourn the death of Mao Zedong at the Great Hall of the People in Beijing in 1976.*

The second liberation

After Mao's Zedong's death, China gradually began to move away from the undeviating revolutionary path he had mapped out. The Gang of Four were arrested and publicly tried, and in 1978 Deng Xiaoping became president amid calls for greater reform. The communes were disbanded, land was redistributed, and farmers were permitted to sell their surplus produce for personal profit. Foreign investment and even some aspects of Western capitalism, such as private ownership, were permitted. More consumer goods appeared in the shops, and attempts were made to modernize industry using Western expertise. With the free market, there were wider disparities in wealth between successful entrepreneurs and their workers in the rapidly growing special economic zones. Zeng Guodong saw these changes. 'Deng Xiaoping said, "Reform is China's second revolution". I was deeply impressed by his comment. It is indeed the second revolution, or second liberation.'

"In the past we had been so cut off, the students knew nothing of the outside world. After the endorsement of the open-door policy, my former students have become liberal.... They can judge, compare and decide what is right. They have enriched their experiences."

SHAO AI LING

SCENE OF VIOLENCE (ABOVE) *A wounded young demonstrator is hemmed in by armed soldiers in Tiananmen Square in 1989, as student demonstrations for greater freedom were suppressed by the military.*

A TASTE OF THE WEST (OPPOSITE) *An American fast food restaurant in the southern town of Shenzhen in 1991 symbolizes China's new economic liberalization.*

Some things did not change. People's hopes that economic liberalism would bring political freedom were dashed by the regime's relentless repression of any dissent. As students demonstrated for democracy and political reform in 1986, rioting spread across the country. In 1989 the government gave orders for tanks from the People's Liberation Army to disperse the crowds of young demonstrators in Tiananmen Square, killing and wounding thousands of people. After forty years the revolution had turned on its own children.

The Chinese now seemed to turn away from their great revolutionary adventure, emerging from years of sacrifice to focus on increasing prosperity. With its rapidly growing economy, China began to occupy a new place on the world arena. Huo Buo, the photographer who had captured the coming of the revolution in 1949, reflected, 'For the last forty-five years our country has continuously made progress. But there are ups and downs, many trials and hardships. It is like the growing up of a human being. There is a Chinese saying that "failure is the mother of success".'

麦當勞
McDonald's

1 9 5 0 – 1 9 7 3

8

New Release

Changing roles for young people

On 14 January 1967 thousands of young people filled Golden Gate Park in San Francisco for an event that for many epitomized the mood of their generation: it was called the 'Human Be-in'. Ron Thelin helped to organize the peaceful gathering. 'We didn't know how many people would show up,' he recalls, 'and when ten thousand people, or maybe more, came out of the woodwork it was just breathtaking, it was earthshaking – this many people were having this experience. There was a sense that something was in the air, this was a new time, a new age.'

The generation of young people who made San Francisco their haven that year felt that the Human Be-In was the high point of what they described as a shared sense of unspoiled liberation. Martine Algier, who was living in San Francisco, took part in the public extravaganza of music and dance. The attitudes and ways of these young people were unlike anything anyone had seen before. 'We felt there was an awakening,' Martine Algier recalls. 'We even used the word among ourselves – mutants. We felt that there was a whole wave of people, specifically young people, who were coming into this awareness. And many of them were isolated in small towns across the country and didn't know there were others like them. We felt we needed to wave and say, "Hey, we're here, you're not alone. Don't be afraid, come on out and *be*, be who you really are".'

Elsewhere in the industrialized world, too – in Australia, Canada, Europe and Japan – young people gained new freedoms in the 1950s and 1960s. They did not all share the 'new age' ideas seen in Golden Gate Park, but almost all did use their new freedom and opportunities to question the authority of their parents, the attitudes and values of society and of the politicians who held power. In their efforts to find new and better ways of living, young people succeeded in challenging long-held conventions and traditional ways of thinking, and came to play a far greater part in society than the young had ever done before.

Shaking off *old restrictions, people gather in the park for a festival of fun and dance.*

Breaking the mould

The world in which the immediate postwar generation grew up was one in which most children were taught to treat their parents and others in authority with unquestioning deference, and to imitate their elders' tastes and values when they themselves reached adulthood. But the dramatic changes of the 1960s had their roots in changes already taking place during the conservative 1950s.

More babies were born in the first ten years after the Second World War in the United States than in the fifty years before it. There were so many 'baby boomers' that school playgrounds and classrooms soon became overcrowded. 'We were the first class to go into a new building because of the growth,' says Bob Bossar, who went to school in Pittsburgh, Pennsylvania. 'I remember the schools, the Salk polio vaccine, how we had to wait in line to get our shots, schools being very crowded.'

In Europe economic recovery from the war was slower, but there too young people were growing up in a very different way from their parents' generation. Prompted by reforms that made education more accessible, young people stayed on longer at school. New schools were built and the number of pupils in them rose, though in the late 1950s only 4 per cent of young people in Britain went to university, 7 per cent in France, 8 per cent in the Netherlands and 11 per cent in Belgium, and as many as 20 per cent in the United States. Beyond Europe – in Australia, Canada, Japan – the same trend could be seen.

In the United States more young people had money to spare than in any previous generation, and they spent it on new leisure opportunities. There were new skating rinks and bowling alleys. There were magazines catering specially for young people. 'The cars were made for us,' says Bob Bossar. 'We had new highways, we had new clothes and music, new schools – just a lot of bright things were going on. Probably a marketer's dream, the baby boomers.' By the end of the decade some two-thirds of American nineteen-year-old males and half of all females were licensed to drive.

Despite the prosperity, as the Cold War between the Soviet Union and the United States intensified it was an anxious time. Living with the fear of a nuclear attack

Musical box

JUKEBOXES became popular during the late 1940s and 1950s, first in the United States – where they had been mass produced since the mid-1930s – and then among young people in Europe as well. Installed in cafés and clubs, they offered a selection of records chosen by the companies that owned them; the selection was regularly updated as new records were released and became chart hits. These coin-operated gramophones were one of the new ways in which the growing incomes of teenagers could be tapped. Wurlitzer jukeboxes, made in the United States, were among the most successful designs.

TIME FOR LEISURE *at the Cock' n' Bull in New York's Greenwich Village, one of the centres of attraction for the young generation of 'beats' or 'beatniks' during the 1950s. Breaking with the traditional attitudes and the conventional dress worn by many young people, they were labelled bohemians.*

raised questions among the young. 'It was scary,' remembers Martine Algier, who lived in a small town in Michigan before moving to the suburbs with her family. 'It was really crazy. It looked like the adults were going nuts – I mean here were these adults who were supposed to be running the world and taking care of us, and yet they'd obviously done something very crazy to put us all in a situation like this.' At school teenagers hid under their desks during air raid drills, and at home they watched their parents store food and dig bomb shelters in their backyards. 'After the Second World War our parents wanted, needed security,' says Ron Thelin, who lived in a small town in California, was an Eagle Scout and attended Sunday School. 'Things were programmed, your future was programmed out....It was like being in a trance.'

For the vast majority of young people everywhere, music helped to break through that trance. Most parents did not approve of the loud, provocative sounds of rock and roll music, which they associated with rebelliousness. Their children felt very differently. While he was still at school in 1955 Ron Thelin watched a film about juvenile delinquency, *Blackboard Jungle*, with its soundtrack featuring music by Bill Haley and the Comets. 'It was a revelation for me. I had never heard the beat before,' he recalls. 'It was totally unlike anything that I'd experienced in my life.'

Rock and roll music had a similar effect on teenagers everywhere who were beginning to question the values their parents tried to impose. 'It seemed like there were ways you were supposed to be and clothes you were supposed to wear, and people who were so concerned with status,' says Martine Algier. 'If you danced there was a way you were supposed to dance....I wanted to dance freely.' When *Blackboard Jungle* was shown in Britain the following year there were riots at some cinemas, and it was banned in certain towns.

Rusty Sachs grew up in a farming community in Norwich, Vermont. Then a rock and roll fan, he used to collect Elvis Presley records. 'The music and the performance were an example to us of how we should move, and how we should let the music dominate us, and be channelled by something other

BOY SCOUTS *in the 1950s were taught the same values – obedience and team spirit – as they had been since the movement was founded early in the century.*

LATEST DANCE MOVES *are demonstrated by a young American couple as West German students attending a dance at the Free University of Berlin in 1953 look on.*

than the standard behaviour patterns that were around us,' he remembers. 'This was something new, this was very out of the ordinary. This was breaking the mould. And it was fun.'

As more and more young people listened to wilder, angrier sounds in music and watched the new films, they began to dance differently and to look different; many of them also felt different. There were some early signs of rebellion as young people began to challenge established patterns of behaviour. In Britain the Teddy Boys broke with postwar conventions of dress, wearing eccentric outfits of narrow trousers and long, tailored jackets. There were similar groups elsewhere: the *Blousons Noirs* in France, the *Halbstarken* in Germany, the *Taiyo-zoku* in Japan, the *Skinnnuttar* in Sweden and the *Stilyagi* in the Soviet Union. In the mid-1960s people in the United States would be shocked by the appearance and unruly behaviour of motorcycle gangs clad in leather, who called themselves Hell's Angels. By 1960 over half the people in the United States were under the age of eighteen, and increasing numbers of them were finding fault with the world around them.

"It was a time of prosperity. We hadn't known poverty....It was a particularly sheltered, very middle-class community. There wasn't a lot of questioning that went on."

PARKER HALL

CULTS OF YOUTH *Many of Britain's Teddy Boys in the early 1950s came from poor backgrounds and were out of school or out of work. Some of them caused trouble; most just enjoyed wearing distinctive clothes as a way of shaping a new and different identity for themselves. David Sackett's brother was one: 'He used to dress up, he had the ties and the crepe soles....He was a little bit out of the ordinary.'*

'TEEN PICS' *described films that were specifically aimed at a young audience. When the leather-jacketed Marlon Brando (far right) starred in* The Wild One, *filmed in 1953, he became an idol of youthful rebellion for teenagers, many of whom adopted a new attitude as well as a new look.*

The generation gap

As economic prosperity came to people in Western Europe at the end of the 1950s, so did the social freedoms and choices that those living in the United States enjoyed. In France, Italy, West Germany and elsewhere there had also been a surge in the number of babies born after the war, and teenagers were growing up in a time of great change. With greater prosperity, they were under less pressure from their families to leave school as soon as they could and start contributing to the family income, though there was plenty of work for those who wanted it.

When he was fifteen years old David Sackett, who lived in London, joined a fashion-conscious group calling themselves Mods. One of them owned a scooter. 'Now we had a bit of mobility,' he says, 'we could go where we wanted.' Every Friday night they watched *Ready Steady Go* on television. 'It was all about the Mod scene, the latest dance craze, the latest footwear, the latest hairstyle,' he says. 'That was a must – the new music, the new sounds, the new groups and the fashion.'

In 1960 compulsory military service in Britain came to an end. Another of the ways in which the values and discipline of the older generation had been instilled was now removed. 'They weren't going to take half a million of us off to France again and ask us to shoot one another,' says Rogan Taylor. 'There was a feeling that we'd had a bloody lousy time and it's about time we had a good time.' In his seaport town, Liverpool, sailors brought back music from the United States, and Liverpool was itself a thriving place to hear the hundreds of bands that performed at popular clubs and dance halls.

One of the bands featured at The Cavern club had changed its name from The Quarrymen to The Beatles. They were sought after by club owners. In 1963 they became hugely successful. 'The music was different from what we were used to,' remembers David Sackett. 'We were listening to something new, that type of music grew on you. We could hardly wait for the next single or album to come out.' Teenagers began to dress like The Beatles, and even copied their 'mop-top' hairstyles. 'Once their hair got long,' recalls David Sackett, 'everybody had long hair, that's what you did.'

THE CAVERN *in Liverpool* (ABOVE) *was a favourite music venue for Rogan Taylor* (RIGHT). *The club was a low-roofed, arched building converted from a warehouse. The noise and the heat under the low ceilings were unbelievable. 'Everything a youngster could want was in there,' he remembers. 'You felt you were at the very heart of it.'*

YOUNG MODERNS – *Mods – prepare for action near the Brighton seafront, scene of a number of sometimes violent confrontations between the scooter-riding Mods and their arch-rivals, the motorcycling Rockers, in 1964.*

Young consumers

For people in the West, the growing affluence of the 1950s bred a new consumer culture, first in the United States and then in Western Europe. For the first time, young people began to be targeted by advertisers and courted by manufacturers, who identified them as a new, potentially profitable consumer group with their own particular tastes, views and preferences.

It was easy for most young people at this time to find work, and they could earn more money than ever before. Businesses were quick to capitalize on their new spending power. Publishers and broadcasters introduced 'pop' columns, music magazines and chart shows, and clothing manufacturers and distributors of consumer goods began to cater for younger shoppers. Some retailers and department stores even despatched their staff on crash courses about the new culture of youth.

Shops were quick to reflect new trends among the young. There was an abundant choice of goods – the latest fashions, the most popular records, soft drinks and cosmetics.

In 1957 some 150 million pairs of blue jeans were sold in the United States, where teenagers were each spending about $400 a year – about $22 billion in total. They bought badges, cars, comic books and clothes as well as guitars, radios, music posters and tickets to attend pop concerts.

In Britain, the Netherlands, Sweden and West Germany teenagers spent between seven and ten times more than those in less prosperous European countries, such as Italy and Spain. By the late 1950s teenagers in Britain were spending about £830 million a year. 'I very much wanted some money to spend on myself,' remembers Penny Hayes from Britain, who left school at fifteen to work in a hairdressing salon. 'I would say ninety-nine per cent went on clothes. We didn't have a very expensive social life, it was down the local coffee bar. If I bought a cup of coffee or Coke it was rare. You just went to meet friends, so it was all clothes....You all looked the same, and that was very important.'

From the late 1950s fashion stores in London's King's Road and Carnaby Street were making large profits by catering for this new fashion-conscious market. Leading boutiques such as Bazaar, Biba and Bus Stop mirrored the characteristic boldness of style that set young people apart from the older generations. There were daring new fashions, such as the ultra-short 'mini skirt', which appeared in Mary Quant boutiques in 1965; it was followed by ultra-long 'maxi skirts'.

Music was by far the biggest seller and teenage consumers, spending hundreds of millions a year on records, accounted for as much as 80 per cent of sales. The film, music and television industries all grew spectacularly, largely as a result of their skill in exploiting the youth market.

In their search for an alternative way of life, the 'hippies' of the 1960s openly rejected these consumer values. Yet despite their efforts to avoid materialism, the culture of consumption prevailed: it was not long before shops were selling the fashions, beads, handicrafts and macrobiotic foods so central to their 'alternative' lifestyles. The *Whole Earth Catalogue*, which set out to teach its readers how to adopt a self-sufficient way of life, sold millions of copies while making a fortune for its editor.

Record sales *of two and a half million were reached in just three months after the release of the* Sergeant Pepper *album by The Beatles in 1967.*

The Beatles had much the same impact elsewhere. In the United States one and a half million people rushed to buy their single in the first weeks after its release in 1964. When the group appeared on the *Ed Sullivan Show* television ratings shot up. 'Everybody was glued to their television set,' says Bob Bossar. On their second tour of the United States, The Beatles performed some thirty-two concerts in thirty-four days across twenty-four American cities, and they caused pandemonium wherever they went, inspiring a whole generation to break with convention and adopt a new look that was unlike anything their parents had.

By the mid-1960s, as the baby boomers everywhere were coming of age, millions of them began to enrol at universities and colleges. With free or virtually free education in many parts of the world, student numbers soared. The number of students in France had doubled since 1945; in West Germany, Italy, the Netherlands and Sweden it was also proportionately larger than before. In the United States there were five million students in 1964, an increase of two million since 1950; they were a sizeable interest group in the country, outnumbering farmers, for example. 'This was a time when everyone went free to the community colleges, to the University of California,' remembers Parker Hall, who grew up in San Luis Obispo, a small town in California, one of the first states to implement new laws offering free tuition. 'Everyone could go.'

In Britain there were a million more people between the ages of fifteen and nineteen than there had been in 1951, and more of them went on to higher education. 'The local authority would pay a grant to allow you to go to university,' Rogan Taylor recalls. 'So bright working-class lads were getting into university and coming out three years later with a degree, and a profession.' The number of students rose by more than one and a half million, and twenty-two universities were built to cater for the explosion.

TEENAGE IDOLS
The Beatles' success in Britain soared after they appeared at the London Palladium (ABOVE RIGHT) *in October 1963. Before long they became the focus of unprecedented teenage adoration. Bitten by 'Beatlemania', teenagers bought glasses and mugs, badges, posters and T-shirts bearing the group's image* (RIGHT). *The police struggled to control the screaming fans* (BELOW).

Angry headlines
In September 1964 the Berkeley campus of the University of California was one of the first to show signs of mounting student unrest. Before Vivian Rothstein enrolled there, she worked to support herself through her studies. For a generation whose parents had never been to university, becoming a student was exciting. 'I wanted to get away from home, I really wanted to throw myself into an environment like that,' she remembers. 'I don't know if I thought of myself as a rebel, I wanted to enter the world.'

Rebels with a cause

There were simply not enough universities to cope with the huge number of students, and many campuses became overcrowded. One of the most congested in France was the Sorbonne, the University of Paris. During the early 1960s a hundred thousand students crammed into its lecture theatres each day, and conditions and standards within them inevitably suffered. Many people found university a liberating experience, but it could also be an alienating one; it was there that many young people felt a growing difference between their own values and those of the rest of society.

In the United States, Vivian Rothstein won a scholarship to study at Berkeley – one of the eight campuses of the University of California, across the bay from San Francisco. Its sheer size added to its impersonality. Vivian Rothstein shared her psychology class with a thousand other students. 'Of all of us who went to Berkeley, many of us were first-generation kids who got to go to college, and we were a big deal in our families, and we'd all got really good grades in high school,' she remembers. 'There were twenty, thirty thousand kids in the school and nobody knew us. Nobody talked to us. We had no counsellor....I felt that I was part of this huge, massive community in which I was unimportant. I started looking for a place to belong.'

It was the same for students on other campuses, prompting the government to increase expenditure on education. Mounting tensions gave rise to new student groups and organizations. The Students for a Democratic Society (SDS) had been set up at the University of Michigan in 1960, and was fast becoming one of the largest student groups in the country. 'We are of this generation, bred in at least modest comfort, housed now in universities, looking uncomfortably to the world we inherit,' read its manifesto. In the United States a 1964 poll estimated that 5 per cent of those between the ages of twenty-one and twenty-five had joined a political group of some kind.

The civil rights movement was what triggered Vivian Rothstein's involvement. 'The whole civil rights effort and the people I met in the civil rights movement became the core of my life at Berkeley. It was harder and harder to stay connected to my studies,' she remembers. 'I had never belonged to anything like that in my whole life....The sense of urgency and community and common mission was very exciting.' At first she took part in local demonstrations outside shops and restaurants that refused to employ black people, and on one occasion she was arrested. In the mid-1960s Berkeley became the site of the first serious student protests for the civil rights movement, which then spread to other colleges around the country.

In many parts of the world, as students grew more aware of global events and issues or watched more television news reports, an increasing number of them began to take a new interest in political and social problems. New courses in the humanities became popular among students; in France the number of social sciences students multiplied by four during the 1960s. Although she was not a student herself, Penny Hayes was working at the University of London. 'It had quite an effect on me,' she recalls. 'It completely opened my eyes to another world. It had been a very closed society in which I had grown up. We didn't have much interest in what was going on outside our own small group. But

"Individually we felt that something was being born, was coming to the boil, and that was very strong."

ROMAIN GOUPIL

Alternative reading

THE 'UNDERGROUND' PRESS *that thrived in Europe and the United States from 1966 became a channel for the younger generation to produce its own alternatives to the more conventional, mainstream magazines that were on sale. Popular magazines such as* Oz, *which was produced in Britain, featured humorous or satirical articles by young writers. There were also underground groups, films and festivals.*

the university really made quite a change.' Penny Hayes soon decided to join the Campaign for Nuclear Disarmament (CND). She joined in protests against the presence of American nuclear weapons in Britain. 'It was a terrific feeling of being a group of people together,' she says. She was also arrested, for her part in a demonstration outside the American embassy in London. As the police ordered the crowds to disperse, Penny Hayes ran right up to the embassy entrance. 'What I thought I was going to do when I got there I don't know,' she says, 'but it was the fact that I had that chance. I ran up the steps and screamed at the top of my voice, "Yanks go home!"'

In France the government's attempt to defeat the Algerian nationalists, which only ended in 1962, had aroused considerable opposition among young people. 'Everyone you met was liable to be called up if they were young,' says Romain Goupil, who lived in Paris and was still at school when he began to take part in peace marches. 'So there would be discussions about torture, about censorship. I remember some extremely violent demonstrations.' As well as joining in the opposition to the government, he and his friends increasingly challenged other authorities ruling their lives. When they grew their hair long, 'We were stopped at the school entrance by an official or a prefect, who said, "If you have your hair like that you can't come to school". From that one little detail,' he remembers, 'we started to question the discipline and the whole organization.' In retaliation they stood outside the school gates and distributed pamphlets that read, 'We aren't sheep, and we won't be shorn!'

The international issue preoccupying most young people was the war being fought by

Voicing opposition *to their government, a group of French students leads a street protest. More young people in France began to take an active interest in national and foreign policies; even school pupils took part.*

Parading for peace (right) *News of the full horror of the Vietnam war reached young people all over the world. Despite its remoteness, it had a direct impact on them. In October 1968 thousands of people turned out for this London peace march.*

the United States in Vietnam from 1965. By the end of that year the military call-up in the United States had doubled, and already 120 000 had been dispatched to fight in the war. Their average age was nineteen. 'We were really involved in a life and death movement,' feels Jeff Jones, who went to Antioch College in Ohio in the autumn of 1965. 'If you were drafted your chances of going to Vietnam and getting killed were very high.' Young men who had gained admission to university on leaving school were able to claim deferment from the draft, and because of this the number of students increased. So did the number of anti-war protests. Some people burnt their draft notices in defiance. 'Everyone you knew was affected by the Vietnam war,' says Parker Hall. 'Every male had some story to tell about the draft. If you were a female you had either a husband, a lover, or a brother – everyone was touched by it. It consumed our generation.'

Many students were arrested as demonstrations spilled over into open confrontations on city streets. In 1966 Parker Hall joined in an anti-Vietnam protest on the campus at Berkeley. 'It was just overwhelmingly powerful to have, in one place, 30 000 people who were opposed to the Vietnam war,' he remembers, 'and up on the stages, the rock and roll bands and great speakers, charismatic people, making a lot of sense.'

News of peace movements in the United States began to reach students in other countries. 'Suddenly I became radical,' says Romain Goupil. He knew what was happening at Berkeley: 'We had a sign that we were working towards the same end, or at least we had a common enemy. This applied to what was taking place in the United States, but also in West Germany, in Italy, in Japan.' Romain Goupil's parents tried to reason with him. 'The more they tried to be reasonable the more I revolted, and this wasn't just true for me, but for my whole generation. We knew that in other countries at the same time people were discussing the same things...that helped us realize we were not alone, and that we were probably right, because there were many other youth groups.'

Elsewhere students shared the same pressing opposition to the war. Some were drawn to more radical groups or left-wing politics, hailing revolutionary figures as heroes. It seemed as though the whole generation was rising against the establishment.

> *“There was a generational optimism....If The Beatles could become the most famous rock and roll band in the world – well, hell, I could go to Nepal if I wanted to, surely?”*
>
> ROGAN TAYLOR

CHANGING APPEARANCES *The hippie culture and lifestyle that produced unconventional ‘psychedelic’ posters* (ABOVE), *exotic new fashions and long hairstyles for both men and women, lured Martine Algier to San Francisco* (RIGHT). *Things had changed a great deal since the day she was ordered to leave a school dance because she had moved her pelvis too much.*

TAKING IT EASY *in Amsterdam* (OPPOSITE), *which acquired a reputation in the 1960s as a European centre for young people looking for tolerance and alternative lifestyles. The availability of cannabis, a popular drug at the time, added to the city's attractions.*

The summer of love

Not all the 1960s generation concentrated on seeking radical political change. Many simply wanted to take advantage of their new social freedoms by having fun or enjoying the opportunity to study. Others who felt disillusioned with society looked for alternatives of their own making. For some, revolutionary politics and a revolution in lifestyle went hand in hand. When Bob Bossar first went to Kent State University it struck him as a college filled with ‘baby boomers’. ‘In the mid-1960s,’ he remembers, ‘people who were dressed a little differently were a little strange....But by 1967 and 1968 it became the norm.’

Changing trends and fashions among the young reflected the ever-widening gap between the generations. In the United States, perhaps more than anywhere else, young people had begun to look more and more distinctive. Their hair was long and untidy. They began to dress flamboyantly in brightly patterned, colourful clothes; some young women wore body stockings and beaded necklaces, and painted their faces and bodies.

‘Hippies’, as they called themselves, talked about love and peace and freedom. Martine Algier was instantly attracted by their lifestyle. She had read and enjoyed the works of the Beat poets and writers of the 1950s, who were in some ways the precursors of this new youth culture. On her way from Michigan to visit her parents she had hitched a lift in a car. Her journey took her to Haight-Ashbury, the district of San Francisco that became the centre of the hippie culture. ‘There was music and dancing and people being free and being wild,’ recalls Martine Algier. ‘I think there was a consciousness that there was a movement happening. There was definitely a sense of being a part of a big wave of something that was coming up.’ When her parents later visited her there, at first they were shocked by what they saw as they drove down Haight Street. ‘I was just so ebullient and so excited and so thrilled with the whole thing,’ says Martine Algier. ‘I remember my mother bursting into tears as somebody wafted across the street in a cape with long, plumed feathers.’

DE BIJENKO
HOTEL
WOLTERING

A culture of drugs

One way in which young people demonstrated their defiance and their desire for new experiences in the 1960s was to take drugs. Although they were illegal, drugs were becoming much easier to obtain.

Several drugs were available. Amphetamines or 'speed', a drug that affected the central nervous system, could be bought at night clubs as 'black bombers', 'French blues' or 'purple hearts'. Hallucinogenic drugs such as mescalin, peyote (derived from 'magic mushrooms') and cannabis (also called dope, grass, marijuana, pot, tea and weed, or hash – hashish – in resin form) could be smoked at 'pot parties', brewed as tea, or baked into cakes.

Cannabis was the most popular drug among students. The hippies' favourite drug was LSD (lysergic acid diethylamide), which induced 'psychedelic' experiences in the people who took it – intense and vivid hallucinations.

LSD was a legal pharmaceutical drug. Discovered in Switzerland in 1938, it was introduced into the United States in 1949 to treat psychiatric patients. In 1960 a psychologist at Harvard University, Dr Timothy Leary, began to manufacture it in large quantities and distribute it to young people at parties, anti-war rallies and on college campuses, urging them to 'tune in, turn on, drop out!' By the mid-1960s LSD was being widely used for recreational purposes.

In California another LSD enthusiast, the novelist Ken Kesey, set out in 1964 with a group of 'Merry Pranksters' in a multi-coloured, dazzling bus to popularize 'acid'. For four dollars they dispensed the 'acid test', an extravaganza of drugs, lights and music to an estimated 10 000 people. 'I was one of those people that LSD had a huge impact on,' remembers Ron Thelin, who was living in San Francisco at the time. 'It was a great experience for me, it was an eye opener, a catalyst to a new awareness....It was an awakening.'

Together the psychedelic, mind-altering drugs became associated with colourful, swirling patterns of psychedelic styles in fashion, fabrics and mixed media entertainment. There was psychedelic art, literature, poetry and poster art. 'Acid-rock' bands such as the Grateful Dead produced chemically inspired lyrics, and a number of musicians died as a result of excessive drug use.

By the late 1960s many countries responded to the increased use of drugs by reinforcing legal restrictions against them. In 1968 a committee set up in Britain to campaign for the legalization of cannabis estimated that up to a million people were using it. In most countries LSD was not an approved drug and there were tight restrictions on experiments with it. It was declared illegal in the United States in October 1966, but by 1968 as many as a million people were thought to have taken it.

Drugs for sale *at the 1970 Powder Ridge Music Festival in Connecticut. For just a dollar anyone could experience the effects of LSD or 'acid', recently made illegal.*

FESTIVAL FANS (LEFT) *Despite torrential rain, the Woodstock music festival drew more than 400 000 people to a muddy farm in upstate New York in August 1969 for an event billed as 'Three days of peace and music'. Similarly vast crowds were drawn to pop festivals held at the Isle of Wight in Britain, at Rotterdam in the Netherlands and to hundreds of rock concerts.*

'It seemed like anything was possible,' reflects Ron Thelin, who had dropped out of college in San Francisco. 'Every kind of character in time seemed to appear on the street, because you could dress however you wanted.' The hippies rejected the social and moral values of their parents and teachers. They were anti-establishment, anti-materialism, anti-war. They were more open in their relationships. They took drugs and gathered at festivals and open-air concerts to listen to songs of protest, folk music, rock or the harsher, drug-induced lyrics of 'acid rock'.

ITALIAN HIPPIES *in Milan staging a hunger strike for seventy-two hours in a cellar in 1967 over restrictions on the distribution of their newsletter, the* Mondo Beat *(Beat World), enforced by the Italian authorities. Youngsters such as these were known as* capelloni *– the 'long-haired ones'.*

Ron Thelin opened a shop in Haight-Ashbury, in which he sold books, crafts, drugs and records. The Psychedelic Shop even had a room for meditation and art shows. 'We put "free" in front of everything,' he remembers. 'We were exploring what freedom was, what a free society was.' There were free stores, free meals in

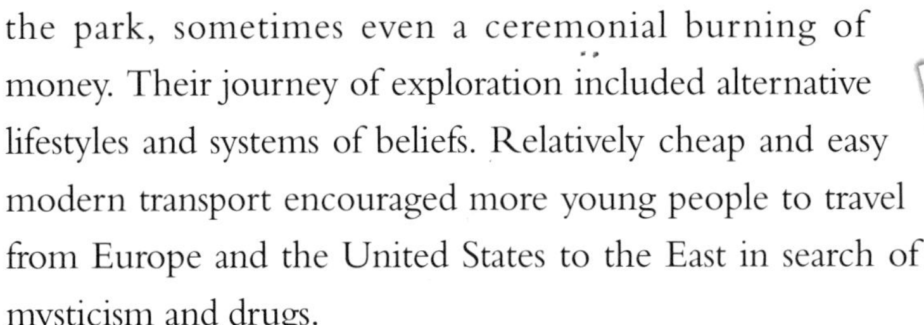

the park, sometimes even a ceremonial burning of money. Their journey of exploration included alternative lifestyles and systems of beliefs. Relatively cheap and easy modern transport encouraged more young people to travel from Europe and the United States to the East in search of mysticism and drugs.

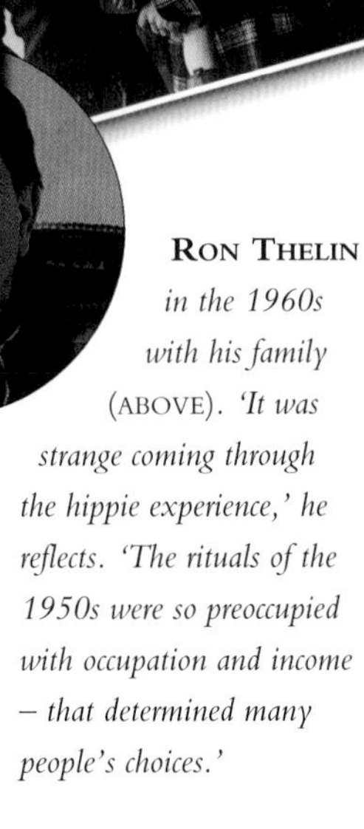

RON THELIN *in the 1960s with his family* (ABOVE). *'It was strange coming through the hippie experience,' he reflects. 'The rituals of the 1950s were so preoccupied with occupation and income – that determined many people's choices.'*

The East attracted Rogan Taylor in Liverpool, who remembers that 'Eastern traditions arrived in the West like a monsoon. Suddenly there was a massive flood of them...you could take your pick from a dozen gods and nobody would turn a hair.' He and a friend decided to set out on the long journey to India. 'The only way a working-class lad travelled before the late 1950s and 1960s was as a soldier or as a sailor,' he says. 'I thought freedom had arrived, coupled with this new kind of confidence, this new optimism – really there wasn't anywhere we couldn't go, there wasn't anything we couldn't do.'

'DEATH OF THE HIPPIE' *Disenchanted with the materialism and false values he felt had become associated with the hippie movement, on 6 October 1967 Ron Thelin closed his Psychedelic Shop and staged a symbolic funeral procession in San Francisco: 'We carried a coffin down Haight Street, filled with beads and lace shirts...and burnt it in a pyre.'*

By the summer of 1967 young people in their thousands were pouring into San Francisco to take part in what was called the Summer of Love. Many more conservative Americans were astonished by reports of the Human Be-In that they read in the national press. As it turned out, the earthly paradise had not arrived. With teenagers from the suburbs of an entire continent bearing down on them in pursuit of happiness, with the mainstream culture taking over their lovebeads and psychedelic clothes, and with the police closing in on their drugs, many hippies began to think their time was up. There were incidences of violence and rape, and the Haight-Ashbury police station appeared to have become a clearing house for teenage runaways.

Meanwhile, on university and college campuses as well as city streets across the world, many young people were becoming increasingly critical of society and of their place in it. In particular, the issue of the United States' continuing involvement in the war in Vietnam provoked a heightened sense of radicalism and anger that was about to reach a new pitch.

Communal living

MANY OF THOSE who became part of the 1960s 'counter-culture' experimented with different ways of living and working. They rejected the conventional lifestyle of the suburban families in which many of them had grown up in favour of communal living.

The influx of young people in the Haight-Ashbury neighbourhood of San Francisco gave a powerful impulse to the setting up of communes in California. 'There was a sense of danger in the city, of things falling apart,' says Martine Algier, who decided to join a rural commune at Big Sur, overlooking the sea in the mountains south of San Francisco. 'In order to get on with making changes, we needed to get to places in the country where we could live together in groups in healthy ways, and have gardens and schools and create the healthy alternative.' In her commune there were seven or eight adults, five children, and a few goats.

In these communes the theory was that no one person was in charge. Instead people pooled their resources and shared ownership, money, duties and responsibilities – for housekeeping, for producing and cooking food, for irrigating land, collecting firewood, even for bringing up children. On most communes, instead of separating work and family life people grew their own food, baked their own bread and made their own clothes. The Drop City commune in Colorado was built of geodesic domes made from recycled materials. Some communes identified with Native Americans, and their members wore – and sold – moccasins and silver and turquoise jewellery. Other communes developed small enterprises such as alternative schools, bookshops or storefront law offices. There were also political communes inhabited by more radical activists. There were some on which people advocated nudity and practised 'free love'; others, set up by religious groups, were strict or even puritanical.

By 1970 there were about 3000 rural communes and a number of urban communes in the United States. Many of them failed. Some ran out of money, and found that they could not survive without some income. Others failed to sustain a free and healthy way of life. 'A lot of people didn't know how to survive, and they didn't know how to grow carrots and dig latrines, and they didn't know how to create alternative schools,' remembers Martine Algier. Some, such as the Hog Farm commune, foundered as a result of drug abuse, malnutrition and even violence.

Communes were also established in Europe. In Germany *Kommune Einz* (Commune Number One), set up in 1967 in West Berlin, was famous for leading radical political action. The idea also spread to Japan, where about fifty communes and hundreds of co-operative villages were set up in the mid-1970s. In Britain by 1972 there were a hundred communes. Some of them were extremely successful, like the Findhorn community; founded in northern Scotland in 1962, by 1972 it had grown into an elaborate organization with over a hundred members, and communal facilities that included a craft centre, a folk singing group and a theatre.

UNDER ONE ROOF *Commune members shared family duties as well as living space.*

Days of rage

As 1967 turned into 1968 youth protests were on the increase in many parts of Europe, both east and west, as well as in Australia, Canada, Japan, Mexico and the United States. The two issues – the Vietnam war and university conditions and organization – ran in parallel, and were often combined. The radical student activity that began in Australia in 1965 at the universities of Sydney and Queensland grew more frequent as students occupied buildings and staged demonstrations calling for reform. In Canada students demanded more representation on university governing bodies, equal access to research facilities, day care centres for their children and a louder voice in academic policy-making. At several universities – Montreal, Ontario and Toronto – students demonstrated, disrupted classes and started a fire.

Peace offering *Flowers became a symbol for young pacificsts opposed to the Vietnam war. At the 1967 peace march in Washington, they were used to confront armed soldiers.*

In the United States anti-war protests were also becoming more violent. One of the largest took place in October 1967, a few months after the government had sent a further 100 000 troops to Vietnam. A march was held in the capital, Washington DC, at the Defence Department, housed in the Pentagon. Jeff Jones, who had joined the leading radical student group, SDS, took part. 'When we got to the Pentagon,' he recalls, 'there were thousands and thousands of people there.' The army was sent in to control the crowd, some 100 000 people. 'Things had reached the stage where the government had to call out the army to protect the Pentagon from the people. It was intimidating,' feels Jeff Jones. 'It was also exhilarating, because the message of alienation and disagreement and contempt had apparently gotten through.'

Later that year the government announced that students who were arrested in anti-war demonstrations would lose their draft deferments. They were not deterred. There were continuing campus rebellions – at Antioch College, at Berkeley, Columbia, Cornell, Harvard, Kent State, Jackson State and others. Students

Rusty Sachs (left) *was initially excited as he enlisted in the United States Marine Corps in 1964. When he returned from Vietnam he felt differently: 'When you're twenty-four and you're coming home from a war with blood on your hands, you don't feel good about it.' He joined other war veterans in discarding his medals. 'It was a cutting of apron strings, a gesture of defiance.'*

had led many of the demonstrations, but the anti-war movement was now far wider, with an estimated thirty-six million people having taken part. The day after the Pentagon protest was held in Washington, 5000 people marched in London to demonstrate against the Vietnam war. Students caused disruption at universities across Britain – at Birmingham, Bradford, Bristol, Essex, Hull, Leeds, Leicester, Manchester and elsewhere – and the government launched an investigation into the causes of the protest.

Students were becoming harder to ignore. There was unrest in Czechoslovakia, in Poland and West Germany. In Italy there were riots and sit-ins at universities in Milan, Rome and Turin. In Denmark, where the number of students at the University of Copenhagen doubled in just five years, violent demonstrations

Public opinion *in the United States had shifted against the Vietnam war. Some still labelled student critics as communists and traitors, but many older people increasingly supported their efforts.*

took place in April 1968. In Japan, where the Vietnam war had fuelled existing anger over education policies, hundreds of students were arrested when they smashed the windows of the Foreign Ministry. Some shielded themselves with gas masks or wore cycle helmets and carried weapons made of sticks and stones as they formed themselves into compact human shields.

The greatest turmoil of all took place in Paris that year, where student demands included an end to the sexual segregation that still existed in university accommodation, wider access to higher education for working-class pupils, reforms in teaching methods, examinations and course content, and the right to appoint class representatives. In 1967 there were more than eight and a half million students in higher education in France. To house some of them, the Sorbonne had built a new campus at Nanterre, in the suburbs of Paris, but even there numbers swelled from 2000 to 11 000 in just four years.

It was there that disturbances began in the spring of 1968, triggered by student protests against the Vietnam war. On 3 May they spread to the Latin quarter in the heart of the city. The Sorbonne was closed and many students were arrested, sparking renewed moves as others, including Romain Goupil, joined in. 'It was an astonishing expression of solidarity,' he recalls. 'Between six thousand and ten thousand students went to the Quartier Latin to surround and open up the Sorbonne....We started to overturn cars,

Students take a stand (LEFT) *in Paris outside the Renault car factory at Billancourt, in an attempt to seize the building in a show of solidarity with the workers. Romain Goupil* (ABOVE RIGHT) *was eighteen when he confronted the riot police, the Compagnies Républicaines de Sécurité (CRS), in May 1968* (ABOVE LEFT *and* TOP). *'We were dealing with tear gas specialists. It was hard to breathe, hard to move about....This wasn't a war, we were students, school pupils.'*

and to set up barricades around the students....We found ourselves behind the barricades saying, "We shall not be moved!" '

On 6 May the riot police were called in. At first they were wary of confronting the students, some of them secondary school pupils, but soon there was violence. 'We had learned a lot of lessons from the United States, from West Germany, from Italy,' Romain Goupil reflects. 'We defended ourselves, which led to a truly violent confrontation. For our generation, this was the first confrontation with the police.' The students prised up heavy paving stones from the city streets and threw a few petrol bombs. They too protected themselves by wearing cycle helmets, covering their faces with cloths soaked in lemon juice against the effects of tear gas. Within a week, 367 people had been injured.

The clashes triggered a nationwide movement, bringing the country almost to a standstill. Millions of workers who had already threatened union action over their own work grievances joined in a national strike, partly out of sympathy for the students. Public services stopped functioning: rubbish piled up in the streets, post was not delivered. Two friends of Charles-Henri de Choiseul Praslin, one of the students, were killed in the violence. 'For two months we demonstrated tirelessly, we spoke with everyone in the street, we fought against the police,' he says. At the height of the general strike nine million people took part. Some feared the country was on the brink of anarchy, but gradually people went back to work as the government reasserted control, undertook to modernize the universities and negotiated with the workers.

In the Netherlands trouble spread from Tilburg to campuses around the country in April 1969. In the United States Jeff Jones took part in a 'Days of Rage' protest in Chicago, organized in October by the radical Weathermen Underground group. 'The first night was the most terrifying thing I was ever involved in,' he says. 'We started down through the streets of Chicago and very quickly it turned into a riot of sorts....People started breaking shop windows and car windows.' As they broke through police barricades, hundreds of people were arrested and six were shot. By the end of the 1960s, says Bill Arthrell, 'It seemed as though every spring we thought the revolution was going to come, that we were going to profoundly change American society.'

WANTED FILE (BELOW) *For his part in causing 'riots and conspiracy', Jeff Jones was wanted by the United States Federal Bureau of Investigation (FBI). He had already been arrested many times on anti-war demonstrations: 'I was always under the jurisdiction of one court or another.' He went into hiding in 1970. 'Some of us had no choice but to go underground, just so we didn't have to waste time and money going on trial.'*

Testaments of youth

In the spring of 1970 two events dramatized how far things had gone. At Jackson State College, Mississippi, two students were shot by National Guard reservists. In May the National Guard fired into a crowd of student demonstrators at Kent State University in Ohio, killing four of them. 'It was a classic confrontation,' reflects Bill Arthrell, who remembers the whole episode. 'On the one side you had student activists, hippies and radicals, the new generation. On the other side was the National Guard, representing the establishment, though they were very young as well, and some of them were Kent State students and some of them were evading the draft, too.' Seventy-five colleges closed, and the students had to wait until December to graduate.

First in line *at the polling station in North Newton, Somerset, a young woman exercises her right to vote in March 1970, after new British laws reduced the minimum voting age from twenty-one to eighteen.*

By the end of 1970 student rebellion had begun to die down. Young people no longer had an immediate, personal reason for opposing the war after the United States government began to withdraw troops from Vietnam, and abolished the military draft in 1973. In some ways the war had acted as a catalyst for them to speak out. 'It was a generational movement,' says Bill Arthrell, 'the first time in history that a whole generation actually stood up against the establishment.'

During the 1960s people under the age of twenty-five had outnumbered their elders. By challenging the old order, they shaped new ideas and brought many changes to society, politics and popular behaviour. Whether they had taken part in the protest movements or not, young people earned new opportunities and rights – to better education, to greater social freedoms, to a wider range of jobs and careers. They had also been admitted into the political mainstream: in many countries the voting age had been lowered from twenty-one to eighteen, and politicians now paid attention to the opinions – and the votes – of young people.

By the mid-1970s the tide was turning towards a new, populist conservatism, and the average age of populations began to rise. But the example of participation and involvement set in the 1960s remained: though the issues were different, people continued to speak out on the environment, nuclear power, equal rights. 'All of a sudden, it was the people who counted,' says Romain Goupil. 'That's what was so extraordinary about the sixties.'

Passport to the future (opposite) *Graduation day at the University of Notre Dame, Indiana. The number of universities in the world doubled during the 1970s to provide for the huge number of young people seeking further education.*

EQUAL PAY FOR EQUAL JOBS
RED TAPE means: WOMEN are RAPED of their RIGHTS

1950–1995

Half the People

Women Fight for Equal Rights

Just before she turned the the corner into Fifth Avenue in New York City, Jaqui Ceballos hesitated. She was there to participate in a public demonstration on 26 August 1970, organized by the women's movement. 'I was afraid we would have only two or three thousand women,' she remembers. 'I'll never forget when I turned the corner at the Hotel Plaza – I could not see to the end. There were thousands of women there!'

All over the city, women stopped what they were doing to join in the huge parade. Some carried placards and shouted out slogans. 'We'd say to the women, "Join us, join us!" ' describes Jaqui Ceballos. 'We just took over the whole avenue, and the horns were beeping, people were lined up on the side, some screaming at us, but most of them were looking at us in real amazement.'

More than 50 000 women are thought to have taken part in that demonstration. The day on which it was held marked the fiftieth anniversary of the constitutional amendment that had granted women the right to vote in federal elections, as men did. Now American women wanted a wider equality, beyond basic political rights. Although many women were better educated, whole areas of life were still closed to them. The equality march was the largest of many that were held throughout the United States that year, as more and more women discovered a stronger sense of identity and began to question their position. 'It was a consciousness-raising day,' remembers Jaqui Ceballos. 'It meant that the possibility of freedom was around the corner....It was the time that the women's movement became a movement.'

It was also the time when women across the world began to serve notice on men that they were no longer prepared to be regarded as second-class citizens. In their shared resolve for change, millions of women began to demand the same opportunities as men, and the right to make their own decisions about their lives. They began to assert themselves, and their collective cause, in society and politics, becoming more ambitious and more determined along the way.

Marching for equality *Protesters throng the streets of New York City in the summer of 1970 to demand equal rights for women.*

> "During the war girls did all sorts of wonderful things.... They flew aircraft and could do almost anything."
>
> GINNIE WHITEHILL

WOMEN AT WORK (ABOVE) *in a Japanese armaments factory in 1940. By 1945 there were more than three million Japanese women in the workforce. The Girls' Volunteer Corps was set up to draft those between the ages of twelve and forty for industrial work. Women who refused could be fined or imprisoned for up to a year. When the war ended women were awarded a number of new rights, including the right to vote.*

'ROSIE THE RIVETER' (OPPOSITE) *starred at the centre of campaigns to recruit women for wartime work in the United States in the early 1940s. Some 80 per cent of them trained in heavy industry.*

New roles for women

By 1970 the lives of many women in the world's developed nations had changed greatly since the beginning of the century. With their families, they had benefited from better health care, better housing and more mobility. They had the same rights to education as men, and many more were going to university. But deeply rooted attitudes and prejudices continued to shape the lives of women. Most women's activities remained confined to the home and family. Those who did go out to work – whether in factories, in offices, or in service industries such as catering or cleaning – were paid far less than men.

On two occasions, it was war that had, indirectly, done most to change the daily lives of women at home. As millions of men left to fight in the First World War, women were recruited into their factory jobs; they also worked in banks, the civil services and insurance companies. For the first time, women became streetcar conductors, carpenters, painters, stokers and tool setters.

Combined with the suffragettes' campaigns, it was women's war efforts that helped persuade many governments to give them the vote. By 1920 women in most northern European countries, in Canada, the Soviet Union and the United States could vote. They claimed new social freedoms, too: to dress differently, to wear makeup, and to smoke in public. In the Soviet Union the communist revolution ushered in reforms for women, and they were now expected to perform the same jobs as men. There were more women in Europe in paid employment than ever before, but in the 1930s both the economic hardship of the Depression and opposition from male-dominated unions meant that women came under pressure to give up their jobs.

During the Second World War, as in the first, the female proportion of the civilian workforce dramatically increased in the combatant nations. In the United States seven million women went to work, many for the first time. 'In the 1940s they called on women to leave those telephone operator jobs and to leave those clerk jobs and come in here and build this engine,' remembers Kay Foley, who grew up in the city of Lynn in Massachusetts during the war. 'They came in and they welded and they did all sorts of things that were typically men's jobs.' By 1942 thirteen million

POST
AY 29, 1943
10¢
BEGINNING—A NEW
KELLAND SERIAL
Heart on Her Sleeve
EDGAR SNOW
REPORTS ON GERMAN
ATROCITIES
ROSIE
Norma
Rockwe

women were at work in the United States, and more than half of them were married.

Women's status in the workplace changed fundamentally during the war. When it was over, the political advance of women continued – in Argentina, China, France, India, Italy and Japan women also gained the vote. In its charter, the new United Nations Organization declared that men and women's rights were equal, prompting its member nations to do the same. Principles of equality were contained in the new postwar constitutions of France, Italy and West Germany.

In the world's less developed nations, despite the principles of equality set out by the United Nations, continuing poverty, the lack of education and enduring social traditions meant that most women's lives did not change. Even in the industrialized world, within a few years traditional stereotypes and restrictions had again reasserted themselves; equal opportunities seemed to be in retreat.

Back to the home front

When the soldiers returned to the United States, four out of five women wanted to hold on to their jobs. But employers felt bound to give jobs back to the men who had left them to fight, and many of the girls who had taken their place married and settled down. 'I did what most girls did,' remembers Ginnie Whitehill, who grew up in a New York suburb. 'I married a war hero. That's what we were supposed to do. And I had children. Every woman was expected to have children. No woman would have ever dared not consider having children.' Hollywood films, radio soap operas and early television serials all reinforced the image of women as housewives and mothers. In some British schools girls were taught housewifery and how to do laundry as part of the curriculum. Television commercials often portrayed women as incompetent.

By 1950 a third of American women still went out to work, the majority of them in poorly paid, unskilled jobs: they could be a domestic maid or work in a textile factory. The better-educated could qualify as librarians or teachers. When Kay Foley left school in 1956 she went to work at an electrical goods factory as a key-punch operator. 'You had to be able to read and transmit that through your brain to the three tips of your fingers, and be able to

Changing places (LEFT) *As the factories reverted to non-military production after the war, so too female veterans of war plants were exhorted to leave the factory behind and return to the kitchen stove.*

Taking a break *from work* (BELOW) *to admire a former colleague's baby is the image on an American magazine cover. The requirement that women give up their jobs on marriage reinforced a common view of women's work as temporary and unchallenging.*

keypunch numbers onto punch cards,' she recalls. 'It never occurred to me to look for something else, because there was nothing else.' A few years later, like most women, Kay Foley gave up her job, married and had a baby. Jaqui Ceballos, who grew up in New York, did the same. 'You could be a secretary for a while, or work in a store. A nurse maybe, a schoolteacher,' she says. 'In any career you took it wasn't really a career, it was a job until you got married.'

The nurseries provided during the war were closed; there were few remaining facilities to help working mothers. Lorena Weeks worked as a telephone operator in Georgia so that she could earn enough to support her three children. 'Telephone operators worked around the clock,' she recalls. 'I worked split hours so that I could be with my children in the afternoon....I'd go back and work from seven until eleven at night, and it was hard. Most men's jobs at that time were eight to five, plus the pay was so much better.'

Rebuilding railroads *was a priority for these women living in devastated Poland. Until conditions improved in the late 1950s, European women played a key role in reconstruction after the war.*

Discrimination in the workplace was widespread. Whole professions were closed to women applicants. Women often could not be promoted above a certain level in the company hierarchy, and some women lost their jobs when they got married. Even after graduating from college, many women were unable to choose the careers they would have liked. Dusty Roads grew up in Cleveland, Ohio close to where the national aviation races were held every year. She had always dreamed of becoming an airline pilot, 'Until I was in high school and found out from my father, "You can't be an airline pilot, darling, they don't hire ladies". It broke my heart,' she says. Instead, when she was twelve years old she decided she would become an airline stewardess. 'I thought, well, if I can't fly in the cockpit at least I can ride in the back.'

Women's wake-up call

By the 1960s increasing numbers of women both in the United States and in Europe were frustrated with the restrictions on the way they could live. For much of the population, especially the young, this was a time of change: there were greater opportunities for education, more open relationships and new social freedoms. But although it was becoming easier for single women in some countries to obtain various forms of contraception, abortion was still against the law. 'One mistake, and you were off in the suburbs, home having babies and starting a family,' recalls Amy Coen, who was a student at the University of Michigan, 'or you were risking your life in a back alley abortion.'

An important development came with the introduction of the birth control pill, by far the most convenient and reliable form of contraception to date. It was sold in the United States for the first time in 1960; six years later, six million women in the United States were taking the pill. Amy Coen's university was one of the first to offer it to students. 'It changed my life, and it changed the lives of my friends,' she says. 'We did not have to worry about being pregnant.' Women could now choose if, and when, they wanted to have children.

Prescription of choice

THE ORAL CONTRACEPTIVE – *known as 'the pill' – took five years to develop in the United States. It was tested on volunteers and approved by the Food and Drug Administration in 1960. It prevented ovulation, and thus pregnancy, by mimicking the body's hormones. The first commercial birth control pill was Enovid-10, produced by the G. D. Searle Company in Illinois. Although the pill was marketed as reliable and harmless to women, it was later discovered to have potentially dangerous side effects; despite this, by 1991 some 200 million women in the world were taking the drug.*

The pill transformed the lives of millions of women everywhere. When it became available in Mexico, Anilu Elias, who already had two children, took it secretly. Her husband wanted to have a third child. 'Without the pill he would have been able to control me,' she describes. 'Taking the pill meant breaking with tradition....It was like stopping the whole mechanism in the world against women and against myself.' Anilu Elias was more fortunate than most women in Mexico, who could not afford to pay for the pill or who had no access to it. In France, Italy and other Roman Catholic countries it was banned altogether.

Without access to safe, reliable methods of contraception, thousands of women still resorted to illegal, sometimes dangerous

FOR MOTHER OF TWO *Anilu Elias* (ABOVE) *the pill meant freedom. 'It was a long time before it got to Mexico,' she recalls, 'but when I read about the pill, I thought it was magic!'*

STEALING A KISS (BELOW) *in New York. Some people blamed contraception for changing social patterns.*

operations. Even in the United States, women sought clandestine abortions. 'No other issue got women involved in the same way, because everyone had experienced something like that,' recalls Jaqui Ceballos. 'There were always thousands and thousands of women looking for abortions. There was such anger that men were dictating what women should be doing with their bodies.... Women began to think, "Why are we going through this?" '

These questions of contraception and abortion and the ethical issues that they raised, added to the less controversial issues of equal pay and equal rights at work. There

Shaping awareness
This British poster of the 1970s used the image of a pregnant man to urge men to share responsibility for contraception and reduce unwanted pregancies. The pill was introduced to Britain in 1961, but was not freely available on prescription to all women until 1974.

Women's mutilation

By challenging traditional approaches to their fertility, women in the West gained new freedoms over their bodies and rights over their reproduction. But in developing countries millions of women still faced potentially life-threatening attempts to control their bodies, and all in the name of tradition. Shortly after Shamis Dirir was born in Somalia, her father left her mother. He had wanted a son. When she was seven years old, she was taken one morning to be circumcised. 'When the time came,' Shamis Dirir remembers, 'I ran away. I was caught and brought back.' They assured her that she was becoming a woman, that without the operation she could never marry and have children. 'I was circumcised with six or seven other girls,' she remembers. 'There was no anaesthetic at all. It was very painful.'

Some ninety million girls are thought to have suffered a similar fate. An ancient practice, female circumcision or 'female genital mutilation' (FGM) – a name used by campaigners against the practice to emphasize the fact that it is a far more radical operation than male circumcision – spread from Egypt to other countries across Africa. It was most widely practised in Central, East and West Africa – including Burkina Faso, Djibouti, Ethiopia, Eritrea, Mali, Nigeria, Sierra Leone, Somalia and northern Sudan – and to a lesser degree in some Muslim parts of Asia.

Despite its popularity among Muslim populations, traditional beliefs and social customs rather than religious rules pressurized parents into forcing their daughters to submit to the practice, in some cases out of fear that they might become social outcasts without it. Some communities believed that it cleansed women and freed them from impurities; others considered it mandatory before marriage, and sought to reserve women's bodies solely for procreation, not pleasure, to ensure their fidelity in marriage; some thought that uncircumcised women could not conceive. Millions of young African girls were victims of female circumcision. Most of them suffered from a host of long-term health problems as a result of the operation, including vaginal and urinary tract infections, pain and permanent scarring; many died in childbirth.

During the 1930s female circumcision was also reported in Australia, Brazil, India, Mexico and Peru, and later among some Christian communities in the Soviet Union. It was used in the United States until 1937 to treat women who had been diagnosed as suffering from 'hysteria' or 'nymphomania'. Female circumcision continued to be clandestinely carried out in the West. In Britain some 10 000 girls from predominantly Somali and Sudanese immigrant communities were thought to be at risk in the 1990s, though the practice had been banned in 1985. Legislation against it was also introduced in Australia, Canada, France, Sweden, Switzerland and the United States, though it often proved difficult to implement.

Women's health organizations and human rights groups around the world campaigned against the practice, which continued to mutilate millions of women in Africa alone. It was local people's efforts to challenge the traditions of their own cultures that offered the greatest hopes of preventing further suffering. In some countries, women's refuges were set up to offer escape for the victims of circumcision, and in Sudan, where an estimated 89 per cent of women were still being mutilated, women's groups began to provide honest information about it in the hope of eradicating the traumatic operation.

In Burkina Faso it was efforts by the government during the 1990s that achieved considerable success in influencing local people's views. National school campaigns, public awareness films, radio broadcasts and posters and village meetings began to transform their long-standing beliefs.

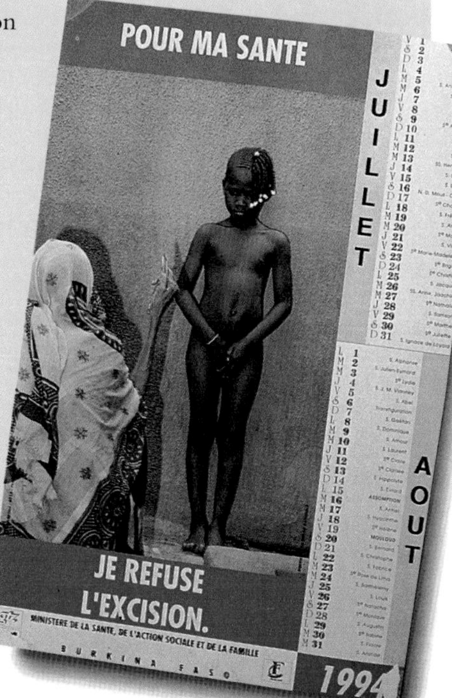

Calendar message *'For my health I refuse circumcision' – the words on a poster against female genital mutilation, pasted onto the walls of a village health clinic in Burkina Faso. More than half of all women in the country underwent the dangerous operation before the government launched the campaign to phase it out.*

were still many hurdles to overcome. When Dusty Roads began to work as an air stewardess, she discovered that it was not a career after all. The airlines viewed it as a temporary opportunity for single, attractive young women. 'They even called it the "charm farm",' she remembers. 'We were supposed to wear girdles, and of course we wore high heels. Occasionally they'd do a girdle check. They'd come up and give you a little tap on your rear end, and if you didn't have a girdle on you would be called into the office.' Stewardesses had to maintain slender figures and, unlike the male pilots, they automatically lost their jobs if they married. 'That made me angry,' recalls Dusty Roads. 'It also violated my sense of fair play that pilots could be fired at age sixty and we were fired at age thirty-two. Something was wrong there.'

With some of her colleagues, Dusty Roads decided to become a lobbyist, and in 1963 she began to protest against the compulsory retirement age for stewardesses. Many other women were also becoming more determined to pursue their quest for change; many of them were helped by an influential book that first appeared in 1963. When Jaqui Ceballos, unhappily married and now with four children, discovered *The Feminine Mystique* by Betty Friedan, she stayed up all night long to read it. 'I'll never forget the way I felt. It changed my life,' she describes. 'I realized that it wasn't my husband, and it wasn't me. It was the society, and the society had to change.'

The Feminine Mystique had the same powerful impact on numerous other women. In it, Betty Friedan drew attention to the way in which women had been thrust back into their traditional roles. She argued that, like men, women could only find their true identity in work that used their full capacities, and not in the dull routine of housework. Within seven years, more than a million copies of this feminist manifesto had been sold in Britain and the United States. It was also read by educated women in developing countries. In Mexico, Anilu Elias had been forced by her husband to give up her job as creative director at an advertising agency. When she read Betty Friedan's book she was overwhelmed. 'I put it away because it felt like keeping a bomb in the house,' she says. 'I knew that after reading that book the only thing I could or should do is to get a divorce.'

Views of women *as the weaker sex were reinforced by advertisements such as these – separated by more than a decade – portraying them as helpless if their cars broke down.*

Service with a smile *Airline stewardesses were expected to be young and attractive. They lost their jobs when the airlines thought their 'charm' might begin to fade, as Dusty Roads* (LEFT) *discovered when she became a stewardess.*

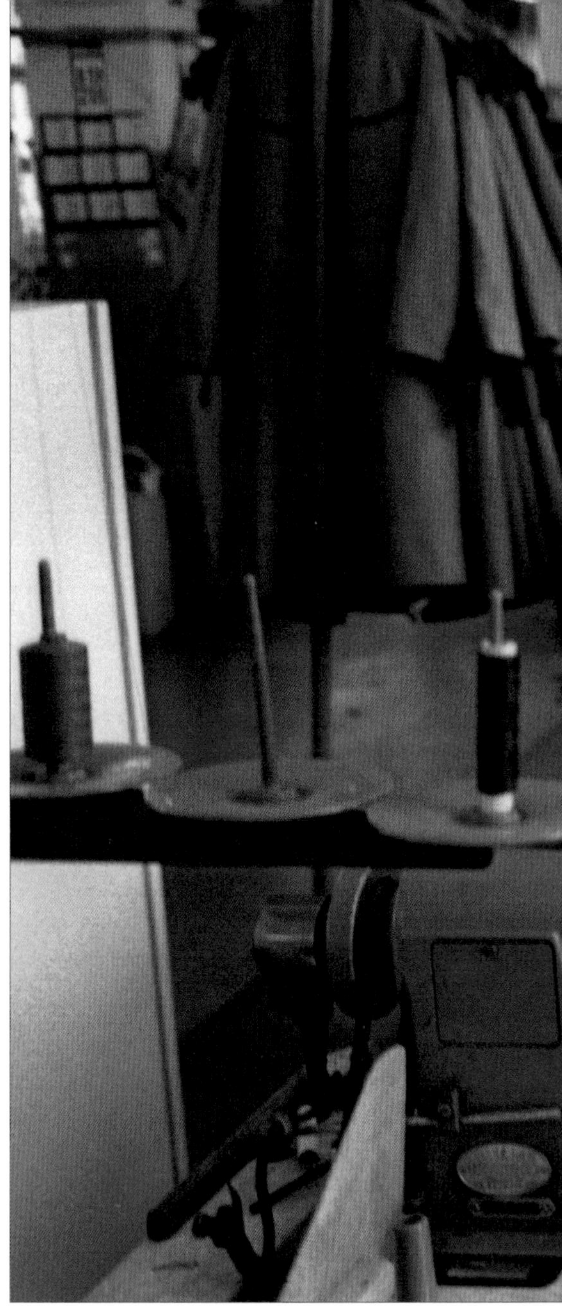

Women's bid for equality

From the mid-1960s the number of women in paid work was on the increase, though they still continued to earn less than men. In Australia and Britain, 45 per cent of women worked. In the United States and Canada the proportion was 49 per cent, and in Denmark and Sweden it was 57 per cent. In the United States, where women were still not legally entitled to receive the same pay as men for doing the same work, the prospect of real change came in 1964 when the Civil Rights Act was passed. It banned job discrimination on the grounds of sex as well as race.

Lorena Weeks was still working long hours as a telephone operator, taking and transferring calls, when she heard about the new ruling. 'I'd watched these men, the toll test men, the switch men, all of them, in work that I felt I could do,' she remembers. 'It was much better pay. The hours were better, the overtime was better....I knew immediately that this was a chance for me to get one of these jobs.'

When she applied for a better job, Lorena Weeks was told that it was being awarded only to men. She then appealed to the union. 'The president told me that he didn't have anything against me,' she recalls, 'but that if I got the job it would mean other women would come into this type of work, and that I was not the breadwinner in the family, the man was the breadwinner.' Next Lorena Weeks decided to take her case to the law courts. The company's lawyer used an obscure ruling – originally intended to protect them – that women and minors should not lift weights in excess of 14 kg (30 lb) to prevent Lorena Weeks from getting the job she wanted. 'It was just foolish to use something like that against women to keep them from drawing these better salaries and having these better-paid jobs,' she insists.

Towards the end of the 1960s more women were beginning to demand changes to such laws. And as they launched a more vigorous campaign for equality, women began to extend their concern to a wider range of issues, such as the environment and nuclear proliferation. Their protests became more committed, and more angry. Jaqui Ceballos was among them. 'It was a fabulous time,' she says. 'It was like a fever of excitement of all the women changing their lives....What we wanted was to be

Graduation day (left) *for Amy Coen and a friend at the University of Michigan. She first joined a feminist group to challenge double standards of admission at the college. 'We were very excited. That was one of the first feminist victories that I remember.'*

Rows of workers (above) *in a clothing factory in Budapest, Hungary in 1980. In Eastern Europe, as elsewhere, the textile and clothing industries employed predominantly women in non-managerial roles. Women's groups in Eastern Europe were disbanded under communism; although many women were as well educated as men, there were fewer opportunities for them in senior positions.*

thinking human beings and take responsibility for running this world equally with men.'

Sensing the changing mood on her university campus, Amy Coen and her fellow students became involved in women's protest groups. 'We understood that women could get together and make a lot of noise and get change,' she remembers. 'We didn't know quite what we were doing in our relationships, but they were going to be equal. Equal was our word.' When they discovered that the university entrance regulations discriminated against women, they succeeded in having them changed.

In the courts, more sexual discrimination suits were being fought by women. After a five-year court case, Lorena Weeks was awarded the job she had wanted for so long. As women continued their individual battles against the establishment, a new women's movement was gathering momentum.

Group force

In 1966 a group of women in New York came together to form a new organization devoted to women's rights. The National Organization for Women (NOW) was the first of its kind in the United States. Jaqui Ceballos became one of the organizers of the group. 'We were beginning to learn how to do things. We did everything ourselves – we wrote our press releases, we put out newsletters, we learned to talk on the telephone, we learned to demonstrate,' she says. 'And so these shy, retiring women who only had their anger...were beginning to learn how to use their power to make changes.'

A CHAIN OF PROTEST *links members of the National Organization for Women as they picket the White House in Washington DC in 1969. The chain, decorated with flowers, was intended to draw attention to the oppression of women.*

The group forced women's issues onto the political agenda by dispatching telegrams to Washington and picketing government offices. The women called for an amendment to the US constitution to give them equal rights and equal pay. They demanded the enforcement of laws that banned sexual discrimination in employment, and repeal of the laws banning abortion. They lobbied for equality for women at work and for the provision of maternity leave and childcare centres. They also targeted newspapers that printed separate listings for women in job advertisement sections, and challenged airline companies over the unfair treatment of stewardesses.

Through the growing number of newspapers, magazines and groups devoted to women's issues, more women discovered that they shared similar problems and they began to organize themselves. 'We used to get together and talk and bare our feelings, which we'd never done before,' says Jaqui Ceballos. 'It was a catharsis, it was just a feverish movement going from meetings to demonstrations, to consciousness-raising groups.' Several of the feminist publications that appeared in Europe and the United States mirrored the enormous impact of Betty Friedan's book.

By 1968 the mushrooming women's liberation movement was becoming increasingly difficult to ignore. In that year NOW chose the Miss America beauty contest in Atlantic City, New Jersey – an annual event that had continued unchallenged since 1920 – as a focal point for its protest. Women arrived from all over the country to take part. 'There were about seven buses leaving from New York City,' recalls Jaqui Ceballos. 'There were buses that came from Canada, from Washington DC, from California, Florida – all these young women. It was really becoming a grass-roots movement.' Outside the hall where the contest was being held the protesters expressed their indignation in unconventional ways: 'We paraded a sheep and we crowned her Miss America. We threw our garments and cosmetics into the trash can,' as Jaqui Ceballos describes. 'We threw bras and girdles and stockings, high-heeled shoes, corsets, false eyelashes – they were oppressive items for women.'

SHOW OF ANGER (ABOVE) *Voicing their disapproval in public, women demonstrate outside the Miss America beauty contest in Atlantic City in 1968. 'The demonstration was against the idea of women being preened to be beauties,' remembers Jaqui Ceballos. Two years later, members of the women's movement in Britain stormed the annual Miss World contest at the Royal Albert Hall in London* (TOP). *They were dragged out by police after hurling stink bombs, smoke canisters, bags of flour and ink pellets onto the stage.*

"It was a feeling of power...that we all want to change society and we can do it."

Jaqui Ceballos

The event was widely reported by the media, which helped to spread awareness of women's issues. The activists encountered some public ridicule, anger and even abuse, but by the time the equality march in New York took place in the summer of 1970, NOW's membership had steadily risen from just 3000 to 15 000. Thousands more women were joining all the time. Some men took part in the marches, too, in support of the women's movement. 'After the march it seemed that everything opened up,' remembers Jaqui Ceballos. 'And it was a worldwide movement – Britain, France, Italy – there were movements all over the world....There was a tremendous feeling of optimism in the 1970s.'

In some parts of Europe, where women's rights had been slow to progress since the 1950s, the women's movement was fuelled by the radical student and worker rebellions that were also taking place during the late 1960s. A French student, Gabrielle Dequesne-Cudenet, had been brought up to believe that women should drink sherry rather than whisky, and that they should smoke only when they were indoors. 'It was an education to mould you as an obedient housewife,' she says. She found that taking part in the student demonstrations that erupted in Paris in May 1968 opened new doors for her. 'Afterwards,' she adds, 'I was no longer the delightful little housewife that I could have been.'

Disillusioned with their low status in a society that still prevented them from divorcing their husbands or having the right to use contraception, Italian women also took to the streets in 1968. Women in Britain formed the National Joint Action Campaign for Women's Equal Rights, and organized an equal pay rally in London's Trafalgar Square in 1969. The following year they convened the first national women's conference. In West Germany women's rights campaigners defiantly hurled tomatoes at their male opponents during a conference, and in Paris women laid a wreath beneath the Arc de Triomphe in honour of 'the unknown wife of the unknown soldier'.

Taking a stand *The Statue of Liberty* (right) *in New York Harbour was used by campaigners to publicize the NOW equality march two weeks before it was due to take place. Jaqui Ceballos* (above) *recalls how they secretly carried two giant banners to Liberty Island and placed one of them on the balcony beneath the statue; it read: 'Women of the world unite'. 'We were so afraid that we weren't going to get people in the streets,' she says, 'this was a way of announcing it.' The striking images carried by the world's press the next day helped spread awareness of the event and of the women's movement.*

Unchanging ways *of life* (opposite) *for women washing clothes in northern Brazil. While women activists in industrial countries fought for equal rights, many poorer women in developing nations were also becoming more active in finding ways to improve their lives. As Serafina Soriana Gallardo, who fought for water to be supplied to San Miguel in Mexico, says, 'Everything has been a struggle. Who are the ones who have carried most of the weight for this struggle? The women.'*

The liberating years

The women's campaigns of the early 1970s led to a series of notable victories. In Europe and the United States it was a time of crucial change as women succeeded in overthrowing, one after another, old laws that had dictated their personal lives. Although in many places unfair attitudes to women still prevailed, new laws affected the lives of millions of women in many different countries and from different social backgrounds.

In Italy women were allowed to seek divorce from 1970, and following further demonstrations, they were able to use birth control legally for the first time in 1972. In Britain a woman government minister introduced an Equal Pay Bill to parliament in 1970. For working women in the United States, whose average earnings were still only 60 per cent that of men, the contentious issue of equal pay continued to be the focus of their campaigns. 'The majority of NOW and the big organizations concentrated on getting the Equal Rights Amendment passed,' remmebers Jaqui Ceballos. They partially succeeded: the conditional amendment to the Constitution, which would guarantee equal rights for women, was passed by Congress in 1972; it was given a seven-year deadline for the ratification by individual states that would bring it into effect.

The laws governing abortion, at that time still illegal in many countries – including France, Germany, Italy, Sweden and the United States – aroused even greater controversy. Demands for free and legal abortion, and outrage over deaths following unsafe operations, triggered local women's movements. In Mexico, Anilu Elias joined a small coalition group to fight for women's rights. 'Abortion was our first and our biggest battle,' she says. 'The first time we ever took to the streets was in a fight for abortion....The first marches were exhilarating. The streets had never been taken over by women's groups before.'

Despite their continued efforts, Mexican campaigners failed to get the laws on abortion repealed. In France and Italy, where thousands of

A steady procession (OPPOSITE) *of Italian women from feminist groups engulfs the broad avenues of central Rome. A series of public marches in the capital, involving 20 000 women in 1975 and 50 000 in 1976, finally succeeded in changing Italy's strict laws on abortion – a crime that had been punishable by heavy fines or even imprisonment – despite continuing opposition from the Roman Catholic Church. France and Spain were affected by similar upheavals.*

Divided interests *Advocates of abortion confront a pro-life campaigner at a rally in Boston* (BELOW). *Reproductive rights were a constant source of dispute, and strengthened the resolve of lobbyist Ginnie Whitehill* (RIGHT) *to overturn the abortion laws.*

Juggling act (RIGHT) *A businesswoman reassures her toddler as she says goodbye at a daycare centre before beginning her professional working day.*

Caring for Children

By the late 1970s Western women had passed what many regarded as an important milestone: the majority of them went out to work. The highest proportion of working married women were in northern Europe, particularly in Denmark and Sweden where 57 per cent of women over the age of fifteen worked, and in Australia, Britain, Canada and the United States. Many of the women needing or wanting to work were mothers, who faced the crucial question of how to look after their young children and earn a living.

One option was part-time work. In the 1970s and 1980s many businesses sought to reduce labour costs by increasing their proportion of part-time workers. Most of these jobs went to women, many of whom welcomed the opportunity to combine working with bringing up a family; part-time work gave them an income without their having to pay for childcare. In 1986 some 90 per cent of part-time workers in Belgium, Britain and Germany were women; in Denmark, France, Luxembourg, Norway and Sweden the figure was almost as high. Women in full-time employment usually had to find alternatives such as daycare centres or nurseries for children too young to go to school.

In the Soviet Union falling birth rates rather than welfare concerns prompted the state to offer maternity leave and other benefits to working women during the 1970s. In Eastern Europe, state provision for childcare was widespread, but low standards drove many women wanting to work to seek part-time jobs, or to work at home.

Childcare varied widely in Western Europe, where it tended to decline with the economic recessions of the 1980s. By the mid-1980s the only countries in Europe where more than 5 per cent of children under the age of five were in government-run childcare centres were France, Belgium and Denmark. In Sweden it became the responsibility of local authorities, not parents, to reserve places for children at the state run daycare centres.

Equal opportunities also meant equal parental responsibility. Northern Europe set a precedent in encouraging fathers to play a more active part in looking after their children. In Norway more men took paternity leave after the government provided them with two weeks' paid leave following the birth of their child, and a Swedish law entitled fathers to paid leave to look after sick children.

Japan offered more daycare facilities than any other industrialized nation in 1991. In the United States working mothers suffered as a result of stringency in public expenditure. Their need was met by a substantial increase in private childcare. In Britain, where only 2 per cent of children under the age of three were in public childcare by the mid-1990s, the situation was worse. Some companies provided crèches, but many working mothers had to rely on friends, relatives, community groups, nannies or private nurseries. Some mothers had to reduce their hours of work or, if they could afford to, give it up altogether.

women took part in demonstrations, the ban on abortion was eventually lifted, in 1975 and 1977 respectively. In 1973, when the last obstacles to legal abortion were removed in the United States, the news was greeted with alarm in some circles, but for the majority of women it represented a huge victory. 'We'd fought for years for the right to have an abortion,' says Lorena Weeks, who had undergone an illegal operation some years before. 'It meant that the pain that I had gone through was something that women did not have to go through any more. It was a big moment.'

By the mid-1970s, with the new sense that anything was now possible if only they felt able to reach for it, people of all ages challenged conventional rules or assumptions that stood in their way. Ten-year-old Fran Pescatore, from Richfield in New Jersey, loved baseball, and was good at the game, but the town had refused to let her join the Little League team. 'Boys and girls in my town were treated totally differently in athletic sports,' she says. 'My dad said to me, "Frances, no one can tell you that you can't do anything just because you're a female".' In 1974 she won a lawsuit brought by her father, and became the first girl to play in the team. 'It was a big deal,' she recalls. 'People started throwing things at me, I remember being hit in the back with rocks and bottles....My brother said to me, "Fran, you don't have to go out there". And I remember saying to him, "No, I want to play baseball, I'm not going to let them stop me!" '

Learning new skills *Claudine Huck became France's first woman woodcutter in 1992. In the thirty years after 1954, the proportion of French working women who were wage earners rose from 59 per cent to 84 per cent, becoming higher than that of men in salaried employment.*

Prime position *Benazir Bhutto, elected prime minister of Pakistan in 1988, waves to a mostly male crowd. The first woman to head an Islamic state, she was one of a growing number of stateswomen; they were also to be found in Britain, France, Iceland, India, Ireland, Israel, Norway, Portugal and Sri Lanka. The Scandinavian countries had the highest proportion of women elected to parliament.*

As the new legal framework helped begin to change people's attitudes, women found they had greater chances of pursuing new careers. Hannah Dadds applied for a job as a train driver in London. 'I was asked a lot more questions than any of the fellows I worked with,' she remembers. 'When I qualified, my friends, my family, all of them thought it was terrific.' When people first saw her in the driving seat, they stared in disbelief. 'Some of the passengers said that we were doing men out of a job,' Hannah Dadds recalls. As new laws were introduced in Britain in the late 1970s to protect working mothers, giving them new rights to maternity leave and maternity pay, the number of women in the workforce rose sharply.

All over the world growing numbers of professional women were succeeding in areas that were once regarded as the exclusive domain of men. They became judges, lawyers, mayors, orchestral conductors, priests and politicians, even heads of government. 'I could be a doctor instead of a nurse, a pilot instead of a flight attendant, a senator instead of a secretary,' points out Dusty Roads, whose lobbying efforts had helped to change the laws on early compulsory retirement for stewardesses. 'It gave me a big thrill when I went up to that cockpit and I saw a girl there, and I knew that I had something to do with it.'

In the cockpit *of a Boeing 767 jet in Sydney in 1992, Sharelle Quinn was the first female pilot to become a captain on Australia's national airline, Qantas.*

Raising their fists (above) *Indian women workers campaign for change. The women's movement had been gathering strength since the early days of India's independence movement, and as they achieved greater political and professional success Indian feminists actively campaigned against the violent oppression of poor women. Resistance to change was strong: the forbidden ritual of sati – suicide on their husband's funeral pyre by Hindu widows – still survived in some places. The poster of an Indian women's liberation group* (left) *announcing International Women's Day, celebrated on 8 March, tells women: 'We will rest only after having broken out of this prison.'*

A decade for women

Since the 1960s the women's movement had developed into an international one. At the beginning of the century there were 200 international women's organizations; by 1986 the number had risen to 18 000. In the developing world, women had long been engaged in their own battles – for better living and working conditions, basic health care and family planning, and education. Women's issues were gaining more worldwide attention, and in 1975 the United Nations announced that it would host three world conferences on women during the UN Decade of Women. Jaqui Ceballos was one of thousands of women who attended the first meeting, held in Mexico City. 'There were women from all over the world,' she recalls. 'There were women from Third World countries who were there to push for other things.'

In poorer parts of the world millions of women continued to be affected by overriding poverty, hunger and illiteracy, but there too they were challenging the systems that oppressed them. Women in many countries had agitated with varying success for

BANKING ON WOMEN

WOMEN IN THE developing world were the most likely people of all to be landless and to face absolute poverty. In 1995 the United Nations reported that of the 1.3 billion people who lived in poverty, 70 per cent were women. In Bangladesh, women in rural districts were among the poorest of the poor. Yet it was there that one of the most promising ideas emerged for helping them to overcome their plight.

In 1976 a Bangladeshi economics professor founded a new development project in the district of Chittagong, with initial funding from local banks. Within ten years, the Grameen or 'village' bank project grew to become a formal, independent bank, branching out to other districts in Bangladesh.

What was unique about the Grameen Bank was that its customers were mostly landless and extremely poor. And 94 per cent of them were women. With a firm belief in everyone's right to receive financial credit, the Grameen Bank operated a pioneering system of 'micro-loans'. Believing that conventional development economics failed because people who most needed cheap credit – the very poor, and especially very poor women – could not get it, the Grameen Bank began to loan money to impoverished, often starving women. They could then buy goats or chickens, perhaps a sewing machine, and use them to generate a regular income, instead of begging. Some could eventually afford to take out a mortgage to buy a small piece of land.

The Grameen Bank preferred to lend to women, who were more reliable borrowers. They did not drink, gamble or squander their money, and children came first in their order of priorities. The bank had remarkably low default rates. It did not ask women for collateral, charged lower interest rates (20 per cent a year compared to the money lenders' rates of up to 20 per cent a month), and offered a much safer alternative to borrowing from other sources.

The bank divided its customers into groups of five women, who encouraged and supported one another when repayment was difficult, and who also had a say in who received bank loans. Bank officials travelled to villages to offer advice to customers as well as to collect loans. When they signed the Grameen Bank's sixteen-point code, borrowers also pledged to keep their families small, to avoid child marriage and wedding dowries, to build and use pit-latrines and to plant as many seedlings as possible. The bank also encouraged more women to vote. It helped empower them in the fight against poverty, and to improve both their living standards and their social status.

By the mid-1990s the Grameen Bank was one of the largest in the country, with more than a thousand branches that loaned millions of dollars every month to two million borrowers living in 68 000 villages. As the micro-loan idea spread, similar institutions were set up in more than thirty countries – most of them in Africa and Asia. In 1995 the Grameen Trust also sponsored 170 worldwide development projects.

BAKING BREAD *outside their new home in Dhaka, one of the many Bangladeshi families who benefited from a local Grameen Bank project to help homeless people build their own houses using local materials.*

the reform of laws that restricted them. They tackled difficult issues such as dowry murder in India and female infanticide in China. In Muslim countries such as Algeria and Iran, where an Islamic revival was taking place, the Western idea of progress was being challenged as traditional attitudes were restored.

Women's achievements faced a new challenge in the West, too, especially in the United States, where powerful religious groups reacted fiercely against the abortion laws. The Equal Rights Amendment to the Constitution had still not been fully ratified by all the states of the Union when the deadline – which had already been granted an extension – expired in 1982, so it failed to become law. Jaqui Ceballos was devastated. 'This was just the right, like men have, to be free and equal citizens, that was all,' she says. 'It was terrible. It was just like rolling up your sleeves and starting all over again.'

Women's Day in Algeria (above) *is marked by a march in the capital in 1994 to honour those killed by the Islamic fundamentalists who threatened women's freedoms.*

Moment of joy (left) *for a newly ordained woman priest in Britain, one of thirty-six women deacons admitted into the Church of England priesthood in 1994.*

Breaking into the ranks (opposite) *New arrivals from the United States army await orders at a Gulf port in 1990. More governments were prepared to admit women into their armed services, though their roles were restricted.*

For the majority of Western women, many aspects of their lives had improved dramatically. More avenues were open to them both at work and in society in general. With marriage no longer an obstacle to professional advancement, women were able to reach new heights in their careers – as pilots, in the navy, as sports umpires, as union presidents, as astronauts. Nearly forty years on, Kay Foley was employed at her local factory once more – and as a chemical processor in the hard hat area alongside the men, rather than as a keypunch operator. 'It never occurred to me in that time frame that I could do what they were doing, that I could make the kind of money that they were making,' she remembers. 'And it came about because these doors were opened by the women who were the activists of their day.'

In 1995 thousands of women delegates gathered for the Fourth UN Conference to discuss women's status. This time they met in the Chinese capital, Beijing. It was a good opportunity for them to take stock. Although there was still much to do, and many women had not yet benefited from the progress made since the 1950s, for American campaigner Amy Coen it was a time to acknowledge what had been achieved. 'I realized that I made a very decent salary, I had a very responsible job, I had wonderful children. I realized how personally I had benefited from all the social changes I had spent my entire life trying to have happen.'

T DOOR

10

1945 – 1989

War of the Flea

The impact of guerrilla wars

IN A LAST BID FOR SAFETY, hundreds of men, women and children struggled to get past the armed guards who surrounded the American embassy in Saigon. Those who did manage to squeeze through the crush joined the scramble to board the tightly packed American helicopter. It was April 1975, and the final evacuation of South Vietnam was under way.

The South Vietnam government, which had been backed by the United States, had fallen. The Vietnamese most closely associated with it were desperate to flee the country, as the American withdrawal would leave them defenceless against the advancing communist forces.

One side's defeat meant triumph for their opponents – the communists of North Vietnam and their supporters in the south. For the Viet Cong troops entering Saigon it was the end of a long struggle: after thirty years they had finally achieved the victory they had been fighting for. Lam Thi Phan was an intelligence officer with the Viet Cong. When the Americans left at last, she recalls, 'I was extremely happy. I had sacrificed my whole life up to that time for the revolution. The Americans had withdrawn – and we had victory.'

The conflict in Vietnam was one example of guerrilla warfare, movements by groups of armed rebels that became increasingly common during the twentieth century. In Vietnam a guerrilla force had undermined one of the most powerful armies in the world. Like fleas on a dog, guerrillas could sap the enemy's strength while their own agility made them too elusive to be confronted.

In many parts of the world guerrilla methods were used to fight for political revolution, national independence or religious freedom. They claimed that they were fighting for 'the people', and grass-roots support was always vital to their success. Mao Zedong, leader of the Chinese communist revolution, believed that guerrillas should 'move like fish in water' among the people. 'With the common people of the whole country mobilized,' he wrote, 'one can create a vast sea of humanity and drown the enemy in it.'

FLIGHT FROM DANGER *Desperate South Vietnamese families clamber aboard an American aircraft in Saigon.*

Revolution in Cuba

Twenty years before the evacuation of Vietnam, and on the other side of the world, a small group of revolutionaries provided a classic demonstration of how an apparently strong regime could be challenged by guerrillas who used the appropriate tactics.

In December 1956 a band of exiles set out from Mexico in a boat called the *Granma*. Their leader was a former lawyer, Fidel Castro, and his aim was to start a popular revolution in Cuba. Arsenio Garcia was among the rebel force that waded ashore on the Cuban coast in the early hours one morning. 'We always think of the arrival of the *Granma* as a shipwreck,' he remembers. 'The boat was grounded, though it didn't sink completely because the water was so shallow. From there we could reach the land through the roots of the mangrove swamp....If one thinks of all the time we spent training, our journey in the boat, getting out of this place and even the two years in the mountains, the landing here was still the most difficult task.'

MEN WITH A MISSION (BELOW) *Arsenio Garcia was among Fidel Castro's rebel army on the journey from Mexico to Cuba in the* Granma (BOTTOM). *It was a voyage beset with difficulties. 'The embarkation should have been with just fifteen people,' Arsenio Garcia remembers, 'but of course there were over eighty of us, along with all the guns and war equipment.' Overcrowded and in a leaky vessel, the tired rebels were easy prey for the Cuban troops when they reached the coast.*

As they clambered through the mangroves, the guerrillas knew the difficulty of their mission. There were just eighty-two of them, and they believed it was their mission to free six million Cubans from exploitation, poverty and repression. Most Cubans in the countryside worked in the sugar cane and tobacco fields of wealthy landowners. They were poorly paid, and were forced to live in crowded, squalid shacks on their landlord's property. There

VIOLENCE ERUPTS (RIGHT) *at Havana University after a presidential decree gives special privileges to the Americans and British. Many Cubans resented American economic and political influence, but fear of military reprisals meant that few people voiced their anger in public.*

were few schools, so many people had little or no education. In stark contrast the capital, Havana, which was only 144 km (90 miles) away from Florida, thronged with American tourists. They used Havana as a playground, pouring money into casinos and clubs, some of which were controlled by the American Mafia. Much of the money being skimmed from Havana's gambling and prostitution businesses was channelled to Cuba's military dictator, General Fulgencio Batista, who maintained his regime with an army of 46 000 men.

When Batista heard that the guerrillas had landed he rushed convoys of well-equipped troops to the eastern province, confident that they could outnumber the rebels and easily overwhelm them. They intercepted and attacked the guerrilla force, showing their captives little mercy. Most of the rebels were killed, but Castro and twenty-one of his men managed to escape. They fled into the most remote and wildest part of the country, the Sierra Maestra mountains. There, deep in the forests, they established a hideout and began the task of rebuilding their forces.

Sergio Fuentes helped to protect the guerrillas and supplied them with food and arms. Eventually he joined them. 'Everything about being a guerrilla was hard,' he remembers. 'We were usually barefoot and had few clothes. We couldn't wash and we had no luxuries like soap. There is no material benefit to be gained from being a guerrilla. It's exhausting and full of hardship.'

But the Cuban peasants were not put off by the privations and dangers. Many were inspired to join the guerrillas when they witnessed the savage reprisals meted out to the rebels by Batista's army. Even some of Batista's soldiers, sickened by the brutality that riddled the Cuban army, deserted to join the guerrillas.

Castro's tiny rebel force soon swelled into thousands. Other underground groups fighting against Batista banded together under his leadership. A strict code of conduct was enforced to ensure that the guerrillas maintained the people's support. 'You had to be respectful to the peasants and their families,' remembers Sergio Fuentes. 'You had to have discipline, and respect what wasn't yours.' Shop owners who were sympathetic gave food to the rebels. 'Sometimes we needed much more than they gave,' recalls Sergio Fuentes. 'So we'd take everything without leaving

"Batista's army were assassinating the rebels as if they were animals. That's what motivated me. I decided that I was not going to kill them. I was going to help them."

SERGIO FUENTES

CUBAN PEASANTS *flock to join the rebel army, inspired by Fidel Castro (centre) and undaunted by the privations of guerrilla life. At first they were hindered by the shortage of arms, but once local sympathy was tapped the movement quickly grew into a force sufficiently powerful to challenge General Batista's army.*

"It was a joyful moment when they said Batista had left. This was real satisfaction for us. We all hugged each other. We toasted each other."

SELESTINO SANCHEZ SANTO

any money, but we'd leave a note. When we got money we would pay them back.' Dishonesty was severely punished. When one of the guerrillas stole for himself, Sergio Fuentes judged him and condemned him to death, even though they were related. 'I was defending the honour of the guerrillas,' he explains. 'This man was creating an atmosphere that undermined confidence in us.'

The young Fidel Castro was an inspiring leader. 'He gave the impression that he was always looking after your needs,' recalls Sergio Fuentes. 'The guerrillas had nothing. Their families needed money and we always tried to send some to them....Fidel tried to help people. That's why we see him, and why we will always see him, as our leader. People who fought with Fidel were prepared to die with Fidel.'

At first the guerrillas were desperately short of weapons. In small, remote clearings camouflaged by jungle foliage they set up workshops to manufacture crude mines and grenades; the weapons were as unreliable as they were makeshift. The rebels depended on the peasants to supply arms. Celestino Sanchez Santo was eager to support Castro. 'He was here to liberate Cuba from the terrible dictator, Batista. That's why we started fighting....We began by looking for arms. We had to go to people who owned land and ask if they would cooperate. We had to try to convince them they should give us weapons.' Women were also important. 'They would tell us this person's got a gun, or that person's got a gun. So that's how, very quietly, we started going to these places....We didn't get anything by force. It was more that we just had to convince people – and that's how we worked.'

JUBILANT CROWDS *in Havana, greeting the triumphant rebel army in 1959, listen to Castro's promises for a fairer and more prosperous Cuba. After his victory Castro gained massive popular support by executing Batista's supporters and instituting radical land reforms.*

One of Castro's most powerful weapons was the mimeograph. It was used to print thousands of propaganda leaflets, circulated throughout Cuba despite efforts by the secret police to stamp out the underground movement. In the cities Castro gained the support of many people, some of whom organized a series of sabotage and bombing campaigns against Batista's forces. These provoked such savage reprisals that local support for Batista diminished further. Gradually the guerrillas controlled more and more of the country, until by the end of 1958 they were fighting on the outskirts of Havana itself. The United States, having initially backed Batista's regime, withdrew its support and General Batista fled from Cuba.

In January 1959 excited crowds lined the streets of Havana to welcome the victorious Fidel Castro and his army into the city. 'We had achieved our aim, our dreams, our triumph,' Arsenio Garcia recalls happily. Fidel Castro was at first to establish a new government that enjoyed mass support from the Cuban people.

Revolutionary fervour spreads

The Cubans had made revolution look surprisingly easy. They had challenged and overturned an oppressive regime in less than two years. The victory achieved by the insurgents, the charisma of their leaders and Cuba's proximity to the United States meant that they had an enormous impact. In Central and South America and also in Europe other revolutionaries, inspired by their example, were encouraged to attempt the same feat, and a number of new guerrilla movements sprang into action.

Some guerrillas tried to adapt guerrilla tactics to the cities, merging into the urban workforce and using this cover to rock the streets with car bombs and stage kidnappings, hijackings and bank raids. Many of these rebels were well educated and from privileged backgrounds. This sometimes distanced them from the very people they believed they were fighting for, and made it difficult for them to gain mass support.

In Argentina from 1974 an urban guerrilla group known as the Montoneros fought a campaign against the radical dictator Juan Perón. Hernan (surname withheld) was an Argentinian who joined the Montoneros. 'We thought we could build a better country,' he recalls. 'It seemed the only way of actually breaking down a government we considered unjust....The great schemes were to nationalize the production and also to socialize great areas of the country. But they were very vague ideas. What we wanted was to end the hunger. We wanted to end the poverty.'

Some of the Montoneros were inspired by events in Cuba. 'The Cuban example was always there for us,' recalls Hernan. 'I

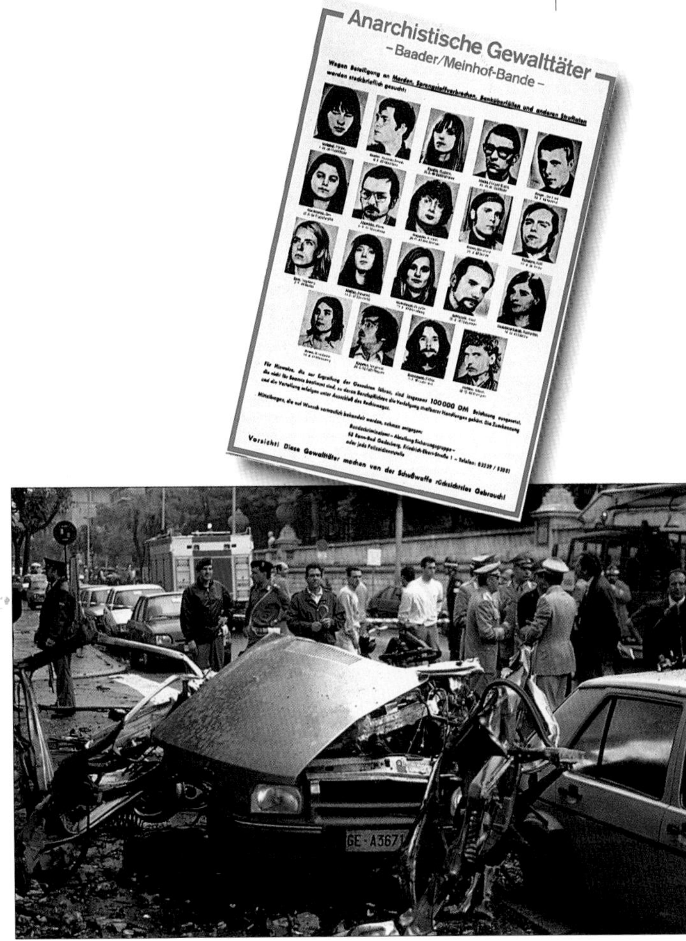

Hitting the headlines *The dramatic acts of violence by terrorist organizations such as West Germany's Baader-Meinhof Gang, also known as the Red Army Faction* (TOP), *and Italy's Red Brigades* (ABOVE) *publicized their cause and attempted to undermine state authority. Attacks in urban areas had the greatest impact, as more people were affected and public outrage ensured that their governments could not ignore the terrorists' demands.*

> *"Che Guevara was like Christ. He had a doctrine and he upheld it all his life. He sacrificed himself....He died for the poor."*
>
> Arsenio Garcia

believe it was the mother of all the revolutions in Latin America.... And the figure of Che Guevara influenced everyone. He was an example of somebody who was untouchable.'

The Montoneros followed traditional guerrilla tactics. 'Our strategy was not to have large battles, but to have small, precise hits at the establishment to wear away the enemy,' remembers Hernan. 'Then we hoped to increase the amount of propaganda so that the working-class people, for whom we were doing this, would begin to take notice and make decisions for themselves.'

Despite the dedication and courage shown by the guerrillas, they failed to win the support of the population. Many people were bewildered by them. Claudia Avila, who lived in the same block of flats as a general whom the Montoneros tried to assassinate (instead, they mistakenly killed his daughter) remembers the public confusion about the rebels' cause. 'I didn't know who the Montoneros were. I didn't know why they were killing people. The press said they were fighting for the workers. But nobody knew exactly why or what for.'

Ernesto Bareira was a member of the Argentinian military intelligence who attempted to infiltrate the guerrilla force. 'The Montoneros were a group of very intelligent, well-prepared men,' he recalls. 'They were of good social origin, and with a good education...but they should have operated with more depth and a political objective, not just with political theory....It was rather a romantic attitude,' he believes, and doomed to failure.

In an attempt to redistribute wealth, the Montoneros gave money to the poor in the cities, particularly in the capital, Buenos Aires. Yet there was no popular uprising in their defence when the army was ordered to annihilate the Montoneros in 1975. 'Most of the population did not help the Montoneros,' remembers Hernan. 'When the most violent time came the Montoneros themselves couldn't put up enough resistance, and the masses didn't back them. That is why revolution failed in Argentina.'

The failure of the guerrillas to bring about revolution in Argentina was echoed elsewhere in South America, as governments – often supported by the United States – learned how to crack down on insurgents, not all of whom were able to gain the allegiance of the very people they believed they were fighting for.

The face *of Che Guevara* (opposite) *on millions of posters, banners and T-shirts became a symbol for a whole generation of radicals who were inspired by his belief that individuals had a crucial part to play in bringing about world revolution.*

Che Guevara

One member of the intrepid band of revolutionaries who clambered through the mangrove swamps in eastern Cuba in December 1956 was a fervent young Argentinian, Ernesto (nicknamed Che) Guevara. The son of an architect, and himself a qualified doctor, Che Guevara had spent many years travelling through Central and South America observing the wretched way of life endured by millions of urban slum-dwellers and rural labourers. Concerned about the social injustice he encountered, and shocked by the United States-backed invasion of Guatemala in 1954, Che Guevara became a passionate and committed revolutionary.

In Mexico Guevara met Fidel Castro, and joined his group of rebel Cubans. He became a close adviser to Castro, and after the revolution's victory was given the powerful post of president of the Cuban National Bank. In 1961 he became minister of industry, but his main preoccupation was still to attempt to set down the ideas and tactics of the Cuban revolution, and to propagate revolution in the rest of Central and South America.

In 1965 Guevara resigned from his comfortable position in government, and set off to lead a revolution among the poor peasants and tin-miners of the Bolivian Andes. Within weeks he was betrayed, ambushed and shot dead by the Bolivian army, with secret United States' backing.

With Guevara's death came immortality. Newspapers around the world carried photographs of him lying on a stretcher, and gave graphic accounts of his mission and his fate. The image of sacrifice for a revolutionary cause caught the imagination of rebels and protesters all over the world. Among them Che Guevara was elevated at that time to the status of a martyr, and he began to exert an influence far greater than it had ever been during his lifetime.

The struggle in Vietnam

In Asia, where 'people's wars' had been far more successful, Mao Zedong's revolution in China had inspired political activists who wanted to try and loosen the grip of colonial rulers or bring down regimes they opposed. It was in Vietnam that the longest, most bitter struggle took place. It engulfed the country for thirty years.

Since the nineteenth century Vietnam had been part of the French empire. After the Second World War the Viet Minh, a communist-led guerrilla movement named after its leader, Ho Chi Minh, launched a revolutionary war against the French, eventually defeating them in 1954. At an international conference it was decided that Vietnam should be formally divided into two states: North Vietnam, led by the communist Viet Minh and supported by the Soviet Union and China; and South Vietnam, which was committed to Western-style capitalism and backed by the United States. The communists declared that the anti-communist South Vietnamese government was just a puppet regime, and pledged to overthrow it by the same means as those they had used against the French. By 1960 at least 5000 communist guerrillas, known as the Viet Cong, had infiltrated into South Vietnam and were fighting against its government.

DRINKING PARTNERS (ABOVE) *In apparent harmony a young Vietnamese boy and an American marine take a break from building a bunker to drink Coke. Most American soldiers believed they were helping to protect the local people, but many of the Vietnamese regarded them more as enemies than as allies.*

For the next twenty years a fierce battle was waged for the hearts and minds of the people of South Vietnam. It was at its most savage in the heavily populated Mekong delta. The government tried to convince the peasants that they should trust the rulers in the capital, Saigon, but the guerrillas told them that only revolution would release them from their poverty and oppression. Many peasant farmers worked in the fields during the day and fought for the Viet Cong at night. Among them was Phan Dinh. 'I followed the Viet Cong because the revolution promised to give

LESSONS OF THE PAST *A veteran militiaman* (LEFT) *shares his experience, gained resisting the French, with fighters of a Viet Cong unit. Both forces successfully used guerrilla tactics, enabling them to defeat opponents far better equipped, financed and trained than themselves.*

us land, rice and clothes,' he declares. 'We were very poor.'

In Phan Dinh's village government forces, known as the ARVN (Army of the Republic of Vietnam), set up a security post to keep a lookout for rebels. The Viet Cong, desperately short of weapons, used trickery to capture the post. 'The soldiers' families all lived in the village,' remembers Phan Dinh. 'We told them they had a duty to call on their fathers, husbands and sons to leave the government post and to come home – and that if the soldiers refused, we would kill them. And we encouraged the villagers to demonstrate....The soldiers gave up. They just handed over their rifles and marched out of the post.'

Thousands of local officials loyal to Saigon were murdered by the Viet Cong, and by 1963 the Saigon government feared it was losing the battle for its own survival. The United States sent 12 000 military and political advisers to stiffen its resistance. Earl Young was one of them. 'We were part of the Kennedy generation,' he says. 'We were prepared to do anything to save South Vietnam from being taken over by the communists.'

Towering over village life (above) *Government security posts were erected to guard against Viet Cong activity. Built to protect the local people, the watch towers were often regarded with suspicion and resentment by the villagers, who frequently collaborated with the Viet Cong to sabotage them.*

The Saigon government soon realized that the guerrillas were heavily dependent on local support, so they decided to move many of the villagers to new settlements. Thousands of peasants, regardless of their age or health, were forced to abandon their homes, gather up their possessions and embark on a long trek to new districts. On arrival they were organized into groups and given the strenuous task of building new communities, under the close scrutiny of Vietnamese officials and American advisers. The new villages were known as 'strategic hamlets', and were designed to be impenetrable by the Viet Cong. 'We provided the barbed wire,' remembers Earl Young. 'We provided the fence posts. We

American advisers *working with government forces. Their attempts to encourage peasant farmers to defend their land against the communist rebels failed. 'They moved the people away from their own land into these hamlets,' recalls Earl Young* (top), *'but it was like the Trojan Horse, because they also brought the Viet Cong infrastructure inside the hamlets.'*

provided training. There was to be a medical technician in every hamlet. It was our belief – if you will, our naivety – that the people would be so thankful for the new school and medical personnel, the drugs and the food, that they would support the Saigon government and cut off their allegiance to the Viet Cong.'

It did not work. The villagers, who felt they had lost their freedom, resented the enforced membership of the militia and the time required to train. Some of them, like Chau Van Nhat, fought in the militia one day and for the Viet Cong the next. 'When I was in the militia I would have one night on duty and then the next night off,' he recalls. 'When I was off duty, I'd contact the guerrillas....I helped them creep into the hamlet undetected.'

New weapons for old (above) *Viet Cong guerrillas dismantle a dud American bomb. They would use its parts to make their own weapons.*

Children help *to make simple but lethal weapons for Viet Cong supporters using traditional local skills. These young boys are preparing a booby trap that would be strung up in the trees above a narrow pathway, and triggered to drop down on an approaching enemy.*

To many people in the West, aware that communist regimes had taken over in Eastern Europe after the Second World War, the conflict in Vietnam seemed more than just a local issue: the whole balance of power in the Cold War world was at stake, and they believed they had a duty to intervene to stem the further advance of communism. In August 1964 the Americans claimed that two of their destroyers had been attacked in the Gulf of Tonkin by North Vietnamese torpedo boats. This incident, and the Soviet Union's increasing involvement with North Vietnam, fired the United States into battle. In April 1965 President Lyndon Johnson ordered US combat troops into South Vietnam. At the height of the fighting they would number 600 000.

The Viet Cong now faced the armed power of the most technologically advanced nation in the world. The Americans and the ARVN set out to defeat the guerrillas using conventional combat methods: mobilizing huge numbers of troops in large groups equipped with heavy weapons, tanks and helicopters, and supported by the world's most powerful bombers, B-52s. But the Viet Cong used hit-and-run tactics, proving too elusive for the Americans to confront and eliminate.

Although short of weapons, the Viet Cong were ingenious in converting the scrap and debris of superpower arms into simple, lethal contraptions such as grenades and mines. They also used natural materials to make traditional fighting weapons. Whole communities were involved in equipping the guerrillas. At the age of eight, Nguyen Thi Be helped to sharpen stakes. 'I'd follow my

mother around and help her with her work,' she remembers. 'I also helped other people by bringing the bamboo sticks to where the traps were being made. The soldiers would often fall into them when they went on patrol.' Poison or excrement was sometimes smeared on the stakes to make wounds turn septic.

Trained to fight a different sort of war, the Americans were living on their nerves. 'The impact on the soldier was psychological,' recalls US army colonel David Hackworth. 'Every time you put your foot down, you didn't know whether you were going to lose a limb or your life. And this was played out for three hundred and sixty-five days going down trails, going down waterways – it took the fight out of you....I took over a battalion down in the delta. It was called the Hard Luck Battalion. In the six months before I took over it had six hundred casualties, all from mines and booby traps. It had never met the enemy.'

South Vietnamese troops *were weighed down with American weapons and trained in conventional Western fighting tactics. They were ill equipped to challenge the speed and agility of the Viet Cong. Most recruits were posted far from their home villages, and desertion rates were high. Between 1954 and 1975 some 200 000 ARVN soldiers were killed.*

Tran Thi Gung *fought with the Viet Cong for many years, living rough in the jungle. 'There were lots of dangers. There were many different kinds of snakes and deadly black ants.... When we were moving through the jungle we had to tie our legs with rubber bands, so that if snakes bit us the poison wouldn't penetrate far into our bodies. The temperature sometimes went up as high as forty-one degrees.'*

Tunnelling for refuge (left) *The Viet Cong dug tunnels to escape enemy troops, but the Americans often pursued them under ground. 'When they got into the entrance we threw grenades or shot at them,' remembers Tran Thi Gung. 'Then we would withdraw to another level.'*

Frustrated American troops (opposite) *try to launch an offensive against the Viet Cong, but are forced into defensive positions against their unseen enemy. Only when the American forces themselves adopted guerrilla tactics did they achieve any measure of success.*

Frustrated in their attempts to confront their opponents, the Americans tried to deprive the Viet Cong of refuge. Entire villages were destroyed and forests decimated. Hundreds of thousands of tonnes of napalm, high explosives, Agent Orange defoliant and phosphorus bombs were dropped. The scale of destruction made it difficult for the peasants to believe that the Americans were really liberating their country. More firepower was ultimately unleashed against the Vietnamese than had been used in all earlier wars put together, and more than a million civilians were killed.

To avoid the shelling and bombing the guerrillas went under ground. They dug a network of tunnels, which they constantly extended. Tran Thi Gung replaced her father in the Viet Cong forces when he was killed; she spent weeks hiding under ground. 'Moving through the tunnels was like crawling in hell,' she recalls. 'You went down and down. When we got really hungry we ate a little dry rice and drank a little water....It was particularly difficult for us girls. We had a lot of problems with hygiene in general because women's ways are different. For men, five days without bathing was fine, but it made us feel uncomfortable, like dirty dogs.' American patrols tried hard to find the tunnel systems and destroy them, but the entrances were well hidden and the tunnel network complex; when tunnels were found, many Americans were simply too large to get into them.

While much of the countryside was in Viet Cong hands, the capital remained the government's stronghold. But the Viet Cong were infiltrating the towns, and many families were split by the same ideological divide that cut across the country. Lam Van Phat had risen to become a general in the South Vietnamese army; his sister, Lam Thi Phan, was a communist. While she was staying with her brother in Saigon she took advantage of his position to pass information to the Viet Cong. 'If I had used my brother for personal gain, then it would have been wrong,' she declares. 'But as I used him for the benefit of the country, for the people, I was right. I am proud of what I did.' Suspecting her, Lam Van Phat reported his sister to the authorities. 'To inform on her like that tore me to pieces inside,' he recalls sadly. 'My heart was in pain because I had betrayed my sister....I was at fault with my family, but the nation's concern came before family.'

Closing the doors of Cambodia

Guerrilla movements conducted in the name of the people sometimes had appalling consequences. Cambodia, like Laos and Vietnam, was a French colony until 1953, but independence failed to bring peace to this troubled region. The Cambodian leader, Norodom Sihanouk, was overthrown in 1970 and replaced by the pro-American military government of the Khmer Republic.

A communist guerrilla force, the Khmer Rouge, led by a group of French-educated revolutionaries, seized its opportunity. Already backed by China, they now allied themselves with Sihanouk, against whom they had rebelled in the 1960s, and launched a guerrilla war against the government. The United States invaded Cambodia in an attempt to suppress the Khmer Rouge forces. Nearly 100 000 people were killed in the fighting, which lasted for five years; millions more became refugees. In April 1975 the government collapsed. The Khmer Rouge quickly occupied the capital, Phnom Penh, and took control of Cambodia in 1976, placing Sihanouk under house arrest.

In the renamed Democratic Republic of Kampuchea the Khmer Rouge leader, Pol Pot, launched an idealistic revolutionary programme to establish a self-sufficient agricultural economy based on collectivization of the countryside. Millions of people were forced out of the towns and cities into rural areas to dig canals and toil in the paddy fields. Everyone, regardless of their particular professional skills or lack of farming experience, had to work on the land to further the agricultural ideal.

As contact with the outside world was cut off, the borders were closed. Foreigners were moved out. Money was banned and the postal system abolished. People were victimized and in many cases executed if they were well educated or bore even slight signs of what the Khmer Rouge condemned as Western influence. Any opposition was crushed. The reign of terror was characterized by mass murders and purges in which more than a million people were killed or died from hunger, illness or sheer exhaustion.

Relations with neighbouring Vietnam, which had already been marred by territorial disputes, grew worse in 1978. Border clashes culminated in a full-scale Vietnamese invasion of Cambodia, which succeeded in toppling the Khmer Rouge. Pol Pot fled, and people began the huge task of rebuilding their country under another new regime.

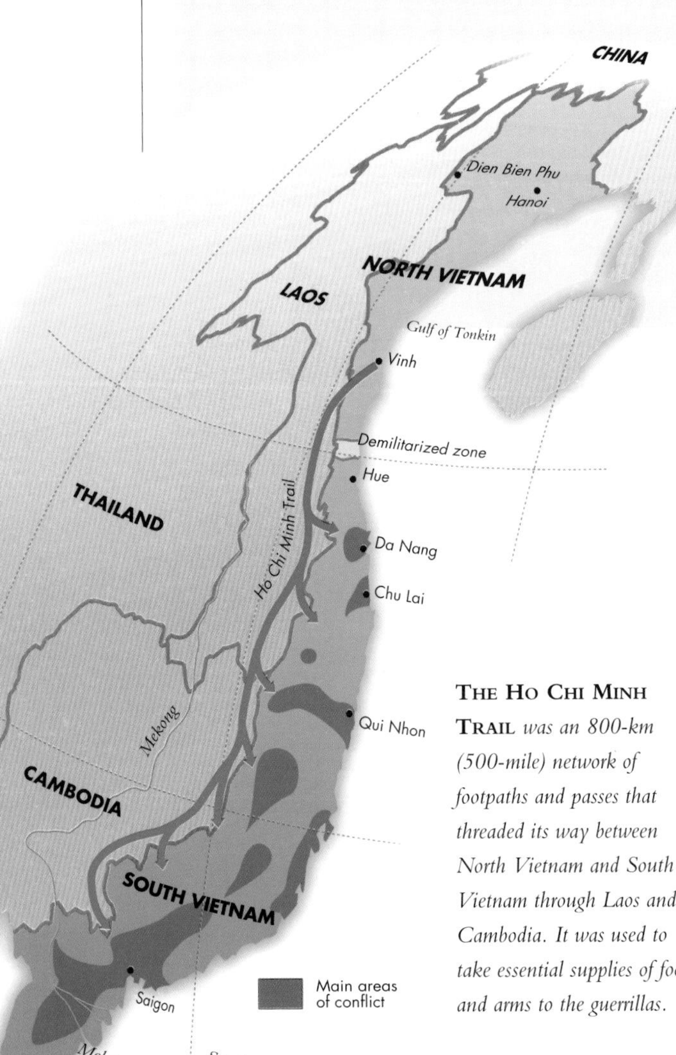

The Ho Chi Minh Trail *was an 800-km (500-mile) network of footpaths and passes that threaded its way between North Vietnam and South Vietnam through Laos and Cambodia. It was used to take essential supplies of food and arms to the guerrillas.*

Lam Thi Phan was captured and, like thousands of others, faced brutal interrogation. 'When they questioned me they attached electric wire to my ears, around my breasts, my feet and even in my vagina. Then they turned the power on so high I thought I was going to die. While the current was running they poured detergent into my mouth. My stomach swelled up and they kicked my stomach until I vomited.' Lam Thi Phan still suffers from the effects of the torture.

In January 1968 the Viet Cong believed they were strong enough to take the fight into the towns. Many soldiers in the South Vietnamese army were celebrating the new year Tet festival when the guerrillas launched a coordinated attack on cities all over the country. In Saigon the Viet Cong invaded the American embassy. Although United States troops and the South Vietnamese army quickly regained control, the attacks had a dramatic effect on American public opinion. Earl Young was back in Washington. 'I thought this was a total disaster, as psychologically the American people were already very uneasy about the course of the war. And when they saw this apparent victory of the communist forces, able to enter every one of the provincial capitals...the American people said, "With all the American troops there, everything we've done in South Vietnam, if we cannot prevent the American embassy from being captured, my God, what are we there for?" '

Television pictures of the savage reprisals inflicted by the ARVN shocked viewers across the world. As the number of American soldiers killed continued to rise – the total was 57 000 – the will to carry on fighting was eroded, and pressure to withdraw grew. In the United States the campaign to end the war intensified until President Richard Nixon signed an agreement with the North Vietnamese government in Paris in 1973, instigating the withdrawal of all American troops from Vietnam.

Triumphant communist forces entered Saigon in 1975. They had shown how a tenacious guerrilla force, with the help of local people and outside support, could defy a great superpower.

FRIGHTENED CHILDREN (ABOVE) *flee the napalm bombing of their village, their plight recorded by news photographers. This attack by South Vietnamese forces was said to be a mistake – it was claimed that their real target was a neighbouring village dominated by the Viet Cong.*

SMILING IN VICTORY (BELOW) *After nearly thirty years of war, Viet Cong troops pose triumphantly in the streets of Saigon, soon to be renamed Ho Chi Minh City. Tran Bach Dan, a leader of the Viet Cong there, had always believed the guerrillas would win: 'They were supported by the people around them, who took care of them, guided and protected them.... They also knew what they were fighting for.'*

Urban guerrillas in Northern Ireland

Violent conflict among the people of Ireland could be traced back over centuries, but the emergence of powerful, highly organized urban guerrilla groups was a twentieth-century phenomenon. A low-intensity civil war had festered ever since the Act of Union in 1801 made Ireland part of the United Kingdom. Its ferocity increased during the twentieth century, as opposing guerrilla factions resorted to terrorism and violence.

Religion was always a fundamental division among the Irish people. The majority of them were formally Roman Catholic, but a powerful minority of Protestants, descendants of English and Scottish emigrants, lived in northern Ireland, particularly in the province of Ulster. Early in the century Irish resentment of Britain's sovereignty and their desire for home rule culminated in the unsuccessful Easter Rising of 1916 in Dublin. Protestants in Ulster were already determined to oppose any severance from Britain, and pledged to fight it with force if necessary.

In 1922 the independent Irish Republic was formed; six of the nine counties of Ulster remained united with Britain. Northern Ireland's prosperity outstripped that in the south, but discrimination against the minority Catholic community in employment, housing and other areas caused much resentment and conflict.

Many civilians in Northern Ireland, including some Protestants, campaigned for equal civil rights in Northern Ireland. When violence erupted in 1969 British troops were sent in; they were to experience at first hand how difficult it was for a modern army to fight anonymous guerrillas who had merged into the community.

The soldiers' original task was to protect Catholics against Protestant aggression, but they soon became the focus of extreme Catholic resentment. The Provisional Irish Republican Army (IRA) and the more radical Irish National Liberation Army (INLA) embarked on a campaign of bombing and shooting attacks on British soldiers and security forces, both in Northern Ireland and on the British mainland. Frustrated by British policy, they aimed to bring their cause to international attention by targeting important members of the British establishment – in 1979 Earl Mountbatten was murdered, and in 1984 the IRA came close to killing the prime minister, Margaret Thatcher.

Many Roman Catholics in Northern Ireland claimed to be Irish nationalists, but only a minority supported Sinn Féin, the political party linked to the IRA. In the Irish Republic Sinn Féin was supported by less than 5 per cent of the electorate. The IRA did receive outside support and funding, much of which came from Irish sympathizers in the United States.

For twenty-five years thousands of British soldiers on duty in Northern Ireland patrolled without ever quite knowing who the enemy was, and in fear of ambush, booby traps and sniper attacks. Terror was returned with equal ferocity by extreme Protestant guerrilla groups, who murdered hundreds of IRA and INLA members and other Roman Catholics. Altogether some 3200 people were killed during 'the Troubles', including 2224 civilians.

Late in 1994 tentative overtures were made between the opposing factions, and a slow, precarious peace process was begun.

Burning resentment *flared into violence in 1969. The suspension of the Stormont (Northern Irish parliament) in 1972 and imposition of direct British rule increased tension and bitterness on both sides.*

Holy war in Afghanistan

Victory in Vietnam had come from a union of communism and nationalism. Conservative guerrillas could use the same tactics with equal success if they too had enough popular support. The clearest demonstration of this came in Afghanistan in the 1980s.

The fifteen million Afghan people had fierce tribal loyalties and were devout followers of Islam; most of them lived in the countryside in a very traditional society. In 1978 the communists seized power in the capital, Kabul, killing the former president. The new communist government was ruthless in its efforts to eliminate potential rivals: all non-communists in positions of authority came under threat, and thousands of religious leaders, teachers and political opponents were killed. The new regime attempted to impose some of the social and political reforms that had been welcomed in Cuba and Vietnam, including measures giving women equal status with men. But many people disliked the changes, which were forced on them with little sensitivity to their traditional beliefs and the customs that had evolved over hundreds of years.

Greeting the troops *Children in Kabul line up to welcome Soviet troops to the city. In reality the majority of Afghans deeply resented the Soviet presence.*

After a popular uprising against the communist government in 1979, the Soviet Union sent in its own troops to support its client Afghan government. The soldiers were said to be there to help defend socialism; soon there were 100 000 Soviet troops in Afghanistan and, as the Americans had done in Vietnam, they greatly underestimated their enemy. To the Afghan guerrillas it was both a war against foreign intrusion and a holy war, fought to safeguard Islam against non-believers. They believed their cause to be worth every sacrifice and deprivation, and that to be killed defending it was an honour. They called themselves the Mujahideen (Soldiers of God). They continued to pray five times a day, and reverently kissed the Koran before going into battle.

Ahmed Shah Massoud was a leader of the Mujahideen, based in the remote scrublands of the Panjshir valley to the north of Kabul. He had read the teachings of Mao Zedong and Che

Guevara; their politics were anathema to him, but he was attracted to their tactics. 'Without mobilizing the people it was impossible to fight against Afghan communists or the Russians,' he recalls. 'We were, as they say, "like fish in water": when the people rally, the enemy doesn't have a chance. The communists were unbelievers and the Russians were invaders. Islam and the independence of Afghanistan were our main rallying cries.'

The people's weapon

The KALASHNIKOV was designed in the Soviet Union and sold or donated to guerrilla movements all over the world. Kalashnikov automatic rifles (AK-47s) were valued both for their power and because they were simple to use and easy to maintain.

The Russians thought that their advanced technology would make it easy for them to defeat the geographically divided and poorly armed Mujahideen. But their weapons and conventional military strategies proved too cumbersome against the agile rebel forces, who constantly outwitted them and always had the support of local people. Oleg Blotsky, a young Soviet infantry lieutenant sent on two missions to fight in Afghanistan, found this out for himself. 'The first time I went for six months. I thought I was doing what was morally correct....I was shocked by what I saw. The second time I knew what was going on in Afghanistan. The officials were lying. In reality we had no friends in Afghanistan.'

YOUNG MUSLIM REBELS (BELOW), *armed with old guns and sticks, prepare to take on the might of the Soviet Union. Ambushes* (OPPOSITE) *were one of the most effective strategies used by the guerrillas to weaken the Soviet troops, who were dependent on supplies of food, weapons and equipment transported by road.*

Both sides committed appalling atrocities. Oleg Blotsky recalls how the Afghan children loved fireworks. 'Once some Soviet soldiers replaced the rocket fuel with explosive and gave the firework to some children who were running around. At night the children gathered to watch this rocket launch. One of them pulled the string and that was it. No boy, and no others.' He remembers how Soviet soldiers feared capture by the Mujahideen, who were renowned for their brutal behaviour. 'One person could be raped repeatedly by up to thirty men, then their stomachs were cut open, their skin pulled off and they were placed, still alive, under the sun to allow flies to settle on them....The Russians hated the Afghans for their cruelty, though at the same time they admitted they were no less cruel during the war.'

Within a few years the guerrilla forces had gained control of most of the countryside, with the Russians governing from heavily armed camps and from the cities. But Mujahideen sympathizers, many of them women, infiltrated the cities. Madar Shawall, whose two sons had been killed by the government

IDENTITY CARDS (RIGHT) *belonging to Soviet soldiers captured by the Mujahideen. Fear of the guerrillas' brutality meant that many soldiers carried personal poison capsules and grenades – a quick death was preferable to torture.*

side, agreed to smuggle weapons across Kabul. 'Hidden under my clothes and tied to my body, I carried two kalashnikovs to my rendezvous....I was nervous because life is sweet and carrying guns in that way was terribly dangerous.' Later, Madar Shawall also relayed vital documents to the Mujahideen; when she was caught she was tortured for three months.

Afghan families (above) *trek through the mountains in search of safety. Up to a third of Afghanistan's people were forced to flee their villages, leaving behind possessions, livestock and land. Three-quarters of Afghanistan's villages were abandoned or destroyed during the war.*

The Soviet forces, like the Americans in Vietnam, tried to obliterate all refuge for the guerrillas. They pursued a scorched earth policy – bombing villages, attacking water wells and driving millions of people out of their homes. Regardless of their age or health, many civilians fled into the mountains for refuge, while others joined the flow of refugees trekking through the mountains to the Pakistan or Iranian frontiers. Altogether five million people were forced to flee.

Huge refugee camps filled with Afghans, and their hatred of the Soviets grew. In 1986 an eight-year-old boy described just one terrible catalogue of events: 'They shot my father with three bullets....My brother and his friend got very angry and fought with them. My brother jumped and grabbed one of the weapons. At this point more Russians came and my brother's fingers were

Mountain passes *on the frontier between Afghanistan and Pakistan provided a supply route for the guerrillas as well as an escape route for millions of refugees. Pakistan offered a safe haven for the guerrillas' families, and also provided a base for exiled Afghan political parties.*

Stone throwers of Gaza

When an Israeli taxi driver carelessly drove into a crowd of Palestinian labourers on 8 December 1987, a powder keg of resentment and humiliation exploded. Resistance to twenty years of occupation by Israeli forces had brought no progress towards independence for the Palestinian people. The death of four Palestinian labourers that day proved to be the last straw, and the entire Arab community in the West Bank and Gaza Strip was quickly galvanized into action. The Intifada was launched.

The Palestinians were committed to bringing about the destruction of the state of Israel, which had been established as a result of the partition of Palestine by the United Nations in 1947. The Israelis' determination that it should survive spurred them to victory in armed conflicts with their Arab neighbours in 1948, 1967 and 1973. After winning the Six-Day War in 1967, Israel had taken control of the West Bank and Gaza Strip; in these occupied territories they subsequently demanded high taxes from the Arab population, confiscated much of their land for Jewish settlers, and made it illegal to hold press conferences without special permission. Flying the Palestinian flag was also forbidden. Years of discrimination and the apparent indifference of the rest of the world to their plight led to the Palestinians taking increasingly violent action on their own behalf.

The Intifada – in Arabic meaning uprising or shaking off – was a mass uprising that involved men, women and children, young and old, in a spontaneous outburst against the occupying forces. Few firearms were used, but there were violent demonstrations, street fighting with petrol bombs broke out, and gangs of children became expert at hurling stones and outwitting Israeli troops. Women played a vital part, often at the forefront of the conflict but also in intelligence work, providing safe houses for the wanted and injured, distributing food in often perilous circumstances and organizing boycotts of Israeli goods.

Faced with the anger of an entire people, and determined to resist any threat to national security, Israeli troops responded in a way that shocked many of their own people as well as the outside world. In the first four years of the Intifada more than a thousand Palestinians, a quarter of them under sixteen years old, were killed by Israeli forces. The reprisals intensified the hatred, and strengthened Palestinian resistance.

In November 1988 Yasser Arafat, leader of the Palestine Liberation Organization (PLO), made the first tentative steps towards peace by finally accepting the existence of Israel. Yet the conflict continued until 1993, when renewed efforts to establish a peace process were achieved through patient Norwegian mediation. Despite these initiatives, there still seemed little likelihood of an independent Palestinian state – the goal for which the Intifada had been launched – being established.

Palestinian civilians and Israeli troops *congregate on each side of the crater made by a petrol bomb.*

cut off. They were cut off by a bayonet – so of course he was helpless. After all his fingers had been cut off they beat him. They shot him in one ear and the bullet came out the other.'

As in Vietnam, the guerrilla fighters were not self-sufficient. Money and support came both from other Muslim countries and from the United States. The path through the mountains from Pakistan was worn by the feet of heavily laden camels and mules in supply caravans bringing food and arms into Afghanistan for the guerrillas. In the final years of the conflict the animals carried the latest American Stinger missiles, designed to shoot down Soviet helicopters and other aircraft.

Brandishing their weapons (opposite), *the Mujahideen celebrate victory in Kabul. After eight years of war the guerrilla forces had fought the Soviets to a stalemate. Faced with the hostility of both Islamic and Western countries, and the opposition of its own fifty million Muslim inhabitants, the Soviet Union finally accepted defeat.*

The Soviet troops transported their own supplies through Afghanistan by road in convoys of trucks accompanied by armed escort vehicles. They frequently had to pass through remote mountain areas that offered ideal opportunities for ambush. Gul Hyder was among the Mujahideen operating in the mountains. 'Once we hit an armoured vehicle with a rocket,' he remembers. 'It went straight through the vehicle and sliced through the heads of the two soldiers inside....Of course, I enjoyed killing Russians because they were invaders. When we were blowing up their tanks and when they were dying, I was really happy.'

The bereaved parents *of a Soviet parachutist mourn their loss. The Soviet withdrawal was greeted with relief by Oleg Blotsky. 'It was clear to everyone that the war was meaningless and we all just wanted to leave....Everyone felt humiliated.'*

By 1989, 15 000 Russians had been killed and a further 35 000 wounded. In the end the tenacity of the Mujahideen and the growing economic and political crisis in the Soviet Union broke the resolve of the government in Moscow. The Soviet leader, Mikhail Gorbachev, finally ordered the withdrawal from Afghanistan. For the second time in fifteen years, the guerrilla tactics of a poorly armed people's army had defeated a superpower.

In all the guerrilla wars, bitterly fought and won at such cost, the fighting left a poignant legacy of grieving families, scarred landscapes and bitter political divisions that would last for many years. And victory alone was no guarantee that guerrilla fighters would rule their people any better than the enemies they had fought so fiercely to defeat.

1945 – 1991

11

God Fights Back

Religion on the Rise

On the evening of 31 January 1979 in a suburb of Paris, Hadi Gaffari was among a group preparing for a long-awaited journey home. 'At midnight, those who were to return to Tehran with the Imam started gathering in the courtyard,' he says. The following morning they boarded an Air France 747 jet. 'We were very happy to return to Iran. All of us had a common feeling....I noticed that the Imam was leaning his head against the window and he had his black cape around him,' Hadi Gaffari recalls. 'As the pilot announced that we had passed the Elburz mountains everybody exploded in tears... everybody started chanting, "*Allah ho Akbar!*" – "God is great!"'

The figure in black at the centre of all this activity was the Ayatollah Ruhollah Khomeini, revered elder leader of the Shia Muslim faith, who had been exiled from Iran for many years. Now he was returning, and three million people poured into the streets of Tehran to welcome him home. Shakoor Lotvi was among them: 'The crowd was so huge that people had no room. They climbed the trees, anywhere they could just to get a glance of the Imam.' Moshen Rafigdoost drove the Imam from the airport. He was so full of emotion that his hands were shaking as he gripped the steering wheel: 'People were sitting on the car, the car was moving and people were being dragged along by it....Those hours are the best memories of my life.'

Khomeini and his followers were intent on carrying out an Islamic revolution that would radically transform people's lives. Yet much more than the fate of Iran was at stake. Across much of the world, religion was on the rise as growing numbers of people began to question the ideas and values of the West, rejecting modernity and turning instead to the alternatives offered by their faith. With mass popular support, increasingly politicized religious movements would challenge established governments. After a century in which progress and modernization had been identified with science and with the rejection of religion, God, it was said, was fighting back.

Religious return *Iranian Muslims in the city of Qom surround the Ayatollah Khomeini's car to welcome him back.*

Old ways and new

By the beginning of the twentieth century most of the world's Muslims had come under the domination of Europeans: the British in India, Russians in central Asia, Dutch, French and Italians elsewhere. Reform movements had swept through the Islamic world, from west Africa to the Indian subcontinent by way of Egypt and the Arabian peninsula, but only the Ottoman empire survived as a great Islamic power – until it was dismembered after the First World War. In Turkey, its former heartland, Mustafa Kemal, better known as Atatürk, created a secular, modern nation modelled on the ways of the West. People who were accustomed to living in a traditional Islamic society now also had to conform to these Western ways. Atatürk abolished the power of the clergy, substituted civil for religious law, introduced changes to the education system, and replaced the Arabic script – essential for reading the Koran – with the Roman alphabet. Hats were to be worn instead of the traditional fez. 'There was a distinct difference between the old Istanbul, the old way of life, and the new way of life,' recalls Altemur Kilic, who witnessed many of these changes. 'People learnt a new script, and street signs changed, shop signs changed ....My mother, who had worn a scarf all her life, threw it away.'

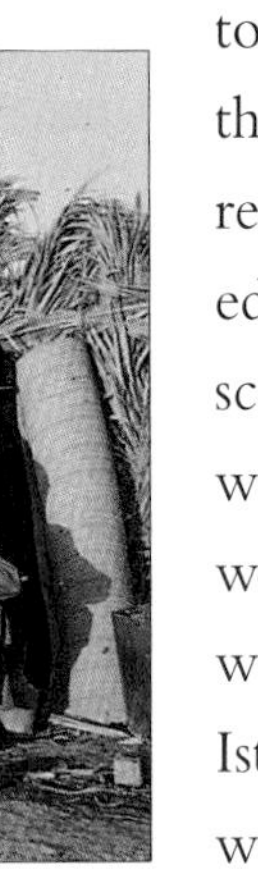

Grounds of discontent *Iran's oil industry was nationalized in 1951, bringing a rich new source of revenue, but many people, such as these refinery workers in Abadan living in makeshift huts, were unable to share in their country's new wealth.*

Similarly, Muslims in Iraq, Lebanon, Palestine, Syria and Trans-Jordan, now under British and French control, found their traditional way of life shaped by the culture of the West. Young people increasingly went to study not in the schools of Islam, but in the universities of the West. An Islamic state was established in Saudi Arabia, home of the holy centres of Mecca and Medina, but there too, the discovery of oil in 1938 was to bring with it many aspects of modern secular society. Britain's plans for the creation of a Jewish homeland in Palestine exacerbated Arab sentiment against Western interference, and strengthened Muslim unity and resolve for independence.

The tide began to turn after the Second World War as many Muslim nations asserted their independence. When British India

Deeds of reform (below) *A man proudly displays his land deeds, acquired under the shah's Land Refom Act of 1962. Land redistribution continued until 1971, benefiting millions of people but weakening the power of the Shiite Muslim clergymen from whom much of the land was taken.*

Codes of dress (left) *Following in Turkey's footsteps, the shah of Iran had decreed in 1928 that men were to wear Western clothes. Women were banned from wearing the veil in 1936. Moloud Khanlary had greeted the ruling with pleasure: 'We started singing songs and dancing.... Then we started kissing each other out of joy.' The policy was sometimes enforced by the police, but as the rules were relaxed in later years some women chose to return to traditional Islamic dress.*

was granted independence in 1947, Pakistan was established as a new Islamic state. In the 1950s first Egypt and then Iraq threw off their British or British-imposed masters. Independence movements were also succeeding in Indonesia, Malaya, and north and west Africa. But although Western power over these territories diminished, much of its influence remained, and many countries maintained economic and strategic links with the West. Several reformist leaders, determined to create modern, secular states, pursued Western-style policies rather than returning to traditional Islamic ways. Islam was even deliberately suppressed in certain countries, such as Syria and Tunisia. While many people enjoyed the new social freedoms that came with a secular society, there was resentment among devout Muslims, who were dismayed by the path their countries seemed to be following.

This was particularly true of Iran, where the former army officer and self-appointed shah, Reza Khan, had initiated a process of Western reform during the 1920s and 1930s. Secular laws were imposed in the courts, and Western curriculums in the schools. The process of modernization was continued by the shah's son, Muhammad Reza Pahlavi, who initiated an economic and social revolution in Iran during the 1960s.

Public parades *were held all over Iran in 1977 to mark the fourteenth anniversary of the shah's rule. The prime minister reviews the Health Corps, sent to work in poor and isolated Iranian villages to help eradicate disease.*

'When the shah started his programme Iran was a backward country,' remembers Daryoush Houmayoun, a journalist at the time of the shah's reforms. 'Land reform, granting voting rights to women, bringing women up to the level of men in our society, literacy drives, bringing new ideas and technology to the villages. Iran was being covered with new factories and public buildings. And everywhere the pace of change was frantic. Iran was really being transformed.' Trade links with Western countries meant that there were many foreigners in Iran; architects and construction engineers from many parts of the world converged on Tehran in search of contracts. There were bars, cinemas and discos. Mashid Amir-Shahy, who came from a secular background, remembers: 'We used to go to cafés, we used to enjoy ourselves, we gave parties and we went to parties. We drank if we wanted to,' she says. Iran's rich oil industry brought new wealth not only for industrial and military development but also for new luxuries: French wines, German cars, Italian fashions.

For a few, the boom brought new wealth. But the dollars did not trickle down to the peasants in the villages, or to the poor manual workers who had crowded into the cities and shantytowns in search of their share in the new prosperity. The life they found was not better than it had been in the countryside – it was often all but unbearable. Grasping landlords, indifferent employers and the police force seemed to be protected by a corrupt political elite whose members used their wealth to import Western luxuries, and who adopted Western attitudes. To many people, Western films, songs and advertising encouraged immorality and blasphemy. Confronted by what they saw, people turned back to the religion of their ancestors; it was to this poorer majority that the religious parties made their appeal.

Most of the population of Iran were Shiites, followers of the Shia branch of Islam. Firm believers in the justice and struggle of Islam, they denounced the Western influences that threatened their Islamic way of life and offended their religious nationalism. The widely respected cleric Ruhollah Khomeini had criticized the shah's father long before for abandoning the traditional ways of Islam, and now denounced the rule of his son. In anti-government sermons and publications, Khomeini and his followers among the

THE PATH OF ISLAM

MANY PEOPLE THROUGHOUT the Muslim world felt uncomfortable with the introduction of a secular way of life because it was in direct conflict with longstanding Islamic tradition. Changing social patterns threatened to prevent them living as true Muslims in a society shaped according to the precepts of the holy Koran – the sacred text held by all Muslims (whether of the Shia or the Sunni branch) to be the word of God.

The Koran lists five basic duties for all Muslims that form the pillars of Islam. They must accept submission to God and the role of the Prophet Muhammad as his messenger. They must undertake to pray five times each day, at the mosque or at home, facing in the direction of Mecca; children are taught to pray at the age of six or seven, and many Muslim countries provide prayer facilities in offices, factories and at airports. The third pillar calls for an annual payment of alms for the poor and needy, which is determined as a fixed percentage of personal wealth and assets. During the holy month of Ramadan fasting from dawn until dusk, which includes refraining from smoking, drinking and sexual activity, is also compulsory, though the Koran excuses the elderly, the ill, young children, menstruating women and travellers. In the fifth pillar, Muslims are required to make at least one pilgrimage to the holiest site of Islam, the Kaabah, at Mecca in Saudi Arabia.

In addition to these basic tenets, Islam has its own laws under the *sharia*, the 'straight path' of Islam. Islamic law calls on all Muslims to defend Islam from aggression. Punishments are specified: lashing for the consumption of alcohol, stoning for adultery, and amputation of hands or feet for theft, though these measures are seldom practised. As well as penal laws there are commercial laws guiding businesses, economic laws forbidding usury and the charging of bank interest, laws on gambling, inheritance, marriage, divorce and polygamy.

Family life is regarded as the basis of Islamic society, and although divorce is permitted, women must seek their husbands' consent and are liable to lose custody of their children. Islam does not exclude women from inheritance or property rights, though it does permit arranged marriages without their consent. Women are encouraged to wear the veil, and men as well as women are urged to dress modestly, according to the traditions of Islam. Islamic law also includes guidelines for eating and drinking, expressly forbidding the consumption of pork or alcohol, and ruling that livestock must be slaughtered according to traditional methods.

The application of Islamic law has varied widely in the Muslim world, and it often clashes with Western-inspired modern aspirations. Because of the Koran's sacred status, its principles and dictates have remained unchanged for 1300 years. Recited in the mosque and studied both privately and at school, it forms the bedrock of Islamic beliefs and way of life, and its doctrine continues to inspire Muslims throughout the world who wish to follow the true path of Islam.

GREAT PILGRIMAGE (LEFT) *Every year, about two million Muslims gather to worship at the great mosque in Mecca. All male pilgrims wear a simple white robe* (RIGHT), *symbolizing their equality before God.*

Party at Persepolis *In 1971 the shah held a party to celebrate 2500 years of monarchy. Five hundred guests were flown in from sixty-nine countries to the ruined city of Persepolis, capital of ancient Persia. They were housed in tents containing several rooms – including two bathrooms – drank the finest champagne from crystal goblets, and ate food flown in from Maxim's in Paris. The estimated cost of the event was $200 million. The celebrations caused great resentment among the Iranian people. 'I saw that billions of dollars needed by our poor country – with no water, no electricity, no hospitals, no roads – was being spent on ceremonies for kings,' says Hadi Gaffari.*

influential Islamic community and clergy began to stir people against the shah, who used his secret police, the Savak, to suppress any opposition. Khomeini's arrest in 1963 sparked a wave of protests. As the military were called in to restore order, many thousands of civilians were killed. The following year Khomeini was forced to flee the country.

Fuelled by widening social and economic disparities and government repression, the determination to root out what were seen as corrupt and decadent customs of the West became a constant theme in the revival of Islam. Abdul Shah Hosseini was clear about what he felt was needed: 'Cease relations with the oppressive Western regimes, discontinue the flow of capital from this country to the outside, rid the country of American military personnel. We wanted no alcohol, no corruption among the young people.' A new, strongly political Islamic consciousness was taking shape. 'The shah's programme for modernization turned into an issue against Islam,' says Ebrahim Yazdi, who supported Khomeini. 'They thought that in order to succeed in modernization, they must combat Islamic resurgence. In turn, Islamic resurgence became a way to resist the oppression of the shah.'

> *"What was so difficult for people was the lack of democracy. Pressure was being imposed on them by the government. This laid the groundwork for establishing Islamic rule as a better hope for the people."*
>
> Said Gonabadi

Calling for revolution

Despite being in exile, Khomeini, who had attained the status of an ayatollah – a religious leader of the highest rank – still had a considerable following among Iran's Muslim population. He had established a base across the border in neighbouring Iraq, in the holy city of Najaf, from where he worked to gather momentum against the shah. 'We had a great goal,' remembers Hadi Gaffari. 'It was to liberate Iran from a regime that was associated with foreigners.... We believed we must be independent, and independence meant we must struggle against the shah's regime. The best way to make the masses aware was to revolt against the shah. Religion and politics are the same thing.'

As Islam became more overtly political, so too did the local mosques where people gathered to pray. The mullah Hadi Gaffari translated Khomeini's words into political action. 'Young people and intellectuals came to the mosque, and it would turn into an ideological meeting, and this would be recorded,' he recalls. 'The courtyard and all the alleys leading to the mosque would be full of people. Some of them would bring pieces of carpet to sit on, and people would bring tape recorders, and it was rumoured in Tehran that the mosque of Hadi Gaffari had recordings of Khomeini's speeches.' Shakoor Lotvi distributed revolutionary leaflets. 'Anywhere we felt these bulletins and leaflets had not reached we would put them up – on the walls of the mosques, at bazaars, in shops and alleys.'

These activities could prove dangerous, but the mosques offered a kind of sanctuary. 'As a result of the brutality of the Savak, practically all the political parties were paralysed,' says Ebrahim Yazdi. 'However, the mosque was

DEMONSTRATIONS OF ANGER *continued throughout the 1970s. Inspired by Khomeini's leadership, people persisted in stirring unrest and openly displaying their resentment towards the shah's government* (ABOVE), *despite the potential dangers they faced from his secret police. Images of the shah and his queen* (BELOW) *are set alight and paraded through the streets.*

"At that time we had no liberties, everything was at the disposal of the government.... We can say that with our revolution we brought the rule of people over people."

MOSHEN RAFIGDOOST

still alive.' Hadi Gaffari sometimes disguised himself as a woman in a *chador*, a cloak covering the body from head to foot. Soroor Moradi Nazari also took precautions. 'If there were even books about Imam Khomeini in our house we would be arrested by the Savak and tortured. I hid pictures inside the kitchen cabinet door.'

In 1977 people began to show their support for Khomeini more openly. 'Religious students took part in the demonstrations, and they started a systematic burning of government buildings,' remembers Daryoush Houmayoun. 'Khomeini became the focus of all the opposition groups. They turned to him more and more.' Not all Iranians supported the campaign. Many educated, liberal families who had welcomed the shah's reforms were alarmed by the Islamic movement for change. When Moloud Khanlary encountered thousands of veiled women marching in one demonstration she could not prevent herself crying. 'I thought of the catastrophe that was falling upon my country,' she recalls. 'If the day of unveiling was a day of joy and happiness, that day was for me a day of mourning and misery.'

BULDINGS ABLAZE *People gather at the site of a cinema that has been set alight by Muslims in the town of Tabriz in northwest Iran after weeks of rioting in February 1978. Many buildings throughout Iran were destroyed as anti-government demonstrations escalated.*

The following year, at the end of Ramadan, the Muslim month of fasting, Khomeini was able to turn the protests into a mass movement. On 8 September 1978 a great crowd of three-quarters of a million people made its way towards the centre of Tehran. 'As we began going towards the city,' Hadi Gaffari describes, 'the people standing in doorways joined the crowd. It was the end of summer, above thirty degrees centigrade, and people were spraying water from their houses to cool down the demonstrators, and distributed refreshments and food.' As the crowd drew nearer they were confronted by soldiers. People tried to appease them with flowers, but their attempts failed. The shah ordered his troops to fire on a crowd of demonstrators in Jalah Square, close to Shakoor Lotvi's home. More than a hundred people were killed. 'As I reached the edge of the square, near the

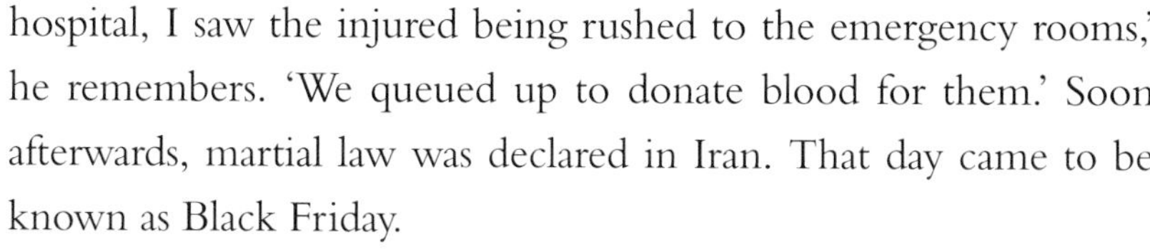

hospital, I saw the injured being rushed to the emergency rooms,' he remembers. 'We queued up to donate blood for them.' Soon afterwards, martial law was declared in Iran. That day came to be known as Black Friday.

The following month, Khomeini was forced to leave his Iraqi sanctuary. This time he chose Europe as his refuge. Paris might be one of the centres of the alien culture of the West, but there he would have access to the Western media. Khomeini settled in a villa in the suburb of Neauphle-le-Château, while mullahs such as Hadi Gaffari travelled between Paris and Tehran. Others used the telephone connections between the two cities. 'When Khomeini had a message,' describes Ebrahim Yazdi, 'there were people in Paris in charge of reading his message down the telephone to people in Iran. There were more people in Tehran and in the provinces receiving that message – recording it, then transcribing it, publishing it and distributing it to people in the mosques through the various mullahs.'

As the street demonstrations in Iran continued, thousands of people were killed. 'They were using tear gas and bullets without any consideration for women or children,' remembers Shakoor Lotvi. 'Our streets were battlefronts in those days....We thought that the shedding of our blood would help the fruitfulness of the revolution.' Twelve-year-old Said Sharifi Manesh enthusiastically

Day of reckoning (top left) *On 8 September 1978 clashes between civilians and the military resulted in the loss of many lives. Hadi Gaffari* (top right) *witnessed that day. 'There were many soldiers, many commandos,' he remembers. 'They had anti-riot gear, they had clubs; they were prepared to beat people and kill people.' A poster showing the bodies of victims of Black Friday* (above) *directs blame at the shah's policies and at his links with the United States president, Jimmy Carter. Anti-American sentiment was to become a familiar feature of Iran's Islamic revolution.*

"When they were gunned down everybody was crying. The whole country was crying. That was the spark of the victory of the Iranian revolution. That was when it was proven that the shah had to leave, because of that day."

ABDUL SHAH HOSSEINI

LEADER IN EXILE *Khomeini and his circle of advisers seated in the garden of his villa in Neauphle-le-Château outside Paris, from where the Iranian revolution was begun. Ebrahim Yazdi spent some time there. 'We needed to have the commmunication with Khomeini in order to bring the body of the masses, ordinary people, into the political struggle against despotism and foreign domination in our country,' he says.*

THE TOWERING MONUMENT (OPPOSITE) *to Iran's Pahlavi dynasty is the site of its downfall, as millions converge there in December 1978 demanding the overthrow of the shah and the return of Ayatollah Khomeini.*

joined in the protests, together with his father, two brothers and one of his sisters. They were injured by the shah's guardsmen on several occasions. 'It was sometimes cold and difficult, but that wasn't important to me,' he says. 'During those demonstrations people were very united – the whole nation. It was like a miracle, all the young and the old. People were working for the triumph of the revolution and the Imam entering the country.'

The whole of Iran was affected. Radio and television both went off the air, and there were widespread industrial strikes that drastically reduced the country's oil production. For Daryoush Houmayoun it was a time of great terror. 'From the winter of 1978 the wave of demonstrations turned into small bands of people who burnt cinemas, offices, liquor shops.' There were instances of unveiled women being attacked by mobs, and demands for the expulsion of foreigners. The climax came in December during the religious holy day of Ashura, as the Islamic cycle of mourning culminated on the tenth day of Muharram, when Shiite Muslims mourn the martyrdom of Husain, grandson of the Prophet Muhammad.

On that day up to five million people converged on the vast square in Tehran where the shah had built the Shayyad monument to the Pahlavi dynasty. Abdul Shah Hosseini was standing on a crowded overpass overlooking the square when a messenger came with new slogans from the central clergy council. 'He asked me to shout these slogans because I have a loud voice,' he recalls. 'So I shouted out, "Why don't you shout what your heart wants, what every single cell in your body is seeking, why don't you shout what is Islamic, what God says? You should all shout, "Death to the shah!" And all the people started shouting, "Death to the shah!" That was the greatest joy of my life up to that time.'

The shah could have ordered his tanks to open fire, but he did not. The game was up. On 16 January 1979, after thirty-seven years of rule, he flew from Tehran airport, having said that he was going on holiday. Mohsan Rafigdoost, who had earlier been arrested for supporting Khomeini, listened to the news that afternoon. 'The radio announced that the shah had left the country,' he recalls. 'People were clapping, they jumped up and down in the streets....That day I bought a lot of sweets and distributed them.'

Society under God

With the departure of the shah, Khomeini's return was only a matter of days away. Millions of people welcomed him back to Iran with songs and slogans. 'One of our slogans was a verse from the Koran which said that goodness comes and falsehood vanishes,' Said Sharifi Manesh remembers. When he saw the Ayatollah arrive at the airport he felt as though, 'My father had gone on a trip and was now returning. The shah was darkness to us; it is a Koranic verse – from darkness, we take you into light.'

Khomeini now declared his vision for Iran. There was to be no Western democracy, no socialism. In the few years of life still left to him, he began to build a thoroughly Islamic society. The revolution's enemies were rooted out; Islamic revolutionary courts dealt harsh verdicts to those who had supported the shah's regime. Many westernized Iranians joined the stream of foreigners and diplomats who fled the country.

Those who stayed found themselves swept up by changes that affected every aspect of their lives. Friday prayers were interspersed with political harangues about the Islamic revolution. Images of the Ayatollah were pasted everywhere – in offices, at schools, in people's homes. Street names were changed. Bars were looted, alcohol burnt, cinemas destroyed. 'There was a liquor store, and my friends and I went and closed it down and put a wall up in front of it so it couldn't operate any more,' remembers Said Sharifi Manesh. 'Gambling casinos, cabarets had been open all night long,' he describes. 'But when the revolution triumphed all of these vanished.' Western music was banned, as was alcohol. Women still had the right to work, but they were encouraged to stay at home and study the Koran. On buses they were expected to use separate doors and to sit at the back; and they were obliged to cover themselves with the *chador*.

Many of the middle-class women who had benefited from the shah's years were appalled by the changes. 'I refused to wear the *chador* to begin with,' recalls Mashid Amir-Shahy. 'I was so outraged that I didn't have time to be frightened of the mullahs,' she says. 'I felt terribly bitter about the whole thing and extremely frustrated. I thought that, after all, the freedom of choosing one's clothing was among the most preliminary freedoms.' But other

women, like Dowlat Noroudi, disagreed. 'Wearing the scarf would enable women to work actively,' she says. 'Socially it created an atmosphere in which you could really participate and express yourself...as a human being, not only as a sex object or as a woman.' Many Iranian men chose to stop wearing Western ties.

But Islam was not just about prayer and styles of dress. In the new constitution of the Islamic republic, which was adopted on 1 April 1979 Islamic law, the *sharia* – which governed every aspect of life – was reinstated. There were even Islamic business codes, which sought to prevent exploitation of the poor. 'Our lives changed a lot,' says Said Sharifi Manesh. Now schoolchildren recited the Koran instead of singing the national anthem. Girls' uniforms also changed. 'They were entering schools wearing veils and Islamic covering – the way we liked it, the Islamic way.'

REACHING OUT (LEFT) *to their new leader, who had won the overwhelming support of the Iranian people. 'Khomeini was the centre of the commotion,' describes Ebrahim Yazdi. 'The enthusiasm of the people was tremendous, almost hysterical.' Khomeini remained at the helm until his death in 1989.*

THE VEIL OF ISLAM *was now a compulsory garment for all Iranian women, in whom modesty and conservatism were encouraged. Women had played a significant part in the revolution* (RIGHT), *and for many of them the* chador *was a symbol of their struggle. Even young girls at school* (TOP RIGHT) *were required to cover their heads.*

The Iran–Iraq War

Martyrs of war
Iranian volunteers about to leave for the front in 1986, as the Iran–Iraq war intensified. They joined thousands of other young men willing to sacrifice their lives in war in return for the glory of martyrdom. Women were also encouraged to become revolutionary warriors.

The loyalty of the Iranian people was put to the test only a year after the birth of their Islamic republic. In September 1980 Iraqi troops, under orders from their president, Saddam Hussein, crossed into Iran at four points along the border, from its northern frontier to the marshlands and rich oilfields of the Arabian Gulf. What followed was to become one of the twentieth century's longest as well as most destructive wars between sovereign states.

Its immediate causes centred on disputes over territory, oilfields and ownership of the Shatt-al-Arab waterway, which carried a large proportion of the world's oil. But there were underlying religious motives as well. Some 55 per cent of the Iraqi population, most of them in the south, were Shiite Muslims. Saddam Hussein felt threatened by the militancy of Iran's Shiite revolutionary leaders, who condemned his socialist Baathist regime, dominated by Sunni Muslims, and called for his downfall. As the war escalated, they appealed to the large Shiite presence in Iraq to defend their faith against the blasphemous tyranny of their president, who had dared to attack the Islamic republic.

Iran launched a series of successful offensives against the Iraqis, and by 1982 Iranian soldiers had entered Iraqi territory. As the fighting grew more intense, hundreds of thousands of Iranians volunteered to fight in what Khomeini declared a *jihad*, a holy war, responding to his calls for would-be martyrs. Many of them, like Said Sharifi Manesh, were boys who were keen to experience what they perceived as the glory of martydom. Although he was too young to fight, he managed to secure a place in the army by forging his papers. 'We were struggling against blasphemy,' he says. 'In the holy Koran it says that if you are killed you are martyrs on the path of God and you will reach high levels.'

After years of deadlocked trench warfare in which thousands of troops were killed, and the use of chemical weapons and long-range missiles by Iraq, Iran's army grew weaker. People suffered greatly from the shortages and misery brought by the war. Iraq succeeded in turning the war into an Arab–Iranian conflict by enlisting the diplomatic and financial support of other Arab countries, including Kuwait and Saudi Arabia. Iran grew increasingly isolated, and had to face the added burden of arms embargoes, while large quantities of arms were supplied to Iraq by Britain, France and the Soviet Union. The United States, keen to contain the spread of Iran's Islamic revolution, also poured billions of dollars into the Iraqi war effort.

The war entered a new phase in 1984, when the United States sent a fleet of warships to the Gulf. In August 1988 Iran reluctantly accepted the terms of a United Nations ceasefire resolution that finally ended the eight-year war. It had exacted a heavy price: both countries faced huge debts, their economies were severely weakened, much of their land was devastated, and there were enormous numbers of casualties. According to one estimate, 367 000 Iraqis and Iranians were killed and about 700 000 were wounded.

Religious awakenings

At a time when millions of people – Christians and Hindus as well as Muslims – were turning to their faith in the search for answers to the moral uncertainties of modern life, Iran's revolution pointed to new possibilities for Muslims in other countries. Arab identity was becoming strongly aligned to Islam, and Islam to politics. A coup led by army colonel Muammar al Gaddafi in 1969 brought a new brand of Islamic socialism to Libya. When rival religious factions fought for control of Lebanon in the civil war of 1975, it was to the Hizbollah, the 'Party of God', that Iran pledged its support. In 1979, when Afghanistan was invaded by the Soviet Union, it was as 'Soldiers of God' that Muslim Afghan guerrillas of the Mujahideen fought. A series of Islamic institutions, world summit meetings and conference organizations had been set up. Millions of people living in the poor and crowded neighbourhoods of cities faced the same social inequalities that had stoked the fires of revolution in Iran – and reached the same conclusions.

THE WORLD OF ISLAM
The Islamic Conference Organization first met in 1969, and was established two years later. It aimed to give political and Islamic unity to Muslim states throughout the world, uniting more than a billion people through their beliefs. About 80 per cent of them are Sunni Muslims. As well as its forty-nine member states, the ICO granted observer status to the unrecognized Turkish Federated State of Cyprus.

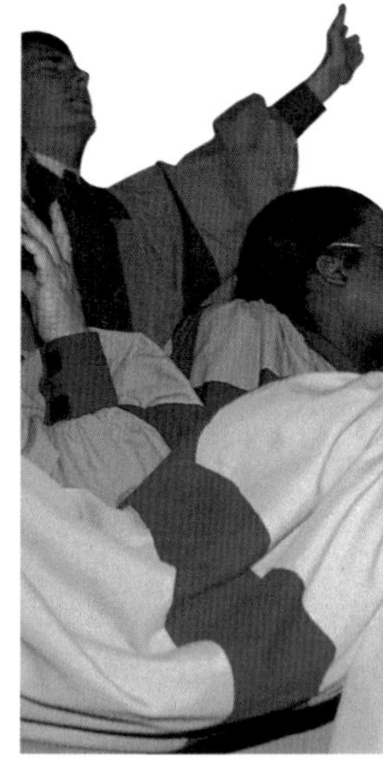

PRAYERS AND POLITICS (ABOVE) *The religious revival in the United States during the 1970s and 1980s extended beyond the churches to rallies and demonstrations in the streets, as thousands of Christians became increasingly vociferous about political and ethical issues.*

RIVAL FAITHS *In the Indian town of Ayodhya in Uttar Pradesh, clashes between Hindus and Muslims led in 1992 to the destruction of a disused sixteenth-century mosque by Hindu extremists. They claimed that the Babari mosque had been built on an important site of Hindu worship. More than 3000 people were killed in the rioting that followed. India's secular, democratic government faced a real challenge in reconciling its diverse religious communities.*

In the Islamic republic of Pakistan, the state established as a new nation for Muslims in 1947, people were in fact governed not by the Islamic laws of the Koran but by a wealthy elite of generals and politicians who pursued modern, secular policies. Seeking to assert the path of Islam as the way forward, Muslim groups succeeded in gaining mass popular support. Following months of rioting in 1977, the Pakistan People's Party was overthrown, martial law was imposed and a new leader took over.

General Zia ul-Haq won many people's confidence by announcing his plans to turn Pakistan into a truly Islamic state. 'We thought that he was a good Muslim,' remembers Hamid Subhani, who worked in a bank. 'Everybody in our family was happy...that at least in Pakistan we have got somebody at the top who was religious, who was a good Muslim, and who would probably deliver his promises to bring Islam to the nation and solve all our problems.' Islamic laws – and punishments – were implemented. Annual payments of alms to the poor, as stipulated in the Koran, were made compulsory. Fasting during the month of Ramadan was strictly enforced. Children

Rallying to Jesus

For many people in the West, it was easy to regard the events taking place in Iran and elsewhere in the Muslim world as a result of Islamic 'fundamentalism'. But in other countries too there were signs of renewed religious fervour in the 1970s and 1980s.

In the United States many people were beginning to look to religion to solve society's troubles. It was largely, though not entirely, among American Evangelicals – Protestant Christians who accept Jesus Christ as their personal Saviour and believe in the absolute authority of the Bible – that Christian fundamentalism took hold. It had avoided involvement in politics as a manifestation of a flawed secular society, but by the mid-1970s the movement became increasingly political. Under the New Christian Right of the 1980s, politically motivated religous groups began to claim a large following.

Many Americans joined its ranks in response to what they perceived as growing social and moral deterioration, even decadence. 'You couldn't watch television or pick up a newspaper without realizing we were constantly, daily in violation of the word of God,' remembers Carol Owen. 'We felt there was real judgement on the nation because of this.' The movement was also fuelled by angry reactions to liberal movements for civil and women's rights; it looked for a return to Christian values, prayers at school, an end to abortion.

It was through the movement of the Christian Right that issues such as abortion, divorce, sexuality and drug abuse entered the political arena. There were mass rallies and public prayer vigils at which some people showed their anger by burning books, magazines and records. One minister, John Gimenez, organized a 'Washington for Jesus' rally in April 1980. 'We didn't know how many people would come. We went out there in amazement when we saw bus after bus after bus,' he says. 'They went home determined that they were going to have a voice, they were going to get involved.'

Church membership, which was especially strong in the affluent parts of the south and southwest, was growing. Membership of the powerful Southern Baptist Convention rose from 10.8 million in 1965 to 13.6 million in 1980. By that year, several surveys suggested that some 40 per cent of Americans regarded themselves as 'born again' Evangelicals, and a similar number attempted to convert others to Christian belief. Many Evangelical schools, and even several universities, were established. Religious groups such as the Moral Majority, established in 1979, used television or direct mail to gain the support of the public. As preachers rose to greater prominence through the media and won financial backing, they presented more of a challenge in the political arena.

The overwhelming endorsement of Ronald Reagan in the 1980 presidential election by Christian supporters who had previously abstained from voting may have contributed to his victory. In 1988 Pat Robertson, one of the leaders of the Christian Right, himself made what was to be an unsuccessful bid for the presidency. Anne Kincaid was one of millions of people who voted for him. 'What those people represented was a ground swell of people saying enough is enough. It is time to stand tall for what we believe. We are tired of watching America just turn its back on God,' she says. 'It was like recognizing that there really is hope – that maybe before the end of this century we could see a change in America.'

who had been taught in English at school were now taught in Urdu. Wearing the veil was compulsory in state schools and in government offices. Cabinet meetings and public ceremonies began with readings from the Koran. 'Zia introduced a law that people should pray while they are in their offices,' remembers Hamid Subhani. 'Normally people used their lunch breaks. Now it became your right.' Many people looked forward to a better way

Living by the book

THE KORAN *plays an important part in the daily lives of Muslims all over the world. Recited at prayer time and in schools, it has remained unchanged since it was revealed to the Prophet Muhammad in the seventh century. It was written and is still read in Arabic, the universal language of Islam; foreign translations of the word of God were traditionally discouraged. The message delivered in its thirty sections, comprising one hundred and fourteen chapters, covers all aspects of life and remains a constant source of guidance for Muslims.*

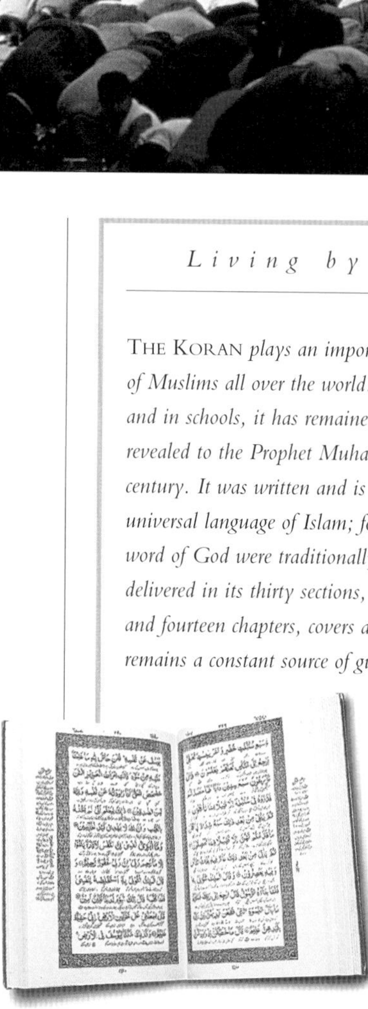

Copies of the Koran are usually wrapped in cloth, and are awarded a place of honour in people's homes. The holy Koran is also sometimes used to administer oaths.

of life. 'They pictured that everybody would be equally treated, they would be provided with food and shelter and education,' says Sheik Khwafa Irshad Razvi. 'They thought that Islam meant bread and butter, and shelter, and self-respect.'

In reality, the new military dictatorship was characterized by corruption and abuse of power under the guise of Islam. The charity payments collected by the government in the form of public taxes often failed to reach the poor. For most people life did not improve under Zia ul-Haq. 'Initially, we had very high hopes,' remembers Hamid Subhani, 'that he would bring changes to society and as a result we would be more Islamic at the end of his period. But later on, he delayed his promises and there were drawbacks in implementing Islamic laws....To remain in power he created a new way to get a vote of confidence from the general public – that if you like Islam, vote for me.'

In Egypt many more people were also turning to Islam. During the 1950s and 1960s President Gamal Nasser, champion of

Culture clash (above)
Egyptian Muslims kneel for Friday prayer on a busy Cairo street. Behind them are signs of the Western-style consumerism that provoked such resentment among many poorer people.

Arab nationalism, had led Egypt in an increasingly secular direction. He had abolished the Muslim Brotherhood, a long-established, influential religious organization, and the Islamic *sharia* courts, and ushered in a period of modernization. Cairo's Al-Azhar University, which had survived for hundreds of years as the Muslim world's most important centre of Islamic learning, became a modern state university. In 1967 Egypt fought a war against Israel in a continuing territorial conflict that had become the focus of much hostility between the Arab nations of the Muslim world and the West. Egypt's defeat heightened Muslim opposition to Nasser's reformist policies. When he died in 1970 a militant form of Islam was winning converts both in the villages and in the teeming neighbourhoods of Cairo.

Egypt's new president, Anwar Sadat, presented himself as a champion of Islam, sometimes joining in prayers at local village mosques. But he believed that the pressures of poverty made it urgent to modernize Egypt, and to do so he adopted an 'open door' policy with the West. He made peace with Israel, and invited Western businesses to invest in Egypt. The shops were flooded with Western consumer goods. For those who could afford them, it was an exciting time, but many people resented the advertisments showing American women using suggestive poses to sell them expensive products they did not need and could not afford. 'Poor people used to watch with regret the expensive suits and shoes in the shop windows,' remembers Aly Abdel Hamed. 'Ordinary people found it difficult to get their basic needs met. The gap between the rich and the poor was very wide....In popular areas there was a lack of educational and social facilities; prices soared....Sadat promised people years of welfare and prosperity after the peace with Israel. But none of those promises was fulfilled.' As they grew more dissatisfied, more people began to take part in anti-government demonstrations.

It was to the mosques that they turned for medical care, education, and other welfare facilities that were dispensed

Muslims abroad
Children of North African immigrants in the French town of Dreux study the Koran at a local mosque. In 1980 there were about two million Muslims living in France, and new communities of Muslims were well established in other parts of Europe and in the United States. Some of them were treated with hostility by local people.

in the name of God, and in return people pledged themselves to Islam. There they were taught the superiority of Islamic laws over the decadent, corrupt secular world. 'This is what we call *dawa*, missionary activity,' describes Yasser Tawfiq. A high school student in his last year, he also taught at the mosque. 'Our job was to teach people the Koran....Every neighbourhood would work to help people, the poor and the needy.' The Islamic awakening spread on student campuses as well as at the mosques. Mona Hamed noticed the changes at her university. 'Girls began to wear the Islamic dress, the *hijab*. Meetings were held at prayer times. Religious books spread in large numbers.' Many people felt inspired by the success of Iran's Islamic revolution. 'When a secular, non-believing regime like the shah's collapses, this brings great hope,' observes Yasser Tawfiq. 'We were hoping to have in Egypt an Islamic state as well.' Religious organizations, including the Muslim Brotherhood, were revived, some of them more radical than others, as Aly Abdel Hamed remembers. 'Members of the Islamic groups tended to describe their opponents as disbelievers, to tear away their wall posters, and use chains and knives to threaten them.'

BEHIND BARS (ABOVE) *Muslims imprisoned as part of a government crackdown on Egypt's Islamic activists. 'These people were from all walks of life – doctors, engineers, people from trade unions, writers and politicians,' recalls Yasser Tawfiq* (TOP), *an Islamic teacher imprisoned in 1981.*

As Egypt's Islamic movement grew more powerful, the government became increasingly hostile. 'The state wanted Islam to be just prayer and nothing else,' says Yasser Tawfiq. 'No awareness, no education, and no reformation.' In September 1981, following street riots in Cairo, President Sadat ordered the arrest of religious activists. Yasser Tawfiq was among the 1500 people who were detained. 'The only thing they hated me for,' he says, 'is for preaching to follow God.' Once in prison, he was out of touch with the outside world: he had no lawyer, no newspapers, no radio. A month later a new arrival to the prison brought him and his fellow prisoners the startling news that President Sadat had been assassinated by Islamic extremists while he was reviewing troops near Cairo on 6 October. The prisoners responded to the news by declaring, '*Allah ho akbar!*' – God is great!

VOTING FOR ISLAM (OPPOSITE) *meant voting for change for the many thousands of Algerians who turned out to demonstrate their support for the Islamic Salvation Front (FIS) in the 1991 elections.*

Algeria's second bid for freedom

The Muslim movement failed to install an Islamic government in Egypt, but what had happened there highlighted how Islamic revivalism had emerged as a strong rival force in Arab politics. When Muslims in nearby Algeria made their formal bid for power, they did so not by militant or extremist means, but through an established democratic process.

As a former French territory, Algeria was one of the most secular Arab states. The Algerian Muslims had won their independence in a bitter, destructive war. But the autocratic rulers of the new socialist government, the National Liberation Front (FLN), failed to fulfil many of the promises of freedom. After an initial period of prosperity, Algeria's economy fell into decline during the 1980s. Oil and gas revenue was used to fund government reform programmes, but economic stability often failed to reach many parts of the countryside and overcrowded cities. People were faced with housing shortages and poor educational opportunities, and often had to queue for bread. 'We started to lose confidence in the government,' remembers Muhammad Ammatari. 'People grew more desperate. The price of oil went down, which affected our economic situation. This created unemployment, and unemployment created corruption, and corruption led to despair.'

In October 1988 thousands of people took to the streets to protest at the contrast between their lives and those of the leaders of the FLN's one-party state. 'They are eating and drinking in their beautiful villas,' one young mother shouted, 'and we have got nothing. We eat dirt in our food.' Another Algerian, Muhammad (surname withheld), watched the demonstrations on television. 'It was impressive for us, I hadn't seen that kind of thing before,' he says. 'Three or four days later it affected our town. At that time, it wasn't really just Islam, it was a revolt against corruption. I was fed up, the people were fed up.'

The Muslim groups among the demonstrators began to gain wider public support. But the government refused to tolerate any opposition, and began a campaign of arrests of the 'Islamists'. The result was popular unrest. Faced with grumbling revolt, continuing violence and mounting terrorism, the government announced its plans to hold what would be Algeria's first democratic elections for

Down with France (above) *Armed Shiite Muslim members of Lebanon's Hizbollah party display their views on foreign intervention, denouncing their former French rulers in a demonstration in southern Beirut in 1987. Heavily embroiled in the Arab–Israeli conflict and ravaged by civil war, Lebanon was divided by the political hostility between its many rival religious communities, and factional fighting continued until 1991. Western fears were heightened by the militant activities of some extremist groups, such as foreign hostage-taking and embassy sieges.*

Facing the direction of Mecca (opposite), *which is compulsory during prayer, Uzbek Muslims attend a mosque in the town of Termez. Uzbekistan was one of the five newly independent central Asian Muslim nations to emerge from the break-up of the former Soviet Union in 1991. Religion had been vigorously suppressed under the communists; now former Soviet citizens were free to worship again.*

thirty years. The Islamic groups founded their own political party, the Islamic Salvation Front (FIS). They delivered political sermons to thousands of people attending Friday prayer, transforming the mosques into campaigning centres. One of the Islamic leaders delivered a speech at Muhammad's school. 'There were twenty thousand people in the courtyard,' he describes. 'He started to talk about things that were real to us, things that no one had said before because they were afraid. That's the first time I had a feeling of being represented by someone. The people listened to him because he talked about people's problems, about their values, everything they had suffered, and he told them, "So follow me, create a multi-party system".'

Elections were to be held first for the legislature, then for the presidency. Thirteen million Algerians voted in December 1991. 'The whole family was thrilled,' Muhammad says. 'It was the first time in their lives they had voted. It was the first time they felt they were really free.' In the first round the FIS won 126 seats; the FLN, after thirty-two years in power, gained just twenty-two.

Despite this overwhelming victory, the Islamic party did not stand in the presidential election: the government cancelled it. Several thousand people, alarmed at the prospect of Islamic rule, took to the streets in anti-Islamic demonstrations. The FIS was banned, and its leaders were among the thousands of people who were arrested. Algerian society was torn apart, and thousands of people were killed, in the civil war that followed.

By this time the man who symbolized Islam's resurgence, Ayatollah Khomeini, had died. News of his death in June 1989 provoked frenzied public grief; on the day of his funeral hundreds of thousands of mourners thronged the cemetery south of Tehran where he was to be buried, and again when the new mosque containing his shrine was opened exactly one year later.

The revolution Khomeini had begun had acquired its own momentum. In some countries Islam now held unchallenged power; throughout the Muslim world, even in states not under Islamic rule, religion had become a formidable political force. As the century ended, God's followers – and not only Muslims but some Christians and Hindus as well – were determined to try to order the lives of others on religious lines.

neutrales Deutschland in Europa!
FORUM
Wer hat uns, das Volk, beklaut?
sagt es jetzt!
und sagt es laut!

12

1970 – 1991

People Power

Collapse of the Communist Empire

On 9 October 1989 journalists were refused entry to Leipzig, East Germany's second largest city. The huge rally described as 'peace prayers' being held that night was expected to attract up to 70 000 East German citizens; the security forces were under instruction to prevent any anti-government demonstration. Many casualties were expected, so hospital wards had been cleared and blood stocks increased.

Two days earlier, returning to Leipzig after visiting Berlin to join in East Germany's fortieth anniversary celebrations, Dietmar Passenheim had watched as lorries were driven into a crowd of demonstrators. On the Monday, 'Ninety-nine per cent of us expected violence,' he remembers. 'We thought the tanks would roll in and destroy us.... But along with the fear was the feeling that I had to go and be with these people in order to change and improve things. It's indescribable, I just knew I had to be there.'

While the crowds gathered in front of the Nikolaikirche close to Karl Marx Square, prayers were said before the demonstration began. In the meantime, military vehicles blocked the side streets, armed and poised for action.

The evening of 9 October proved to be a decisive moment in the history of East Germany, and had far-reaching repercussions. No shots were fired, no violence erupted. The Soviet president, Mikhail Gorbachev, had visited Berlin for the anniversary celebrations and had made it clear to the East German government that he would not support those who refused to accept the need for change. For the communist leaders in Berlin, the end was near.

The Leipzig demonstrations were part of a pattern of protest accelerating in Eastern Europe. Within a month the Berlin Wall, since 1961 a symbol of the division between capitalist Western Europe and the communist East, had come down. The power of the Soviet Union, which since the 1940s had held Eastern Europe in its grip, was now being challenged. The monolithic empire of Soviet communism was soon to be shattered.

Waving banners *of protest, the people of Leipzig demonstrate against communist rule in East Germany.*

Living under communist rule

In the early 1970s the world was still divided into the spheres of influence of the two superpowers that had dominated international relations since the end of the Second World War. Each represented a polarized ideology. The United States saw itself as the guardian of democratic freedom and the champion of capitalism, while the Soviet Union proclaimed the glories of communist society and the benefits of controlled economies. The Soviet Union dominated Eastern Europe; the United States jealously guarded its influence in the West. Conflict in countries outside Europe often drew on the resources and support of the superpowers, each eager to prevent an expansion of the other's influence.

The state continued to shape the lives of people living under communist rule. In some countries it decided how many children people could have, where they were educated, what job they could pursue, where they lived, what information they were exposed to, what allegiances they had and what opinions they were allowed to express.

Communist ideals were introduced to schoolchildren from a young age. Dasha Khubova, who later became Moscow's leading oral historian, remembers her education in the Soviet Union in the 1960s and 1970s. 'From your first day at school you were taught about your country and told that you must be proud of it. They told you about the revolution and you felt it was all for you....From when you were a small child you heard and read about it. There was no choice, no option, you believed it....This mania, this feeling that we were the best and that we had the best of everything – we never doubted it.'

Some people believed that the communist state justified its existence because of the security and welfare it provided. Harold Jäger, a border guard in East Germany (the German Democratic Republic, GDR), recognized the benefits this could bring. 'We enjoyed cheap rents, money for holidays, free education....Even if I hadn't been a member

THE COMMUNIST STATES (BELOW) *in Eastern Europe were – with the exception of Albania and Yugoslavia – for forty years dominated and largely controlled by the powerful Soviet Union, which was itself made up of fifteen republics. Eastern Europe provided a buffer zone between the Soviet Union and the capitalist nations of the West.*

Nina Motova (above), *who worked in a ball bearings factory in the Soviet Union, was an ardent believer in the communist state. 'The work, the government and the Party are my life,' she says, 'and I am proud of them all.'*

Official celebrations (top) *were staged each year on May Day. The cream of the nation's workers and athletes, military personnel and weaponry, followed by cheering crowds, paraded before the Soviet leaders in Moscow's Red Square.*

of the state security, I would never have been scared of unemployment or of having too low a pension....I really appreciated that feeling of security.'

Others felt that they were having to live a double life. When Carmen Blazejewski was a child she believed, 'Socialism meant peace and no difference between rich and poor.' As she grew up her parents told her that they did not agree with everything they were told. This knowledge was dangerous. 'I had to learn from an early age not to let the kindergarten teacher know anything about the knowledge I had from my parents,' she recalls. Children in East Germany were tested at school to check whether they watched the forbidden West German television. Carmen Blazejewski's mother was a teacher. 'She warned me that we would have to draw a clock like the one shown on TV,' she says, 'and that I must draw the one on GDR television, not the one from the West.' One clock used dashes to display the minutes, the other dots.

Governments bombarded their citizens with evidence of the success of communism, but some Eastern European nations were close to economic collapse by the early 1970s. Millions of people still endured great hardship: food was often scarce; housing was desperately inadequate; people had to wait up to ten years for a flat or to buy a car; industry was inefficient and wages were low. Western clothes and consumer goods were highly prized, but were unobtainable except at huge expense through the black market.

Shopping in the market (right) *in Moscow. Buying food was a daily chore for many people in communist states. There was little choice, and people living in the cities sometimes faced shortages of basic goods such as bread and meat.*

Access to the West was strictly limited, and it was difficult to gain any information about the outside world, particularly in the Soviet Union. But many people yearned for something more than the hardships and the monotony of communist life. Natasha Kusnetsova lived in the town of Rostov. 'We didn't have enough food,' she says. 'All you could buy were carrots, cabbage and potatoes.' She became intrigued by the liveliness in Western music. 'I imagined the meaning of the words,' she recalls. 'I felt the sense of freedom even without the words ....Later I saw pictures, and was fascinated. I couldn't forget them; I wanted to know all about the world they came from.'

A captive audience *Potential buyers choosing televisions in a Moscow store. Few consumer goods were available to people living under communist rule, but most citizens had access to television, which was controlled by the state.*

It was dangerous to try to find out about that world. Any communication with Westerners was strictly forbidden, and no criticism of the Communist Party was tolerated. Citizens were kept under close surveillance by the secret police, and informers were encouraged to report any deviation from the communist line by neighbours, colleagues at work, friends and even members of their own family. In East Germany there were 86 000 secret police (Stasi) agents, and another 100 000 people who were tempted – or pressurized – into acting as informers. Stasi files were kept on six million of East Germany's eighteen million citizens.

Dietmar Passenheim (below) *was a member of a cooperative that assembled prefabricated housing* (below right) *in East Germany as a young man. He was later employed by the transport police* (below left)*, and then worked as an informer. 'A precondition of the job,' he says, 'was being a Party member... another was that we didn't have any relatives in the West.'*

Dietmar Passenheim worked in Leipzig. He was a police informer who searched trains that ran through to West Germany, looking out for anyone who might be trying to escape to the West and checking on the passengers for 'subversive' intentions. 'We always made the assumption that every West German was an agent,' he says. 'He was an enemy, and we had to find out what he was doing here.' Suspicious-looking people were first identified on the station platform. Posing as an ordinary citizen, Dietmar Passenheim would get into the compartment with them. 'I would

just start talking to them and try to build up a bit of a relationship,' he recalls. 'Then I would ask what they were going to do in West Germany, and whether they enjoyed their time in the GDR....A superior officer walked up and down the corridor, and we had a sign language...if I pulled my right ear lobe it meant that I wanted to talk to him, and we would meet farther down the corridor.'

Some agents and informers had to work between twelve and seventeen hours a day. After ten years Dietmar Passenheim tried to resign, claiming that the hours were too long and the job too stressful. 'If I had told them the real reasons,' he says, 'I would have been imprisoned immediately. I would have been regarded as an enemy of the state.' His resignation was rejected.

Challenges to communist rule

Millions of citizens living in Eastern Europe resented and feared the regimes under which they lived. There were several occasions when people had tried to stand up to them. In 1953 there were riots in East Berlin, and three years later an uprising in Hungary. In 1968 the Red Army marched into Czechoslovakia to put an end to the reforms introduced during the 'Prague Spring'. In country after country forces of the communist regimes, backed by the Soviet Union, ruthlessly suppressed all signs of discontent or rebellion among their peoples.

The people of Poland had long resisted Soviet-dominated communism. Protests in 1956, 1968, 1970 and 1976 had all been crushed with the use of force. The disturbances in 1970, triggered by sudden price increases on many foodstuffs, were most serious in the Baltic ports and shipyards, and particularly in Gdansk, once the German port of Danzig.

Alena Borusewicz was a nurse in the Gdansk shipyard where her father also worked; her husband, Bogdan Borusewicz, became a member of the dissident group KOR (Committee to Defend the Workers). She realized the difference between the Polish government's propaganda and what was really taking place. 'The press was portraying the shipyard workers as hooligans and idle workers,' she remembers, 'but I knew that my father was a very different kind of person.' She started to write articles for the underground publications produced by the resistance movement; for the first time many workers were able to read uncensored material about health and safety at work, occupational diseases, and political and historical events in Poland and in the outside world. 'We wanted to give the people courage to do something,' she says. 'We tried to break the censorship so that people could read what they wanted.'

By early 1980 the Polish economy was close to collapse. with nearly half the state's budget spent on food subsidies. Foreign debts were crippling the economy, wages were low, and there were acute food shortages. When the government again announced an increase in food prices – the price of meat was almost doubled – spontaneous strikes broke out. As before, the centre of resistance was Gdansk. In the shipyards a strike committee was formed, led by Lech Walesa, an electrician. Strikers from all over Poland joined

the committee, which called for political as well as economic change: for freedom of the press, the right to form independent trade unions, the release of political prisoners and the right to strike.

Taking part in the strike was dangerous, and not all the Gdansk shipyard workers did so. But enormous numbers of people from other occupations did gather outside the shipyards to show their support. Alena Borusewicz remembers seeing a woman out walking one Sunday morning with two smartly dressed little girls. At first she assumed they were going to visit someone. 'I suddenly realized that this woman was taking her children to the shipyard gate,' she remembers. 'I felt like crying. I felt it was a symbol of support for those of us who were on strike.'

Henryka Krzywonos was a tram driver. Her fellow workers sent her to represent them at Gdansk. When the strikers in the shipyard considered returning to work, she stood on a truck and shouted anything she could think of that might persuade them to stay. 'I tried to explain that if they left, if they went home, they would be betraying all the other striking workers,' she recalls. Henryka Krzywonos was convinced that the strikers had a responsibility towards all Polish citizens. 'Beyond the gates were more than a million people,' she remembers. 'The square was full of people.... Without them we wouldn't be able to do anything, but we knew we had their

Joining forces (LEFT) *Workers inside the Gdansk shipyard, and their supporters outside it, united in their efforts to bring about change in Poland. The strikers were led by Lech Walesa (in the centre of the photograph, on the far side of the railings). Members of Solidarity, the federation of trade unions, included doctors, engineers, manual workers, shopkeepers and teachers, and some 900 000 former members of the Communist Party. Their demands included 'Work for bread', as the banner they are carrying declares* (RIGHT). *Most of Solidarity's demands were eventually conceded by the Polish government.*

A HOLY ALLIANCE

SPONTANEOUS CELEBRATIONS broke out all over Poland on 16 October 1978 when a Polish cardinal, Karol Wojtyla, was elected Pope, head of the Roman Catholic Church. He was the first Polish Pope ever, and the first non-Italian one for more than 450 years.

Seven months later more than 500 000 Poles gathered in Warsaw's Victory Square to listen to Pope John Paul II, as he was now known, address his countrymen. 'The future of Poland will depend on how many people are mature enough to be nonconformists,' he told them. His words brought inspiration to the deeply religious Polish people, most of whom were still practising Roman Catholics despite the communist government's attempts to discourage religious worship.

More than a quarter of Poland's population turned out to hear the Pope preach in public as he toured the country on his nine-day visit. Its enormous impact was played down by the government-controlled media, but there was a huge resurgence of religious activity, including services held in public. 'The mass united the people,' remembers Henryka Krzywonos. 'People were standing together and creating a kind of community....We were not afraid.'

The Church played a subtle but important role as the Polish people fought against communist rule. Its aim was to survive within the communist system that it wanted to see overthrown. At first it condemned the strike, but later supported Solidarity's demands. 'The Church's involvement with the conflict gave us extra security,' recalls Bogdan Borusewicz. 'The authorities allowed priests to enter the shipyards and conduct mass....It was an important experience for the community, and it consolidated us. We were convinced we were doing the right thing. If the priests were with us, we believed no harm could come to us.'

When martial law was imposed in December 1981 the Church continued to support Solidarity, providing refuge for hunger strikers and medical, economic and moral support to union members. Its part in the opposition movement made the Church a target for government attack. The abduction and murder of a popular radical priest, Father Jerzy Popieluszko, provoked worldwide condemnation, and increased the pressure on the Polish government to listen to its people.

support....The strike unified us. We started to be a nation for ourselves.'

After intense negotiations between the strike committee and the Polish government, on 31 August 1980 the Gdansk Agreement was signed. Workers were given the right to form trade unions and to strike; an economic overhaul was promised, including a rise in wages; and the Catholic mass was to be broadcast on the radio each Sunday. The strike committee formed the basis for a national trade union and political movement, *Solidarnosc* – Solidarity – which rapidly grew to have more than ten million members. It was an extraordinary victory for the workers. The confrontation between them and the leaders of the workers' state that claimed to represent them had been closely followed all over the world; many strikers believed this would protect them from reprisals by the Polish authorities. They were wrong.

LINED UP *against the people, the Polish militia in riot gear* (TOP) *oppose crowds of demonstrators. Zbigniew Lelental* (ABOVE) *was a trainee officer in the police when martial law was declared in December 1981. 'We didn't know what to expect,' he remembers. 'But we knew that if we didn't maintain order ourselves, it would end tragically for Poland.' Soviet military intervention was probably averted by the severity of the Polish authorities' action.*

The political crisis in Poland continued. In February 1981 the defence minister, General Wojciech Jaruzelski, took over as premier; he was appointed first secretary of the Communist Party in October. As union militants, advised and supported by the Roman Catholic Church, continued to press for change, further strikes caused upheaval throughout the country. They also began to have an impact further afield; governments elsewhere in Eastern Europe were extremely alarmed at the possibility of their own peoples following the Polish example. In December, under intense pressure from Moscow, Jaruzelski imposed martial law. Solidarity was banned, its members imprisoned or intimidated.

POPE JOHN PAUL II *addresses his fellow countrymen during his tour of Poland in 1979.*

Henryka Krzywonos continued her work for Solidarity, but in secret. She knew that she would eventually be found out. 'The fear was indescribable,' she says. Eventually, 'They came and broke my door down. The fact that I was pregnant made no difference to them. They beat me, throwing me around like a ball, then left me bleeding.' She lost her baby. Her flat was searched, and she was forced to leave the area. Despite the fear and the harsh repression, Solidarity survived underground. Within six years – though only after a change of government in Moscow – it would re-emerge.

"The Soviet Union was the Big Brother. We thought that if they can do things then so can we. We identified with glasnost *and* perestroika*...it played a major role."*

CARMEN BLAZEJEWSKI

FACE TO FACE *Mikhail Gorbachev* (ABOVE) *was the first Soviet leader to talk directly to the people. Yevgeny Mahaev* (LEFT) *was enthusiastic. 'We had hopes that there would be changes....I liked it.' Gorbachev's plain speaking and personal charm at first brought him popularity and widespread support.*

THE OLD GUARD *ended with the funeral* (RIGHT) *of Konstantin Chernenko, who died on 10 March 1985 after only a year as president of the Soviet Union. He and his predecessor, Yuri Andropov, were in poor health during their time in office. Chernenko maintained the hard line of President Leonid Brezhnev, who died in 1982.*

Reforms and revolutions

It was not until Mikhail Gorbachev became leader of the Soviet Union that the situation in the communist world began to change. In 1985 he succeeded Konstantin Chernenko. Fifty-four years old, Mikhail Gorbachev was the youngest member of the Politburo, the Communist Party's ruling committee. Yevgeny Mahaev, who sold fish in Moscow, was among many people who welcomed the news of Gorbachev's appointment. 'When Gorbachev came, everyone said that because he was young and had a lot of energy life would improve,' he remembers. 'Life in the early 1980s had stagnated. We needed change.'

Within days of taking office Gorbachev was already talking about the need for change. The new policy came to be known as *perestroika* (restructuring): the whole Soviet economy needed to be made more efficient. Gorbachev put into practice his own belief that leading Party members should get closer to the people. He spoke openly about the dire economic crisis facing the nation, acknowledging the fact that the quality of its products was low, that management was riddled with corruption, and motivation among workers was poor. In a country where the state controlled everything, Gorbachev now encouraged a degree of free enterprise. Yevgeny Mahaev remembers: 'He said that we could work

SUPERPOWER RECONCILIATION

When Mikhail Gorbachev became leader of the Soviet Union in 1985 few people foresaw that the appointment would spark off an explosion of change affecting not just the communist empire but the whole balance of international politics. There had been previous attempts to improve relations between the two superpowers – the Soviet Union and the United States – but they had foundered in 1979 with the Soviet invasion of Afghanistan.

Gorbachev was a pragmatist. He believed that communism must evolve and change if it was to survive. He recognized that one of the most vital changes was a scaling down of the arms race between the superpowers. The Soviet Union was spending a quarter of its total revenue on arms, and this was crippling the economy. Gorbachev injected new vigour into arms talks with the United States, and embarked on a series of summit meetings with President Ronald Reagan. The Cold War was beginning to thaw.

The first summit was held in Geneva in 1985, and despite mutual suspicion the two leaders agreed to continue cautious exchanges. They met again at Reykjavik in October the following year, though the talks broke down when President Reagan refused to give up his Strategic Defence Initiative (SDI). By 1987 the Soviet Union's need to reduce its arms expenditure had become urgent, and when Reagan visited Moscow in 1988 to sign an arms reduction treaty it was apparent that Gorbachev would pay almost any price to bring about an end to superpower competition.

Gorbachev was the first Soviet leader to acknowledge the cost of the communist empire. He knew that the Soviet Union could no longer pursue its interventionist policy in other East European states. Opposition groups within the Eastern bloc were encouraged by Gorbachev's abandonment of the 'Brezhnev doctrine', by which Moscow had justified Soviet involvement in the defence of socialism wherever it might be under threat.

This dramatic change in foreign policy, the scaling down of the arms race and the radical domestic reforms in the Soviet Union made Gorbachev a hero in the eyes of many people living in both East and West. Carmen Blazejewski remembers the excitement created by Gorbachev's visit to East Berlin. 'The news of the visit spread fast,' she recalls. 'Normally everything had to be organized: people were given flags to wave and had to take the day off work. But when Gorby came the state didn't have to organize anyone – people wanted to see Gorbachev anyway. They filled the streets, chanting "Gorby! Gorby!" ' Much of Europe was swept by 'Gorbymania'; in 1990 Gorbachev was awarded the Nobel peace prize.

and earn money for ourselves. The people believed him and soon founded their own small enterprises and businesses. I quit my shop and became independent from the state.'

Reforms within the Party structure enabled Gorbachev to push through new measures. In order to rally the public behind *perestroika*, Gorbachev introduced a policy of *glasnost* or 'openness', in which the media, the people and the state were all encouraged to be more open and honest. People found their newspapers full of stories about inefficiency, bad management and nepotism. Disturbing facts about current events, such as the devastating nuclear accident at Chernobyl, were matched by revelations about previous leaders and their policies. The works of banned writers were published, and many political prisoners were released. Some people found the revelations too much for them. Nina Motova was a factory worker in the Soviet Union, and had won awards for her work. She was intensely proud of the nation's achievements. 'When *glasnost* came they began to tell us things we didn't want to hear,' she recalls. 'They told us bad things about Lenin and how he ruined the history of the world. Well of course Lenin could make mistakes, but the life was good and we were moving towards a very bright future. Now I am ashamed to hear the criticism of our economy and our country.'

Gorbachev's reforms were soon extended to relations with other states in the communist bloc. The 'Brezhnev doctrine', which had been used to justify Soviet intervention in the affairs of other communist states, was replaced by the 'Sinatra doctrine' – they could do it their way. In Hungary opposition groups were legalized, and reformers within the Communist Party gained more power. Market reforms replaced the old centralized economy, and in early 1989 the Communist Party declared its support for the transition to a multi-party political system.

Dismantling the barrier *A barbed wire fence had separated Hungary and Austria since 1969. When Hungary opened the border in May 1989, large numbers of East Germans took the opportunity to escape to the West. In September Hungary declared all its borders open – the first Eastern European state to open its borders to a non-communist neighbour.*

The wall comes down (right) *Jubilant crowds at the Berlin Wall after the East German government announced the opening of the border in November 1989. The wall divided the city and people of Berlin for twenty-eight years; many people had died when they attempted to cross it to reach the West. Now people chipped away at the wall by hand before equipment could be brought in to demolish it.*

One of the most dramatic and welcome changes came in Poland. In January 1989 Solidarity's legal status was restored, opposition to the Communist Party was allowed, and parliament reformed. These initiatives swiftly led to multi-party elections; by the summer of 1989 a coalition government led by Solidarity was in power, the first non-communist government in Eastern Europe for forty years.

Encouraged by the changes initiated by Mikhail Gorbachev, opposition groups in East Germany also grew stronger. When Hungary opened its borders with the West early in 1989, thousands of East Germans made their way to Hungary, which they could visit legally, and from there left for the West. This mass exodus shocked some East German citizens. Bärbel Reinke, who was a waitress in East Berlin, thought that 'What these people were doing was leaving a sinking ship. I was torn in two about it... not everyone could run away, otherwise the country couldn't change.' The official press denounced those who left as enemies of the

LONG LIVE

Gateway to freedom (ABOVE) *Large crowds flocked to the Brandenburg Gate in Berlin on the night of 9 November when the border between East and West was opened. Bewildered border guards allowed people to pass through the gate without identity papers or passports.*

state. Bärbel Reinke recognized the consequences of the exodus: 'We didn't have a proper workforce any more. The doctors were leaving, and soon we didn't have enough nurses either.'

In October 1989 Mikhail Gorbachev came to Berlin for the GDR's fortieth anniversary celebrations. In a thinly veiled warning to the East German leader, Erich Honecker, he declared, 'He who is too late is punished by life'. It was a clear indication that Moscow would not back the East German government in repressing the people's call for reform. Reassured by this message and by the peaceful demonstration in Leipzig, protesters gathered in the other major East German towns; on 4 November half a million people rallied in East Berlin to call for an end to communist rule.

Faced by this overwhelming pressure, on 9 November the East German government announced that the border was to be opened. People were free to visit West Berlin. Andreas Höntsch, a film-maker in East Berlin, heard the news flash. 'We just couldn't believe it,' he says. 'Then we saw pictures on television showing people at the border crossing...they were waving...it seemed impossible.' At first there was confusion. Bärbel Reinke went to the wall immediately, and decided to visit West Berlin by walking through the Brandenburg Gate. 'Nothing would stop me,' she says. But when she arrived she found her way was blocked. 'I became terribly frightened,' she recalls. 'I thought they had tricked us and simply shut the wall again....I started to shout and panic.' Eventually she was allowed to go through; an officer escorted her. 'It was dangerous,' she reflects, 'but looking back everyone behaved very calmly.'

Carmen Blazejewski and Andreas Höntsch were also determined to see for themselves, so the next day they bundled their sleeping child into their car and drove to the border. They were concerned that it might be closed again before they could get there, but when they reached it the guards waved them through. 'People were getting out of their cars and giving flowers to the guards. It was a very peaceful sight,' says Carmen Blazejewski. 'Someone greeted us with a bottle of sparkling wine, and chocolate for the child....We were in the West. I was shaking, I was so excited....The streets were full of people, and everybody was embracing each other ....There was a feeling of great joy.'

Bärbel Reinke (left, *with her children), like thousands of other East Berliners, regarded the Brandenburg Gate as a symbolic entrance to the West. When concerts were held and political speeches delivered in West Berlin close to it, 'We would go and stand at the gate and listen,' she says. 'We weren't allowed to, but we still did it.'*

Destroying the evidence *In January 1990 East German citizens broke into the Berlin headquarters of the secret police and tore up thousands of Stasi files. The Stasi had accumulated files on a third of the East German population and more than half a million foreigners.*

Harold Jäger was on duty at the border on 9 November. He was bewildered by what was happening. 'We had no instructions, no orders during that critical situation,' he recalls. 'That was proof to me that everything was lost....The desire and will of the people was stronger than the power of the state. It was the end of the GDR.' In October 1990 the GDR did come to an end. After an overwhelming vote for unification, the political boundary between East and West Germany was dissolved.

Revolution spreads

In Czechoslovakia the communist regime was also struggling against massive popular rebellion. Dissidents such as the playwright Václav Havel became increasingly prominent in the resistance movement. Andrej Krob had long been friends with Havel. He was a handyman and Havel's driver, and as a stage hand helped Havel to put on some of his controversial plays secretly in flats and barns. He continued to work with Havel in the underground movement. 'We knew it was no joke working for something that was disliked by the Bolsheviks,' he recalls. 'It could easily ruin our lives. But I had a sense of justice, so I had to make my decision, despite the consequences.'

In the late 1980s Andrej Krob began to work as a cameraman for an underground video journal. He recorded dissident meetings and protests, and some sympathetic people who worked for the official Czech television station helped to edit them. 'We would make a master copy, and then make multiple copies and distribute them,' he recalls. 'They would be screened in pubs and even factories, all over Czechoslovakia and abroad....We wanted to spread information among the local public. That way the people would come together and could become more organized.'

Petr Miller was a blacksmith working for a large company, CKD, in Prague. Like many others with an adequate standard of living, he was at first reluctant to join a revolutionary movement. People remembered the Soviet invasion of their country in 1968, and were afraid to risk change. Their fears were allayed when Mikhail Gorbachev made an official visit to Prague in 1987. Petr Miller was impressed by him. 'He started to talk about things in a new way,' he says. 'It was very engaging, and his new policies were widely discussed in the workplace....It was transparent that something big was happening in Eastern Europe. It seemed that the Iron Curtain was bound to fall.'

On Friday 17 November 1989 a peaceful crowd gathered in Prague's Wenceslas Square for a memorial demonstration in honour of a student killed by the Nazis fifty years earlier. Andrej Krob filmed the demonstration; he was expecting trouble. 'We saw the militia gathering,' he remembers. 'I carried my camera under my coat and mingled

Andrej Krob (left, *talking to Václav Havel) set up an underground video journal in Czechoslovakia. His contact with Havel was vital. 'Havel's role is undeniable,' recalls Andrej Krob. 'He was the initiator, he put us together and made us think things through.'*

Candles of hope (above) *in Wenceslas Square in Prague were lit as a symbol of peaceful protest against government policies in November 1989, while state riot police assembled in the side streets. There were daily demonstrations in support of political change.*

with the crowds....We knew the government would have to act.' The demonstration was violently suppressed. On the Saturday and Sunday some 200 000 people demonstrated in protest at police brutality. It was also on Sunday that Václav Havel and his fellow dissidents formed an official opposition group, Civic Forum, after a series of meetings. Petr Miller went to the Magic Lantern theatre to listen to their discussions. He asked Havel, 'Who is representing the workers here?' He remembers how Havel 'pointed his finger at me and said, "Well, you are going to".' Petr Miller was swept into the reform movement, organizing strikes and later participating in negotiations with the government. Members of Civic Forum, including Petr Miller, were pursued by a growing number of journalists. 'Suddenly there was a huge number of foreign press reporters, television photographers, film producers...all seeking our views. We were not groomed for this role. We tried hard not to let it show, we tried to present ourselves correctly, but we were really complete amateurs.'

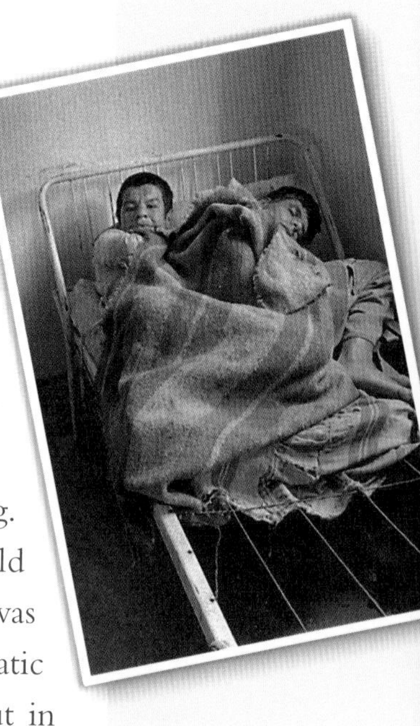

Abandoned children (above) *Many thousands of Romanian orphans were barely able to survive the terrible conditions in which they had to live.*

The Communist Party had lost all hope of continuing. By the middle of December the old regime had been swept away, and was replaced by a newly elected democratic government. Change had come about in Czechoslovakia so quickly and peacefully it became known as the 'velvet revolution'.

Burning the flag *of the Romanian Communist Party, demonstrators in Bucharest give vent to their anger and bitterness during a memorial in January 1990 for victims of the violence.*

It seemed as though the entire edifice of communism might be toppled without bloodshed. But the revolution in Romania was to prove far from peaceful. Romanians were kept as isolated as possible from the events taking place elsewhere in Eastern Europe, and the regime there refused to countenance any changes. Nevertheless, on 17 December 1989 a crowd of Romanians demonstrated in the city of Timisoara, in Transylvania, demanding civil rights and political reform. The president, Nicolae Ceausescu, ordered his security forces, the Securitate, to fire into the crowds. More than a hundred people were killed that week, and many more injured.

Four days later Nicolae Ceausescu and his wife Elena appeared before a crowd of 80 000 people outside the Central Committee building in Bucharest. Instead of giving their usual organized ovation the crowds shouted, 'Down with the murderers!' Television cameras filmed the scene, but transmission was cut off so viewers did not see Ceausescu's bewilderment. He then realized that he had lost even the simulated support of his people. Soon the army went over to the opposition, while the Securitate started shooting. Ceausescu and his wife escaped by helicopter. They were later captured, tried and executed.

A CULT OF REPRESSION

THE PEOPLE OF Romania endured one of the most tyrannical regimes anywhere in the communist world. For a time their ruler, Nicolae Ceausescu, was regarded as a liberal in the West because of his attempts to promote nationalism and throw off the Soviet yoke; less was known about the ruthless domestic policies he inflicted on his people, sacrificing their welfare for national prestige and personal glorification.

In the early 1980s the Romanians suffered acute food shortages as Ceausescu increased food exports to reduce the country's foreign debts. Fuel was rationed so that oil could be exported; anyone who burnt fuel when the state declared the temperature to be above 10°C (50°F) was liable to prosecution. Ceausescu ruled the country with an iron hand: all the media were censored, contact with foreigners was strictly forbidden, faxes and photocopiers were banned, and every typewriter in the country had to be registered with the state so that any subversive printed material could be traced to its originator.

While the people suffered material deprivation and were denied any civil and political rights, public money was squandered on gigantic architectural projects. Thousands of Bucharest citizens were forced into slum housing on the outskirts of the city so that a large area could be cleared to build a new palace for Nicolae Ceausescu and his family. Any sign of resistance by the people was immediately quelled by Ceausescu's personal security forces, the Securitate. Numbering more than 100 000, the Securitate terrorized the Romanian people into submission. It was rumoured that every telephone was bugged, and that a quarter of the population were 'informers' working for the Securitate.

The regime penetrated every aspect of people's lives. When the birth rate dropped, abortion was made illegal and contraceptives were banned. All women under the age of forty-five were expected to have at least five children, regardless of their income, health or personal wishes. The legislation was enforced by compulsory regular gynaecological inspections.

The result of this policy was that women already struggling to feed and clothe their families resorted to illegal, often dangerous abortions, or abandoned babies they could not provide for. Hundreds of thousands of children were left in overcrowded, squalid orphanages run by inadequate numbers of untrained staff who lacked the resources to provide proper care for them. Lack of sterile medical supplies and the traditional practice of injecting newborn babies with extra blood meant that the AIDS virus soon gained a foothold, and by December 1989, when the Ceausescu regime was brought down, half the babies in Europe with AIDS were Romanian.

CENTRAL AVENUE (BELOW), *built in central Bucharest by Nicolae Ceausescu. Ordinary citizens, some of whose homes had been razed to clear the land, were denied access to this part of the city.*

The empire crumbles

While the people of the communist satellites struggled to assert their independence, the heart of the Soviet system was faltering. Mikhail Gorbachev's radical reforms had alarmed traditional Party members, while most people found themselves faced with even longer food queues, more acute shortages, rising prices and a surge in crime. In 1989 a wave of strikes swept across the Soviet Union, from the Ukraine to the Arctic. In August more than a million people in the Baltic states – Estonia, Latvia and Lithuania – joined hands, forming a human chain to protest against Soviet domination.

Miners on strike (BELOW) *in the Ukraine in 1989 demanding political change. The Ukraine was the second most populous republic in the Soviet Union, and also one of the most conservative. But once the forces of change were unleashed, resentment of Soviet domination grew into widespread public protest.*

Many Russians who had initially supported Gorbachev felt disillusioned. 'The reforms were so great that life had changed and the people had changed,' says Yevgeny Mahaev. 'Now it was money that was important, rather than friends.' Andrei Ozerskii, a physicist working in Zelenograd, the Soviet electronics centre, at first believed that Gorbachev would strengthen the nation; then he too began to have doubts: 'By 1988 and 1989 I knew that the changes in the leadership and party were not good for the country. 'Gorbachev's words were empty....But my final disillusionment came in 1990 when he met the leaders of the seven capitalist countries. I realized that it would not bring any benefit to our country.'

Gorbachev, struggling to appease both the Communist Party hardliners and the restless radicals, satisfied neither faction. On May Day 1990 the people of Moscow gathered in Red Square, where every year they turned out to cheer military parades and political leaders. But on this occasion jeers and chants rang round the square. Gorbachev and the Politburo were shouted down, and had to retreat.

Boris Yeltsin, a prominent member of the group demanding faster reform, began to overtake Gorbachev in popularity, and in February 1991 he publicly challenged the president, declaring that he should either increase the pace of reform or resign. In

Gesture of defiance (above) *Lithuanian protesters impaled their passports on the barricades to symbolize their rejection of Soviet citizenship.*

June Yeltsin became the first democratically elected president of the Russian Federation.

As the situation continued to deteriorate, Communist Party conservatives decided to take matters into their own hands. People watching television on 20 August 1991 knew that something was wrong when the usual programmes were replaced by the ballet *Swan Lake*, interspersed with announcements that Gorbachev was 'undergoing treatment' at his holiday home in the Crimea. In fact there had been a coup: a self-appointed emergency committee announced that it was in control, and tanks moved into the centre of Moscow. 'We were horrified,' remembers Dasha Khubova, who listened to a foreign radio station to find out what was happening. 'At first we didn't speak, we just listened. Then my mother said, "I

Civilians surround *a Soviet tank* (above) *in Moscow during the coup in August 1991. Boris Yeltsin, the Russian president, defied the coup, challenging its leaders – the Emergency Committee – and calling for a general strike. The planned attack on the White House, the parliament building, did not take place.*

had hoped that your life would be better, but it's the end".'

Boris Yeltsin was in his dacha outside Moscow when the coup took place. He heard the news on his return, and made his way to the square in front of the White House, the parliament building. Joined by thousands of supporters, he climbed onto a tank and urged people to resist. Within hours, crowds of civilians had surrounded the White House to protect the rebels. Natasha Kusnetsova was among them. 'I wasn't afraid,' she says. 'I couldn't just stand by. I knew that if I had to live behind the Iron Curtain again I would do something extreme....I would rather die.'

Sergei Evdikimov was one of the officers in the tank regiment that had been ordered to the White House. 'Moscow was flooded with troops,' he recalls. 'Civilians gathered all around them and talked to the soldiers. The people built barricades right in front of my tank.' Uncertain of his orders, and having lost all radio contact with his commanding officer, Sergei Evdikimov found out about what was happening by reading the resistance leaflets distributed by the White House. 'One young guy climbed on my tank and we started discussing the situation...."Why don't you come over to our side?" he asked.' After an appeal from the White House, and despite his fear of reprisals, Sergei Evdikimov decided he would join them. 'I could tell that the public supported Yeltsin,' he says. 'I was joining the people.'

Standing together *Civilians in Moscow befriended those sent to threaten them. They gave the soldiers gifts of food and cigarettes, and persuaded them to support the people rather than fight them.*

Communism brought down (right) *The people of Moscow celebrated the collapse of the coup and Boris Yeltsin's challenge to the power of the KGB in Russia by toppling the huge statue of Felix Dzerzhinsky, founder of the Soviet secret police. The numerous statues of Vladimir Ilyich Lenin all over the country were later also removed as the Communist Party he had led was banned, and the Soviet Union he had founded more than seventy years earlier was dismantled.*

Without the support of the public, the army or the police, the coup failed. It proved to be a beginning, not an end. Mikhail Gorbachev returned to Moscow still defending the Party, but it was Boris Yeltsin who took charge during the final months of the communist empire, transforming Soviet institutions into Russian ones. Other republics declared their independence from the Soviet Union. On 25 December 1991 Gorbachev resigned, and the red flag of the Soviet Union was lowered from the roof of the Kremlin. It was an extraordinary moment. 'I had such mixed feelings,' says Dasha Khubova. 'All my generation had been born under this flag ....It was the symbol of our life, and now it was coming down. It was frightening because it seemed like the end of everything, but it was also exciting. We knew that things were changing.'

13

1980–1995

Back to the Future

Towards the Millennium

When the armies of Iraq crossed over the border into Kuwait in August 1990, the world held its breath. After issuing threats over many weeks, Saddam Hussein, the Iraqi president, had decided to invade Kuwait and take over its immense oil wealth for himself.

Less than a year after the Soviet empire had begun to crumble, the Gulf war was a reminder that although the Cold War might be over, the world was far from peaceful. The Iraqi invasion was condemned in the United Nations, and by January 1991 forces had assembled in Saudi Arabia to challenge it. Tens of thousands of people – most of them Iraqis – died as the international army, three-quarters of a million strong, forced the invaders back to Iraq.

The Gulf war reflected many of the issues facing the world as the century ended. It had been fought over a key energy source – oil. The pall of black smoke that hung over the burning oil wells, visible for hundreds of kilometres, was a reminder of the damage being inflicted on the environment not just in the war, but by human activities across the globe. The war was fought using sophisticated military technology, by forces often so far removed from the fighting that they never saw the suffering it inflicted. It was closely followed on television all over the world. Edwin Nerger, who watched in Fort Wayne, Indiana, says: 'Just about everybody in the country and a lot of the rest of the world actually lived that war....I'll never forget it.'

In the century's last decades there were many local conflicts that had international implications. Growing ethnic tensions mirrored the nationalism that had proved to be one of the principal causes of the First World War. Many people's lives were affected by economic upheavals far beyond their control in the world's repeated cycles of expansion and recession. The technological optimism of the age of electricity reappeared in the age of the computer. In some ways, people's hopes, fears and expectations at the end of the twentieth century seemed remarkably similar to those of their great-grandparents at its beginning.

Deserted landscape *Kuwaiti oil wells burn on the horizon following the Gulf war.*

New nationalisms

In 1900 many peoples, subjects of the European empires, were beginning the long struggle for independence for their nations and a voice in the political process for themselves. As the century ended, this was still true. From 1945 the Cold War that had divided much of the world into two ideological camps made national identities seem less important than whether to be communist or anti-communist. But by the mid-1980s the rigid polarization of the Cold War years began to ease, and from 1989 in Eastern Europe and the Soviet Union political independence was gained by many people, citizens of the new states established when the Soviet empire collapsed.

The voice of minority peoples was increasingly being heard: Basques and Catalans in Spain, Belgian Flemings, Bretons, German-speakers in northern Italy, Scots and Welshmen all demanded more self-government or autonomy. Sometimes this led to bloodshed and civil war. In 1991 the people of Chechnya, an autonomous province in the Russian Federation, declared their independence. At first the Russians responded by imposing economic sanctions; those did not subdue the Chechens, and in December 1994 a military invasion was launched. It was fiercely resisted, even when Chechen villages were shelled and Grozny, the capital, reduced almost to rubble.

Kashmiris stand *in front of the ruins of their home. Possession of Kashmir, situated on the mountainous northern border between India and Pakistan, remained a source of conflict between those two countries, as it had been ever since Indian partition in 1947.*

There were many other ethnic groups still hoping for greater recognition, among them the people of Kashmir, mostly Muslims, who were forced to remain part of predominantly Hindu India by an army of more than 600 000 Indian soldiers; the plebiscite that should have been held after the 1949 intervention by the United Nations had never taken place. One of the largest stateless nations remained that of the Kurds, who made up nearly a quarter of the population of Iraq and Turkey, and about a tenth that of Iran and Syria; their homeland straddled the borders of these countries. The revolt in Iraqi Kurdistan, which had begun in the 1960s, was brutally put down in the late 1980s.

The most poignant reminder of the century's early years came on 5 February 1994, when a mortar bomb exploded in the

Waving the flag
Chechen soldiers in Grozny celebrate outside the presidential palace after successfully beating off an attack by Russian forces in January 1995. Hundreds of ethnic and local groups within the Russian Federation demanded more autonomy after the Soviet Union collapsed in 1991.

old market square in the Bosnian city of Sarajevó, killing sixty-nine people. The bomb had fallen within a few metres of where a Serbian nationalist, Gavrilo Princip, had assassinated Archduke Franz Ferdinand of Austria eighty years before. In the spring of 1991, realizing that the federal state of Yugoslavia was doomed, Serbs and Croats had tried to forge independent states, seizing as much territory as they could from their neighbouring Yugoslav republics. Among the first outsiders to realize how dangerous this process might be was a group of Italian tourists, who found themselves in the middle of a gun battle between Croatian police and Serbian nationalists. A Croatian policeman and a Serbian butcher were killed, the first of some 200 000 people to die in the bitter ethnic conflicts between the peoples of Yugoslavia, whose rivalries had been submerged under communism. The fighting took the heaviest toll in Bosnia, where the Serb forces intimidated and murdered Muslim inhabitants whom they tried to expel from areas they controlled, a process known as 'ethnic cleansing'.

Muslim refugees *at the Tuzla camp near the Bosnian town of Srebrenica. Bosnia was an ethnic patchwork of Croats, Muslims and Serbs. As the conflict continued, hundreds of thousands of refugees fled or were forced to leave their homes; as evidence of mass graves, concentration camps and other atrocities emerged, it became increasingly clear that a new generation would inherit the old legacies of fear and hate.*

The atrocities committed in the breakup of Yugoslavia were dwarfed by events in Rwanda. One of the most densely populated countries in the world, this small African state was inhabited by two principal ethnic groups, who had lived together peacefully before it became first a German, then a Belgian colony. Since Rwanda had gained its independence in 1962 the minority Tutsi dominated both Rwandan society and the majority Hutu people. Attempts to resolve the conflict between them in the early 1990s seemed to be making progress, but on 6 April 1994 the presidents of Rwanda and neighbouring Burundi, returning from negotiations in Tanzania, were killed when their aircraft was shot down by a surface-to-air missile. The old enmity erupted afresh – the result was genocide. In the bloodbath more than half a million Tutsis and any Hutus who were suspected of supporting them were killed – men, women and children were hacked or bludgeoned to death by axes, machetes and any other weapons that could be found. Fearing reprisals, millions of Hutus fled Rwanda hoping to find safety in neighbouring Tanzania and Zaire; those who managed to survive the difficult journey and reached the border had to endure terrible conditions in the refugee camps.

Hillside of hunger *Food supplies from the International Red Cross are handed out to Rwandan refugees in the Goma camp in Zaire. Diseases such as cholera quickly spread in the unhygienic conditions of the camps, despite the help of aid workers from many international charities.*

Peacekeeping force *American soldiers under the auspices of the United Nations in Somalia in 1993. The UN's role as international peacekeeper was becoming more difficult – and more expensive: in 1988 the peacekeeping budget was $230 million; by 1995 it was more than $3 billion. In the decade from 1985 the UN was involved in twenty-five peacekeeping operations.*

People across the world watched and listened in horror as news of events in Bosnia, Rwanda and the world's other trouble spots was brought to them. It was television – the medium that more than any other tended to make the world a smaller, more homogenized place by allowing everyone to watch the same films, be seduced by the same advertisements, and desire the same lifestyle – that also ensured that everyone knew of the tragedies taking place. They were a grim reminder of the high price being paid by those who identified themselves with ethnic struggles and the new nationalism, which often denied them both the political stability and the economic opportunities that many people elsewhere in the world were able to take for granted.

The Million Man March *in Washington DC on 23 October 1995 was the largest black rally to be held since the civil rights march led by Martin Luther King in 1963. Issues of race and inequality had still not been resolved. Many black Americans found their identity in their race rather than in their citizenship of a country that they felt still denied them an equal place.*

Capitalism takes over

In Western Europe, where during the first half of the century many millions of people had lost their lives and livelihoods in war, a new spirit of cooperation had been established. Through the close economic ties established among members of the European Community, it was hoped that the political hostilities that so often in the past had led to war could be ended for ever. The six states that had founded the European Community in 1957 – Belgium, France, Germany, Italy, Luxembourg and the Netherlands – were joined in 1973 by Britain, Denmark and Ireland, and during the 1980s first by Greece and later by Spain and Portugal. In 1995 Austria, Finland and Sweden also joined; by this time Cyprus, Malta and Turkey had also applied for membership. So had Hungary, Poland, Romania and Slovakia, which looked westwards once the Iron Curtain had fallen.

The end of communism in Eastern Europe in the late 1980s brought economic and political change, and new hardships as well as new opportunities for the people living there. Three hundred million people were affected; many of them had skills comparable to those of people in the West, but continued to earn far less. The contrast in prosperity was most startling in Germany, a divided nation from 1945 until 1989. It was estimated that the economy of the eastern part of the country would not catch up with that of the west for at least ten years, though 150 billion Deutschmarks were being invested in its economy each year.

Since the Second World War, both the socialist states under communism and the Western democratic nations had been more closely involved in their citizens' lives than ever before. In the communist bloc, state control still limited individual rights and freedom of speech, but it ensured full employment, free education and health care for all. A social welfare programme had also been introduced in the capitalist democracies, funded by the prosperity of the boomtime years of the 1950s and 1960s. But in the late 1970s and 1980s politicians and voters began to question whether the state was the best owner of industries and services such as coal, electricity and railways. In the United States President Ronald Reagan declared: 'Government is not the solution to our problem – government *is* the problem'. Margaret Thatcher, the British

prime minister, said, 'There is no such thing as society'. Public services and welfare were cut back. The 'enterprise culture' was supposed to replace the promise that the state would take responsibility for its citizens' well-being 'from the cradle to the grave'.

In the former Soviet Union the political revolution that ended communist rule was followed by equally dramatic economic change. As well as democracy, people were to have capitalism. As subsidies were removed from factories, and the safety net that had protected the people was suddenly removed, pensioners were impoverished, miners and soldiers were not paid for months, and increasing numbers of people experienced the bitterness of unemployment – unknown under communism. Others found that their enterprise could make them millionaires.

In China, where almost a quarter of the human race still lived under a communist regime, the economy was also changing with the times. China's leaders embraced the market, and instead of insisting on equality said that the Chinese should try to make themselves rich; individual enterprise and increased spending on consumer products was the only way China would be able to fulfil its 'Four Modernizations' policy and become a major economic power by the end of the century. While the Chinese came to resemble Western capitalists in the ways they acquired and spent money, with production soaring by some 10 per cent a year, their elderly leaders remained in unchanged political control, determined to stamp out any sign of dissent or desire for democracy.

China's economic growth depended on the manufacture of consumer goods for export to the rest of the world. By 1995 some

Mall of America (left) *in Bloomington, Indiana. The largest shopping mall in the United States, it could offer 7 km (4.3 miles) of shop fronts, a wedding chapel, Legoland, amusement arcades and restaurants – the ultimate shopping experience.*

Capitalism comes to Moscow (right) *Fast food outlets such as Pizza Hut and McDonald's catered for a vast new market in the former communist world. In 1992 a Big Mac hamburger bought in Pushkin Square cost the average customer a day's wages.*

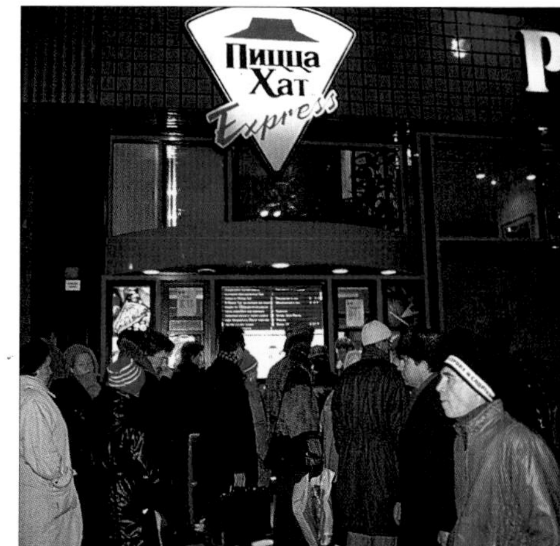

Signs of the times *Hong Kong* (ABOVE), *one of the most successful economies of East Asia, was due to be returned to China by Britain in 1997. The small, crowded islands represented a triumph of capitalism on the communist coast. China gave assurances that Hong Kong's autonomy would be respected; its promise of economic partnership is shown on the poster at the border* (BELOW).

60 per cent of toys for the international market were made in southern China, where 3000 factories were staffed by more than a million workers, most of them young women. Their wages were lower than those that would have been paid to workers in most other countries, but they were for the first time earning money that enabled them to make consumer choices of their own.

Some of the companies whose products were being made in Asia were household names in the West. They were part of a new approach to manufacturing that no longer heeded national or even continental boundaries. The rapid developments in international communications systems and the removal of trade barriers meant that multinational companies could choose where to process raw materials, where to make the components, and where to assemble goods of all kinds – from toys to cars. These companies grew ever larger and ever richer; by 1992 the 500 largest companies between them accounted for nearly a third of the world's total gross domestic product, and nearly three-quarters of world trade; more than half of the 'greenhouse emissions' produced by global industry

were the result of their activities. In 1993 up to 90 per cent of trade in a wide range of commodities – cocoa, coffee, copper, cotton, iron ore, pineapples, tea, tobacco – was controlled by no more than six giant corporations, whose activities affected numerous small farmers, craftsmen and shopkeepers in the developing world. As the wealth of the multinationals grew, so did their economic power. Accountable only to their shareholders, these companies began to replace governments as shapers of the world economy. At a time of rising unemployment, people in industrialized countries were also affected: as the multinationals sought cheaper labour for their factories, unemployment in developed nations increased.

Eager to play their part in the world economy, and to improve trade as a way of acquiring foreign currency and reducing their debts, many developing countries set up special Export Processing Zones (EPZs) to attract multinational corporations. While there were benefits for the host nations, conditions for the workers were often poor, and the countries themselves became more vulnerable to fluctuations in world markets. This was true in predominantly agricultural countries as well, where farmers were encouraged to abandon subsistence crops such as maize or sweet potatoes in favour of cash crops such as coffee or exotic vegetables to stock the shelves of Western supermarkets. Their customers had an ever greater range of goods to choose from, and once-seasonal fresh foods could now be obtained all year round.

Toys for export
Barbie dolls being packed in a toy factory in Indonesia. By the end of the 1980s no Barbie dolls were made in the United States: they were all manufactured in South America and East Asia.

These efforts ensured that during the 1980s and 1990s more countries – in Central and South America and particularly in parts of Asia – began to share in the new prosperity, though much of Africa was being left behind. The poorest developing countries came under pressure from the international lending organizations such as the World Bank to carry out what was called 'structural adjustment': cutting public expenditure to reduce state budgets, deficits and inflation. Investment in education and welfare was reduced; the one area where cuts were not made was in defence budgets – they absorbed ever higher proportions of national wealth in many countries, including those that could least afford it.

The result of all these economic and political changes was that across the world in almost every country, developing and developed, the gap between rich and poor widened.

Children of the Street

THE PLACARD LEFT BY THE BODY of a boy killed on a beach in Rio de Janeiro read: 'I killed you because you had no future'. In the 1980s and 1990s in the cities of Brazil, where many street children died violent deaths at the hands of the authorities, it was the police, rather than poverty or loneliness, that those whose home was on the street most feared.

As the populations of the world's cities grew during the century, so the numbers of young people living in them rose. Both in industrialized and in developing countries, the numbers of children working and even living on the streets also grew. By the mid-1990s there were millions of them; it was impossible to calculate exactly how many. The highest number, about two million children, were estimated to be in Brazil; there were large numbers elsewhere in some countries in Central and South America, particularly in Colombia, Guatemala and Mexico. There were street children in India, many of them belonging to families known as 'pavement dwellers'; and others in Ethiopia and Sudan, in Sri Lanka and Vietnam.

Most of the children were forced onto the streets by poverty, having to help support their families by selling roasted peanuts, cleaning car windscreens or 'guarding' cars, shining shoes or begging. These children went home at night. A small minority had abandoned or been abandoned by their families, and had to find what care and companionship they could among other street children. In industrial countries they were most often runaways escaping family discord. An estimated 80 per cent of North American homeless children had left because they had been physically or sexually abused; this was said to be true of only 20 per cent of street children in Central and South America. In the developed world there were about the same number of street girls as street boys, whereas in cities of the developing world the vast majority were boys.

Concern for the children's fate led to a number of projects to help them, and they also took initiatives of their own. In 1985 the National Movement of Street Boys and Girls was founded in Brazil. The second national meeting, in 1989, exposed the authorized killing of children; the resulting publicity forced the government to recognize what was taking place. In Guatemala the staff of Covenant House (Casa Alianza), an organization set up in the mid-1980s to offer shelter to street children, decided to document the violence after a child was kicked to death by four policemen. When they publicized the violence and attempted to prosecute the perpetrators, the workers themselves received death threats.

Many children encountered hostility not only from the authorities but also from the general public, who saw them as drug-abusing, violent delinquents. But the street children – like all the other children whose childhoods were being disrupted by famine or exploitation, or the traumas of war – did not create the world in which they were growing up. Living on its margins, they merely reflected it.

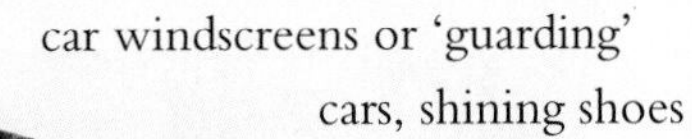

HANGING ON *Street children in Rio de Janeiro, Brazil. All street children were at risk of violence, abuse and exploitation by adults and older children. Many of those with no other prospects drifted into crime as they grew up.*

THE INTERNATIONAL AIRPORT *at Orly, near Paris. In the early 1990s it was Europe's third busiest airport – after London Heathrow and Frankfurt am Main in Germany – with more than twenty-three million passengers a year. As air traffic increased, airports became increasingly congested not only in the terminals but in the air above, and computer-controlled air traffic control systems became more sophisticated and complex.*

The shrinking world

The changing patterns of world trade would not have taken place without the technological revolution that accompanied them. At the beginning of the century it had been the discovery and the many applications of electricity that had the greatest potential and brought about the most dramatic technological change. In the 1990s technological innovation continued, and at an increasingly rapid pace. The exploration of space, developed during the Cold War years, had led to a greater understanding of the outer world; this was being matched by an unparalleled exploration of our inner world: the workings of the human body.

The most dramatic impact on people's lives was to come through the electronics and computer revolution. The computer developed from advances in mathematics, miniaturization, silicon chemistry, engineering and many other fields. In the 1980s the manufacture and widespread use of personal computers made it possible for individuals as well as companies to link up around the world faster and more cheaply than ever before. The giant dustfree

SURFING THE NET *at the Cyberia Internet Café in London. It was impossible to establish how many people were using the Internet by the mid 1990s; estimates varied from sixteen million to forty million, and the number was said to be doubling every year. Users could gain almost instant access to an extraordinary range of information and activities.*

mainframe computers of the 1960s had centralized power in large institutions, and had to be operated by white-coated specialists; the personal computer dispersed power to individuals. Anyone able to afford the hardware (which became cheaper every year) could word-process, calculate, operate spreadsheets, and access databases of every kind. Huge amounts of information could be processed and transmitted in seconds. By the early 1990s people in almost every field – from shopkeepers to doctors and tyre-fitters to financiers – were using computers in their work. Children were taught how to use them in school, and enjoyed the games that could be played on them at home.

By the early 1990s the personal computer was being transformed from a self-contained desktop tool to a gateway to every other computer in the world via the Internet. People around the world could now communicate directly and instantaneously with each other for little more than the cost of a local telephone call. The Internet began as a United States military project to develop a communications system that would not be destroyed in the event of a nuclear attack. In the late 1970s the system was opened up to other government departments, and to research organizations and universities. In 1992 permission was granted to private companies to offer subscriptions giving individuals access to information on the Internet. Access to the Internet began to grow most rapidly in the prosperous West, and also became available elsewhere in the world: India and South Korea opened up a full service; and it was spreading in Indonesia and the Philippines.

It was too early to predict the full impact of this technology. Among its probable consequences were the increasing dominance worldwide of 'American' English in business, and the dispersal of 'office work' from city centres to people living and working in small towns and villages. It was already possible to ignore national boundaries and employ people for clerical work in countries where labour costs were lower: American airlines used computer operators in the Caribbean to prepare their tickets, and British banks sent figures to be processed overnight in India.

By the mid-1990s it was clear that the computer revolution was still only beginning. In addition to numerical data (military and intelligence information,

GREEN FUEL *While the roads became ever busier, attempts were made to reduce the noxious effects of vehicle exhaust emissions. One of these was unleaded petrol.*

The silver disc

COMPACT DISCS *were first launched in 1980; by the end of the decade the sale of discs was already overtaking that of vinyl records. They offered improved sound quality, and because they were read by a laser beam rather than having a needle running in a groove, did not wear out. They could store vast amounts of information, and were soon used not just for music recordings but as an alternative to books and videos, combining text, graphics, sound and animation.*

ROBOTS ON THE LINE (ABOVE) *The heavy, hot, repetitive work of making cars, such as this Porsche in Germany, was undertaken faster and more accurately by robots than by humans.*

SCANNING THE BRAIN (RIGHT) *A medical technician examines the brain of a patient at a New York hospital. Non-invasive diagnostic techniques were a valuable medical tool.*

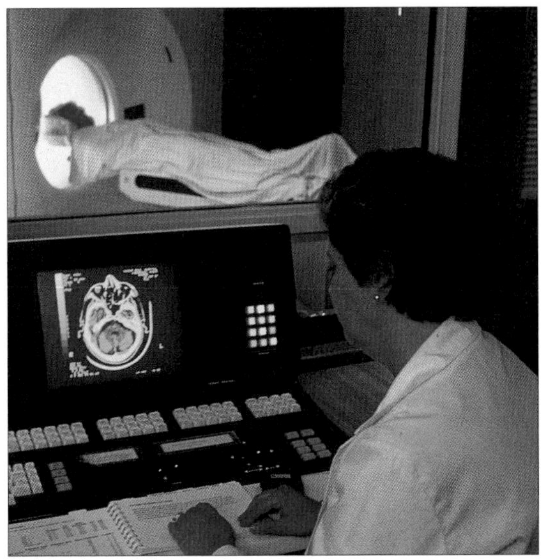

Mapping our genes

For much of the twentieth century, the exploration of space was one of the most exciting scientific adventures. By the late 1980s another kind of exploration was taking place that was likely to have a huge impact on the future of the human race.

The instruction manual of the human body is written in a chemical code found in the nucleus of cells. These coded messages determine our biological inheritance: our appearance, our inherent abilities, our predisposition for different diseases, and much more. This chemical instruction manual is known as DNA – deoxyribonucleic acid. The structure of DNA was discovered in the 1950s; within its structure, which is like a spiral ladder, are the units – called genes – that carry the coded instructions for the individual characteristics of every organism. During the 1980s a research project was initiated whose aim was to map the genetic code of human beings. Such a huge and costly venture needed international cooperation, and in 1988 the Human Genome Organization (HUGO) was established; by 1990 it already had 250 members – all research scientists – from twenty-three countries.

A complete genome map would cover the whole of the DNA sequence, but this would be prohibitively expensive. As only 2 per cent of the entire sequence of DNA consists of active genes, about 100 000 in all, it was decided to concentrate on these. The messages of the genetic code are 'written' in pairs of chemical bases; a short message would consist of a few hundred bases, while long ones require many thousands. By the end of 1995 more than five million bases had been identified – still only a fraction of the total.

From the outset the most compelling reason for the research was to help eradicate inherited disease. There are thousands of these diseases, including asthma, certain cancers, cystic fibrosis, haemophilia and sickle-cell anaemia. It is 'mistakes' in the message of a particular gene that can trigger the disease in an individual.

While some scientists undertook the painstaking work of mapping the genes, others developed techniques to change them. Genetic engineering speeds up the process that naturally takes place in any sort of selective breeding – long used to produce more fragrant or colourful flowers, crops with greater yields or improved animal breeds. Selective breeding works only within a species; genetic engineering can transfer characteristics between very different species – a process was developed to produce insulin, the hormone humans need to regulate sugar in the blood, within genetically engineered bacteria. By the mid-1990s the possibilities of gene therapy were offering new hope to many thousands of people. There was some concern about the ethical implications of genetic engineering, yet it might also prove enormously beneficial, perhaps improving the health of entire populations by correcting the faults in genes that carry disease from generation to generation.

FROZEN CONTINENT (ABOVE) *A biologist undertakes research in the harsh conditions of Ross Island on the coast of Antarctica. Activities other than scientific research were banned for fifty years in 1991. The continent is of particular interest to environmental scientists, as its thick covering of ice – an average of 2000 metres (6500 feet) deep – holds the history of the Earth's atmosphere.*

VIRTUAL REALITY (LEFT) *first became available in March 1993. This uniquely interactive form of computer entertainment was hailed as an exciting new experience – and as an addictive hi-tech hallucinogen.*

SPACE LAUNCH (OPPOSITE) *A satellite is released from a space shuttle cargo bay. The first manned space flight took place in 1966; in 1981 the space shuttle, the first manned spacecraft designed to be reused, was launched. Space programmes were developed for both military and scientific purposes.*

telephone banking, scientific calculations, commercial transactions) voice communication, music, maps, still and moving images could be translated into digital information, stored, retrieved and reproduced at amazing speed.

The computer was not the only important technology of the late twentieth century. During the previous hundred years, people's lives had been changed as much by the achievements of medical scientists as by those of engineers and physicists, and now biotechnology promised further possibilities for curing disease. Some people embraced the new possibilities; others urged caution, and called for more stringent ethical and environmental controls.

By the 1990s concerns about the environment had become a constant reminder that the development of new technologies could be dangerous as well as beneficial, and that their effects were often not understood at the time; like so much else, it had become a global issue. Scientists and environmentalists increasingly agreed that uncontrolled human activity was damaging the Earth, and that the carbon dioxide emissions resulting from industrial activity were likely to bring about dramatic, potentially disastrous climatic change. It was feared that over-consumption of water would threaten whole regions, and water shortages provoke conflicts as dangerous as earlier wars over land and oil.

On the brink of the new millennium, humans could for the first time truly be said to be living in the global village, where the actions of people in one country directly impinged on those in other countries. Technological advances challenged the power of institutions; governments could no longer so easily restrict their citizens' access to information, or pursue policies in isolation. Fast, cheap communication enhanced people's opportunities to take part in the global economy, and education and skills became increasingly important: in time, the world would be divided between the information haves and have-nots. Many people faced an ambiguous future, and lived poised between fear and hope in a world of rapid change. As Donald Hodge, who had grown up in the early years of the century, reflects, 'It is an entirely new world ....Everything has changed – the outlook of people, aspects of communication. The world has shrunk down to a tiny ball now, where once it used to extend so far.'

Acknowledgements

Television

Executive Producers
Peter Pagnamenta (BBC)
Zvi Dor-Ner (WGBH)

Archive Producer
Christine Whittaker

Programme Producers
Archie Baron, Charles Furneaux, Bill Treharne Jones, Marian Marzynski, Max Whitby, James A. Devinney, Peter Ceresole, Jenny Clayton, Mark J. Davis, Anne Moir, Angela Holdsworth, Ben Loeterman, Angus MacQueen

Assistant Producers
Rosalind Bain, Robi Dutta, Harry Gural, Nathan Z. Hendrie, Nancy Fraser, Kevin Huffman, Lisa Jones, Marcus Kiggell, Gabrielle Osrin, Dominic Ozanne, Sun Shuyun, Eddie Tulasiewicz

Film Researchers
James Barker, Michaela Barnes, Maggi Cook, Alex Cowan, Carol Davis-Foster, Deborah Ford, Hilary Goldhammer, Susan Levene, Jill McLoughlin, Lynn Mason, Alf Penn, David Thaxton, Masha Oleneva

Film Editors
Guy Crossman, Sally Hilton, Alison Lewis, Roderick Longhurst, Jon Neuburger, James Rutenbeck, Charles Scott, David Simpson, Beth Solomon

Supervising Film Editor
Stephen Sampson

Series Managers (London)
Carol Harding, Candida Pryce Jones

Production Managers (Boston)
Carol Osterer, Kathleen Shugrue

Core Team
Laura Azevedo, Sheoko Badman-Walker, Sally Ball, Alexandra Branson, James Dobel, Jill Flippance, Sue MacGregor, Fiona Mellon-Grant, Rachel Solman, Alison Whitlock

Publishing

People's Century was produced for BBC Worldwide Publishing by

B·C·S Publishing Limited, Chesterton, Oxfordshire

Editorial Director
Candida Hunt

Art Director
Steve McCurdy

Editors
Deena Daher, Jenny Roberts

Assistant Editor
Tabitha Jackson

Picture Research
Alexander Goldberg and James Clift of Image Select (London), David Pratt

Index
Sarah Ereira

Picture credits

10 Image Select/Vioujard, **12** *(top)* Corbis/Bettmann, **12** *(bottom)* Corbis/Bettmann, **13** *(top)* Image Select/Dickman, **13** *(bottom)* Hulton Getty, **15** *(left)* Aleksei Kondratiev, **15** *(right)* Popperfoto, **16** *(top)* Thomas Saffer, **16** *(bottom)* Thomas Saffer, **16/17** US National Marine Archive, **17** Popperfoto, **18/19** Advertising Archives, **19** Popperfoto, **20** *(top)* Sheldon Johnson, **20** *(middle)* Sheldon Johnson, **20** *(bottom)* US National Archives, **21** *(top)* Periodicals Art Library, **21** *(middle)* Periodicals Art Library, **21** *(bottom)* Popperfoto, **22** *(top)* Corbis/Bettmann, **22** *(bottom)* Hulton Getty, **22/23** Popperfoto, **24** *(top)* CND, **24** *(bottom)* Hulton Getty, **24/25** Kobal Collection, **26/27** Image Select/Gilbert Uzan, **27** Image Select/De Bugey, **28** *(top)* Valery Staradumov, **28** *(bottom)* Valery Staradumov, **29** Novosti/Image Select, **30** Image Select/Deville, **31** *(left)* Leonid Teliatnikov, **31** *(right)* Leonid Teliatnikov, **32** Image Select/Sultun, **33** Image Select/Kurita, **34** Hulton Getty, **36** *(top)* Corbis/Bettmann, **36** *(bottom)* Hulton Getty, **37** *(top)* Hulton Getty, **37** *(bottom)* Hulton Getty, **38/39** Magnum, **39** *(left)* Hulton Getty, **39** *(right)* Werner Bischof/Magnum, **40** Werner Bischolf/Magnum, **41** Magnum, **42** Image Select/Sony, **42/43** Corbis/Bettmann, **43** Spectrum, **44** Spectrum, **44/45** Magnum, **45** *(left)* Magnum, **45** *(centre)* Nobuko and Taisuke Sato/Tim Humphries, **45** *(right)* Japanese Embassy, London, **46** Hulton Getty, **46/47** Hulton Getty, **47** *(top)* Hulton Getty, **47** *(bottom left)* Takunori Nagaoka, **47** *(bottom right)* Takunori Nagaoka, **48** Hulton Getty, **48/49** Images, **50** Hulton Getty, **51** *(top)* René Burri/Magnum, **51** *(bottom)* Philip Jones Griffiths/Magnum, **52** Marilyn Silverstone/Magnum, **52/53** Image Select/Lochon, **53** *(top)* Yi Chong Kak/ Tim Humphries, **53** *(bottom)* Yi Chong Kak/Tim Humphries, **54** René Burri/Magnum, **54/55** James Nachtwey/Magnum, **55** *(left)* Kang Sung Ro, **55** *(right)* Kang Sung Ro, **56** Hutchison, **57** Image Select, **58** Ian Berry/Magnum, **60** *(top)* Publisher's Photo Source, **60** *(bottom)* Popperfoto, **61** Corbis/Bettmann, **62/63** Popperfoto, **63** *(left)* Popperfoto, **63** *(right)* Popperfoto, **64/65** Corbis/Bettmann, **65** *(top)* Corbis/Bettmann, **65** *(bottom)* Bernard Lafayette, **66/67** Corbis/Bettmann, **67** *(top)* Ernest Green, **67** *(bottom)* Corbis/Bettmann, **68** Popperfoto, **69** *(top)* Floyd Mann, **69** *(middle)* Floyd Mann, **69** *(bottom)* Magnum, **70** Hulton Getty, **71** Corbis/Bettmann, **72** Popperfoto, **72/73** Camera Press, **73** *(top)* Popperfoto, **73** *(middle)* David Bruce, **73** *(bottom)* David Bruce, **74/75** Magnum, **75** Popperfoto, **76** *(top)* Hulton Getty, **76** *(bottom)* Image Select/Chambeau, **77** Image Select, **78** Hulton Getty, **79** *(top)* Image Select/Bouvet, **79** *(bottom)* Image Select/De Keerle, **80** *(top)* Popperfoto, **80** *(bottom)* Nomathamsanqua Koha, **81** Image Select, **82** Image Select, **84** Magnum, **85** *(top)* Toshio Hamada, **85** *(middle)* Hidenori Yamashita, **85** *(bottom)* Hidenori Yamashita/Max Whitby, **86** Hulton Getty, **86/87** BBC, **87** *(top)* Hulton Getty, **87** *(bottom)* Olga Penrose, **88** Lloyd Kiff, **88/89** Hulton Getty, **89** Corbis/Bettmann, **90** Rex Features, **91** *(top)* Magnum, **91** *(bottom)* Magnum, **92/93** Environmental Picture Library, **93** Panos Pictures, **94** Press Association, **94/95** Environmental Picture Library, **96** Environmental Picture Library, **96/97** Liaison, **97** *(top)* Lois Gibbs/Max Whitby, **97** *(bottom)* Liaison, **98** *(top)*

Image Select/Dupuis, **98** *(bottom)* Image Select/Biblis, **99** Image Select/Piel, **100** *(top)* Image Select/Bartholomew, **100** *(bottom)* Image Select/Alain Mingam, **101** Image Select/Mecca, **102** *(top)* F. Sherwood Roland, **102** *(middle)* F. Sherwood Roland/Max Whitby, **102** *(bottom)* Image Select/Liason, **103** Image Select/Ribiero, **104** Image Select/Malis, **105** Image Select/Patrick Piel, **106** Popperfoto, **108** Hulton Getty, **108/109** Archive Photos, **109** Hulton Getty, **110** *(top)* Corbis/Bettmann, **110** *(middle)* Peter Robinson, **110** *(bottom)* Corbis/Bettmann, **111** AKG London, **112/113** Hulton Getty, **113** Archive Photos, **114** *(top)* Lenore's TV Guide, **114** *(middle)* Hulton Getty, **114** *(bottom)* Popperfoto, **115** *(top)* Magnum, **115** *(middle)* Kamila Mouchkova, **115** *(bottom)* Associated Press, **116** *(top)* Alex Azar, **116** *(middle)* Corbis/Bettmann, **116** *(bottom)* Corbis/Bettmann, **117** *(top)* Hulton Getty, **117** *(bottom)* Hulton Getty, **118** *(top)* Hulton Getty, **118** *(bottom)* Advertising Archives, **119** *(top)* Dorothy and Benjamin Berger, *(middle)* Corbis/Bettmann, *(bottom)* Corbis/Bettmann, **120** *(top)* Popperfoto, **120** *(bottom)* Australian National Film & TV Archives, **120/121** Allsport, **122** *(top)* The Vintage Magazine Company, **122** *(middle)* Steliana Stefonoiu, **122** *(bottom)* Corbis Bettmann, **124** Suman Film Company, **124/125** Mark Edwards/Still Pictures, **125** Children's Television Workshop, **126** Associated Press, **127** Camera Press, **128** *(top)* Image Select, **128** *(bottom)* BBC, **129** Network, **130** Hulton Getty, **131** *(top)* Hulton Getty, **132** *(bottom)* Hulton Getty, **133** National Labour Party, **134** Hulton Getty, **134/35** Hulton Getty, **135** *(top)* Marjorie Cave, **135** *(bottom)* Marjorie Cave, **136** *(top)* Corbis/Bettmann, **136** *(bottom)* Corbis/Bettmann, **136/37** Corbis/Bettmann, **137** *(above)* Deborah Runkle, **137** *(bottom)* Deborah Runkle, **138** *(top)* World Health Organization, **138** *(bottom)* Hulton Getty, **139** Hulton Getty, **140** Image Select/Peterson, **141** *(top)* World Health Organization, **142** *(bottom)* UNICEF, **142** Image Select/Xinhua/Nouvelle, **143** Image Select/Santosh Basak, **144** *(top)* Image Select/Santosh Basak, **144** *(bottom)* World Health Organization, **146/47** Environmental Picture Library, **148** Image Select/Jean Michel Turpin, **148/49** Hector Mata/Image Select, **149** Hulton Getty, **150** Image Select/Daher, **150/51** SIPA Press, **151** *(top)* Image Select/Vioujard, **151** *(bottom)* Peter Staley, **152** Image Select/Bartholomew, **152/153** Art Directors, **154** Peter Newark, **156** Popperfoto, **157** Popperfoto, **158** Cartier Bresson/Magnum, **158/159** Hulton Getty, **160** Popperfoto, **161** Peter Newark, **162/163** Sun Shuyun, **163** *(top left)* Shao Ai Ling, **163** *(bottom left)* Shao Ai Ling/Jenny Clayton, **163** *(right)* Camera Press, **164/165** Cartier Bresson/Magnum, **165** *(top)* Peter Newark, **165** *(bottom)* Camera Press, **166** *(top)* Camera Press, **166** *(bottom)* Camera Press, **167** *(top)* Sun Shuyun, **167** *(bottom)* He Jin Lua and Lian Tianyun/Jenny Clayton, **168** Camera Press, **168/169** Popperfoto, **169** Popperfoto, **170** Hulton Getty, **171** *(top)* Image Select, **171** *(bottom)* Image Select, **172** *(top)* Topham, **172** *(bottom)* David King, **173** *(top)* Tong Xiang Ling, **173** *(middle)* Tong Xiang Ling/Jenny Clayton, **173** *(bottom)* Hulton Getty, **174** Image Select/Chince, **174/175** *(top)* Popperfoto, **174/175** *(bottom)* Popperfoto, **176** Corbis/Bettmann, **177** Image Select/Lil Liais, **178** Corbis/Bettmann, **180** Christie's Images, **180/181** Corbis/Bettmann, **181** *(top)* Hulton Getty, **181** *(bottom)* Corbis/Bettmann, **182** *(top)* Marc Ribould/Magnum, **182** *(bottom)* Kobal Collection, **183** *(top)* Hulton Getty, **183** *(middle)* Rogan Taylor, **183** *(bottom)* Hulton Getty, **184** Apple Corporation, **184/185** Hulton Getty, **185** *(top)* Camera Press, **185** *(bottom)* Rex Features, **186** *(top)* Image Select, **186** *(bottom)* Vivian Rothstein, **187** Andromeda (Oxford) Ltd, **188** Image Select/Rey, **188/189** Popperfoto, **190** *(top)* Rex Features, **190** *(bottom)* Martine Algier, **191** Camera Press, **192** Leonard Freed/Magnum, **192/193** Redferns, **193** Hulton Getty, **194** *(top)* Ron Thelin, **194** *(middle)* Ron Thelin, **194** *(bottom)* Corbis/Bettmann, **194/195** Rex Features, **196** *(top)* Rusty Sachs, **196** *(middle)* Rusty Sachs, **196** *(bottom)* Marc Ribould/Magnum, **196/197** Leonard Freed/Magnum, **198** *(top left)* Image Select, **198** *(top right)* Romain Goupil, **198** *(bottom)* Popperfoto, **198/199** Rex Features, **199** Jeff Jones, **200** Press Association, **201** ZEFA, **202** Corbis/Bettman, **204** Corbis/Bettmann, **205** Norman Rockwell/Advertising Archives, **206** Advertising Archives, **206/207** Advertising Archives, **207** Magnum, **208** *(left)* Schering Health Care, **208** *(right top)* Anilu Elias, **208** *(right middle)* Anilu Elias, **208/209** Corbis/Bettmann, Advertising Archives, **210** Claude Sauvageot, **211** *(top left)* Advertising Archives, **211** *(top right)* Advertising Archives, **211** *(middle)* Dusty Roads, **211** *(bottom)* Advertising Archives, **212** *(left)* Amy Coen, **212** *(right)* Amy Coen, **212/213** Magnum, **214** Corbis/Bettmann, **215** *(top)* Popperfoto, **215** *(bottom)* Image Select/Laffont, **216** *(left)* Jaqui Ceballos, **216** *(right)* Corbis/Bettmann, **217** Popperfoto, **218** *(top)* Ginnie Whitehill, **218** *(bottom)* Corbis/Bettmann, **218/219** Image Select/Fornaciari, **219** Telegraph Colour Library, **220** Image Select/Kobbel, **220/221** Camera Press, **221** Corbis/Bettmann, **222** Vibhuti Patel, **222/223** Raissa Page/Format, **223** Aga Khan Trust for Culture/Anwar Hossein, **224** *(top)* Popperfoto, **224** *(bottom)* Corbis/Bettmann, **225** Corbis/Bettmann, **226** Image Select/Claude Francolon, **228** *(left top)* Arsenio Garcia/Peter Sainsbury, **228** *(left middle)* Arsenio Garcia, **228** *(left bottom)* Arsenio Garcia, **228** *(right)* Acme Photo, **229** Popperfoto, **230** Corbis/Bettmann, **231** *(top)* AKG London, **231** *(bottom)* Image Select/Fornaciari, **232/233** AKG London, **234** *(top)* Corbis/Bettmann, **234** *(bottom)* Camera Press, **234/235** Popperfoto, **235** *(top)* Earl Young, **235** *(bottom)* Earl Young, **236** Popperfoto, **236/237** *(top)* Duong Thanh Phong, **236/237** *(bottom)* Popperfoto, **238** *(top)* Tran Thi Gung, **238** *(middle)* Duong Thanh Phong, **238** *(bottom)* Duong Thanh Phong, **239** Popperfoto, **241** *(top)* Corbis/Bettmann, **241** *(bottom)* Image Select/Labbe, **242/243** Image Select/Lochon, **243** Image Select/Novosti, **244** *(top)* Courtesy of the Ministry of Defence Pattern Room, **244** *(middle)* Hulton Getty, **244** *(bottom)* Image Select/Liason, **245** Image Select/Gregory, **246** *(top)* Image Select/Gaal, **246** *(bottom)* Image Select/Nagakura, **247** Image Select/Zoom 77, **248** Image Select/Dison, **249** Image Select/Mingam, **250** Rex Features, **252** *(left)* Popperfoto, **252** *(right)* Popperfoto, **252/253** Image Select, **253** Popperfoto, **254/255** Image Select/Mohamed Lounes, **255** Image Select/Mohamed Lounes, **256** Popperfoto, **257** *(top)* Rex Features, **257** *(bottom)* Rex Features, **258** Popperfoto, **259** *(top left)* Popperfoto, **259** *(top right)* Hadi Gaffari, **259** *(bottom)* Rex Features, **260** Image Select/Uzan, **261** Image Select/Abbas, **262/263** Image Select/Abbas, **263** *(top)* Image Select/Goodman, **263** *(bottom)* Image Select/Michel Artault, **264** Rex Features, **266** Image Select/Bartholomew, **266/267** BBC, **268** Popperfoto, **268/269** Rex Features, **269** Rex Features, **270** *(top)* Yasser Tawfiq, **270** *(bottom)* Rex Features, **270/271** Image Select/Vioujard, **272** Image Select/Taher, **273** Image Select/Reza, **274** Image Select/Bouvet, **276/277** Magnum, **277** *(top)* Nina Motova, **277** *(bottom)* Nina Motova, **278** *(left)* Hulton Getty, **278** *(right top)* Dietmar Passenheim, **278** *(right bottom)* Dietmar Passenheim, **279** *(top)* Magnum, **279** *(bottom)* Dietmar Passenheim, **280/281** Image Select/Apsteguy, **281** Image Select/Czarnecki, **282/283** Magnum, **283** *(top)* Image Select/Czarnecki, **283** *(bottom)* Zbigniew Lelental, **284** *(top)* Image Select, **284** *(bottom)* Yevgeny Mahaev, **284/285** Image Select/Francolon, **286** Image Select/Bouvet, **287** Image Select/Piel, **288** *(bottom)* Bärbel Reinke, **288/289** Image Select/Bouvet, **289** Image Select/Bouvet, **290** *(left)* Andrej Krob, **290** *(right)* Andrej Krob, **290/291** Camera Press, **292** *(left)* Associated Press, **292** *(right)* Magnum, **292/293** Camera Press, **294** *(top)* Image Select, **294** *(bottom)* Image Select/Saussier, **294/295** Magnum, **295** Magnum, **296** Camera Press, **297** Magnum, **298** Camera Press, **300** Camera Press, **300/301** Paul Lowe/Magnum, **301** Magnum, **302** Camera Press, **303** *(left)* Image Select/Turpin, **303** *(right)* Image Select/Peterson, **304/305** Martin Parr/Magnum, **305** C. Steele-Perkins/Magnum, **306** Ian Berry/ Magnum, **306/307** Camera Press, **307** Image Select/Hernandez, **308** Image Select/Ghislaine Morel, **308/309** Image Select/Alain Buu, **309** Paul Lowe/Magnum, **310** *(top)* Spectrum, **310** *(bottom)* Images, **310/311** Images, **311** Spectrum, **312** *(top)* Images, **312** *(bottom)* Image Select/Howell, **313** Images

The publishers would like to thank all the people who took part in the making of the programmes and kindly lent their own photographs for use in this book.

Index

Page numbers in italic type refer to picture captions.

A

Abe, Chikara, 44
Aboriginals, Australian, 77
abortion, 208, 209, 215, 218, 220, 224, 293
Abrell, Joe, 114
acid rain, 98, *104*
advertising, 110, 112, 115, 121, 303
Afghanistan, Soviet intervention, 243-6, 248, 265, 285
African National Congress (ANC), 74, 76, *78*, 79-80
Afrikaners, 61, 62
Agarwal, Anil, 92, 93
Agent Orange, 238
Agnew, Harold, 12, 22
AIDS, 150, *151*, 152, 293
aircraft: atomic bombing, *12*, 13-14; pilots and stewardesses, 207, 211, 215, *221*; B-52 bombers, 236; Vietnam, 236, 238
Alaska, 100
alcohol: advertising, 112; Islamic law, 255, 262
Aldermaston march, 23-4
Aleutian islands, 90
Algeria: television, 114; women's status, *224*; Islamic politics, *270*, 271-2
Algier, Martine, 179, 181, 190, 195
Altshuller, Lev, 15
American Broadcasting Company (ABC), 121
American Nuclear Society, 26
Amir-Shahy, Mashid, 254, 262
Ammatari, Muhammad, 271
Amoco Cadiz, *100*
Anacapa island, 88
Andropov, Yuri, *284*
Anghel, Badea, 127
Antarctica, *312*
antenatal care, 132
apartheid, 61, 62-3, 72-4, 79-80
Apollo 8, 83
Apollo 11, 118
Arafat, Yasser, 247
Argentina: women's suffrage, 206; Montoneros, 231-2
arms race, 16, 23, 24, 32
Army of the Republic of Vietnam (ARVN), 235, 236, *237*, 241
Arora, Shyam Sunder, 124
Arthrell, Bill, 199, 200
Asanuma, Inejiro, *120*
Asian Games (1986), 55
Atatürk, Mustafa Kemal, 252
atom bomb, 11-16
atomgrads, 15
Atomic Energy Commission (AEC), 20
Australia: anti-nuclear protest, 24; Aboriginal land rights, 77; television, 112, 114, 120, 122; Olympics (1956), 114; immunization, 136; food aid, 149; young people, 179; education, 180; youth protests, 196; women's status, 210, 212, *221*; childcare, 219
Austria: Green Party, 99; borders, *286*
Avila, Claudia, 232
Ayers Rock, 77
Ayodhya, religious riots, *266*
Ayres, Richard, 83
Azar, Alex, 113, *116*, 128

B

Baader-Meinhof Gang, *231*
baby boom, 180, 185
Bagge, Carl, 84, 85, 98-9, 100
Baird, John Logie, 108
Bantu, 63
Bareira, Ernesto, 232
Batista, General Fulgencio, 229, 230, 231
Beatles, The, 117, 183, 184, *185*, *190*
beatniks, *181*, *193*
beauty contests, 215
Beijing: revolution (1949), 159; Cultural Revolution, *172*; Tiananmen Square massacre (1989), 176
Belgium: radioactive fallout, 26; Green Party, 99; education, 180; women's status, 219
Bell Telephone Laboratories, 108
Benes, Alexandra, 122
Berber tribesmen, *141*
Berger, Benjamin, 119, 120
Berger, Dorothy, 117, 119
Berkeley students, 186-7, 189
Berlin: Olympics (1936), 109, 121; Free University, *181*; communes, 195; Wall, 275, *286*; riots (1953), 280; border opening, *288*
Bharatiya Janata Party (BJP), 124
Bhatt, Kalpana, 144
Bhopal, toxic leak, 100
Bhutto, Benazir, *220*
Biafra, 149
Big Sur, commune, 195
Bikini atoll, 21
Biko, Stephen, 76
birth control, 48, 142-5, 208, 209, 293
Black Friday, *259*
Black September, 120
Blackboard Jungle, 181
Blazejewski, Carmen, 277, 284, 285, 289
Blotsky, Oleg, 244, *248*
Boer War, 61
bombing: nuclear, *12*, 13-14; Vietnam, 236, 238
Borusewicz, Alena, 280, 281
Borusewicz, Bogdan, 280, 282
Bosnia, 301, 303
Bossar, Bob, 180, 184, 190
Brandenburg Gate, *288*, 289
Brando, Marlon, *182*
Brandt, Marjorie, 107, 113, 119
Brazil: fuel, 103; television, 122
Brezhnev, Leonid, *284*, 285, 286
Brish, Arkadi, 15-16, 23, 32
Britain: nuclear research, 12, 16; nuclear energy, 19, 26; civil defence, 22; nuclear testing, 23; anti-nuclear protest, 23-4; nuclear waste, 27; *Torrey Canyon* disaster, 87-8; Green Party, 99; television, 108-9, 110, 112, 114, *118*, 121, 122; coronation, 114; health care, *132*, 133, *134*; education, 180, 185, 187-8; young people, 181, 182, 183, 184, 187-8, 192; pop festivals, *193*; communes, 195; Vietnam demonstration, 197; student unrest, 197; voting age lowered, *200*; women's status, 206, 212, 216, 218, 219, 220-1; contraceptive pill, *209*; childcare, 219; ordination of women, *224*; Northern Ireland policy, 242; Middle East involvement, 252, 264
British Broadcasting Corporation (BBC), 110
Brixner, Berlyn, 11
Brown, John O., 109
Bruce, David, 73, 78
Brundage, Avery, 46
Bucharest: television, *127;* demonstrations, *292*
Buenos Aires, 232
bullet train, *47*
Burundi, 303
Bush, George, *151*
Buthelezi, Chief Mangosuthu, 79

C

Cable News Network (CNN), 128
cable television, 121, 128
Cambodia, 240
Campaign for Nuclear Disarmament (CND), 24, 188
Campbell, Bonnie, 83
Canada: nuclear power, 19; pollution, 102, *104*; health care, 132, 136; food aid, 149; young people, 179; education, 180; youth protests, 196; women's suffrage, 204; women's status, 212; childcare, 219
cancer, 31, 56, 96, 311
cannabis, *190*, 192
Cape Canaveral, *117*
cars: Japanese industry, 41, 44; Japanese ownership, 44, *45*; South Korea, *52*, 55; Hong Kong, 56; pollution, 86, *310*; unleaded fuel, *310*; robot manufacture, *310*
Carson, Rachel, 86, 88
Carter, Jimmy, *259*
Castro, Fidel, 228-31, 233
Cave, Marjorie, 135, 152
Ceausescu, Elena, *127*, 292
Ceausescu, Nicolae, 127, 292, 293
Ceballos, Jaqui, 203, 207, 209, 211, 212, 214, 215, 216, 218, 222, 224
CFC gases, 102
Chau Van Nhat, 236
Chechnya, conflict, 300
Cheliabinsk atomgrad, *15*
chemicals industry: Japanese, 41, 49; pollution, 86, 94, 96, 97-8, 100; explosions, 100
Chernenko, Konstantin, 284
Chernobyl, 28, 31, 285
Chiang Kai-Shek, *see* Jiang Jieshi
Chicago, 'Days of Rage', 199
child: labour, 156; care, 207, *218*, 219; marriage, 223; homelessness, 308
China, 155-76; nuclear weapons, 24; Korea, 49; television, 114; birth control, 142; population, 145; Communist revolution, 155, 159-60; history, 156-9; Long March, 157; People's Republic, 160-6; health, 163; education, 163; food production, 165, 168-9; Great Leap Forward, 166-8; communes, 166-7; famine, 169; occupation of Tibet, 170; Cultural Revolution, 171-2, 174-5; Peking Opera, 173; economic reforms, 176, 305-6; women's suffrage, 206; infanticide, 224
Chipko movement, 93
Chisso Corporation, 84-5, 91
Choshane, Magdeline, 75
Christian Right, *266*, 267
Chun Doo Hwan, *54*
circumcision, female, 210
Civic Forum, 291-2
civil defence, 22
Civil Rights Act, 66, 212
civil rights movement, 65, 66, 67-71, 117, 187
Clarke, Tony, 108
Clean Air Acts, *86*, 89
clothing industry, *213*
coal industry: Japanese, 41; US, 98-9; environmental issues, 98-9
Coen, Amy, 208, 213, 224
Cold War: arms race, 23; ending, 32, 285, 299, 300; effect on Japanese economy, 39; fear of nuclear attack, 180; Vietnam, 236; space exploration, 309
collectivization, 165, 166, 170
Columbia Broadcasting System (CBS), *115*
Commissariat of Health, 133
Committee to Defend the Workers (KOR), 280
Commoner, Barry, 20-1
communes, 166-7, 195
Communist Party: East German, 278; Polish, *281*, 286; Czech, 292; Romanian, *292*
compact discs, *310*
computers, 309-10
Congress of Racial Equality, 68
consumer culture, 184
consumer goods, 44, 47, 52, 86; environmental concerns, *98*
contraception, *see* birth control
Correa Camacho, Luis, 148
Council Against Atomic and Hydrogen Bombs, 21
Croats, 301
Cronkite, Walter, *115*
Cuba, revolution, 288-31
Cultural Revolution, 162, 170-5
Cyprus: Turkish Federated State, *265*
Czechoslovakia: pollution, *104;* Soviet invasion (1968), *115*, 280; displaced persons, *134*; student unrest, 197; velvet revolution, 290-2

D

Dadds, Hannah, 220
Daewoo, 53
Dalai Lama, 170
Dallas, 122, 125
danchi, 44, *45*
Daoud, Abu, 120
dazibao, 174

DDT, 86, 88, 134, 140
de Choiseul Praslin, Charles-Henri, 199
de Klerk, F.W., 80
Deng Xiaoping, 171, 172, 176
Denmark: radioactive fallout, 26; Green Party, 99; student unrest, 197-8; women's status, 212, 219; childcare, 219
Depression, 204
Dequesne-Cudenet, Gabrielle, 216
Devi, Amravati, 142, 152
Devi, Dhanari, 138
Dirir, Shamis, 210
divorce, 216, 218
Dix, Harry, 108
Djibouti, 210
DNA, 311
Dobynes, Elizabeth Fincher, 107, 116, 117, 122
Dr Strangelove, *24*
Doganis, Sally, 23
Doordarshan, 124
dowries, 223, 224
Drop City commune, 195
drugs, *190*, 192, 193
Dutch Reformed Church, 61
Dzerzhinsky, Felix, 296

E

Earth Summit (1992), 103
Earthday, 89
Easter Rising (1916), 242
Eastern Europe: television, 115, 127; collapse of communism, 127, 300, 304; health, 137; women's status, *213*, 219; childcare, 219; Soviet control, 276, 286
education: Japan, *38*, *44*; South Africa, 63, *74*, 75; US integration, 67-8, 71; television, *125*; literacy, *156*, 163, *165*; China, 163, *165*; postwar expansion, 180; women, 204, 206; Iran, 253; Islamic, 267, 269-70; Soviet, 276
Egypt: independence, 253; secular state, 268-9; Islamic movement, 269 71
Eisenhower, Dwight D., 19, 67
electricity, 19, 26, 86,
electronics, 41, 43, *56*
Elias, Anilu, 208, 211, 218
Elizabeth II, Queen, 114
Ellis, Les, 135, 136, 152
Employee's Health Insurance Scheme, 133
Environmental Protection Agency, 89
Equal Opportunity Law, 43
Equal Pay Bill, 218
Equal Rights Amendment, 218, 224
Estonia, 294
Ethiopia: energy, 103; famine, 149;
'ethnic cleansing', 301
European Community, 304
Evdikimov, Sergei, 296
Export Processing Zones (EPZs), 307
Exxon Valdez, 100

F

factory workers, *41*, 43, 56, 306, *307*
famine, 149, 169
farming: pesticides, 86; influence of television, 120; Chinese collectives, 165; Great Leap Forward, 168-9
female genital mutilation (FGM), 210
Feminine Mystique, The, 211
festivals, pop, *193*
Findhorn community, 195
Finland, Green Party, 99
First World War, *see* World War, First (WWI)
Fleming, Alexander, 132
Foley, Kay, 204, 206, 207, 224
forests, *92*, 93, 102, 104
Fort Wayne, Indiana, 110, 113
France: nuclear power, 16, 19, 27; nuclear weapons, 24; radioactive fallout, 26; radioactive waste, *26*; Green Party, 99; oil pollution, *100*; television, 108-9, 110, 112, 122; AIDS, 151; education, 180, 187; young people, 182, 183; student protest, *188*; 1968 disturbances, 198-9; women's suffrage, 206; women's status, 206; birth control and abortion, 208, 218, 219; empire, 234, 240, 252, *272*; Middle East involvement, 264; Muslim community, *269*
Freedom Riders, 68-9
Friedan, Betty, 211, 215
Friends of the Earth, *90*, 94
Frost, Conrad, 107, 108, 109
Fuentes, Sergio, 229, 230

G

Gaddafi, Muammar al, 265
Gaffari, Hadi, 251, 256, 257, 258, 259
Gandhi, Indira, 142
Gandhi, Mohandas (Mahatma), 65, 93
Gang of Four, 171, *174*, 175, 176
Garcia, Arsenio, 228, 231, 232
Gaza strip, 247
Gcbashi, Tandy, 63
Gdansk, shipyard strike, 280-1, 283
genetic: defects, 20; research, 311
German Democratic Republic (GDR), *see* Germany
Germany, Federal Republic of, *see* Germany
Germany: nuclear research, 12; anti-nuclear protest, 24, 27, *98*; Green Party (Die Grünen), 99; pollution, 102; television, 108-9, *110*, 112, *122*; Munich Olympics (1972), 119; health care, 133, *134*; young people, 182, 183, 184; students, 185, 197; communes, 195; women's status, 206, 216, 218; Baader-Meinhof Gang, *231*; collapse of communism, 275, 286-9; Berlin Wall, 286; life in East Germany (GDR), 276-7, 278-9; reunification, 289; economy, 304; car industry, *310*
Gimenez, John, 267
Girls' Volunteer Corps, *204*
glasnost, 284, 285-6
Goldberg, Dennis, 74
Gomes, Diaz, 122
Gonabadi, Said, 256
Gorbachev, Mikhail: arms reduction treaty, 32; withdrawal from Afghanistan, 248; Berlin visit (1989), 275, 288; leadership, 284-6; reforms, 284-6, 294; Prague visit, 290; coup attempt (1991), 295, 296; resignation, 296
Goupil, Romain, 187, 188, 189, *198*, 200
Grameen Bank, 223
Granato, Virginia, 137
Granma, 228
Grateful Dead, 192
Great Leap Forward, 166-8, 171
Green, Ernest, 67, 68
Green movement, 98, 99
Green Revolution, 149
greenhouse effect, 102
Greenpeace, 90, 94
Group Areas Act, 63, 73, 74
Grozny, conflict, *300*
Gruhl, Herbert, *99*
Guao Xiuying, 163
guerrilla warfare, 224-48
Guevara, Che, 232, 233, 243-4
Gulf War, *128*, 299
Guomindang (Kuomintang), 156
Gupta, Mukesh, 104

H

Hackworth, David, 237
Haight-Ashbury, 190, 193, 194, 195
Haley, Bill, 181
Hall, Parker, 182, 185, 189
Hamamoto, Tsuginori, 84, 89, 91
Hamed, Aly Abdel, 269, 270
Hamed, Mona, 270
Hanada, Toshio, *84*
Haq, Zia ul, 266-8
Harku, Budu, 152
Hashimoto, Yoshiko, 36, 39, 44
Havana, *228*, 229, 230
Havel, Václav, 290, 291
Hayes, Denis, 89
Hayes, Penny, 184, 187, 188
He Jin Lua, 167, 168
health, 131-52; effects of radiation, *13*, 14, 20, 21, 31; Japan, 37, *39*, 48; factory workers, 43; blood transfusions, 63; effects of pollution, 84, 96; polio vaccine, 131, 136-7; penicillin, 132-3; epidemic disease, 132-4; insurance, 133, 134; tuberculosis (TB), 134-6; smallpox, 138-41; malaria, 140; family planning, 142-5; population explosion, 145, 146; cholera, 147-8, 150; famine, 149; AIDS, 150-2; barefoot doctors, *163*; Chinese campaigns, 163; medical technology, *310*, 312; genetics, 311
Hell's Angels, 182
Henry, Frankie, 65
Hewitt, Don, 109, 116
Hill, James, 12
Himalayas, 93
Hindus, 124, 265, *266*, 272, 300
hippies, 184, 190, 193, *194*, 200
Hirohito, Emperor, 12-13, 35, 38
Hiroshima, bombing, *12*, 13, 14, 21, *32*; rebuilding, *38*
HIV, *see* AIDS
Hizbollah, 265, *272*
Ho Chi Minh, 234
Ho Chi Minh Trail, *240*
Hodge, Donald, 312
Hog Farm commune, 195
Honecker, Erich, 288
Hong Kong, 56, *306*
Höntsch, Andreas, 289
Hooker Chemicals Company, 94
Hosseini, Abdul Shah, 256, 260
Houmayoun, Daryoush, 254, 258, 260
housing: Japan, *36*, 44, *45*; South Korea, *51*; South African shantytowns, 60; Mexican settlements, *96*; East Germany, 277-8; Romania, 293
Howard, Winifred, 24
Hu Benxiü, 156, 159, 163, 168
Hubova, Dasha, 276, 295, 296
Huck, Claudine, 220
Huhn, James, 113
Human Be-In, 179, 194
Human Genome Organization (HUGO), 311
Hungary: women's status, *213*; uprising (1956), 280; reforms, 286
Hunter, John, 22
Hunter, Robert, 90, 94
Huo Buo, 155, 176
Husain, Zafar, 140, 141
Hussein, Saddam, 264, 299
Hutchison, Patty, 90
Hwangbo Gon, 54
Hyder, Gul, 248
hydrogen bomb (H-bomb), 16, 21, 22, 23, 24
Hyundai, *52*, 53, 54, *55*

I

Ichihashi, Masaaki, 41
Ikeda, Hayato, 42, 47
Immorality Act, 63
Independent Television (ITV), 112
India: nuclear testing, 24; Chipko movement, 93; Bhopal disaster, 100; television, 114, 120, 122, 124, *125*; life expectancy, 132, 152; health care, 137-41, *152*; family planning, 142-5; population, 145; immunization, 131, 136-8, 163; women's suffrage, 206; women's status, *222*, 224; British rule, 252; independence, 252-3; Hindu–Muslim relations, *266*; Kashmir issue, 300
Indonesia: economic growth, 56; rainforests, 102
infant mortality, 133, 146
information processing, 310, 312
Inkatha movement, 79
International Atomic Energy Agency, 19
International Drinking Water

Supply and Sanitation Decade, 146
International Olympic Committee, 46
International Red Cross, *303*
International Women's Day, *222*
Internet, *309*, 310
Intifada, 247
Iran: women's status, 224, 255, 262, *263*, *264*; Afghan conflict, 246; Islamic revolution, 251, 260, 265; shah's rule, *252*, 253-6; opposition 257-60; war with Iraq, 264
Iran–Iraq War, 264
Iraq: British mandate, 252; independence, 253; war with Iran, 264; invasion of Kuwait, 299
Ireland: guerrilla warfare, 242; EC, 304
Irish National Liberation Army (INLA), 242
Irish Republican Army (IRA), 242
Ishida, Akira, 12, 13, 14, 32
Islam: women's status, *220*, *224*, 255, 262-3; Afghanistan, 243, 244; European domination, 252-3; Iran, 251, 253-60, 262-3; law, 255, 263, 266-8, 269
Islamic Conference Organization (ICO), *265*
Islamic Salvation Front (FIS), *270*, 272
Israel: nuclear weapons, 24; Munich Olympics (1972), 119; women's status, *220*; Six-Day War, 247; Intifada, 247
Italy: use of DDT, *88*; Green Party, 99; television, 110, 112; malaria, 140; young people, 183; students, 185, 197; hippies, 193; women's suffrage, 206; women's status, 206; birth control and abortion, 208, 218; Red Brigades, *231*
Iwamoto, Hiroki, *84*

J

Jäger, Harold, 276, 289
Jang Chang Sun, 49, 55
Japan: WWII, 12, 35, *159*; surrender, 14, 35, 36, 158; US nuclear tests, 21; nuclear programme, 32; Allied occupation, 35; postwar, 36-9; health care, 37, 39, 133; industry, 38-43; education, 38, *44*, 180; work, 43; life expectancy, *39*, *152*; housing, 44, *45*; prosperity, 44, 47; Tokyo Olympics (1964), 46, 47; economy, 47, 49; Western influence, 47, 48; tourism, 48; pollution, 49, 84-5, 89, *91*; whaling, 94; television, 108, 110, 112, *120*, 122; young people, 179; communes, 195; youth protests, 196, 198; women's suffrage, 206; childcare, 219
Jaruzelski, General Wojciech, 283
Jiang Jieshi (Chiang Kai-shek), 156, 157
Jiang Qing, 171, 173
Jiao Shouyun, 162
Jim Crow system, 64, 71
Jin Jingzhi, 158, 165, 174
Johannesburg, 72, *73*
John Paul II, Pope, 282, 283
Johnson, Lyndon B., 236
Johnson, Sheldon, 14, 20, 31
Jones, Jeff, 189, 196, 199
Joshi, Madan Lal, 120
jukeboxes, 180

K

Kabul, 243, *248*
Kalashnikov rifles, *244*, 246
Kampuchea, *see* Cambodia
Kang Sung Ro, 51, *55*
Karma, Bi, 138
Kashmir, conflict, 300
Kennedy, John F., 71, 107, 116, 117
Kenya: fuel consumption, 103; AIDS, 150
Kesey, Ken, 192
Khan, Reza, 253
Khanlary, Moloud, 258
Khmer Rouge, 240
Khomeini, Ayatollah Ruhollah: return to Iran, 251, 262; opposition to shah, 254, 256-8; arrest, 256; exile, *257*, 259, *260*; Islamic revolution, 262-3, 272; death, 263, 272; war with Iraq, 264
Kiff, Lloyd, 88
Kilic, Altemur, 252
Kim Bok Soon, 50, 51-2
Kincaid, Anne, 267
King, Martin Luther, 65, 66, *71*, 72
Klein, Hans, 119
Kleinberg, Howard, *120*, 128
Koha, Nomathamsanqua, 60, 63, 76, 80
Kondratiev, Aleksei, *15*
Koran, 255
Korean War, 39, 49
Krishen, Radan, 120
Kriz, Bohumir, 138, 141
Krob, Andrej, 290, *291*
Krzywonos, Henryka, 281, 282, 283
Ku Klux Klan, 68
Kuomintang, *see* Guomindang
Kurchatov, Igor, *15*
Kurds, 300
Kusnetsova, Natasha, 278, 296
Kuwait: invasion, *128*, 299; Iran–Iraq War, 264
Kwak Man Young, 50

L

Lafayette, Bernard, 65, 66, 67, 69
Lam Thi Phan, 227, 238, 240
Lam Van Phat, 238
land: Japanese reforms, 38; Australian Aboriginal rights, 77; Maori rights, 77; Chinese landlords, 160; Cuba, 228, *230*; Iran reforms, *252*, 254; conflicts, 312
Land Fund Commission, 77
Land Reform Act (Iran), *252*
LaPratt, Paul, 67
Latvia, 294
Leary, Timothy, 192
Lebanon: French mandate, 252; civil war, 265; religion, *272*
Leipzig, demonstrations (1989), 275, 288
Lelental, Zbigniew, *283*
Lenin, Vladimir Ilyich, 286, *296*
Lenya, Rowlands, 150
Lewin, Hugh, 72, 73
Lewis, James, 132
Lian Tianyun, 167
Libya, coup (1969), 265
life expectancy: Japan, *39*, 152; US, 132; India, 132, 152
literacy, *156*, 163, *165*
Lithuania, 294, *295*
Little Rock, Arkansas, 67
Liu Shaoqi, 171, 172, *174*
Llana Rudas, Maria, 147-8
London: smog, *86*; television, 108, *114*, 118; coronation, 114; fashion stores, 184; university, 187; Vietnam protest, *188*; Miss World, *215*; women's rights, 216; Internet Café, *309*
Long March, 157
Lotvi, Shakoor, 251, 257, 258, 259
Love Canal, 94, 97
Lovell, James, 83
LSD, 192
Lucky Dragon, 21, 27
Luo Shifa, 160, 169, 174
Lusaka, *128*
Luxembourg: Green Party, 99; women's status, 219

M

Ma Gennan, 155, 156, 158, 160, 163, 169
Maalin, Ali, 141
MacArthur, Douglas A., 36
McDonald's, 48, *176*, *305*
Mafia, 229
Mahaev, Yevgeny, 284, 294
Malan, Daniel, 62
malaria, 132, 134, 140
Malaysia: electronics industry, 43; economy, 56; health care, *141*
Manchu dynasty, 156, 170
Manchuria, Japanese invasion, 158
Mandela, Nelson, 74, *79*
Manesh, Said Sharifi, 259, 262, 263, 264
Manhattan Project, 12, 19
Mann, Floyd, 68, *69*
Mao Zedong (Mao Tse-tung): establishment of People's Republic, 155; Long March, 157; peasant support, *157*, 158, 160; leadership, 159, 162, 165, 171; land reforms, 160; Marriage Law, 160; Great Leap Forward, 167, 168, 169; Cultural Revolution, 171-5; Little Red Book, 171, 172, 174; arts policy, 173; death, 175, 176; on guerrilla war, 227; influence, 234, 243
Maoris, 77
maquiladoras, 96
March of Dimes, *136*
Marx, Karl, 162
Massoud, Ahmed Shah, 243
Matsuda, Tomiji, 104
Maysiels, Constance, 59
measles, 137
Mecca, 252, 255
Medicaid, 133
Medicare, 133
Melbourne Olympic Games (1956), 114
Melescanu, Felicia, 127
metal poisoning, 84, 96
methyl mercury, 84
Mexico: chemical pollution, 96; water supply, *146*, *216*; food supply, 149; youth protests, 196; birth control, 208; women's status, *216*, 218
Mexico City, 145
Miller, Petr, 290-2
Million Man March, 303
Minamata Bay, 84, 89, 91, 104
Mods, 183
Montgomery, Alabama, 65, 66
Montoneros, 231-2
moon landing, 118, 119
Moral Majority, 267
Morocco, health care, *141*
Moscow: May Day parades, *23*, *277*, 294; White House attack, *295*, 296; fast food, *305*
Motova, Nina, 277, 285-6
Mouchkova, Kamila, 115
Mountbatten, Earl, 242
Muhammad Reza Pahlavi, shah of Iran, 253, 254-60
Mujahideen, 243, 244, 246, 248, 265
multinational companies, 306-7
Munich Olympic Games (1972), 119-20, 121
music: rock and roll, 181; youth market, 184; Western influence, 278
Muslim Brotherhood, 269, 270
Muslims, 255, 265, 266, 272, 300, 301; Shiite, *252*, 254, 255, 260, 264, 272; Sunni, 255, 264, *265*; *see also* Islam
Mutually Assured Destruction (MAD), 23

N

Nagaoka, Takunori, *47*
Nagasaki: bombing, 13-14, 21; shipyard, 41
napalm, 238, *241*
Nasser, Gamal, 268-9
National Committee for a Sane Nuclear Policy (SANE), 24
National Guard (US), 66, 67, *69*, 200
National Health Service (NHS), 133
National Joint Action Campaign for Women's Equal Rights, 216
National Liberation Front (FLN), 271, 272
National Movement of Street Boys and Girls, 308
National Organization for Women (NOW), 214, 215, 216, 218
nationalism, 299, 303
Nationalist Party (South Africa), 60, 61, 62
Native Land Act (1913), 61
Native Urban Area Act (1923), 61
Nazari, Soroor Moradi, 258
National Broadcasting Company (NBC), 121
Nelson, Gaylord, 88, 89
Nepal, energy, 103
Nerger, Edwin, 113, 119, 299
Netherlands: radioactive fallout, 26; anti-nuclear protest, *31*; Green Party, 99; pollution, 102; television, 112; education,

180, 185; young people, 184; student unrest, 199
Nevada desert, nuclear testing, 16-17, 20, *21*, 22, 31
New York: Earthday, 89; World's Fair (1939), 109; women's movement demonstration, 203
New Zealand: Maori land rights, 77; television, 112, 114
Nguyen Thi Be, 236-7
Nissan, 44
Nixon, Richard, 89, 116, 241
Nobel Peace Prize, 66, 285
Noroudi, Dowlat, 263
North Korea, 39
North Vietnam, 234, 236
Northern Ireland, 242
Norway: whaling, 94; women's status, 219, childcare, 219; Middle East mediation, 247
nuclear: power, 11, 14, 19; testing, 11, 16-17, 20-2, 24, 90; fission, 14; war, fear of, 22-3, 180-1; power stations, 26-31, 86, *98*; waste, *26*, 27, 90; non-proliferation treaty, 24; *see also* atom bomb

O

Oak Ridge, Tennessee, 12
O'Donahue, Chuck, 98
Ohba, Miyoshi, 35, 36, 37, 48
oil: crisis, 53; pollution, 86-8, 100; Iranian industry, *252*, 254; Algerian revenue, 271; Gulf War, 299
Oishi, Matashichi, 21, 27
Olympic Games: Tokyo (1964), 46, 47, 49; Seoul (1988), 55; Berlin (1936), *109*, 121; Melbourne (1956), 114; Munich (1972), 119-20, 121; Barcelona (1992), 121
Oppenheimer, Robert, 12
Oswald, Lee Harvey, 107
Ottoman empire, 252
'Our World', 117
Owen, Carol, 267
Oz, *187*
Ozerskii, Andrei, 294
ozone layer, 102

P

Pacific: nuclear tests, 21; whaling, 94
Pai, Dutta, 144, 145
Pakistan: nuclear weapons, 24; health care, *138*; food supply, 149; Afghan conflict, 246, 248; independence, 253; Islamic state, 266-8; Kashmir issue, 300
Palestine, 252
Palestinian Liberation Organization (PLO), 247
Palestinian terrorists, 119, 120
Papworth Sanatorium, 135
Paris: students, 186, 198-9, 216; women's movement, 216; Khomeini's exile, 259, *260*
Park Chung Hee, 50
passbooks, 73, 74
Passenheim, Dietmar, 275, 278-9
Patterson, Walt, 86, *87*
peasants: China, 156, 157, 158, 160, 162; Cuba, 229; Vietnam, 234-5
Peking Opera, 173
penicillin, 132, 133
Penrose, Olga, 87
People's Liberation Army, 155, 158
perestroika, 284, 285
Perón, Juan, 231
Persepolis, 256
Peru: water supply, 146-7; cholera, 147-8, 150
Pescatore, Fran, 220
pesticides, 86
Phan Dinh, 234, 235
pharmaceuticals, 112
Philippines: Japanese trade, 56; television, 114; sanitation, *147*
pill, the, 208; *see also* birth control
plutonium, 20, 27
Pohang Iron and Steel Company (POSCO), 53, 54
Pol Pot, 240
Poland: student unrest, 197; women's status, *207*; Gdansk strike, 280-1; Solidarity, *281*, 282-3, 286; role of Church, 282; elections (1989), 286
police: South African, 73, 78-9; Iranian, 254, 256; East German, 278-9; Czech, 291
polio, 131, 136-7
pollution: nuclear waste, 26, 27, 90; Japan, 49, 84-5; US, 85; chemical, 86, 94-8; oil, 86-8; levels, 92; Green movement, 98; population explosion, 145
Popieluszko, Father Jerzy, 282
population: rising world, 103, 142, 145; ageing, 133, *152*; control, 142-5
Population and Registration Act, 63
Prague: Soviet invasion, *115*, 280; demonstrations (1989), 290, *291*
Prague Spring (1968), 280
Pratt, Ann, 64
Presley, Elvis, 181
Prianichnikov, Veniamin, 27, 28, 31
Princip, Gavrilo, 301
Pripyat, Ukraine, 28, 31

Q

Qin Yongchang, 167
Qom, *251*
Quant, Mary, 184
Queverdo Linares, Cesar, 146
Quimby, Barbara, 94
Quinn, Sharelle, *221*
Quotations from Chairman Mao, 171, *172*

R

race relations: racial laws (South Africa), 59, 63, 74, 75; apartheid, 61, 62-3; Rwanda, *148*, 303; 'ethnic cleansing' (Bosnia), 301
Radebe, Nomphiti, 78
radiation: sickness, *13*, 14, 21, 31; fallout, 16, *17*, 20, *21*, *28*, 31, 32, 86; contamination, 26, 28, 31; waste, 26, 27, 90; materials transported, *26*
radio, transistor, *42*
Rafigdoost, Moshen, 251, 258, 260
Raghuvir, Tegu, 137
railways, *166*, 220
rainforests, 102, 104
Ram, Panchu, 139
Ramayana, 124
Ratana Church, 77
Razvi, Sheik Khwafa Irshad, 268
Ready Steady Go, 183
Reagan, Ronald, 32, 100, 267, 285, 304
Red Brigades, *231*
Red Flag Canal, *165*, 169
Red Guards, 171, 172, 174
refugees, *134*, *148*, *149*, 246, *303*
Reinke, Bärbel, 286, 288, 289
religion, 251-72; Japan, 38; Tibet, 170; abortion issue, 208, 224; women's status, *220*, 224, 255, 262, 263; Northern Ireland, 242; Poland, 282, 283; *see also* Christian Right, Hindus, Islam, Muslims, Roman Catholic Church
Ren Fuqin, 158, *159*, 163
Ren Yangchen, 169
Renault, *198*
Rhee, Syngman, 49-50
Rhine, pollution, 102
Rio de Janeiro, Earth Summit, 103; street children, *308*
Roads, Dusty, 207, 211, 221
Robben Island, 74
Robertson, Pat, 267
Robinson, Peter, 110, 114, 117
robots, *310*
rock and roll music, 181
Rockers, *183*
Roh Tae Woo, 54
Roland, F. Sherwood, 102
Roman Catholic Church, 208, *218*, 242, 282
Romania: television, 122, 125, 127, 128; revolution, 127, 128, 292; orphanages, *292*, 293; Ceausescu regime, 293
Rothele, Eric, 76
Rothstein, Vivian, 186, 187
Runkle, Deborah, 136, *137*, 152
Russian Federation, 295, 300
Rwanda, *148*, 303

S

Sachs, Rusty, 181, *197*
Sackett, David, *182*, 183
Sadat, Anwar, 269, 270
Saemaul Undong, 50
Saffer, Thomas, 16, 31
Sahel region, *149*
Saigon: American evacuation, 227; Tet offensive, 240; renaming, *241*
St George, Utah, 20, 31
St Louis, Missouri, 20-1
Sakharov, Andrei, 16
Salk, Jonas, 136, 180
Samsung, 53
San Francisco: peace treaty (1951), 35; Golden Gate Park, 179; hippie culture, 190, 193, 194, 195
Sanchez Santo, Selestino, 230
satellite television, 121, 120, 128
satellites, 117, 118, 119
Sato, Nobuko, 44, *45*, 47
Sato, Taisuke, 44, 48
Saudi Arabia: Islamic state, 252; Iran-Iraq war, 264
Savak, 256, 257, 258
Schonfeld, Reese, 121
Schweppes, *94*
Second World War, *see* World War, Second (WWII)
Securitate, 293
Sellafield nuclear reprocessing plant, 27
Seoul, *50*, *54*, 55
Serbs, 301
Sesame Street, *125*
shah of Iran, *see* Muhammad Reza Pahlavi
Shao Ai Ling, *163*, 165, 171, 172, 174, 176
Sharia, 255
Sharpeville massacre, 59, 73
Shawall, Madar, 244, 246
Shiite Muslims, *252*, 254, 255, 260, 264, 272
Shinto religion, 38
shipbuilding: Japan, 41; South Korea, 54
Shuba, Elizabeth, 60
Sickness Insurance Act, 133
Sihanouk, Norodom, 240
Silent Spring, 86
Silva Marin, Sennefelder, 147, 148
Singapore, 56
Sinn Féin, 242
Sisulu, Albertina, 73, 74, 80
Sisulu, Walter, 74, 80
Six-Day War, 247
slavery, 64
soap operas, 122, 125
Solidarity, *281*, 282, 283, 286
Somalia: smallpox, 141; famine, 149
Sony Corporation, 41, *42*
Sophiatown, 72-3
Sorbonne, 186, 198
Soriana Gallardo, Serafina, *216*
South Africa: nuclear weapons, 24; Sharpeville, 59; apartheid, 61, 62-3, 72-6, 78-80; diamond mines, 62, 63; elections, 79, 80; health care, 136
South African Institute of Race Relations, 62
South Korea: Korean War, 39, 49; governments, 49-50; New Village Movement (NVM), 50-1; modernization and reform, 50-4; textiles industry, 52; lifestyle, 55;
South Vietnam, 224, 227, 234
Southern Baptist Convention, 267
Southern Christian Leadership Council (SCLC), 66
Soviet Union: atomic weapons, 15, 16; nuclear energy, 19; arms race, 16, 23; civil defence, 22; nuclear power stations, 26; nuclear waste, 27; Korea, 49; training South Africans, 78; whaling, 94; television, 108, 109, 110; health care, 133, 137; aid to China, 165, 169; young people, 182; women's suffrage, 204; working women, 219; influence in Vietnam, 236; Afghanistan, 243-6, 248, 265, 285; political crisis, 248; Iran-Iraq War, 264; religious policies, *272*; communist ideals, 276; *perestroika* and *glasnost*, 284-6; collapse, 294-6, 300; economy, 305

Soweto, 76, *78*, 80
space shuttle, *312*
Spain: Green Party, 99; abortion laws, *218*
sponsorship, sport, 121
sport, 119, 121, 128, 220; *see also* Olympic Games
Srebrenica, *301*
Sri Lanka, 103
Srivastava, Vasanti, 144
Staley, Peter, 151
Staradumov, Valery, *28*, 31
Stasi, 278, 289
steel: Japan, 41; South Korea, 53; China, 167-9
Stefonoiu, Steliana, 122, 125, 127
sterilization, 144-5
Stern, Sharon, 131
Stormont, *242*
Strategic Defence Initiative (SDI), 285
street children, 308
strikes: Gdansk shipyard, 280-1, 282; Ukraine miners, *294*
Strong, Maurice, 88, 91, 104
strontium-90, *20*
structural adjustment, 307
student protest, *54*, *76*, *79*, 186-9, 196-200, *228*
Students for a Democratic Society (SDS), 187
Subhani, Hamid, 266, 267, 268
Sudan, famine, 149
Suffragette movement, 204
Sugawara, Hisako, 48
Sunni Muslims, 255, 265
sustainable development, 103
Sweden: civil defence, 22; nuclear energy programme, 27; Green Party, 99; Natural Step programme, 103; young people, 182, 184; education, 185; women's status, 212; abortion, 218; childcare, 219
Switzerland: Green Party, 99; chemical pollution, 100
Syria, 252

T

Tabriz, *258*
Taiwan, 56, 159
Takehora, Akimoto, 41, 42
Tange, Kenzo, 46
Taniguchi, Sumiteru, 13-14, 32
Tanzania: energy, 103; Rwandan conflict, 303
Tawfiq, Yasser, *270*
Taylor, Rogan, *183*, 185, 190, 194
technology, 309-10, 312
Teddy Boys, 182
telenovelas, 122
teleshopping, 128
television, 107-28; ownership of sets, 44, 55, 110, 113; colour, 44, 118; development, 108-9; advertising, 112, 113; political importance, 115-17, 128, 277; sport, 119, 121, 128; news, 119-20, *127*; educational uses, 120; satellite and cable, 121, 128; soap operas, 122, 125; religion, 124
Teliatnikov, Leonid, *31*
Teller, Edward, 16, 32
Telstar, 117
terrorists: Palestinian, 119, European, *231*
Tet offensive (1968), 240-1
Thailand: trade, 56; government, 56; television, 114
Thatcher, Margaret, 242, 304-5
Thelin, Ron, 179, 181, 192, 193, *194*
Three Mile Island nuclear power station, 26
Tiananmen Square massacre, 176
Tianjin, *159*, 167
Tibbets, Paul W., *12*
Tibet, 170
Timisoara, demonstration (1989), 292
Tinian Island, 12
Tod, Jonathan, 87
Tokyo: traffic, *37*, *49*; housing, 44, *49*; Olympics (1964), 46, 47, 49; expansion, 49; demonstrations, *91*
Tong Xiang Ling, 173
Tonkin incident (1964), 236
Torrey Canyon, 87, *100*
Toyota, 39, 44
trade unions: Japan, 38, 42; South Korea, 53, 54
Tran Bach Dan, *241*
Tran Thi Gung, 238
Trans-Jordan, 252
transport: railways, *47*, *166*, 220; trailer ride, *51*; hitching, *62*; racial segregation, *65*, 68; toxic cargo, 100; *see also* cars
Truman, Harry S., 12
tuberculosis (TB), 134-6, 152
Turkey, 252
TV Globo, 122

U

Uchida, Suezo, 41
Ukraine, miners' strike, *294*
Ulster, 242
underground press, *187*
unemployment, 277, 307
Union Carbide, 100
unions, *see* trade unions
United Nations: General Assembly, 19; Security Council, 59; environment conference (1972), 91; marketing guidelines, 112; sanitation programme, 146; charter, 206; conferences on women, 222, 224; poverty report, 223; Palestine partition, 247; Iran–Iraq War ceasefire, 264; Gulf War, 299; Kashmir intervention, 300; peacekeeping role, *303*
United Nations Conference on Environment and Development (UNCED), 103
United Nations Environment Programme (UNEP), 92
United Nations International Children's Emergency Fund (UNICEF), *134*, *141*
United Nations Population Fund, 145
United States of America (US): nuclear testing, 11, 16-17, 20-1, 31, 90; atomic bombs, 12-15; arms race, 16, 23; civil defence, 22; anti-nuclear protest, 24; nuclear power stations, 26; nuclear waste, 27; occupation of Japan, 35, 36-9; debt to Japan, 49; Korean War, 49; racism and civil rights, 59, 64-71; chemical pollution, 86, 88, 100, 104; television, 108-9, 110, 112, 121, 122, *125*; advertising, 112, 113; effect of TV on politics, 115-17; Vietnam War, 117, 189, 194, 196-8, 200, 227, 234-41; health care, 132, 133, 140, 152; life expectancy, 132; food aid, 149; AIDS, 151; young people, 179, 180, 182, 183, 184, 187, 194; education, 180, 185; Human Be-In, 179, 194; pop festivals, 193; communes, 195; anti-war protests, 196-7, 199-200; women's status, 204, 206-7, 212-15, 218, 224; contraceptive pill, 208; abortion issue, 209, 218, 220, 224; childcare, 219; influence in Cuba, *228*, 229, 231; Mafia, *229*; influence in South America, 232, 233; Cambodia invasion, 240; influence in Northern Ireland, 242; influence in Iran, *259*; religious revival, *266*, 267; political ideology, 276; shopping, *305*; manufacturing, *307*; information technology, 310
universities: expansion, 180, 185, 200; student unrest, 186, 196; women, 204, 213; Muslim students, 252, 269
uranium, 14, 27
Uzbekistan, religion, *272*

V

vaccines, 131, 132, 136-7
Vause, Wendy, 114, 118, 119
Viet Cong, 224, 234-6, *237*, 238, 240, 241
Viet Minh, 234
Vietnam War, 234-41; TV news bulletins, 117, 241; anti-war protests, *188*, 189, 194, 196-8, 200; ends, 227
virtual reality, *312*
Vivien, Reverend C.T., 71
Voting Rights Act, 66, 71

Walesa, Lech, 280, *281*
Washington: peace march (1967), 196, 197; religious rally (1980), 267
waste, toxic, 90, 94, 97-8; *see also* radiation
water supply, *139*, *146*, 312
Weathermen Underground, 199
Weeder, Michael, 72, 78, 80
Weeks, Lorena, 207, 212, 213, 220
West Bank, 247
whaling, 90, 94
White, Quentin, 62
White House, Moscow, *295*, 296
Whitehill, Ginnie, 204, 206, *218*
Whole Earth Catalogue, 184
Wild One, The, *182*
Williams, Zekozy, 65
Windscale nuclear reactor, *19*, 26
women, role of: Japan, 38, 43, *204*; Malaysia, 43, 56; Singapore, *56*; Chipko movement, 93; China, 156, 160, *173*, 206, 306; changes, 203-24; women's movement, 203, 215; US, 204, 206-8, 212-15, 218, 224; wartime work, 204; contraceptive pill, 208, 209; equal pay and equal rights, 209, 212-15, 220-1; circumcision, 210; childcare, 219; Grameen Bank, 223; soldiers, *224*, *264*; position in Islamic societies, 255, 258, *262*; *see also* abortion, birth control
Woodstock festival, *193*
World Bank, 307
World Commission on Environment and Development, 103
World Health Organization (WHO), 112, 134, 138, 140-1, 146, 151
World War, First (WWI), 204, 299
World War, Second (WWII), 12-15, 132, 158, 204

X-rays, *134*, 135

Yamashita, Hidenori, 84, *85*
Yazdi, Ebrahim, 256, 257, 259, *260*, *263*
Yeltsin, Boris, 294, 295, 296
Yeon Bong Hak, 50, 52, 53
Yi Chong Kak, 52, *53*
Yi Sung Hwan, 54
Yokohama, 49
Yoshida, Shigeru, 36
Young, Earl, 235, 241
youth market, 184
Yugoslavia, 301

zaibatsu, 38
Zaire, Rwandan conflict, 303
Zambia, television, *128*
Zende, Alaim, 76, 78
Zeng Guodong, 166-9, 174, 175, 176
Zhang Pingan, 172
Zhou Enlai, 173, 175
Zulus, 79
Zwerg, Jim, 68